Orientalism and Islam

European Thinkers on Oriental Despotism in the Middle East and India

Through an historical analysis of the theme of Oriental despotism, Michael Curtis reveals the complex positive and negative interaction between Europe and the Orient. The book also criticizes the misconception that the Orient was the constant victim of Western imperialism and the view that Westerners cannot comment objectively on Eastern and Muslim societies.

The book views the European concept of Oriental despotism as based not on arbitrary prejudicial observation, but rather on perceptions of real behavior and processes in Eastern systems of government. Curtis considers how the concept developed and was expressed in the context of Western political thought and intellectual history and of the changing realities in the Middle East and India. The book includes a discussion of the observations of Western travelers in Muslim countries and analysis of the reflections of seven major thinkers: Montesquieu, Edmund Burke, Tocqueville, James and John Stuart Mill, Karl Marx, and Max Weber.

Michael Curtis is a Distinguished Professor Emeritus of political science at Rutgers University. He is the author of approximately thirty books, most notably *Verdict on Vichy* (2004), *Three against the Third Republic* (1959), *Totalitarianism* (1979), and *Antisemitism in the Contemporary World* (1973). For many years, he was the president of American Professors for Peace in the Middle East and editor of the *Middle East Review*.

Contents

Acknowledgments

It is a pleasure to acknowledge the advice and counsel of a number of friends and colleagues who read parts of this work at various stages and helped shape it to its present form. I am particularly grateful to Kenneth Bialkin, Robert Garber, Jonathan Kapstein, Suzanne Keller, Leonard Moss, Renee Winegarten, the two readers who were consulted by Cambridge University Press, the Syndicate of the Press of the University of Cambridge, and my editor Lewis Bateman and his assistant Emily Spangler for helpful comments. Above all, my thanks to my wife Judith K. Brodsky, the embodiment of splendor in the grass, the glory in the flower.

Introduction

What's Past Is Prologue

In 1743 Dr. Samuel Johnson commented that "a generous and elevated mind is distinguished by nothing more certainly than an eminent degree of curiosity; nor is that curiosity ever more agreeably or usefully employed than in examining the laws and customs of foreign nations." Fifty years later he added, "There are two objects of curiosity, the Christian world and the Mahometan world. All the rest may be considered as barbarous." The six major Western European thinkers from Montesquieu to Max Weber, and other commentators discussed here, exemplify his aphorisms in having been "usefully employed" with their varying " degrees of curiosity" about the Muslim world. This book addresses their perceptions and conclusions about the particular style of politics in the past history of the countries of the Middle East, and the nature of Islam and its impact on political behavior in those countries as well as in North Africa and Mughal India. That style has been characterized as Oriental despotism; a concept derived from the Greek word *despotes*, the master of the household who held complete power over his family and slaves. Using this concept allows one to distinguish analytically that style of autocratic and absolute government from other more moderate forms of rule.

This work is based on the premise that Western analysts and observers of Middle Eastern and Muslim societies can discuss and interpret them without being biased or racist. The discussions by the authors covered in this book implicitly refute the simplistic and reductionist argument that all European writing about the Muslim Orient is racist, imperialistic, or totally ethnocentric. If their views are controversial, they are not examples of historical partisanship. Without claiming that their views and perceptions of Muslims and of the countries in the Orient discussed by our writers are directly relevant to the resolution of current problems in the area, and without making explicit comparisons between the past and the present, their perceptions and diverse views are nevertheless helpful in providing a background for understanding the nature of contemporary Muslim societies and the cultural identities of the peoples in the Orient, particularly at a moment when Western countries are being challenged by groups and organizations stemming from the Middle East, and when the number of Muslims resident in Western countries has been increasing.

Clarification of the terms used here is desirable. An epigram usually attributed to Winston Churchill, though by some to Oscar Wilde or George Bernard Shaw, is that the United States and Britain are "two nations divided by a common language." The term *Orient* exemplifies the jest. American and European, including British, usage of *Orient* often differs on the precise definition of the borders of the Orient, the term adopted from the Latin *oriens*, the land of the rising sun. Traditionally, in Western European parlance the term refers to the area of what is now called the Middle East, or, alternatively, the Near East. The adjective *Oriental* similarly refers to the peoples and cultures of those countries. The French terminology makes the point clear: the Eastern Question, the diplomatic and political issues relating to the decline of the Ottoman Empire, is named *la question d'Orient*. At variance with Western Europe usage is the customary American parlance, certainly since the late nineteenth century, of applying the term *Orient* to East Asian countries, or what is now often referred to as the Far East. What is important in all this is that the words *West* and *East* from the beginning suggested geographical as well as cultural and religious differences, though the frontiers between the two could neither easily be demarcated nor could the terms be defined with precision.

For discussion in this book, the West is regarded as synonymous with Europe, an entity embodying a number of geographical, cultural, political, religious, and moral features. Though divisions and frictions existed, and to an extent still do, among the political components of that entity, a certain sense of solidarity among the peoples of the West has resulted from common historical experiences allowing them to regard themselves as different from most other regions of the world. Europe as we now know it is little more than three hundred years old. It is the progeny of that part of the Western world once known as Christendom, which was a physical area inhabited by Catholics and, later, Protestants but excluding Orthodox, Byzantine Christians, and also a political and social entity in which people shared a common religious heritage and destiny. Acknowledging the complicated history of the area, with its unexpected turns, advances, and retrogressions, it is nevertheless a plausible argument that it was the Muslim attacks on that area and resistance to them between the seventh and ninth centuries that, despite lingering theological differences, helped lead to the concept and the realization of a specific physical territorial region with a common Christian community. That region defended itself against the Muslim attacks, and part of it was successful in remaining Christian; by contrast the peoples of Persia and Central Asia were less successful and were conquered and converted by those Muslim forces.

The Muslim advances and repulsions in the West had important consequences. Whether or not one accepts the controversial argument of Henri Pirenne, best expressed in his influential book, *Mohammed and Charlemagne*, that it was the rapid advance of Islam in the West that caused the break in the Mediterranean-based trading economy, the countries in the European peninsula developed an economy in which wealth was derived from land rather than water, thus leading to a feudal system.[1] More important for our present purpose was the emergence of a more distinctively Western type of Christendom that included the non-Roman as well as Roman areas but excluded Byzantine territory. Its earliest important manifestation was a Christian universality and orthodoxy with Charlemagne, the king of the Franks, being crowned on Christmas Day in 800 as Holy Roman Emperor by Pope Leo III, who switched his allegiance away from the Byzantine emperor in Constantinople. Pirenne's own famous conclusion is still worth pondering: "without Islam, the Frankish Empire would probably never have existed; without Muhammad, Charlemagne would have been inconceivable."

Christendom as a political unit gradually became more ineffectual as a result of significant events and changes: the Reformation, the 1648 Peace of Westphalia, which recognized the right of each prince to determine the religion of his own state, the decline of the Holy Roman Empire as an effective political unit, and the rise of sovereign nation-states. In its place, modern Europe, the West, emerged, the historic result of diverse factors beginning with the polities of ancient Greece and Rome, and developed into advanced, increasingly democratic states. This book deals with some prominent intellectuals in this political West.

Marcel Proust once remarked that the real voyage of discovery consists not in seeking new lands but in seeing with new eyes. In these days when many perceive the possibility of a hostile and dangerous confrontation between Islam and the West, and when the figure of Osama bin Laden is as least as challenging today as the Great Sultan of the Ottoman Empire was in the past, it is beneficial to examine how the two sides have perceived each other over time and what can be learned from those perceptions. The premise of this book is that the study of past perceptions represented here by six major Western European thinkers, from Montesquieu to Max Weber, and the observations of travelers, Western scholars of Oriental societies, and earlier political theorists from Aristotle on, who influenced those major thinkers, shed light on the true picture of political and religious life in the Middle East, still useful for understanding that area today, and on the nature and motivation of Islam.

The six major Western theorists examined here were all brilliant and celebrated figures who made important contributions to intellectual history and to political discussion in general. Here, in their contributions to the advancement of knowledge of, and conclusions about, politics and societies in Muslim countries, they address and provide an understanding of a specific type of political regime and a set of relations between ruler and ruled that are significantly different from those in their own countries, Britain and France. Their contributions have been important for the variety and perspicacious nature of their ideas, which incidentally reveal that the Western attitude to the Orient was not monolithic; the depth and range of their influence in the continuing Western discussion, perceptions, and opinions of despotism in the Orient and of the impact of Islam on societies and cultures; and their assessment of the meaningful differences between East and West.

Our six writers illustrate a syndrome of characteristics of political beliefs, leadership, and administrative and government structure in the Orient that contrasts sharply with the values and principles of Western systems. The Western world, usually understood as an amalgam of influences – Greek philosophy, Roman law, the concept of a legal person, Judeo-Christianity, secular Enlightenment, and political development leading to the creation of territorial nation-states – has incorporated values and ways of life different from both the historical and contemporary Orient. In the West, understandably imperfect as are all systems, one finds democratic principles, individual rights, balance of power, division of power, and limits to authority. One is aware of the past glories, the prominent role played in the past, or the multiple contributions to knowledge, art, scholarship, and science made by Oriental societies. One such contribution was that, between the eighth and tenth centuries, almost all nonliterary and nonhistorical secular Greek books available in the area of the Middle East were translated into Arabic. The subjects covered included astrology, alchemy, geometry, astronomy, music, Aristotelian philosophy, physics, and medicine. Five centuries later, sultan Medmed II (1541–81) called for Arabic translations of Greek works.[2] Nevertheless, the Western political and cultural values were absent or negligible in Muslim Oriental regimes where individuals were subject to rulers whose power had fewer institutional restraints. The Koran (4:59) makes this latter point clear: "Obey God, obey his Prophet and those who hold authority over you."

In contrast to the normal Western relationship of religion and politics the Prophet Muhammad was a political and a spiritual leader, promulgating the holy law of Islam and founding and ruling the first Muslim state. Within a few years he had unified the Arab tribes in Arabia around his persona and the religion he founded, and warred against Bedouin and Jewish tribes and the Byzantine Empire. He had fused the two spheres of politics and religion in such fashion that separation of them in later Muslim states has been difficult. In another telling contrast between East and West, while Muslims are not forbidden from Christian and Jewish holy places, non-Muslims by the edict of Caliph Umar, the second successor of Muhammad, were not allowed to live in, or even visit, the holy places of Islam, Mecca, and Medina.

Since the advent of Islam in the seventh century, political leaders in Middle Eastern societies have linked religion and politics in formulating policies toward everyone but especially toward Christendom and the Western world, which was seen as Islam's only serious rival. The fact that this is still the case suggests that the contemporary Middle East and the nature and significance of Islam today can only be fully understood in the light of evaluations of past history. The discussion in this book of Oriental despotism is not simply an episode in intellectual history but is a reminder that thoughts and events have antecedents as well as consequences.

Certain questions, relevant for our own times, can be posed. In view of the analysis and conclusions about past despotism in Muslim societies, are contemporary Arab Muslim societies compatible with democratic political systems or with governments based on principles of human rights? Are those societies willing or able to follow the path of modernization? If mainstream Muslim societies signify loyalty to Allah and to the Prophet Muhammad (570–632) and are based in practice on the *sharia* (the law that, in principle, regulates all aspects of Muslim communal and private life and is derived from the Koran, a text in Arabic, and amplified by the words and deeds of the Prophet and later by Islamic jurists) can they owe genuine allegiance to a territorial state not constructed on a religious basis or to a national civic society?

A challenging contemporary issue is how Muslims, if religion essentially defines their identity, should live and behave in a community under non-Muslim rule. In a manner still relevant today, our six main writers and their predecessors discuss these questions that concern, among other things, the relation between religion and political power, the parameters of religious zealotry, the role and place accorded to women, the degree of civil liberties, and political participation in the Orient. Whether these contemporary problems should be regarded as illustrative of a clash of civilizations between an Occidental and an Oriental, largely Muslim world is arguable, but less disputatious is recognition that meaningful differences did and still do exist between the two worlds.

These questions were long considered, usually in nonsystematic fashion, by the numerous early European travelers, missionaries, diplomats, cultural historians, and political theorists, many of whom had firsthand information and observations of Eastern countries they visited or wrote about, especially regarding the Ottoman Empire and Persia. This book's first chapters focus on these observers not only because of their own inherent interest but also because of their considerable influence on our six main writers. These figures, some highly learned, some captivating because of their attention to detail, some eccentric, provided important contributions to European understanding of the nature of Eastern societies and the continuing encounters and conflicts between Christian Europe and the Muslim East, particularly the Ottoman Empire, which at one point stretched from the frontiers of Persia to those of Morocco, and from Hungary to Yemen. In the early encounters, the West's problem was how to resist the Muslims, not how to impose imperial domination over them.

Before turning to actual Western perceptions of the Orient it is pertinent to suggest that the study by Westerners of Eastern countries is not inextricably linked to desire for power over the Orient, which implies a hegemonic imperialist or colonial attitude. Nor is it axiomatic that knowledge and perception of truth are inherently linked to the desire to impose power. Obviously scholars and commentators reflect the values and cognitive styles of their own cultures, but many, including myself, come to the study of other cultures out of enthusiasm and curiosity.

However, a now widely held and influential view is that such study by Westerners of Eastern systems cannot be truly objective.[3] Inherently such study, it is postulated, contains cultural bias and inability to form conclusions in a disinterested fashion. An Arab proverb asks what camel ever saw its own hump. One can agree that the observer's subjectivity and cognitive biases inevitably influence political, ethical, or aesthetic judgments that stem from a wide range of variables, beliefs, customs, and circumstances. This is true no matter how sincere the observer's attempt to be objective, how rigorous the mastering of relevant empirical data, how careful the analysis of political, social, economic, and religious issues, and how scrupulous a comprehensive gaze cast over an intellectual landscape. An early warning came from Gunnar Myrdal, in his magisterial study, *The American Dilemma*, which stated that bias in social science cannot be erased "simply by keeping to the facts."[4] Another came from George Orwell who, in his graphic essay, "Looking Back on the Spanish War," feared that the very concept of objective truth was fading out of the world, and who, in another essay, "Why I Write," declared that no book was genuinely free from political bias.

Nevertheless, it is one thing to acknowledge that the values and the preferences of an analyst may shape the outcome of an inquiry, or end in a debatable interpretation, or even at an extreme, into a distorted presentation of reality. However, it is another matter to contend that objectivity is a concept that is only relative to the contingent schemes of individuals, or that what is called truth is merely the outcome of the subjectivity or the "narratives" of the writer.[5] It would appear prejudiced and arrogant for critics to imply that Westerners are ignorant of or lack appreciation of cultural diversity in the world in general or cannot be objective about conditions in the Orient in particular. This would be to deny Westerners the right to search for new knowledge or ignore their concern to correct inaccurate information, an activity inherent in Western scholarly enterprise. That search is pertinent to Pascal's aphorism: it is not certain that everything is uncertain.

The late Maxime Rodinson, the distinguished French scholar of the Middle East who was also a committed Marxist and Communist all his adult life and thus no defender of Western imperialism, made the point very well. He understood that "under the influence of decolonization and anticolonialist ideology the great temptation today, especially by the younger generation, is to reject the acquired wisdom of the past as tainted by Eurocentric and colonialist mentality." This rejection meant forgetting that "until now it has been the West that has applied the most refined scientific methods in its approach, even if the practice of those methods had already been initiated within the non-European civilizations studied." While acknowledging that an intimate knowledge of a society and its culture by a member of it gives that person a privileged position, Rodinson maintains it is also true that individuals outside a particular society have certain advantages in studying that society, and that an outsider's distance from prevailing local ideologies is in itself a factor of utmost importance. The consequence of that distance is manifest in the contributions made by European writers, including those in this book, to the study of Muslim societies that include a critical approach to primary sources, recognition of cultural pluralism and its consequences, and a separation of scholarship from religious or political dogmatism.[6]

The core of the criticism of Western views of the Orient stems from postmodern theory. Since Nietzsche, the notion of objective reality, and scholarly attempts to portray that reality, has been regarded as suspect and truth held to be a social construct.[7] One late-twentieth-century exponent of this school of thought, the influential French philosopher Jean Baudrillard, proffered the concept of "hyper reality," the view that individuals today can no longer discern what reality is because they are lost in a world of "simulacra," images and signs created and presented as "real" by the mass media, information technologies, and entertainment events.[8] Spectacle is seen as crucial in creating our perception of the real. At an extreme, Baudrillard's concept may also suggest that reality does not exist independently of human representations.

If this postmodern view emphasizes the power of seduction, an argument, more polemically pointed regarding the possibility of objective political and historical analysis, is that knowledge and the perception of truth are inherently linked to the seduction of power. In the terminology of the late influential French intellectual Michel Foucault, the production of knowledge and the exercise of administrative power intertwine. For him, knowledge and "discursive practices" are social ideologies that function as forms of exerting power and disseminating the effects of power.[9]

In a more intemperate and polemical fashion this Foucaultian argument has been applied by disciples to the intellectual and cultural interactions between Western Europe (the Occident derived from the Latin *occidens*, west or setting) and the Orient. The basic assertion is that Western Europe, and then an extended West including the United States, has not only dominated and exercised colonial or imperial rule over the Orient but also that, through intellectual and aesthetic means, it has created an essentialist, ontological, epistemologically insensitive distinction between a "West," materially developed and self-assured about its superior civilization, and an "Orient," which it regards as inferior, backward, and not modernized. The conclusion of this argument, in reality unwarrantable self-abasement, is that investigation by Westerners of Eastern societies and politics, and the search for knowledge about them is and always has been inextricably linked with desire for power over the Orient.[10] It insinuates that this distorted perspective of Eastern peoples and politics by Western scholarship is, implicitly or otherwise, in essence a justification of imperial control over the Orient.

Yet objective analysts deconstructing this argument may well conclude that it is both a credulous caricature of the true nature of Western perceptions of Eastern systems and a fallacious attribution to them of an Orient that is immutable and inferior. At its most absurd, the children's picture books of Barbar the Elephant that have been written by Jean de Brunhoff since 1931 have been viewed as imperialist propaganda indicating the desirability of French colonialism. For anyone cognizant of the genuine and sincere efforts (many are included in this book) of Western writers in books, articles, reports, journals, diaries, letters to investigate, understand, and interpret Eastern cultures, customs, and political behavior, it is unreasonable to argue that Western study of the Orient is little more than a form of colonial power. Curiosity and a desire to contribute to the advancement of knowledge are not tantamount to cultural or intellectual forms of colonialism or disguised Western hegemony. In the main, the serious Western writers here have adhered to the aphorism of Edward Gibbon: the duty of a historian is not to impose his private judgment on an issue.[11]

The neo-Foucaultian argument, sometimes couched in arcane opacity, conveys a monolithic and binary view of what has been and remains today, in reality, a complex and knotty process of understanding and interpreting foreign cultures.[12] In this intellectual debate a justifiable response is that if one assumes an essentialist, automatically prejudiced, and unchanging "West" and a hostile "Other," one also assumes implicitly an "East" that can be seen in equally simplistic and essentialist fashion.[13]

These monolithic and binary views do not take into account the diversity of the historical Middle East political and military reality and the periods of change both in Europe and in the Islamic lands caused by the incorporation of different peoples and cultures. They are a simplification of a complicated series of historical events and encounters. It serves little purpose to posit a perpetual conflict between a "West" and a "Muslim Orient" in simplistic terms. One might recall that the majority of conflicts in which Islamic peoples were involved were with other Muslims. Relations between Europeans and Muslim countries were only part of the network of interactions, and interrelationships between Muslim rivals were often more important. Struggles in the sixteenth and early seventeenth centuries, for example, between the Sunni Ottomans and the Shi'ite Persian Safavids were more intense, continuous, and important than conflict with Europeans.

Earlier, Muslim writers paid less attention to the Crusades when they were occurring than to intra-Muslim rivalries and immediate external enemies such as the Byzantium Empire and the more dangerous Mongol invasions in the mid-thirteenth century, which captured Baghdad in 1258 and slaughtered thousands and destroyed the Abbasid caliphate. The Crusades received so little attention that there was no Arabic term for *crusade* until modern times. Historical analysis also shows alliances changing for geopolitical reasons. France was linked to the Ottomans against the Hapsburgs; Russia was allied with the Muslim Khanates; and the Iranian Safavid dynasty sought alliances in the West. Though the argument has been forwarded for partisan purposes, it appears misguided to posit the relatively short Western dominance in the Middle East in the nineteenth and twentieth centuries as if it were the norm of historical relationships.

Another consequence of the neo-Foucaultian argument is the tendency to minimize or even totally neglect the significance of the Byzantine Empire, which was the eastern part of the Roman Empire and had been Christian since the conversion of Constantine, who founded a city on the site of Byzantium, and then in 330 made it his capital naming it after his own name. In essence the empire was a Mediterranean state with a common faith that lasted until 1453. The neo-Foucaultian argument thus ignores the reality that the Byzantines dominated the eastern Mediterranean for several centuries and shared with Muslims cultural and economic contacts as well as the conflicts that forced them to surrender territories to the Muslim conquerors. Such a reductionist argument also neglects the impact of the heirs of Byzantium: Greece, Orthodox Christianity, Russia, and the Slavic world. It ignores or denies the coexistence of a fluid interaction and cross-fertilization of cultures with continuing rivalry between Europe and Muslims and the Orient. This has long been the case. The first Islamic dynasty, the Umayyads (661–750), centered in Damascus was influenced by Byzantine traditions as well as by the Zoroastrian Sasanid Empire (224–651) in Iran and Iraq.

A recent insightful view of this cultural interaction is an analysis of the series of thirty-three prints, now known as the *Tauromaquia*, which Francisco Goya began etching in 1815 and which depicts the bullfight in Spain. These etchings reveal sympathetic portraits of Moors within the framework of Spanish history.[14] His analysis suggests that the nine centuries of Muslim presence in the Iberian Peninsula had a considerable role in shaping the identity of the Spanish pastime, that the Moorish past was integral rather than alien to the Spanish national identity. The fluid cultural interaction is apparent in many areas, not only the aesthetic exchanges in Iberia and in Sicily but also in the icons and images shared by the East and the West even in times of conflict. Islamic rugs are prominent in some of the paintings of Hans Holbein and Van Dyck. Other well-known examples include the interaction of Ottoman Sultan Mehmed II with Italian artists, the European-style furniture in part of the Topkapi Palace, and, later, the baroque and rococo style in the Dolmabahce Palace in Istanbul. Cultural cross-fertilization in the arts and architecture between East and West, and the interaction of cultural counterpoint and conformity illustrate the permeable boundaries and shared undertakings between the two sides.[15] A familiar illustration of this is the culture between the tenth and thirteenth centuries of Andalusia (al-Andalus) in Spain with its cross-fertilization of Islamic, Jewish, and Christian thinkers. In Spain, especially in Toledo, and in other European countries, Western scholars benefited from translations of Islamic scientific texts, including those on mathematics, into Latin. Historians have noted that ideas from the East permeated the Renaissance in Europe. William McNeill wrote that at that time "Westerners discovered that the Muslims possessed a sophistication of mind and richness of learning far surpassing that available in Latin."[16]

One particular illustration of the complex interaction of the two cultures is the Great Church of the Holy Wisdom, St. Sophia in Constantinople-Istanbul, which served for nine centuries as a church and for five more as a mosque and is now a secular museum. Within it are Byzantine Christian mosaics and large green medallions around the walls with Arabic monograms in gold of Muhammad and the first four caliphs. The interaction sometimes took a personal form; one example was the flamboyant William Beckford, the wealthy and eccentric English writer and politician who, while in Madrid for a time in the late eighteenth-century, took a young Muslim named Muhammad as a lover. Another enticing example of the interaction is that of Giuseppe Donizetti, musician, adventurer, friend of Napoleon, and brother of the more celebrated composer, who was appointed in 1827 to conduct the Imperial Band in the Ottoman Palace.

A changing balance of political and military power has existed during the centuries between East and West. Periods of war and virulent expressions of religious zeal on both sides alternated with eras of peace, during which skirmishes continued, and arrangements such as the financial tributes, in essence indemnities, paid by Western rulers to the Ottoman Empire existed. These eras witnessed mercantile arrangements, frequent deals between the two sides, diplomatic encounters, and the granting by the Ottomans of capitulations, agreements that can be seen as early versions of "most favored nation" arrangements that extended trading, economic, and diplomatic privileges to some European countries.[17] Moreover, the history of that empire was marked by internal and external conflict and by continuous evolution during the centuries, which therefore led to changing relationships and cultural, political, and economic contacts with the West.

Much of the criticism of Western commentary on the East is concentrated on Western presentations of Oriental life in art, literature, music, theater, and films, which are seen as voyeuristic, portraying Oriental life as exotic and dwelling unduly on questionable and demeaning aspects of behavior. Critics of this persuasion contend that the Orient was depicted in art, particularly in the nineteenth century, as an enchanting, picuresque setting exhibiting eroticism, cruelty, and opulence. Certainly in that century, erotic titillation, fantasies regarding women and their sensuality especially in the harem, and exotic images appear in Western art portraying Oriental life. No one looking, for example, at Eugène Delacroix's *Death of Sardanapalus* or Jean-Léon Gérôme's *The Snake Charmer* can deny this. Yet it is one thing to acknowledge the attitude and sensibility exhibited in these paintings but quite another to suggest they are active participants in an ideology of imperialism. They ought more properly to be assessed in terms of their aesthetic quality and historical interest.

A number of things are pertinent about this general criticism of Western artistic presentations. Those presentations that are criticized for their portrayal of Oriental life, particularly its exotic and erotic elements, are not dissimilar from the hundreds of images of Western life that have long appeared in Western art and continue to the present day. Ingres, for example, has been criticized for his harem scene, *Odalisque with a Slave*, but he also portrayed similar nude female figures in other important paintings not concerned with the Orient. Secondly, the images of Oriental life are not related to any desire to exercise Western political power over the Orient. Many of them, such as those by David Roberts and David Wilkie, in the early nineteenth century, touch on archaeological or topographical aspects, and even on the real-life experiences of Muslims as is clear in some of the paintings of Delacroix, John Frederick Lewis (who spent ten years in Cairo in the 1840s), Eugène Fromentin, and, later, Etienne Dinet who converted to Islam. Other images feature historical events and characters, landscapes, and street scenes illuminated by a bright sun, as Auguste Renoir displayed, and the color of barren earth. If in French art of the nineteenth century there was Romantic fascination with a supposed exotic Orient, also present were images of a lost original Muslim culture.[18] The criticism of Western presentations neglects the significant cross-cultural artistic contacts between East and West. A poignant, in view of later German history, illustration of this cross-cultural contact and Arabic influence was the Neue Synagogue built in Berlin in 1866, which resembled the Moorish building style of the Alhambra in Granada. After desecration by the Nazis in 1938 and destruction by Allied bombing in 1943 the synagogue was partially reconstructed in 1995 essentially in the original style.

The history of art, and more particularly of architecture, reveals not only that Muslim civilization has benefited by absorbing the culture its colonialists found in Spain and in Constantinople after Islamic forces conquered those areas, but that the Orient has been depicted sympathetically by artists since the Renaissance. Gentile Bellini, who lived in Istanbul from 1479 to 1481, is probably the most well-known example of this sympathetic attitude with his great painting, now in the National Gallery in London, of Sultan Mehmed II; the painting is an Oriental iconic image in which the sultan is represented as a ruler even more powerful than a Venetian doge. The impact of Oriental life on Bellini is noteworthy; when he arrived back in Venice he was dressed in Oriental costume. A painting, *The Reception of the Ambassadors*, traditionally attributed to Bellini though now labeled in the Louvre as anonymous, portrays a group of nobles visiting the sultan. About the same time another Italian artist,

Constanzo da Ferrara (patronized by the sultan who had invited Venetian craftsmen to his court), made a medallion of the ruler.[19] Melchior Lorchs published an engraving of Suleiman the Magnificent in 1536. Attempts were made, though unsuccessful, to bring Leonardo da Vinci and Michelangelo to the Ottoman court, which had been, certainly until the 1530s, a source of enthusiastic patronage of European artists. This patronage was to a considerable degree one outcome of the perception by the Ottomans of their enhanced role and stature in the world after their conquest of Constantinople in 1453 and the stirring of Muslim ambition to reunite Constantinople with Rome.

Oriental narratives featuring Muslim settings, costumes, and luxury goods, and portraits of the rulers of the Muslim world appear in the works of many other Renaissance masters, including Vittore Carpaccio, Giovanni Mansueti, Lorenzo Lotto, Piero della Francesca, and Bartolomeo Bellano.[20] A cogent analysis of sixteenth-century artistic and literary artifacts controverts the argument that the West's perception of the East, based on imperialistic Eurocentrism, was of an alien "Other." On the contrary, using illustrations such as Edmund Spenser's *Faerie Queene*, Carpaccio's paintings of St. George, Benozzo Gozzoli's frescoes of the *Adoration of the Magi* in Florence, and Hans Holbein's *The Ambassadors* (1553), it argues that cultural products of the sixteenth century reveal an "engagement between East and West."[21] Some indications of the fact that this engagement was mutual in character are shown by Western imitations of Turkish carpets in the late sixteenth century and by the Ottoman use of Western status symbols such as official royal portraits, crowns, gold helmets, scepters, and royal tapestries. Iconography of this kind fulfilled a propagandistic illustration of Ottoman power.[22] If nineteenth-century European painters, such as the German Gustav Bauernfeind and the Austrian Rudolf Swoboda, illustrated the life of the Orient, a Turkish artist, Osman Hamdy Bey, adopted a Western style in his portrait, *A Lady in Constantinople*.

Western artists admired the style of Islamic art in its decoration of flat surfaces with appealing patterns and arabesque calligraphy. One might well argue that the Western rococo style had some roots in the arabesque, a style that spread in Europe chiefly through engravings, metal objects, pottery, textiles, and bookbindings with arabesque ornament. Great artists – Veronese, Delacroix, who visited Morocco in 1832, Gérôme, Chassériau, Rogier, Ingres, and, in more recent times, Kandinsky and Matisse – and many less well-known artists have been stimulated by Oriental or Islamic culture. Rembrandt collected and copied Indian miniatures. European craftsmen emulated Eastern styles, patterns, and techniques; assimilated Eastern skills and motifs; and absorbed fabrication of metalwork, glass, leather goods, damascening (inlaying gold and silver in brass), marbling (decorating paper), porcelain figurines, and marquetry into the West. They acknowledged that fellow craftsmen in Persia excelled in textiles, ceramics, tanning, and stone cutting, among other crafts. Europeans were also aware of the sophistication of Indian chintz, Chinese silks, Japanese lacquer, and painted screens. The Western adoption of Oriental motifs and practice is clearly evident to all tourists who visit San Marco and the Doge's Palace in Venice or the Royal Pavillion in Brighton, England, or towns such as Dubrovnik, or even Kew Gardens in London.

Similarly, musical compositions, to mention only the most well-known operas such as Mozart's *Die Entführung aus dem Serail* and *Die Zauberflöte*, Delibes's *Lakmé*, Borodin's *Prince Igor*, Rossini's *Semiramide*, Verdi's *Aida* and *Nabucco*, Berlioz's *The Trojans at Cathage*, Bizet's *Djamileh* and *The Pearl Fishers*, Saint-Saens's *Samson and Delilah*, and Puccini's *Turandot* and *Madame Butterfly*, may portray fascination and fear of the Orient, but they also reflect the complex and varied relationship between East and West, and in some cases the benevolence of the Muslim ruler. Some of Mozart's operas imply an Enlightenment sensibility in the Orient: in *Seraglio* the Turkish Pasha Selim appears as a virtuous and magnanimous individual who grants his Western captives their freedom and broadens their emotional horizons by his kindness and noble behavior. In Mozart's *Cosi fan tutte*, the two women are fascinated by the Muslim Albanian disguise of their lovers. One aspect of the cultural interaction of East and West is illustrated in music by the adoption by European rulers from the end of the seventeenth century of the instruments and techniques, the rhythmic beat of the percussion battery (*batterie turque*), and the Ottoman janissary band into their own military music.[23] Turkish-style music appeared in Western ballets and opera-ballets, the most well known of which is Rameau's *Les Indes Galantes* of 1735. Eastern influence on Western music has been shown during the last three centuries in the works of many Western composers, from the eighteenth century to Stravinsky, Holst, Britten, and Messiaen in the last century, who introduced aspects of Oriental music, different sonorities, instrumental color, and rhythmic complexity into their compositions.

Western literature is replete with fanciful tales and negative images of Eastern countries, particularly Turkey, of cruel Oriental rulers, of Tamerlane, and of the nature of Islam. Yet it is salutary to recall that major writers through the centuries such as Ariosto, Molière, Racine, Marlowe, Shakespeare, Dryden, Byron, Chateaubriand, Flaubert, Oliver Goldsmith, and Horace Walpole have been fascinated by the Orient in positive as well as negative fashion. An amusing example of the former is seen in Molière's comedy-ballet of 1670, *Le Bourgeois Gentilhomme*, with its Turkish sequence and where the ambitious

Monsieur Jourdain is happy to consent to his daughter's marriage to the supposed Turkish prince, son of the sultan. The protagonists, advised by an elderly Muslim, in Voltaire's *Candide* find peace in Constantinople. Nearly two centuries later, Sir Walter Scott in *The Talisman* wrote more sympathetically of the style and behavior of the Saracen than of the Christian knight. However, critical comment about the Orient, such as the works of pseudotravelers, especially the *Letters Writ by a Turkish Spy* (1684) by Giovanni Paolo Marana, which influenced Daniel Defoe and Montesquieu's *Lettres Persanes* (1721), and occasional pornography, such as the *Lustful Turk* (1828), are also part of Western literature.[24] In this regard it is interesting that Defoe's *Robinson Crusoe* was influenced by the English translation of an Arabic philosophical novel about a man living alone on a desert island. Many European writers did view the Orient as a contrast to Christian virtues and European ways of life. Even the moderate Montaigne, who saw the Orient in a positive light, regarded the Turkish state, "the strongest in the world," as one where the people were simultaneously trained to esteem arms and despise letters, and where rulers did not observe promises and were cruel conquerors.[25]

Nevertheless, to accept negative commentary or exotic presentations in art, music, and literature as the only images of the Orient held by the Western world is deliberately to ignore or to minimize not only the positive writings about it but also the remarkable contributions to knowledge, scholarship, and understanding of the area by erudite Europeans, historians, and philologists and by inquisitive scrupulous travelers, who were disinterested in power relationships or colonial control and sought for truth without concern for any ideological framework. These individuals collected information through a variety of methods in different degrees: reliable historical research about the past and the present in the Eastern countries with which they were familiar; honest reporting on their personal observation and sightseeing; their knowledge of the oral tradition of peoples in those countries; and, following the path that Arnaldo Momigliano termed "the Herodotean approach," a trustworthy, respectable, objective account of their encounters, contacts, and relationships with the East and the increasing Western information about it.[26]

Critics who have referred disparagingly and in negative language and stereotypes to Western study and portraits of Eastern societies and cultures as prejudiced interpretations of those societies aiming at intellectual and political domination of them, neglect the complex Western approaches to the Orient and the wide, varied, and eclectic range of opinions of Western writers that belie any simplistic contention of an inexorable Western hostility or condescension toward the Orient, which is portrayed in fanciful fashion as a consequence of Western pathologies. These critics, in discourse frequently monolithic in character, have had some success since the 1980s in converting the previously honorable word *Orientalist*, a term coined in the latter part of the eighteenth century in both England and France to define the student of the history, archaeology, languages, literature, culture, and social and religious life of the East, which would help Europeans understand the Orient, into a pejorative term, and sometimes used the term as a political tool or for polemical obfuscation.

Critics of this kind disregard the reality that writing by scholarly Orientalists and observation by pilgrims, merchants, and travelers arose independently of any Western imperial or colonial interests in the Orient and from a variety of motives: natural curiosity about foreign areas; pursuit of objective new knowledge; empathy; and the desire to make comparisons with political, economic, or religious traits in the writer's own country or in the West generally.[27] From the Orient the West acquired methods and tools and knowledge of science, medicine, and philosophy, and acknowledged its borrowings. Europeans acquired Muslim scientific knowledge through the Latin translations of Arabic works. Under Muslim Moorish rule in Spain the cities of Toledo and Cordoba were notable intellectual centers.

Robert Schwoebel concludes his important work by suggesting that individuals of different kinds in the Renaissance period demonstrated not only that writing about Turks was acceptable, but also that a foreign culture could be studied successfully by an outsider.[28] Even a simple list of a few of the more notable Westerners, some admittedly eccentric characters, who contributed to the study of the Orient and of Islam is impressive.[29] One early example was the baptised Jew Pedro de Alfonso who compiled the first objective work about Muhammad in the early twelfth century. Starting with the considerable scholarship in medieval Spain, the list would include holders of chairs in Arabic: Guillaume Postel, a distinguished scholar and eccentric mystic, in Paris (1539), Edward Pococke in Oxford (1638), Simon Ockley, translator of works by Arab theologians and philosophers and author of *The History of the Saracens*, in Cambridge (1711), Adrien Reland, who published an account of Islam drawn from Islamic sources, in Utrecht (1701), and Silverstre de Sacy, an exacting Jansenist philologist, in Paris (1795).[30] To this can be added the scholars who studied the Orient at the Collège Royal, later the Collège de France, founded in 1529; Barthélemy d'Herbelot de Molainville, student of Oriental languages and author of the majestic *Bibliothèque Orientale*, an immense bibliography of Arab and Turkish works and manuscripts, completed posthumously in 1697 by Antoine Galland, translator of *The Arabian Nights* and professor of Arabic in Paris in 1709; and William Jones, student of Sanskrit and Indo-European languages who presided over the Asiatic Society of Bengal set up in 1784.

To take one example of Western contributions, William Jones founded the Asiatic Society, which he conceived of as playing an important role in scientific analysis of Asia's society, history, antiquities, and environment. The society was to study the governmental and religious institutions of Asia, as well as its scientific skills, literature, and art. That contribution has been well acknowledged. One hundred and thirty years later, the president of the newly founded India Science Congress spoke of Jones and the society as "the principal source of inspiration in the organization and advancement of scientific research of every description in this country."[31] Equally impressive as the contribution by Jones are those by the considerable list of distinguished scholars during the last two centuries as well as the emergence of societies and journals concerned with specialized research on the Middle East. Some of these scholars have been noticeably sympathetic to Arab and Islamic causes: Edward G. Browne, critic of British foreign and imperial policy who was associated with the campaign for Egyptian nationalism and for Persian liberty, W. S. Blunt for Arab nationalism, Louis Massignon for the Palestinians, and Ignaz Goldziher was critical of foreign control of Egypt and of Western denigration of Islam.[32] The first major European journal specializing in the area was the *Fundgruben des Orients*, founded by the Austrian Josef von Hammer-Purgstall (1774–1856). In 1821 the Société Asiatique of Paris was started; two years later it issued its *Journal Asiatique*. Similar societies and journals began in England in 1823 and 1834, in the United States in 1842, and in Germany in 1847.

Even if Western scholars did not all exhibit sympathy for Arab or Islamic causes, they nevertheless could be genuinely concerned with scholarship on the area. An important example was the consequence of the invasion of Egypt in 1798 by General Napoleon Bonaparte with fifty-five thousand troops to fight against Murad Bey, the leader of the Mamluks who ruled the country though it was technically a province of the Ottoman Empire. This invasion, the Expédition d'Egypte, was undertaken to control the country, undermine British relations and trade with Britain, and challenge British access to the route to India. More idealistically, Bonaparte, in his proclamation to the people of Egypt, which had been under Ottoman suzerainty since 1517, said he was a defender of Islam and had come to liberate the population from tyranny, and in practice would try to modernize Cairo, at that time a larger city than Paris. Bonaparte defeated the Mamlukes at Mount Tabor in the Holy Land but failed to capture the port city of Acre. His armada of 335 ships was defeated at the mouth of the Nile in August 1798 by a British fleet under Horatio Nelson. Bonaparte did introduce reforms in political institutions, health service, taxation, and postal system. Nevertheless, the Expédition has often been regarded as an imperialistic adventure, militarily unsuccessful and often savage in character, and as a forerunner of France's conception of a *mission civilisatrice*, introducing civilization to a backward people, in the Middle East as elsewhere.

Yet it did result in the *Description de l' Egypte* (1809–1828). This extraordinary publication, in ten volumes of explanatory text and thirteen volumes of engraved folio plates, containing information, accurate and detailed, on archaeology and antiquities, Egyptian society, demography, medicine, sociological issues, and geography was produced by 150 leading scholars, artists, engineers, and architects, including Claude Berthollet, the eminent chemist, and Gaspard Monge, the famous mathematician (whose name is still present in a street in Cairo) who accompanied Bonaparte's troops. No objective commentator can suggest that the work was merely an adjunct of imperialism or that an ideological West had implicitly presented a prejudiced portrait or fantasy of the Orient.[33] This exceptional scholarly work, based on empirical observation and taxonomy, is now considered the foundation of modern Egyptology in its presentation of all aspects of the country, ancient and modern. It laid the basis for further archaeological study of the country. It also starkly poses the larger question of the manner of the recovery of the pre-Islamic past, buried and forgotten by Muslims, which was largely the achievement of Western Orientalists, and to a lesser extent of Western travelers. It was the French, who in 1799 discovered the Rosetta stone (which was captured by British troops two years later), the key to translating hieroglyphics, excavated the ruins at Karnak, and established the Institute of Egypt in Cairo. The declared purposes of the institute were to advance and propagate enlightenment in Egypt, to study and publish information on industrial, historical, and natural phenomena in Egypt, and to offer opinions when asked by the French government.

HISTORICAL CONTEXT OF THE ORIENT

Our writers were observing the Orient at different historical moments, some at the height of the Ottoman Empire and some as it was declining when the Mediterranean was no longer an Ottoman lake as it had been for more than a century, when the empire had lost its naval hegemony in the Levant area, and when it had been stopped at the gates of Vienna in 1683. They were also concerned with issues of Muslim societies in India and Algeria. The perceptions of our writers must be understood in this changing historical context. European interest in the Oriental Islamic world coupled with fear of that world long antedates the era of our six main writers and those of the travelers and observers in this book. From the founding of Islam and the forming of Bedouin warriors into a unit in Arabia and their early military conquests, Europeans perceived the threat of the Orient and Muslims in a variety of ways, including moral, intellectual, religious, political, and military, at least until the late seventeenth century when the Ottoman Empire was weakening.

That fear and concern can in many ways be traced back to the early years of Islamic rule when at the battle of Yarmuk (636), near what is now the border between Jordan and Syria, the forces of the Islamic caliphate defeated those of the Byzantine Roman regime. The following year they defeated the Persians at the battle of Qadisiyya: this victory was noticeably evoked by Saddam Hussein in 1980 during the Iran-Iraq war. This first wave of Muslim conquests outside the Arabian Peninsula then led to the rapid advance of Islam into areas that were Christian: Palestine, Syria, Mesopotamia, Egypt, Spain, and North Africa. Muslim forces also advanced into the areas of Iran, Central Asia, and India. In 711 Muslim forces crossed the Strait of Gibraltar and invaded Iberia; by 720 they had conquered most of it from the Christian people. Not until 1492 was the whole of Iberia under Christian rule. During the ninth century Sicily had been conquered and parts of southern Italy harassed by Muslim forces.

Muhammad, the Prophet of Islam, had during his short rule founded a state maintaining and advancing his faith by military means, a state that later Muslim rulers and thinkers have regarded as a model to be emulated. The challenge to the Christian world of these early Islamic conquests was quickly recognized. One of the first to convey critical perceptions of Islam and its power was the Anglo-Saxon monk, known as the Venerable Bede. Probably referring to the victory of Charles Martel at Poitiers in 732, he wrote that the "swarm of Saracens (Muslim forces) ravaged Gaul with horrible slaughter but not long afterwards they paid the penalty of their wickedness in the same country."[34]

In his first inaugural address President Lincoln spoke of "the mystic chords of memory stretching from every battlefield and patriot grave to every living heart and hearthstone." These chords, stemming from seventh-century history when Muhammad had ordered his adherents to fight the unbelievers until they accepted Islam or submitted to its rule were evident when Osama bin Laden and his colleagues, in their 1998 declaration, called on Muslims everywhere to fight the United States and its allies and specifically referred to the 636 victory at Yarmuk. Many Muslims knew the significance of the reference and the allusion to past glory. Similarly, chants in Lebanon, in the internecine feuding among rival groups in recent years, of "We serve you, Hussein" are references to the killing in 680 of Imam Hussein, the grandson of the Prophet. The twentieth-century Saddam Hussein idolized Saladin, the acclaimed conqueror of Jerusalem, as a hero.

Historians still attempt explanations for the remarkable early success of Islamic forces, which on the east approached the frontiers of the Tang dynasty in China, and in the west clashed with the Merovingian princes of the area that is now France. Those forces were perhaps fortunate to have attacked when both the Byzantines and the Persians had been weakened by previous wars. Those two empires were further weakened by the presence within them of Arab tribes who had converted to Islam. A frequent explanation for Islamic success has been the qualities of the followers of the new faith, courage, and moral superiority. Muslim Arabs were united in a single political and religious community. More mundanely, jihad, defined here as armed struggle against nonbelievers rather than as moral striving, promised earthly and heavenly rewards; martyrs were promised a special place in paradise, while on earth soldiers kept most of the captured booty. Regardless of the explanation, the Islamic success not only conquered substantial territory, the periphery of which largely remains today, but also uprooted native religions, Zoroastrianism, the state religion of the Sasanid dynasty in Persia, Buddhism in Central Asia, and Hinduism in the Indus valley, as well as controlling the Christian majority in the Levant. Arabic became a major world language. The caliphate, under the Umayyad clan from 661–750 when it was defeated by the Abbasids who at that time were based in Damascus, extended to Cordoba in the West. The Islamic forces had been stopped from taking Constantinople from 674 to 676, and again from 717 to 718, and had been halted at the Pyrenees from 733 to 740, but they had not been confined to Arabia.

Confrontation between European and Oriental Islamic countries, with periods of coexistence and intervals of complex relationships between the two sides, lasted more than a thousand years. In the early confrontations the Muslim stereotype of the European Franks was of a people dirty, deceitful, sexually loose, filthy in their personal habits, though courageous and redoubtable in war. Inscriptions in the Dome of the Rock, which was built by the caliph Abd al-Malik in Jerusalem from 691 to 692 on the Temple Mount, a place holy for both Christians and Jews, explicitly reject the Christian doctrines of the Incarnation and the Trinity. The Dome of the Rock and the mosque built nearby fifty years earlier were a symbolic display of Islamic success on ground that had been occupied by the first Jewish temple (Solomon's in the tenth-century BC) and the second (destroyed by the Romans in AD 70), and by the Church of the Holy Sepulchre, the sanctuary established by Constantine close to it, which is the place alleged to be where Christ's tomb was discovered, a tomb Constantine was eager to protect.

At the same time the mutual need for trade was recognized. Europeans wanted Oriental spices, especially pepper and ginger, ivory, perfumes, and jewelry. The Muslims wanted timber and iron for ships and weapons, linens, and woolens. Reminders of that trade are evident in the use in English of words of Arabic, Persian, or Turkish origin: *check*, *tariff*, *douane*, *damask*, *cashmere*, and *muslin*.[35] Ottoman commercial competitiveness and its interest in setting up trading networks, as well as its expansionist ambitions and changing political alliances, were facilitated by its sea power in the Mediterranean.[36]

After Muslim forces had thrust themselves into the West and, especially after they had raided Ostia and Rome in 846, Christian dignitaries spoke of the need for a counteroffensive. Pope Leo IV (847–55) promised a heavenly reward for Christians fighting the Muslims; a generation later Pope John VIII (872–82) made similar promises for those who would fight the infidel. But no serious action was taken until the eleventh century. In 1009 the Fatamid caliph Al-Hakim, purportedly annoyed by Christian Easter pilgrimages to Jerusalem, had destroyed the Saint-Sepulchre church as well as other churches in the area. Pope Gregory VII (1073–85) announced in 1074 his plan to lead personally a force to help the Christians of the eastern Mediterranean. Twenty years after this abortive project Pope Urban II (1088–99) at the Council of Clermont in 1095 gave a sermon, proclaiming that the Muslims had seized Jerusalem, the Holy City of Christ, and called on Western Christians to retake the Holy Land and the Holy Sepulchre, and to help the beleaguered Eastern Church. He denounced the Muslims as a "race utterly alienated from God."

Historians legitimately differ on the genesis of the first Crusade in 1096 and on why the call for it was implemented although calls two centuries earlier went unheeded. Certainly Pope Urban II was a persuasive advocate and skilful publicist for his cause. The summons to liberate Jerusalem caught the imagination of sufficient parts of Christian society, aristocratic families and their dependents, households linked to monasteries, lay courts, some people interested for mercenary reasons or disparate ambitions, and others who were disturbed by reports of the persecution of pilgrims going to Jerusalem and believed that the treatment of pilgrims and their access to the Holy Land had worsened because of the actions in the area of the Seljuk Turks from the 1070s. The Crusades were justified on the basis of a common Christian faith directed against Islamic enemies seen as threats to the faithful.[37] They were not launched for greed for Arab wealth and territory. On the contrary the Crusades were a costly enterprise for the participants. Nine Crusades took place sporadically before the last official one in 1291, which ended with the loss of Acre, the last Crusader stronghold, after Syria and the area of Palestine had been gradually lost by Christians during the thirteenth century.

Jerusalem experienced a checkered history from its founding about four thousand years ago. King David, circa 1000 BC, had made it the capital of his Israelite kingdom, and Solomon built the temple there. The city as well as the Jewish temple were destroyed by the Babylonian King Nebuchadnezzar in 586 BC, bringing an end to the kingdom of Judah. After the fall of the

Babylonian empire to the Persians fifty years later, Jerusalem was controlled in succession by the Persians, Greeks, and Romans. In the fourth century AD Constantine made Jerusalem a Byzantine Christian city. In the seventh century, Muslims, who built the Dome of the Rock there, began their control of the city. The Crusaders captured it in 1099 and founded the Latin Kingdom of Jerusalem, which suffered from personal and political rivalries and which lasted only eighty-eight years. Saladin (1138–93), founder of the Islamic Ayyubid dynasty in Syria and Egypt, captured Jerusalem after the battle of Hattin in 1187, as well as other cities in the Holy Land, from the Crusaders. Saladin, a Kurd born in Tikrit who came to rule over the lands of Syria, Palestine, and Egypt, has become a legendary figure in the Arab world as a symbol of resistance to and for overcoming "European imperialism" as a result of his capture of Jerusalem. Europeans have had a more nuanced perspective of this complex figure. Dante put him in limbo together with the actual and legendary figures of Troy and Rome. Immediately after the fall of Jerusalem he was "the scourge of the Lord"; later, he was seen as generous, chivalrous, magnanimous, and noble, the epitome of knighthood. Voltaire expressed this complexity; Saladin was at the same time conqueror and philosopher. His reputation as a superb diplomat and humane leader is reflected in chivalric romances, most memorably in Sir Walter Scott's *The Talisman*. Saladin was also a holy warrior and an upholder of the orthodox Islamic faith but was allegedly a patient of Moses Maimonides, the great Jewish rabbi, philosopher, and physician.

In 1229 Jerusalem was ceded to Frederic II, the Holy Roman Emperor, by negotiation with the Ayyubid ruler, Al-Malik al-Kamil, and in 1244 it was again lost to the Muslims when the Khwarizim Turks sacked the city and massacred the Christian population, thus ending Crusader rule. Muslim rule over the city would last until December 1917 when the British army arrived. Though some Crusaders had mixed motives and were interested in trade, influence, and dynastic rivalries, the stated goal and the primary purpose of all of them was to recapture Jerusalem, defend Christianity, end Islamic rule in the Holy Land, and stop Islamic territorial expansion. That expansion continued elsewhere, but it had been halted temporarily in the West by Charles Martel, grandfather of Charlemagne, at the battle of Poitiers (Tours) in 732, and in the Iberian Peninsula where, after seven centuries of struggle, the Reconquista, the gradual recapturing of Spain by Christians, gained victories in Toledo in 1085 and finally in Granada in 1492. An unanticipated consequence of the Christian capture of Granada was that Sephardic Jews expelled from Spain settled in Salonika, helping it become the most important commercial city of the Eastern Mediterranean.[38] Though there is some dispute on the significance of the battle of Poitiers for saving Christianity from the Islamic threat, if Charles Martel had not won it, Western history would have been quite different. The graphic comment of Edward Gibbon on the alternative history is pertinent here: "the interpretation of the Koran would now be taught in the schools at Oxford, and her pulpits might demonstrate to a circumcised people the sanctity and truth of the revelation of Muhammad." Curiously, Adolf Hitler, not generally recognized as a scholar of Islam, mused in his table talk on August 28, 1942 that "had Charles Martel not been victorious at Poitiers . . . then we should in all probability have been converted to Islam, that cult which glorifies the heroism which opens up the seventh Heaven to the bold warrior alone."[39]

Though European observation and analysis during the years covered all the Middle East, and to some extent, India and China, much of it focused, as in this book, on Turkey and the Ottoman Empire. Before that empire existed the inhabitants of the territory were variously regarded by Westerners, and at different periods appear in European literature and art, as Saracens and Moors as well as Turks. The word *Turk* was sometimes a simple appellation or identification, but often was used in a derogatory fashion, connoting cruelty and lasciviousness, and also as a synonym for the word *Muslim*.[40] During the eleventh century the Seljuk Turks had emerged as an important political and military power; in 1055 they conquered Baghdad and much of Asia Minor, and soon occupied Syria and Palestine. In 1071 they defeated the Byzantine emperor at Manzikert and expanded into Anatolia. After the Seljuk Empire declined in the twelfth century, it was succeeded by the Osmanli Turks who in the fourteenth century became controllers of the area of Anatolia, and were soon to create the Ottoman Empire and to become official protectors of the sacred sites of Mecca and Medina.

The concentration of European interest in and fear and concern about the Ottoman Empire, its political and military might, economic resources, and Islamic religion, was understandable. It was the great military power of early modern history and, dating its foundation circa 1300, it lasted for 622 years, into the twentieth century. Christian European countries had been able to regain some of their territory lost to the Moors and Arabs. Now they faced a new attack from the Islamic world, partly from the Tartars but mainly from the Turks and their empire in the fourteenth century. The Ottoman military force crossed the Dardanelles, entering European territory in 1354, and within a few years conquered Gallipolli, Adrianople, and a large part of the Balkans, reaching the Danube. In the fifteenth century, after Sultan Bayezid I (1389–1401) had incorporated all of Anatolia under Ottoman rule, the empire scored victories over the Greeks, Serbs, and Hungarians. Memories of the Serbian defeat at the battle of Kosovo in 1389 and the consequent Ottoman rule in the area have played a role in influencing local inhabitants in recent conflicts in the Balkans six hundred years later. The Islamic threat to the West lasted from the seventh to the late seventeenth century, antedating any evidence of imperialist aggression by the West.[41]

At the same time, as already mentioned, periods of peace ensued between the Ottomans and the West during which some Western political regimes such at that of Venice pursued trade, made commercial and economic agreements, and even sought diplomatic relations, which were important not only in themselves but also for guaranteeing the security of Italian shipping.[42] The Ottomans in turn negotiated alliances and engaged in diplomatic activity as well as in commercial ties. From the fifteenth century, Venice had a permanent diplomatic presence in the Ottoman Empire.[43] In the complicated tangle of diplomatic relations in the sixteenth century Francis I of France in 1536, wanting to prevent the Hapsburgs from dominating Europe, entered into a temporary alliance with Turkey, and also in 1544 allowed the Turkish fleet to winter in the port of Toulon.[44] Among other things the 1536 treaty granted French subjects the same commercial and legal privileges that the Venetians had in the Ottoman lands. It laid the basis for a French resident ambassador in Constantinople. One consequence of this agreement was that France gave some support to the Turkish navy in its victory over a Christian alliance at Prevesa in 1538. Elizabeth I, the British queen in the 1580s, viewing the Ottomans as a counterbalance against the Spanish and a Catholic threat to England, the major Protestant power, considered an alliance with them.[45] Her policy appeared to be, better the turban than the tiara. Significantly, though the Ottoman sultans received European resident ambassadors, they sent none of their own except on ad hoc missions.[46]

Another telling instance of comparable disparity was that although some Europeans, especially in the seventeenth and eighteenth centuries and even later, dressed like Ottomans (so-called Turkish dress became fashionable) and wore turbans, which entered into English imagery and attire, the Muslim sultans did not allow their subjects to dress like Europeans. Among the more well-known portrayals of Europeans with turbans are the self-portrait of Jan Van Eyck (1433), paintings by Cima da Conegliano (1459) and Vittore Carpaccio (1511), Rembrandt in the mid-seventeenth century, Vermeer's *Girl with a Pearl Earring* (c. 1665), Elizabeth Vigée-Lebrun and William Hogarth in the mid- and late eighteenth century, and Allan Ramsay's painting of Jean Jacques Rousseau (1766). In English literature perhaps the most well-known reference to Turkish attire is Othello's final speech; "Where a malignant and turban'd Turk beat a Venetian and traduc'd the state."

Even those nations that negotiated with the Turks still talked of the need for common Christian cause against the Turks, as was shown by the language in the nonaggression pact among major European countries signed in London in 1518, and the peace treaty signed in Calais, between England and France, in 1532. Despite the temporary alliances with the Ottoman Empire and the continuing wars among European countries, those countries still insisted, at least publicly, on the solidarity of Christendom against the Islamic Turkish infidel. Some examples can illustrate the point. Henry VIII in 1544 urged a universal peace in all Christendom for possible action against the Turkish common enemy. James VI of Scotland in 1590 similarly called for a league of all Christian powers against the Turks; in 1598 he wrote of the poor state of Christendom, torn and vexed by the Turkish wars and their internal feuds.

Despite the peacetime initiatives, threats of different kinds continued to exist for Europe. The Ottoman Empire reached its peak, its moment of glory, with the conquest by Mehmed II of Constantinople, the seat of the Byzantine Empire, in 1453, Athens in 1456, and the Greek principalities of Trebizond and Morea and the absorption of much of Hungary and control of areas in Eastern Europe in the sixteenth century. Mehmed made Constantinople a Muslim city by building mosques and pious foundations though he also patronized Italian artists. The military threat of the Ottomans remained great with its conquest in 1517 of Egypt, which then became an Ottoman province. The empire maintained its naval hegemony in the Mediterranean, at least until its defeat by the Holy League (Papacy, Spain, Venice, Knights of Malta) in Lepanto in 1571, the largest naval battle in the Mediterranean and essentially one between forces of Christendom and the Ottomans.[47] Lepanto can be seen in essence as the Christian response to the Ottoman siege of Malta in 1565 and attack on Cyprus in 1570. The empire controlled most of the coastal area of North Africa, Algeria, Tunis, as well as Cyprus, and attempted to capture Vienna in 1529 and 1683; both efforts were unsuccessful. Muslim forces from Turkey were still invading central Europe in the seventeenth century. However, defeats of the Ottomans at the end of the seventeenth century, including the final unsuccessful Turkish assault on Vienna in 1683, led to the Treaty of Karlowitz in 1699 between the empire and the Holy League according to which the Ottomans had to cede considerable territory in Eastern Europe. This was followed in 1718 by the Treaty of Passarowitz between the empire and Austria and Venice by which the Ottomans lost more territory in the Balkans. The European powers after counterattacking then, with varying success, began the process of invading and controlling lands once in Muslim hands. The Ottoman forces, better prepared and more numerous than their Austrian opponents, did gain a victory, after a fierce battle, in July 1739 in Glocka and took the city of Belgrade. The consequent treaty fixed the border between the Habsburg monarchy and the Ottoman Empire, with the Habsburgs ceding North Serbia to the Turks.

If the direct, aggressive military danger posed by the Ottomans had been curbed, the threat to the West, its people, and goods by Muslims was not over. Fernand Braudel wrote of the important place of piracy and the positive correlation between it and the economic health of the sixteenth-century Mediterranean economy.[48] This was important for both Christians and Muslims.[49] The history of the trans-Atlantic slave trade by which about ten to twelve million Africans were transported to the Americas is now a familiar and significant part of American culture. By contrast, and much less well known, though it was used as a literary trope by writers including Cervantes (himself a slave in Algiers, 1575–80) in two plays and especially in *Don Quixote*, Defoe in *Robinson Crusoe*, and Voltaire in *Candide*, is the large-scale slavery of European Christians, which became important and existed for three centuries at the same time as the Atlantic slave trade.[50] This capture and slavery of Europeans was conducted by the corsairs operating from the North African coastal regions known as the Barbary, stretching from Morocco to Libya (Tripoli); except for Morocco the three regencies of the Barbary were nominally under the suzerainty of the Ottoman sultan but had a certain degree of political and commercial autonomy. Recent research suggests that during the sixteenth and seventeenth centuries more individuals were taken to the Barbary Coast than were transported across the Atlantic during the same period. The two forms of slavery differed, however, in two important ways. The Atlantic trade in Africans was much larger in the long run and more important in world history than the enslavement of Europeans. Moreover, black slaves were taken to the Americas for purely commercial reason for profit, while enslavement of Europeans was not only concerned with material gain but also had a religious Muslim component.

For more than three centuries, from the sixteenth century until the nineteenth, the Barbary corsairs, who should not be considered as pirates but as privateers of the Muslim governments operating from North Africa, preyed on and captured large numbers of ships from Christian countries such as Britain, France, and Spain, plundering commercial ships and desolating coastal towns. Anxiety about the corsair practice of raiding coastal settlements, especially Italian ones, during the night and capturing some individuals is still echoed in the Italian slang phrase *pigliato dai turchi* (taken by the Turks).The corsairs, the most well known of whom in the sixteenth century is Barbarossa or Redbeard, who was given the title of Defender of Islam by the sultan, regarded themselves as warriors engaged in a holy war against Christians; they captured Christian men and women to sell at slave markets, the most important of which was in Algiers. Writings of this early period recount the story of this slavery. Father Pierre Dan, the French priest of the Order of the Redemption, in his book published in a French edition in 1649 concluded that between 1530 and 1640 about a million Christians had been put in chains. Father Emanuel d'Aranda, a Flemish individual who had been enslaved in Algiers in the 1640s, thought that six hundred thousand Christians had suffered the same fate.[51]

Contemporary writers have come to a similar conclusion. Though the exact statistics are perhaps tentative, Robert C. Davis, in his recent book *Christian Slaves, Muslim Masters*, has carefully calculated that between 1530 and 1780 about one million and possibly one and a quarter million European Christians were captured by the Barbary corsairs, brought to North Africa, and sold as slaves.[52] He also suggested that because of deaths, escapes, ransomings, and conversions, about one quarter of slaves (about 8,500) had to be replaced every year to maintain the numbers. The city of Algiers, a major center of the slave trade, had a continuous population of European slaves of about twenty-five thousand between 1550 and 1730. The narratives and sermons of those who escaped or were ransomed, such as Saint Vincent de Paul who was sold as a slave in 1605 and escaped two years later, had an important impact on European perceptions of Muslim societies. The Muslim corsairs in the early seventeenth century learned from Europeans the technique of building and using sailing ships that could make long-distance journeys. The result was that the corsairs attacked European countries as far north as Iceland, where in 1627 dozens of people were killed and nearly four hundred residents were captured and became enslaved. A fascinating account of that experience, newly translated from Icelandic into English, was written in 1628 by a Lutheran minister, Reverend Olafur Egilsson, in his sixties at the time, who was taken captive and was able to negotiate a ransom agreement.[53] Other places such as Baltimore in Ireland, Madeira, the Italian and Iberian Peninsulas, Carloforte on an island off the coast of Sardinia, and the Thames estuary suffered similar experiences. One of those places was Penzance in England where corsairs were shipwrecked in 1760; a century later the episode was turned into the comic opera, *Pirates of Penzance*, by Gilbert and Sullivan. The corsairs at one point played a decisive role in controlling much of North Africa and the Mediterranean, and levied blackmail on European traders who were forced to pay tributes or give them costly gifts.[54] To help with this problem the Roman Catholic Order of Mathurins (Trinitaires), founded in France in 1198, for centuries raised money to free Christian slaves captured by the corsairs.

The corsairs also attacked the sea routes to New England, capturing ships and enslaving some Americans. Before the independence of the United States,

American ships and sailors had been protected by Britain and then France. After the 1783 treaty of independence the United States had to defend itself. In 1784 Thomas Jefferson, then American minister in Paris, proposed a coalition of European countries and the United States to deter the corsairs from their assaults. He failed to persuade the Europeans to join in an effort to compel the Barbary Coast to engage in perpetual peace. Paying tribute or, in modern language, appeasement, Jefferson believed would only invite more demands. However, American action was not immediate. John Adams, then American minister in London, wrote to Jefferson on July 31, 1786 that "Congress would never, or at least for years, decide to fight the corsairs." Equally frustrating for Jefferson and Adams was the refusal of the pasha of Tripoli to make peace. Instead he replied that "It was written in the Koran that all nations who had not acknowleged the authority of the Prophet Muhammad were sinners, that it was the right and duty of Muslims to make war on whoever they could find, and to make slaves of all they could take as prisoners, and that every Muslim who should be slain in battle was sure to go to Paradise."[55]

The U.S. Congress had been allocating money as tribute to the corsairs, which at one point amounted to almost one-fifth of annual reveue, until the newly installed President Jefferson refused to pay the sum demanded. In the late 1790s the United States had began constructing frigates to protect U.S. commerce. In 1801 Jefferson sent some frigates and forces to Tripoli (as the area of what is now Libya was then called); the hostilities against the corsairs that began during 1804 and 1805 can be seen as America's first overseas war. The rallying cry was "millions for defense, but not one cent for tribute." The marines acted in February 1804 in the attempt to free the USS Philadelphia, which was burned, and its crew that had been captured by the corsairs. The role of the U.S. Marines in those hostilities is immortalized in the line "to the shores of Tripoli" in the *Marine Corps Hymn*. That role is also commemorated in the Tripoli monument, depicting ideas of glory, fame, and commerce, carved in 1806, the oldest military monument in the United States, now at the Naval Academy in Annapolis.

Yet, the problem for the United States had not ended. The U.S.-Barbary Coast treaty of 1805 still required the United States to pay a sum of $60,000 for the three hundred Americans imprisoned by the corsairs. Jefferson diplomatically drew a semantic difference between paying tribute and paying ransom. After more American ships and sailors were captured, the United States in 1815 engaged in a second set of hostilities leading to the capitulation of the dey of Algiers and the end of the practice of enslaving Christians. About the same time, in August 1816 a squadron of the British fleet arrived off the shore of Algiers with the goal of compelling the rulers of Barbary to stop seizing and selling

European captives. After a one-day bombardment of the city, the ruling dey, Omar Pasha, surrendered and agreed to release all the 1,642 European Christian slaves in Algiers and promised to abolish Christian slavery. Yet it was not until after the French conquest of Algeria in July 1830, which is discussed in Chapter 6 of this book, that Christian slavery and corsair activities were ended.

Though it had suzerainty over North Africa up to Morocco and extended its control to the borders of Persia, the Ottoman Empire saw its main antagonist as Europe, the rival religious and political system that did not accept the universal mission of Islam, though Europe also benefited from the empire as a rich economic market.[56] By the eighteenth century, the empire and its institutions were in decline: weak both militarily and economically when compared with the West and less competent in administrative efficiency. Control by the sultan and his servants over large areas of the empire became weak, and powerful interests not amenable to central control became stronger in the provinces.[57] The empire suffered from serious internal problems, including the breakdown of authority, loss of control over manpower and revenue sources, lack of economic development, shortage of timber, and incompetent sultans and ministers. It was unable to modernize as Europe had done through the rise of science and technology, the creation of nation-states and efficient government organization, and the industrial revolution or capitalist enterprise. The series of capitulations granted to the West, from the sixteenth through the eighteenth centuries had weakened Ottoman economic independence, Mediterranean trade was taken over by Italian cities, European merchants captured economic markets, and the Ottoman Empire lost many European territories.

The Ottoman military threat had been met by Europe, which had ended its internal wars of religion between the various Protestant and Catholic churches, and had begun the secularization of politics in many countries. At the battle of Navarino in 1827 the combined Ottoman and Egyptian armada was destroyed by an allied naval force of Britain, France, and Russia. Land battles from 1828 to 1829 between Russia and Ottoman forces led to further defeats for the empire. Reforms in the Ottoman Empire began in the nineteenth century. By then there was no reason to fear the weakened empire as in the past. The period of Western control or dominance in the Muslim Arab world had begun. A cutting remark by Tsar Nicolas I in 1853 about the empire was that, because of the Ottoman loss of territory and his view that the empire was controlled financially by European powers, it was "the sick man of Europe."[58] The witty response of Sir George Hamilton Seymour, the British ambassador to whom the remark was addressed, was that the Ottoman Empire should be treated gently; it needed a physician, not a surgeon.[59]

The fear of Muslims by Christendom persisted for centuries past the Crusades, a fear more virulent at some times than at others. By the end of the eighteenth century that fear was being reduced as the European Christian powers began dominating most of the Muslim world and controlling it directly or indirectly until the twentieth century. The Ottoman Empire, which had engaged in continual warfare, finally ended as a result of World War I after which it lost almost all of the territories it once held. Yet as late as the mid-fifteenth century, Pope Pius II (1458–64) called in 1464 for a new crusade, even wanting to lead it himself, against the infidels whom he regarded as a danger to the Christian faith. For a time Florence and Venice were interested, but the call for what was an abortive attempt to lead a crusade was not implemented. Paradoxically and somewhat inexplicably, Pius II, though arguing that Islam raised false expectations of salvation and that Muhammad was a fraud and a heretic, nevertheless wrote a cordial letter to the Sultan Muhammad II, urging him to convert to Christianity. Not surprisingly Muhammad did not heed the request. Such cordiality was rare, and Western fears focused on religious differences as well as territorial ones. Until the eighteenth century, relations between the Muslim Orient and the West were often seen on both sides in terms of religious confrontation. The Muslim Ottoman headdress, the turban, was regarded in Renaissance England as representative of the challenging religious power and as the most feared symbol of Islam and of Ottoman power and authority. "Taking the turban" was synonymous with becoming a Muslim. Some Europeans kept calling for Christian unity against Islam and the Turks. Clarence Rouillard, indicating the degree of Western concern, calculated that of the numerous books and pamphlets on Turkey in the seventeenth century, many had the words *Christian* or *Christianity* in the title: only one had *Europe*.[60] Interestingly, Pius II helped make the word *Europe* interchangeable with *Christendom*. Understandably, our six writers, and the travelers and Orientalist scholars discussed in this book were concerned to address the religious as well as the political aspects of the Orient, and the interrelation between them. European perceptions of Islam and of its correlation with despotic government are the themes of Chapter 1.

I

European Views of Islam and Their Correlation with Oriental Despotism

As summarized briefly in the introduction, commentary by Europeans on the nature of Eastern social and political systems was commingled with their conception of the Islamic religion, though their knowledge of it was imperfect. Criticism by Christians of its rival religion was voiced soon after the advent of Islam starting with St. John of Damascus in the late seventh century, who wrote of "the false prophet," Muhammad. Rivalry, and often enmity, continued between the European Christian world and the Islamic world, whether the latter can be regarded as consisting of Islamic societies or societies only partly molded by Islam.[1] For Christian theologians, the "Other" was the infidel, the Muslim. Despite changing Christian images of Islam it was generally regarded as theologically false and as the basis of a hostile, different, and dangerous civilization. Theological disputes in Baghdad and Damascus, in the eighth to tenth centuries, and in Andalusia up to the fourteenth century led Christian Orthodox and Byzantine theologians and rulers to continue seeing Islam as a threat.[2]

In the twelfth century, Peter the Venerable, the Abbot of Cluny, who had the Koran translated into Latin, regarded Islam as a Christian heresy and Muhammad as sexually self-indulgent and a murderer, and as a person who was not the Lord but a messenger. However, he called for the conversion, not the extermination, of Muslims. A century later, St. Thomas Aquinas in *Summa contra Gentiles* accused Muhammad of seducing people by promises of carnal pleasure, uttering truths mingled with many fables and announcing utterly false decisions that had no divine inspiration.[3] Those who followed Muhammad were regarded by Aquinas as brutal, ignorant "beast-like men" and desert wanderers. Through them Muhammad, who asserted "he was sent in the power of arms," forced others to become followers by violence and armed power.

Norman Daniel has argued that between the twelfth and fourteenth centuries a "medieval canon" of Islam became firmly established in Europe.[4] The canon included a number of key points: the fraudulent claim of prophecy by Muhammad, who was considered a schemer and sexually promiscuous; Islam as a form of Christian heresy, especially regarding the Trinity; reliance on force; laxity in sexual matters; and the idea, which the canon saw as absurd, of the Koranic paradise. With the Ottoman Empire advance into Europe, and as Turkey became equated with Islam in the sixteenth century, Islamic countries were seen as a military and political as well as a religious threat, in spite of the lure of profit from Eastern trade and diplomatic relations. Islam continued to be viewed as at least partly responsible for Oriental despotism, the degradation of women, slavery, and a passive, obedient population subject to cruelty and violence.

Philosophers and poets voiced these concerns. Leibniz wrote of an ideal polity, a kind of medieval Christian republic, and he sought to persuade Louis XIV to attack the Ottoman Empire, the main opponent of European Christianity, in Egypt. John Milton, in *Paradise Lost*, compared the Ottoman ruler, anxious to conquer Christendom, with Satan. He wrote of Satan sitting exalted, "high on a throne of royal state, which far outshone the wealth of Ormus (in the Persian Gulf) and of India, and of the gorgeous East with richest hand showering on her kings barbaric pearl and gold." Milton referred to the spear of the great sultan directing the course of the fallen angels.[5]

Though serious and disinterested observation and analysis by Europeans was taking place, at the same time there were harsh statements, misunderstandings, or insensitive remarks by Western commentators or political figures regarding the Orient. An incidental passage by Francis Bacon in the early seventeenth century refers to the Turks as a "cruel people, who nevertheless are kind to beasts." He pictured them "without morality, without letters, arts or sciences; a people that can scarce measure an acre of land or an hour of the day; base and sluttish in building, diet and the like, and in a word, a very reproach to human society."[6] In a familiar passage, in canto XXVIII, Dante located Muhammad in the eighth circle of hell with other "sowers of discord and scandal." Montaigne, in his essay on virtue, indicated that the Assassins (an extremist sect) were esteemed among "the Muhammedans of a sovereign devotion and purity of customs: they hold that the most certain way to merit paradise is to kill someone of a different religion."[7] In effect however, Montaigne was incorrect; most of the victims of the Assassins were fellow Muslims, and they were not esteemed among Muslims.

In general, European medieval romances and humanist writers added to a critical portrait of the Orient.[8] The romances, promoting an ideal Europe through the incorporation of myth, chivalric legends, fact, and propaganda in literary tropes, presented images of gallant Christian knights fighting the Saracen foe. Renaissance humanists, using ancient history, classical texts, and rhetoric, referred to the Ottoman Empire in negative terms when addressing secular political and culture issues. Petrarch, circa 1350, believing the Christian West was the bastion of civilization against the East, suggested that if Julius Caesar returned he would not allow the "Egyptian thief" to possess Jerusalem, Judea, and Syria, and even Egypt. A century later, Bruno equated the Turks with the Barbarians of ancient Roman history, both having destroyed cities, learning, and books. Muslims, in essence Ottoman Turks, were thus seen as barbarians and equated with the Goths, Vandals, and Lombards, who were responsible for the fall of ancient Rome.

Accurate information about Islam percolated into the West with the translations of the Koran, first into Latin, and then directly into English by George Sale in 1734, though one version had been translated from French into English in 1647. Appraisals of Islam that were critical of its immoral nature, and particularly of the character of Muhammad (spelled differently by authors), continued to appear in Europe. One such appraisal was by Michel Baudier, French historian (1585–1645) to the court of Louis XIII in one of the first works in French on Islam. Writing of the Muslim enemy he was particularly caustic, as Pascal was to be, about Muhammad: "his voluptuousness and brutal mind only feeds on the dirty delicacies of sensuality, and is blind to those of the soul ... not content to have had a bordello on earth ... he lifts it up to heaven." He wrote of the impostures of Muhammad, "the vanity of his sect, the ridiculous and brutal doctrine." Baudier, author of three books on Turkey (1617–1625), was caustic about the abominable vice, sodomy, the greatest evil in the Ottoman Empire. Many others later wrote of other vices in a system marked by existence of concubines, boys used for pleasure, profligate lust, and the use of opium. Guillaume Postel in 1560 was almost a lone voice in writing that most Turks were not polygamists.

About the same time as Baudier, Sir George Sandys in *A Relation of a Journey*, provided an uncharitable view of Muhammad as a Saracen lawyer. He described him as a man of obscure parentage who pretended he had been divinely appointed for leadership to give a new law to mankind and by force of arms to reduce the world to his obedience. Muhammad had subjected the gross Arabians to a superstitious obedience. Naturally inclined to all villainies, including insatiable lechery, Muhammad "countenanced his incontinency with a law" to couple with whomsoever you liked.[9] The "Muhammadan religion," derived from a person who was wicked and worldly in his projects, disloyal, treacherous, and cruel, allowed men the enchantments of fleshy pleasures, but controlled them with tyranny and the sword.

Blaise Pascal (1623–62), in the scattered notebooks collected after his death as *Apology for Christianity* in the *Pensées*, sought to show that religion was not contrary to reason, but rather was venerable and attractive. However, for Pascal that meant Christianity because that religion alone, "with its blend of external and internal," was suited to all.[10] He contrasted Christianity with Islam. Muhammad's reasons had no validity; they stood only on their own authority. Unlike Jesus Christ, Muhammad had no witnesses and was a false prophet. When Pascal compared Jesus Christ and Muhammad, he concluded that whereas the latter had chosen the path to worldly success, Jesus had chosen immortality through death.[11] Any man could do what Muhammad did; he wrought no miracles, his coming was not foretold, he taught no mysteries: "What sign has he that no man lacks who chooses to call himself a prophet. . . . What moral system, what happiness?" By contrast, Pascal held, "no man can do what Jesus Christ has done."

In the mid-seventeenth century, Islam was used in the context of intense theological disputes on the origin and nature of Christianity. During the Christian religious ferment in Europe at that time, Catholics and Lutherans accused one another's religion of possessing Islamic characteristics and its adherents of being Turkish infidels. Nevertheless, both Christian camps were aware of problems: the conversion to Islam of captured and enslaved Christians and the lure of Islam for some Christians. They consequently called for Christian unity in opposition to the Turks and their Islamic religion, which they regarded as one of violence and lust.

Publications on the Ottomans and on Islam became more numerous, and many were critical. The English version of the French translation of the Koran appeared in the 1650s, Francis Osborn's *Political Reflections on the Government of the Turks* in 1656, and Paul Rycaut's *Present State of the Ottoman Empire* in 1668. Probably the strongest and most influential criticism of Islam was by Humphrey Prideaux in *The True Nature of Imposture Displayed in the Life of Mahomet* in 1697. As the title indicates, Prideaux denounced Muhammad as an illiterate barbarian, licentious and wicked, the model of a true imposter, and referred to "Muhammad divinity" as odd stuff, compared with Christ and Christianity, which had none of the marks, characteristics, or properties of imposture.[12] Prideaux, an Anglican minister who became Dean of Norwich, warned about the dangers of Deism and Catholicism, and wanted to overcome the "giddy humor" of youth and the apathy of those uninterested in religion, but his chief concern was Islam, which meant both political and religious tyranny. His book was a great success and was rapidly reprinted in a number of editions.

Yet some literature looked favorably on Muslims. In Spanish writings, at one point, the image of the Moor was in part one of nobility, chivalry, and refinement. Some Europeans expressed moderation in their opinions of Islam. One of these was Henry Stubbe, writing a generation earlier than Prideaux, who in *An Account* (1674), wrote probably the first work in English sympathetic to Islam, attempting to show the similarity between Islam and Unitarian Christianity. Stubbe, a learned librarian and physician and opponent of trinitarianism, rejected the charge that Islam was the "vilest imposture" and approvingly claimed that Muhammad was the "wisest legislator that ever was."[13]

In his long *Dictionnaire historique* (1697), Pierre Bayle, skeptic of Christian orthodoxy and an advocate of tolerance, wrote twenty-three pages on Muhammad. Like his predecessors, Bayle regarded Muhammad as a man devoted to sensuality and the sword, an imposter and a false teacher who used religion to enhance himself. But he also displayed some sympathy for Islamic societies, their tolerance of other religions, and the modesty of their women. His sympathy for Muslim societies stemmed from his views on the complexity and variety of monarchical systems. Bayle has habitually been considered a defender of French royal absolutism against the dangers of civil disorder, though some suggest his position on the issue was more complex and that it changed in his later writings.[14] He postulated the distinction, to become more common in the eighteenth century, between absolute and limited monarchies. In evaluating the Ottoman system, Bayle thought that perhaps the sultan was not an absolute despot because he ruled through laws. Despotism for Bayle was a matter of degree rather than an absolute phenomenon, suggesting that analysis based on empirical observation rather than stemming from a simple generalization was appropriate for accurate interpretation.

During the next two centuries, the view of Muhammad as an imposter continued to be held by many, though some differed on the extent of his virulence. Among them were Barthelemy d'Herbelot, who compiled the *Bibliothèque Orientale*; Henri Boulainvilliers in his *Life of Mahomet*, which portrayed the Prophet in a rather sympathetic manner; and Voltaire in his play, *Le Fanatisme ou Mahomet le prophète* (1742), translated into English two years later as *Mahomet, The Imposter*. Using impassioned language, Voltaire wrote that no one could excuse the behavior of Muhammad, "the merchant of camels." Voltaire declared that Muhammad had excited a revolt in his town; persuaded people he had held conversation with the angel Gabriel; boasted he received from Heaven part of what Voltaire called his unintelligible book, which affronted common sense at every page; put his own country to fire and the sword to make his book respected; and only given the vanquished the choice between conversion to Islam or death. Interestingly Voltaire, however, who wrote of the Prophet's cruelty, fanaticism, sexual lust, and ambition, sought to separate the imposter, Muhammad, "the terrible and powerful man" who played on the credulity of his followers and imposed his message by brute force, from the Islam of his own eighteenth century, which he saw moving toward greater tolerance.

In the eighteenth century, critics of Islam stressed that Islamic doctrine had been propagated by the sword. They considered the interconnection between temporal power and religion. Some wrote of a benign Christianity confronting a malevolent Islam. Diderot in his article, "Sarrasins ou Arabes," wrote that Muhammad could be viewed as the greatest enemy that human reason had ever known. He imposed his will on ignorant people and "cut the throats of those who hesitated to regard those chapters (from the Koran) as inspired work." Diderot regarded the Koran as an absurd, obscure, and dishonest work. Like Voltaire he also thought Muhammad offered a choice of either converting to his religion and having access to beautiful women, or facing death.[15] Similarly, Louis de Jaucourt described Muhammad as achieving a victory over Mecca and then conquering all Arabia with a scepter in one hand and sword in the other forcing people to embrace Islam or pay tribute. He saw Muhammad and his immediate successors, the Arabs, as committed to the expansion of Islamic civilization. The Arabs "swarmed from their country to spread the religion and empire that Muhammad had founded." They were emboldened by the Koran, which contained all the precepts of Islam.[16]

In Chapter 50 of *The Decline and Fall of the Roman Empire*, Edward Gibbon offered a mixed portrait of Islam and its founder. He contended that Muhammad, sword in one hand and the Koran in the other, had erected his throne on the ruins of Christianity and of Rome, and had led a memorable revolution that had imposed a "new and lasting character" on the nations of the world. Interestingly enough, Gibbon remained undecided whether this "extraordinary man" was an enthusiast or an imposter. Gibbon was equally ambivalent about Islam.[17] He considered Islam unsatisfactory because it was intolerant of other religions and conducive to despotism. Gibbon did make some complimentary remarks about Islam, but with his exquisite sense of irony wrote of the promised paradise that, instead of inspiring "a liberal taste for harmony and science, conversation and friendship," celebrated idle luxury and sensuality. He described Arabs as rovers who were allured by the promise of paradise and plunder: "the enjoyment of wealth and beauty was a feeble type of the joys of paradise prepared for the valiant martyrs of the faith." Gibbon understood that religion and government were inextricably interwoven. He held that Muhammad exercised both royal and sacerdotal office, and that it was impious that the decrees of a judge were supposedly inspired by the divine wisdom. Gibbon conjectured that Muhammad's conscience was soothed by the persuasion that he alone was absolved by the Deity from the obligation of positive and moral laws.

Major nineteenth-century European philosophers also viewed Eastern societies and political structures of despotism as intertwined with Islam. Karl Friedrich Schlegel contrasted German tribal activities, which, as he saw it, had led to Christianity, peace, and civilization, with Arab activities, which had produced Islam, hatred, anger, and lack of civilization.[18] Jacob Burckhardt remarked that Islam, while it had a rich past, had led to only one type of state, despotism.[19] Practically from the beginning the caliphate was a despotic system. He argued that a fusion between religion and government, which had not occurred in the West, had taken place in Islam. The whole of Islamic culture was, he wrote, dominated, shaped, and colored by it; Islam has only one form of polity, of necessity despotic, the consummation of power, secular, priestly, and theocratic. This aridity, this dreary uniformity of Islam, he concluded, probably did more harm than good to culture.

Johann Gottfried Herder, presenting a balanced view of Eastern societies and praise for past cultural and scientific contributions made by the Arabs, regarded the Koran as a wonderful mixture of poetry, eloquence, ignorance, and sagacity.[20] Yet he regarded Arab monarchy as "Khalific," despotic in the highest degree. The powers of the Western emperor and pope were combined in the position of the Khalif, and the Islamic beliefs in inevitable destiny, in the word of the Prophet, and in obedience to the Koran, promoted total submission to the rulers. Following Islam led to a passive state in which subjects accepted the arbitrary rule of the Khalif. Herder's general view of Asia was that it lacked conditions for further development or pursuit of knowledge. In particular he regarded China as an "old ruin," a static social system, and a stationary state; it was "an embalmed mummy wrapped in silk and painted in hieroglyphics."

The writers in this chapter believed that the precepts of Islam gave credibility to despotism, and they were deeply critical of those despotic governments they thought were committed to an Islamic mission to conquer the world. Commentaries of this kind are still relevant for consideration in our contemporary world even though written centuries earlier. Similarly, it is still useful to examine the observations of some of the many travelers to the Orient and India who not only played a significant role by their adventurous and mercantile activity but also provided valuable empirical information about those countries, which helped the major writers in this book, especially Montesquieu and Marx, to frame their generalizations about despotic systems.

2

Observant Travelers

Herodotus, explaining the writing of his *History* circa 444 BC, commented that he wanted to preserve the rememberance of what men have done. For purposes of this book it is invaluable to consider the writings of the many Western European travelers who provided valuable information about the Middle East and India. Many wrote critically of their experience in those societies; others were more sympathetic.[1] To posit that Western analyses of the Orient are hegemonic in their approach, or always suffer from doctrinaire attitudes, or duplicitously explain Muslim societies and culture in terms of an unchanging Islam is an essentialist argument.[2] If some Westerners had insufficient or inaccurate information, made mistaken generalizations about the realities of Eastern societies, or were prejudiced from a religious perspective, many others sought objective, empirical data and tried to formulate unbiased conclusions about Eastern societies and about the real, understandable fear of Muslim expansion.[3]

A wide variety of people during the centuries wrote about Eastern countries, especially about Turkey and India where at its peak in the seventeenth century the Mughal Empire ruled more than one hundred million people, a number five times larger than in the Ottoman Empire. These people included pilgrims to the Holy Land; travelers and adventurers; diplomats, notably Venetian envoys to Turkey in the fifteenth and sixteenth centuries; physicians; commercial agents and merchants; artists; Christian missionaries, friars, and French Jesuits who wrote sympathetically of China; former prisoners in Turkey; and historians. This interest in the area, taking both positive and negative form, stemmed from different and mixed motives: curiosity about non-Western societies, and often about their supposed exotic character; simple pleasure; religious propaganda resulting from the recognition of theological differences between Christianity and Islam;

commerce including a search for gold, silver, and gems; the desire of Christian missionaries to convert Muslims; eagerness to expand practical mercantile opportunities with rich Eastern countries and to obtain capitulations from these countries; appreciation of past achievements in the Orient in medicine, such as the technique of inoculations against smallpox brought to England by Lady Mary Wortley Montagu from Constantinople in the 1720s; the advances in mathematics, mechanics, and astronomy, among other fields; increasing study of Arabic and other languages with the establishment of university chairs in Arabic; repugnance at the cruelty of Turkish rulers; and a fear of the "malignant and turbaned Turk" and of the ongoing aggression and expansion of conquest by the strong and disciplined army of the Ottoman Empire.

The early perceptions of Oriental regimes and societies were made by these travelers, all of whom were Christians, though of varying denominations. Many of them were gifted and articulate writers, who dealt with both secular and religious issues, including Marco Polo in the late thirteenth century and John Mandeville, the latter of questionable authenticity, in the mid-fourteenth century. Even if the accounts of their experiences by travelers from the sixteenth to the eighteenth centuries cannot all be fully trusted for accurate observation, and if sometimes those accounts were confined to personal adventures or were religiously prejudiced, they nevertheless provided both valuable empirical information and systematic analysis, secular in character, sober and unemotional. This was not only valuable in itself, but it was also influential both on contemporary European images of the Middle East and on Islam, and also, directly, on later writers, especially Richard Jones, Montesquieu, and Karl Marx, and on many subsequent perceptions of the Orient.[4]

Some of those travelers are not well known except to specialists.[5] More well-known and influential European individuals are Ogier Ghiselin de Busbecq (1520–92), a native of Flanders who became ambassador of the Habsburgs to Constantinople (1554–62), and who is said to have introduced the tulip to the West; Giovanni Botero (1540–1617), a Jesuit priest who served rulers and Cardinal Borromeo in Italy; Jean-Baptiste Tavernier (1605–89), a merchant, trading in jewels and other precious goods; Paul Rycaut (1629–1700), a merchant and trader, originally from Antwerp who settled in London and became ambassador to Turkey; François Bernier (1625–88), a French doctor and philosopher who traveled to Syria, Egypt, and India, and was a physician at the court of the Great Mughal for eight years; and Jean (John) Chardin (1643 –1713), a French Protestant jeweler who visited and wrote on Persia.[6]

Each traveler told his own individual story but all described similar features of Oriental politics and societies. The mostly negative views held by these travelers coincided with three factors: the beginning of the shift in power from the Ottoman Empire to Western Europe, the domestic problems the empire was encountering, and the growing dissimilarity between Western and Eastern societies. Western systems had passed through a stage of feudalism and, with certain qualifications in some countries, were developing political regimes with limited monarchies, privileged aristocrats with some independent authority, and institutional arrangements that could restrain the central ruling power.[7] By contrast, Oriental systems lacked such general restraints of this kind as well as the separate corporate bodies that could limit the power of rulers.

The travelers emphasized a number of themes: the absolute and arbitrary rule by an individual who had often come to power through a brutal and ruthless process involving, at times, the murder of members of his family; the total submission and obedience of subjects; the lack of an hereditary aristocracy; the opulence, extravagance, corruption, and cruelty of the rulers; the existence of slavery and the dependence of the ruler on slaves and mercenaries, especially Janissaries, fighting for the glory of the sultan and for their new faith, for military and defense activities; the subjection of women; the lack of private property; the backward or stagnant society; and the role of Islam.

THE FRENCH AND ITALIANS

Ogier Ghiselin de Busbecq, while ambassador in Constantinople (1555–62), a time which according to his memoirs he did not much enjoy, was concerned about the threat to European Christendom from the Ottoman Empire.[8] In his *Letters*, which began to be published in 1581, he wrote, among other matters, of his diplomatic efforts to negotiate a truce and then a peace agreement between the Holy Roman Empire and the Ottomans, the gossip about the imperial court, Turkish costumes, exotic plants, and dancing elephants in Constantinople. On arrival in Istanbul, Busbecq, while looking at the "marvelously handsome dresses" thought it was the most beautiful spectacle he ever saw. He admired certain aspects of Turkish life: the court dress; modesty of behavior; absence of distinctions based on birth, wealth, or sale of office; the honest judicial system; the military and administrative skills; the absence of poverty; the fact that those who held the highest posts under the sultan were often the sons of shepherds and herdsmen; and the self-denial and discipline of the soldiers, the Janissaries, whom he contrasted with the behavior of European soldiers, more often drunk, debauched, and contemptuous of discipline. In the Ottoman Empire no person "owed his dignity to anything but his personal merits and bravery." Nevertheless, on balance Busbecq was critical of the absolute power of the sultan; the opulence and extravagance of the court;

and the intrigues and murders involved in the power struggle for succession to the throne. He also argued that the ultimate objective of the Turks, whom he regarded as devoted to a false faith, was to prepare the way for the extinction of Christianity.

Giovanni Botero, in his comparative study of major social systems in the world, provided considerable geographical and anthropological information, in addition to an account of political economy and religion, all of which was helpful in explaining the degree of power of the different states and societies.[9] Like some other writers, and anticipating one of the major propositions of Montesquieu, Botero argued that the large size and the climate of Asia were likely to lead to the formation and existence of great empires while the moderate climate of European countries favored smaller, diverse nations. Also, Botero believed that the peoples in the two areas had different skills and characters, those in Europe being superior, technologically and politically, to those in Asia. Thus, for reasons both of geography and the human qualities of their populations, the West had superior strength relative to Asia.

Botero did use "despotic government" to refer to Eastern systems, except Persia, and also included other countries such as Ethiopia, Siam, India, and China. Botero saw the Ottoman Empire, within its territorial limits, as completely despotic, and the Great Turk, the sultan, as absolute master of all things including private property because he owned everything. He generalized that Oriental systems were marked by excessive concentration of authority and control of revenues. Inhabitants of Ottoman society were slaves, not subjects; they were dependent on decisions by the despotic *Gran Signor* whose will was law. No person, however important, was safe or secure because all depended on the whim of the *Gran Signor*. Botero explained that the ruler maintained himself in absolute power by two means: not allowing his subjects to have weapons, and using, in order to protect himself, renegades, Janissaries, taken as children from their countries who were then raised to become loyal soldiers.[10] The Ottoman Empire had become great, partly through the success of these fighters and its own resources, and partly through the discord of Christian states at the time.

Botero, a Jesuit who left the order in 1579, regarded, as did Busbecq, the Ottoman Empire as the terror facing Christian nations.[11] Differing from some other travelers, he characterized Russia, the Muscovy of Ivan IV, as well as Turkey and India as Oriental despotisms, but took a kindlier view of Persia where he saw the people as sociable, there was an honored nobility, and subjects took delight in cultural activities. By contrast, Botero's portrait of the Ottoman Empire was totally negative. He saw the people there as slaves and as exploited; commerce was in the hands of foreigners; state officials were corrupt; and order and discipline were so extreme as to foster injustice and lead to weakness. His empirical observations of the Ottomans were influential; they were seen by many as an accurate picture of Oriental despotism.[12] He clearly distinguished between Eastern regimes, in which liberty and the right to property did not exist, and Western regimes with legal constraints on power and where individuals had private property.

Between 1631 and 1668 the Protestant merchant-ambassador Jean-Baptiste Tavernier traveled six times to Turkey, Persia, and particularly India, the country on which he wrote most in his *Six Voyages* (1676) a publication reprinted twenty-one times by the mid-eighteenth century.[13] He wrote not only about the political system but also about a variety of aspects of life in India, politics, the differences between Sunnis and Shi'as, art, architecture of towns, food, markets and trade, and very knowledgeably about precious and other metals. Tavernier, who had been invited to the emperor's grandiose birthday festival in 1665, was one who, like Jean de Thévenot and Edward Terry, marveled at the opulence and the power of the Great Mughal. This ruler was "the richest and most potent monarch of Asia, the greatest power in Asia, comparable to what the King of France is in Europe." His enormous principal palace contained fine-cut stone, thirty-two marble columns, and thrones covered with diamonds, rubies, emeralds, and pearls. When the emperor went out he had a bodyguard of five or six hundred armed men; when he went to the mosque, eight elephants announced by trumpet fanfares marched in front of him.[14] Differing from Botero in his appraisal of Persia, Tavernier saw the government there as purely despotic: the king had the right of life and death over his subjects and was not limited by any council or procedures that might provide advice or by the kind of restraints customary in Europe.[15] The ruler killed members of his own family he suspected of wanting to assassinate him. Like many other commentators on the Orient, Tavernier concluded that the Eastern systems lacked hereditary nobility, a landed aristocracy, and private property in land.

Perhaps the most influential of the late seventeenth- and eighteenth-century writers on the Orient was Paul Rycaut, a diplomat of Huguenot extraction, who represented England for five years in Istanbul, during which he said he explored Ottoman registers and records to ascertain the true nature of the system. In an implicit warning to English decision makers of the pernicious nature of excessive absolutism, Rycaut portrayed the Ottoman Empire as an arbitrary, violent, cruel, corrupt, tyrannical regime where the ruler, devoid of reason or virtue, was absolute and above the law.[16] Ownership of all property, except religious property, was vested in the sultan: no independent control of lands and revenues existed. All the wealth of the empire went to satisfy the appetite of a single man whose will and lusts were served. Unlike European countries, no noble class with "title of blood" was present to occupy high positions. In this system men were raised by adulation, chance, or the arbitrary favor of the ruler. Officials labored as slaves for their great patron and master. For Rycaut, the Turks exemplified the dictum of Francis Bacon, "a monarchy where there is no nobility at all, is ever pure and absolute tyranny." The whole composition of the Turkish court was "a prison of slaves . . . a fabric of slavery."

In his analysis Rycaut was implicitly optimistic that the West would prevail over the Ottoman Empire, which was in a bad condition, economically and politically, though the military was strong. He saw this decline of the empire as a sign of divine displeasure. The empire would disintegrate: "This mighty body would burst with the poison of its own ill humors." One of these "humors" was the "flattery and immoderate subjection" that had caused the decay of Turkish discipline in the sultanate of Ibrahim when women were very influential (part of the "Sultanate of Women" in the sixteenth and seventeenth centuries); in his own time Rycaut believed the contemporary Sultan Mahomet was advised chiefly by his mother, blacks, eunuchs, and handsome young male favorites.[17] Rycaut ends his "epistle to the reader" by offering thanks to God for his having been born a Christian, in view of the "superstition, vanity, and ill foundation of the Mahometan religion," and for having been born in a country, the most just and fair in all the world, instead of in a state (Turkey) exhibiting tyranny, oppression, and cruelty, and where reason "stands in no competition with the pride and lust of an unreasonable minister."

Similar conclusions about Asian systems, particularly about Mughal India, appear in the writings of François Bernier, who spent fourteen years, between 1655 and 1668, in various countries in Asia. His argument, in his *Travels in the Mughal Empire, 1656–1668*, which was to influence later writers, was that those systems were in rapid decline in a ruined and depopulated land.[18] In India the Grand Mughal maintained his power with a large military force: two hundred thousand cavalry and three hundred thousand infantry. The financial situation of the Mughal Empire was not healthy. The ruler's expenditure was about the same as his revenue. Much of the revenue went into jewelry. The power of the ruler (Aurangzeb) was cruel and oppressive. Unlike the French situation, in India, and in other Eastern countries, private property, hereditary nobility, and parliaments or judges of local courts did not exist. Royal authority was sadly abused. The ruler claimed the property of all rents from the lands in the empire though, in arbitrary fashion, he made conditional grants to the military leaders, governors, and tax farmers of the provinces. For Bernier, the crucial fact was that the right to private property was not acknowledged.

For Bernier, the effects of the despotic power of the ruler were a disastrous economy, desolate regions unfit for human habitation, and poor cultivation of the land, which was seldom tilled except by compulsion. There was no incentive to engage in profitable activities. The state of slavery obstructed the progress of trade and led to profound and universal ignorance. The country was ruined by the need to defray the enormous charges required to maintain the splendor of a vast court and to pay for a large, expensive military establishment. Moreover, independent chiefs and princes in the country added little to the revenue.

In this corrupt system the people, having no legal or institutional protection, were in subjection, suffering from the "use of the cane and the whip." The Great Mughal was surrounded by slaves, who were ignorant, and by parasites raised from the dregs of society, unfamiliar with loyalty and patriotism. The king sat on his throne in the most magnificent attire surrounded by a vast collection of precious stones. In the East, the only law that decided all controversies was the cane and the caprice of the governor. Like other observers around the same period, Bernier wrote of the cruel process of succession to the throne during which brothers of the new ruler were killed.

Bernier knew India best, but he broadened his remarks to apply to other countries. The effects of despotic power, unrelentingly exercised, were to be seen by the condition of "Mesopotamia, Anatolia, Palestine, the once wonderful plains of Antioch." The three countries, Turkey, Persia, and Hindustan (India), had no idea of private property, "the foundation of all that is good and beautiful in the world." They all had the same faults and must, sooner or later, experience the same pernicious consequences: tyranny, ruin, and misery. Bernier warned that "actuated by a blind and wicked ambition to be more absolute than was warranted by the laws of God and of nature, the kings of Asia grasp at everything until at length they lose everything." In what was perhaps an indirect warning or advice to Jean-Baptiste Colbert, minister of Louis XIV, who incidentally in the 1660s encouraged the teaching of Oriental languages in Paris as well as trying to increase trade with the Eastern countries, Bernier called for moderation in economic policy, especially regarding taxation and private wealth. He concluded, "God forbid that our monarchs in Europe should also be the sole owners of all the lands which their subjects now possess" and held that the decline of Asian states was due to the absence of private property and incentives. Bernier argued that European monarchs, contrary to the situation in Oriental despotisms, should ensure the existence in their regimes of private property and legal and civil rights.

Jean (John) Chardin, a Huguenot merchant and jeweler, and friend of Bernier, traveled to Persia, in whose language he became fluent, and India between

1665 and 1679, and then immigrated to England in 1681, where he was knighted by King Charles II, appointed a Fellow of the Royal Society, and became the East India Company's representative to the Dutch. He was another observer to stress the impact of climate, writing that "the cause or the origin of the customs and habits of the Orientals" lay in the nature of their climate.[19] Hot climates, present in Asia, enervated the mind as well as the body. This, Chardin believed, helped to explain the fact that Asian systems were despotic. The government of Persia, extravagant and arbitrary, was monarchical, despotic, and absolute; all authority rested entirely in the hands of one man, in both spiritual and temporal matters, who was in all respects the master over the life and goods of his subjects.[20] Chardin saw the King of Persia as the most absolute in the world, able to do whatever he said, and to see that his commands were always exactly executed. He was raised in an atmosphere of sensuality. Asians, living in these systems ruled by one person, were incapable of conceiving of the administration of sovereign power by several men of equal rank.

Chardin, however, was more cautious than Bernier in generalizing about Oriental despotism and ownership of land. He implied that his view about despotism was pertinent only to the Safavid dynasty in the sixteenth and seventeenth centuries in Persia; it did not stem from the slavish nature of Asian peoples, but rather from the Shi'ite doctrine of the country derived from the authority of Muhammad. At one point Chardin suggested that for most people other than the great lords, the Persian government might more properly be termed military, arbitrary, and absolute rather than despotic. For the most part, the government was regulated by civil laws. He even said the condition of the Persian people was "more secure and gentle than in many Christian states."[21] Chardin differed from other writers of the period such as Botero and Bernier in stating that land revenues went not only to the ruler but also to others in the country. He referred to Persians as tolerant, hospitable, pleasant tempered, the most civilized people of the East. Yet Chardin also wrote that the Persians did nothing out of magnanimity, a virtue almost unknown in the East.[22] Seemingly contradicting his own opinion, and anticipating Montesquieu, he wrote that as fortune and bodies were enslaved by an utterly despotic and arbitrary power, so were hearts and minds, which know only fear and hope.

THE ENGLISH TRAVELERS

Like the French observers, English travelers also made important contributions to empirical data about and understanding of the countries they visited or inhabited. The opinions of Eastern societies and politics by English writers of the seventeenth and eighteenth centuries, some of whom did not travel to the Orient, in many ways resemble those of the French observers discussed above.[23] A few examples of the many travelers can illustrate the point: Richard Knolles (1545–1610), British historian; Fynes Moryson (1566 –1630), travel writer; George Sandys (1578–1644), traveler and poet; Sir Thomas Roe (1581–1644), diplomat in India and Turkey, and his chaplain for three years, Edward Terry; Charles Eliot, British diplomat; William Hunter; William Roberson (1721–93), Scottish historian; and William Eton.

Richard Knolles, who never left England, produced the first major work in English on Ottoman history, *The General History of the Turks* (1603–04), a work that was extended by Paul Rycaut to become *The History of the Turkish Empire*, which accompanied his own book, *The Present State of the Ottoman Empire*.[24] Knolles wrote of the power of the empire and its ambitious ruler, the emperor, lord of all: the regime "had no other limits than the utmost bounds of the earth from the rising of the sun until the setting of the sun." Conscious of the religious and military challenge to Europe, Knolles coined the phrase he thought applicable to the Turks: "the present terror of the world."

Knolles held that the expansion by the Turks into Europe resulted from craftiness, deceit, and the use of cunning rather than strength; he warned of the danger of trusting promises made by "the Turk devoid of all faith and humanity." In a striking passage, Knolles held that the sway of the Turks revealed "the secret judgment of the Almighty, who in justice delivered into the hands of these merciless miscreants, nation after nation to be punished for their sins."[25] The Turk was also ruthless, "like a greedy lion lurking in his den, lay in wait for them all," and was treacherous with "snares to entangle other princes in" to devour them. In portraying the reality of power in the Ottoman court Knolles noted its theatricality with its "slothful and effeminate attributes." He saw the court dominated by luxury, cruelty, voluptuousness, religious hypocrisy, as well as by despotism. In a striking passage on the callousness of Ottoman rulers, Knolles, aware of the fratricide of nineteen brothers strangled at the accession of Mehmed III (1595–1603), wrote "of the common matter among the Ottoman Emperors, the brother becoming the bloody executioner of his own brethren."[26]

Fynes Moryson, one of the first professional travel writers, referred, in his comprehensive narrative on the Ottoman Empire, to it as "absolute and in the highest tyrannical, using all subjects as born slaves," lacking a true nobility.[27] Those who lived under the tyrant were little sponges to be squeezed when they were full.[28] The Turks were brave, but cruel, idle, and addicted to sexual pleasure, especially sodomy. The Italian and Irish Catholic populations were bad enough, but the Turks were the lowest point of barbarism. Moreover, though they were trading partners of the West, the Turks also posed a threat to European Christianity.

About the same time, George Sandys, poet, translator, travel writer, who visited Istanbul in 1610, wrote *A Relation of a Journey, 1615*, in which he was critical of the Ottoman Empire and of Islam, "the creation of a mutinous and epileptic Byzantine soldier."[29] The empire, ruled by slaves, the upstart creatures of the sultan with no nobility of blood or people with hereditary possessions, bordered on stagnation. In the past the area had been renowned, the seat of most glorious and triumphant empires, the stage where acts of valor and heroic actions took place, the location where arts and sciences had been invented and perfected.[30] It had become "the most deplored spectacles of extreme misery: the wild beasts of mankind having broken on them, and rooted out all civility, and the pride of a stern and barbarous tyrant possessing the thrones of ancient and just dominion." The tyrant ruled through terror and violence. The Turks, Sandys found, were also incredible takers of opium, carrying it with them both in peace and war. He thought it made them "giddy headed and turbulent dreamers."[31]

Sandys was equally critical of Islam and viewed its founder as an imposter. Muhammad pretended that he became the leader of the new religion not by military means but by divine appointment, and had been sent by God to provide a new law for mankind and by arms to reduce the world to obedience. He had a subtle wit, viciously employed, was naturally inclined to all villainies, and was insatiably lecherous.[32] His laws were an excuse for self-indulgent sexual license. The Koran was full of fables, legends, visions. It promised a paradise, full of palaces with silk carpets and amorous virgins. Sandys concluded that "the Mahometan religion, being derived from a person in life so wicked, so worldly in his projects, was supported by tyranny and the sword, and rooted out all virtue, all wisdom and science, all liberty and civility."

Sir Thomas Roe, courtier, parliamentarian, and English representative of James I in Constantinople, and agent of the East India Company to the Mughal court in India (1615–18), was one of the many who were bedazzled by the opulence and splendor of the court in which the Mughal "sat on cushions very rich in pearls and jewels," waiting to receive presents.[33] Echoing the theatrical predilection of the late sixteenth and early seventeenth centuries, especially in Marlowe and Shakespeare, for using themes and images of the Orient for dramatic effect, Roe recorded that the Mughal's council had "so much affinity with a theater, the manner of the king in his gallery, the great men lifted on a stage, as actors, the vulgar below gazing on." In his account of the birthday festivities in 1617 for the emperor, whom he saw as a complex figure both cruel and gentle, Roe painted a setting of incalculable riches and unrivalled magnificence.

In his letter of January 17, 1616, to Lord Carew on the state and customs of India, Roe wrote of the absence of written law, an observation he reiterated in a letter of January 29 to the Archbishop of Canterbury. Instead, the king was both ruler and judge, rendering judgments once a week. Those who rose to prominence, including governors of provinces, were people who were his favorites; they rose by giving him rich and rare presents; they were not born nobles but ruled by the emperor's command. All the land was the ruler's; he was everyone's heir, a fact that made him very rich. Though most of Roe's writings were on Mughal India, he also made clear his view that the Ottoman Empire was in decline: it was like an old body, crazed through many vices that were revealed when youth was gone and strength decayed.

Edward Terry, chaplain to Roe, echoed his master's view of Mughal India in his own comprehensive picture of conditions there.[34] He remarked, in similar fashion to Tavernier, that because of his great treasure and large territory, the Great Mughal was the most powerful and richest king of the East, if not of the whole world. Like Roe, Terry commented that, because there was no written law, the will of the ruler was law. Government was arbitrary, unlimited, and tyrannical. No one possessed any land or title except by the king's will. He appointed people to a combined military and civil service, making sure no subordinate remained in one place too long lest he become too popular.Terry painted a disparaging portrait of the court. The Great Mughal, descended from Tamerlane, styled himself the king of justice, the light of the law of Muhammad, the conqueror of the world. He sat on a glorious throne with rich jewels, traveled with no less than two hundred thousand men, women, and children in the camp. Terry saw the Great Mughal as an overgrown prince, like a huge pike in a great pond that preyed on all his neighbors.[35] The Protestant Terry also condemned the Mughal's sexual habits and his religion. The inhabitants of the king's house included only his women, eunuchs, and little boys whom he kept about him for pleasure. Terry compared Muslims to priests of Baal and misled Papists. Islam promised gratification "because it contains much in it very pleasing to flesh and blood, and soothes up, and complies exceedingly with corrupt nature, it wanted no followers presently to embrace and assert it."[36]

Sir William Eton, in *A Survey of the Turkish Empire, 1799*, wrote that the government of Turkey could truly be characterized as despotism.[37] He defined the concept in this way: "a power originating in force and upheld by the same means . . . a power scorning the jurisdiction of reason, and forbidding the temerity of investigation . . . a power calculated to crush the growing energies of mind and annihilating the faculties of man in order to insure his dependence." Turkey exemplified despotism: the system wielded both "the temporal and spiritual sword, converted fanaticism itself into an instrument of sovereignty, and united in one person the voice and the arm of the Divinity." Yet qualifying this stark view to some degree, he suggested there were two restraints on the sultan's power. Although the *Gran Signor* could appoint and depose the Mufti, he usually became the tool of the religious dignitary. Another check came from the great council (Divan) formed by the leading military officers, heads of the ulema, and ministers of the empire. Eton made an interesting comparison between social relations in Turkey and those in Europe. Much of the civilization of modern Europe, he argued, was attributable to the influence of female society, from which came the high and noble passions that excited men to deeds of active patriotism and benevolence and the softer pleasures that ornament and endear the social circle. By contrast, the Turks were barbarians, whose love was based on sensuality without friendship or esteem.

A similar argument to that of Eton was made by William Robertson, Scottish ordained minister and distinguished historian, who reiterated a strongly critical view of Turkish society and politics. He held the Turks were "cruel and fierce barbarians" and argued that the genius of the policy of the Turkish government was purely Asiatic and could properly be termed despotic.[38] The sultan was the supreme power in a system with no courts, no body of hereditary nobles, and no other institutions that could limit or moderate his monarchial power. The distinguishing and odious characteristic of Eastern despotism was that it annihilated "all other ranks of men in order to exalt the ruler." To be employed in the services of the sultan was "the only circumstance that confers distinction."[39] The only relationship between the ruler and his subjects was that of master and slave, the former destined to command and punish, and the rest to tremble and to obey. However, like Eton, Robertson qualified his position by arguing that restraints might exist, imposed by religion, obedience to the Koran, and, even more importantly, by the military power of the Janissaries, the only power in the empire that a sultan or his vizier had reason to dread. The great art of the Ottoman government, therefore, was to obtain the fidelity and the loyalty of the Janissaries. These qualifications in Robertson's argument reflect the fact that he was writing in the eighteenth century when radical changes were occurring, or being proposed, in the Ottoman Empire.

Among the many other English travelers from the eighteenth century on who wrote about the Middle East a few may be mentioned to illustrate the nature of their interest. They include Lady Mary Wortley Montagu, the remarkable wife of the English Ambassador to Istanbul in 1717–18, who wrote valuable letters about her experience there and specifically about the positive aspects of the harem; Lady Hester Stanhope (1776–1839), wife of a later English Ambassador to Turkey, who not only lived in the area but also for a time dressed as a Bedouin and traveled accompanied by a caravan of twenty-two camels, and considered Arabs to be the boldest people in the world, tender and kind; Richard Francis Burton (1821–90), British explorer and linguist, who translated *The Arabian Nights*, and also wrote of Bedouin independence and individualism; Wilfred Scawen Blunt (1840–1922) who thought Bedouin society was free from bureaucracy and criticized the British occupation of the Sudan and Egypt, the inhabitants of which he thought should rebel against the Ottoman Empire; Gerald de Gaury (1897–1984), British soldier and diplomat, who wrote a number of books sympathetic to Islam and Arab life; Freya Stark (1893–1993), the unusual lady who was one of the first Western women to travel through the Arabian deserts, in southern Arabia, and in the territory of the Syrian Druze, learned Arabic, and found the hidden routes of the ancient trade in incense; Sir Wilfred Thesiger (1910–2003), explorer of remote areas of Arabia, who wrote of the life of the Bedouins and the marshlands of southern Iraq where he lived for eight years; Gertrude Bell, the rich adventurer and scholar fluent in Arabic and Persian, who designed accurate maps of the Syrian desert and Mesopotamia, before helping the British government in World War I; and, of course, the enigmatic T. E. Lawrence.

3

Political Thinkers and the Orient

"Without comparisons to make," wrote Alexis de Tocqueville, "the mind does not know how to proceed." Comparative political analysis addresses the similarities and differences in past and present political systems. On the basis of empirical data such analysis searches for existing patterns of behavior and formulates theories, concepts, generalizations, models, and typologies to understand and interpret them. The observation and comparison of political systems together with the study of history is not only an intellectually valuable exercise in its own right but may also be of practical importance, as James Harrington the seventeenth political theorist implied, as the means by which one can learn the craft of the statesman.

An inevitable dilemma in comparative politics, however, is that a model or typology is unlikely to encompass without qualification the multifarious nature of the political and social reality in all places and times. In addition, as the philosopher Karl Popper pointed out, an inherent problem in social science analysis, including that of framing typologies is distinguishing between the essential and accidental aspects of political or social entities and what should be considered pertinent to generalizations about them.[1] Nevertheless, even with awareness of these pitfalls, one can employ the term *despotism*, sometimes associated and even confused with other terms such as *tyranny* and *dictatorship*, to refer to a particular kind of nondemocratic rule or society in any comparative study, and more particularly the term *Oriental despotism* can be used to refer to that kind of rule prevalent in Eastern countries.[2]

The term *despot* and the adjective *despotic* were rarely used until the late sixteenth century. The term *despotism* became more familiar in the seventeenth and eighteenth centuries and was used to criticize absolute monarchical rule, especially that of Louis XIV. In France the word was first defined in a dictionary in 1721, and then by the Académie Française in 1740.[3] Increasingly, the word and its derivative equivalent, *Oriental despotism*, were applied to Eastern systems and specifically to the Ottoman Empire with the growing conviction that they were of a different order from Western systems and had rulers who were absolute, arbitrary, and corrupt, and had societies that were stagnant. Unlike tyranny, which was seen to have some positive features, Oriental despotism was described negatively. This chapter traces how the West came to define the "Other" as Oriental despotism.

In his work *The Statesman* Plato outlined a sixfold classification of forms of government, three of which are law-abiding and three of which are corrupt versions of the form. However, the real starting point and fount of comparative political analysis is Aristotle in *The Politics* who combined empirical investigation of existing constitutions and political systems with speculation and generalizations about the nature of systems. In this regard a starting point is his differentiation of three types of political systems in terms both of the number of the ruler, whether it is one, few, or many, and also in terms of the quality, good and corrupt versions, of those systems.[4] Through this classification Aristotle pursued the study of what was the best political system. He envisaged good rule as that which was in the public interest, based on general regulations and not arbitrary, and accepted by willing subjects. He indicated that the authority of a constitutional ruler over subjects was differerent from that of a master over slaves.

In addition Aristotle compared systems in other ways, by climate, by people, by geography. One passage (1327b), pertinent to our examination of the origins of Western perceptions of the Orient, is his comparison of three peoples: those in the colder regions of Europe, those in Asia, and those in Greece. The first are deficient in skill and intelligence but have spirit, and that is why they continue to remain comparatively free; the second have skill and intelligence but are deficient in spirit and thus continue to be subjects and slaves; the Greek people, geographically between the other two, have spirit and intelligence. Aristotle contrasts the Hellenes, the Greeks who were inherently free, with non-Hellenes, implicitly Persians, or barbarians who were slaves by nature. The "Other" for Aristotle was the Persians. He equated the Hellenes with the master, *despotes*, head of the household exercising appropriate rule over slaves who, because of their nature, were not capable of ruling themselves.

Examining five different kinds of kingship, Aristotle (1285 a) made a crucial distinction, one that was to affect subsequent political thought. He wrote that a particular form of kingship was present among some uncivilized (non-Hellenic) peoples. This form possessed an authority similar to that of tyrannies, but it was, he argued, "constitutional and hereditary." Aristotle's explanation for this kind of regime was that these uncivilized peoples were more servile in character than were the Greeks, as the peoples of Asia were more servile than were Europeans and would therefore tolerate "despotic" rule without any complaint. Therefore this form of kingship was stable. His assertion that Asians unlike Greeks (Europeans) had a servile nature was to be of singular influence in political thought. Aristotle's differentiation between Greeks and Persians (the Orient) was to metastasize into the contrast between "West" and "East" for all subsequent political thinkers comparing systems and societies in the Orient with those in the West.

All the same, Aristotle did not clearly differentiate the terms *tyrant* and *despot* especially when dealing with non-Greek kingships. The title "despot" had appeared in ancient Greek terminology, sometimes as a title of honor. This usage continued into early Christian liturgy in churches where Jesus was referred to by the words, "In the name of the Lord (*Tou despotou*) Jesus Christ." Aristotle (1285 a/b) described some ancient Greek monarchies as dictatorships, which could be called *elective forms of tyranny*. These dictatorships were tyrannical, but they differed from the regimes among uncivilized people because they rested on the elective consent of their subjects and were nonhereditary. Another of Aristotle's forms of kingship was the absolute type where a single person was sovereign on every issue; it corresponded to paternal rule over a household because this kind of kingship could be regarded as paternal rule over a polis, tribe, or collection of tribes. This would be the closest that Aristotle came to discussing our notion of Oriental despotism.

Despotism was not originally used as a derogatory term. By contrast, *tyrant* was a title used among the pre-Hellenic inhabitants of Greece and had a negative connotation. Unlike tyranny, despotism did not entail illegal rule over involuntary subjects. The crucial difference for Aristotle appears to be that tyranny was illegal rule or abuse of power or rule in the interests of a particular person, while despotism implied a legal system of arbitrary rule, appropriate for subjects, and often accepted by them as legitimate. As already described, the despot acted as he did because of the servile nature of the people. Parenthetically, a similar lack of clarity to that of Aristotle lasts into the eighteenth century and appears in the American Declaration of Independence where, in one paragraph, the justification for the overthrow of British rule is based on "absolute despotism" and then "absolute tyranny."

For theorists after Aristotle, the term *tyranny* appears in general to mean lawless, illegitimate rule by one person who had acquired power by usurpation, irregular, nonconstitutional means, while the Greek word *despot* has the connotation of master or *seigneur*. Important intellectual figures – Aquinas, Marsillius, William of Occam, and Nicolas Oresme – and translators of Aristotle in the Middle Ages occasionally used versions of the Greek word, such as *monarchia despotica* or *despoticum* or *despotizare*, often with no derogatory meaning. More frequently, the terms used for similar regimes were *dominator* or *dominatio*, and then *monarchie seigneuriale*. The concept of tyrant in medieval political thought was generally applied to a ruler who did not abide by fundamental law (6). An important distinction was made by John of Salisbury in his *Policraticus* in 1159, the first systematic treatise on politics in the Middle Ages, when he wrote, "between a tyrant and a prince there is this single or chief difference, that the latter obeys the law and rules the people by its dictates, accounting himself as their servant."

Political concepts, in the past as in the present, have often been used for partisan or polemical purposes. Marsillius (Marsiglio of Padua, 1280–1343), William of Occam (1290?–1349), and Nicole Oresme (1323–82), all used *despotism* to refer to the Papacy in its struggle with contemporary monarchs. In *Defensor Pacis*, Marsillius wrote of despotic power in Asia, and condemned attempts of the Popes to exercise similar unlimited power and "unjust despotism."[5] Quoting Aristotle, he argued that citizens, men who participated in the civil community, must be free, and not be subject to another's despotism or slavish domination. The ruler must be accountable for actions contrary to the law, or his principate would become despotic, and the life of the citizens would become servile and insufficient.

William of Occam contrasted a "regal principate," where the king was lord of all things, which existed for the sake of the common good, with a "despotic principate," which existed principally for the private good of the ruler. The latter ruler could use slaves for his private good so long as he attempted nothing contrary to divine or natural law. Occam attempted to clarify the terminology of Aristotle. A bad king becomes a tyrant when he begins to rule his subjects against their will for his own good, but if he begins to rule them with their consent for his own good he becomes a despot. Occam argued that Aristotle had sometimes called the latter regime a tyranny, but there was a distinction between despotism and tyranny. However, both tyranny in the proper sense and the despotic principate were the opposite of the regal principate.

Critical comments, in a sense making John of Salisbury's generalization more specific, are those about the nature of Eastern systems that appear in political discussions, sometimes in incidental remarks, by prominent European writers. Perhaps the sharpest, earliest, and most influential of such remarks on the distinction between Western and Eastern systems, essentially contrasting France with the Ottoman state, was made by Machiavelli in *The Prince* published in 1532.[6] All principalities, he argued, in history have been governed in one of two ways: either by one prince with all other persons as his servants, or by a prince and barons who hold positions as ministers not by grace of their master but because of their noble birth. The Turkish emperor exemplified the first kind; the king of France, the second. The latter was subject to laws, had a group of established nobles who had hereditary rights and could not be removed by the king without danger to himself. By contrast, the Turkish kingdom was ruled by one master whose ministers were his servants; he could remove and change those ministers as he pleased. Subjects were all slaves and were dependent on the ruler.

Machiavelli's important distinction between the two types of regime was the forerunner of future contrasts between Western European systems, incorporating legal and political restraints on the ruler, and Eastern regimes where such restraints were absent or not invoked. Symbolically, France represented the tradition of European liberty while the Ottoman Empire represented the Orient where royal power was not restrained by law.

Some sixty years after Machiavelli, the influential French theorist Jean Bodin (1530–96), writing during the Huguenot revolt in 1576 that threatened the French monarchy, and wanting to protect the state and strengthen the power of the king, argued that in all political systems, sovereignty was absolute and undivided.[7] Sovereign power is what distinguished the state from all other organizations. It was supreme power over citizens and subjects. The French monarchy could, therefore, exercise that absolute power.

Bodin's book, *Six livres de la république*, is somewhat haphazard and poorly organized, but nevertheless, in some passages that in essence separated civil liberty from political liberty, he differentiated the French type of monarchical rule from "seigneurial monarchy." The latter was Bodin's term for despotism, a regime typified by Turkey, which resulted from conquest and which had discretionary power over the lives and goods of subjects. In European absolute monarchies, subjects obeyed the monarch who was circumscribed by the laws of nature and divine law. He granted his subjects their natural liberty and private property. By contrast, the "Grand Seigneur," the despotic seigneurial monarch, in Turkey was a prince who was lord of all goods and all persons. He governed his subjects by virtue of conquest and a just war, and as absolutely as a father ruled his slaves. At the same time, Bodin, writing during a bitter period in the religious wars in France, at one point thought that the "the king of the Turks ... permits everyone to live according as his conscience allows." Occasionally, Bodin added "the Muscovite monarch" to the list of "seigneurial monarchies" or "lordly Monarchies." But the Ottoman sultan was the person who wielded "authority worthy of the name of empire or of authentic monarchy." He was the only power "who with justification can lay claim to the title of universal ruler ... only he can justifiably claim to be the descendant of the Roman Emperor."

Bodin never used the word *despotism*, and his themes and language lack complete clarity. This is apparent in one of the influential aspects of his argument, that concerning the consequences of just and unjust wars. He argued that a regime was appropriate when the prince, who had defeated his enemies in a just war, then assumed an absolute right to their goods and was entitled to govern his subjects as his slaves. But the ruler, who, by an unjust war or any other means, enslaved a free people and seized their property, was not a despot but a tyrant. For Bodin then it is against the law of nature to enslave a free people and to seize their goods, but he also said that what was won in a just war was the property of the victor, and that the vanquished were his slaves.

The distinction between two types of systems, absolute government and arbitrary government, the latter resembling Bodin's "seigneurial monarchy," was more clearly made by Jacques Bossuet (1627–1704).[8] In his *La Politique Tirée de l'Écriture Sainte*, published in 1679, Bossuet wrote of that arbitrary government that "is not found with us (France) or in perfectly civilized states." In this kind of system the subject peoples were born slaves or serfs; no one possessed property; the prince could dispose of the lives, as well as the goods, of subjects; and there was no law except the will of the prince. He described such government as barbarous and odious. This system was different from absolute government, which could compel but that was subject to the will of God and in which everyone had legitimate possession of his own property.

By contrast with the theorists justifying absolutism, the pamphlets, *Les Soupirs de la France esclave*, published anonymously, but usually attributed to a Huguenot exile Michel Le Vassor (1648–1718) in Holland (1689–90), though at times analytically confusing, were critical of the French system, likening the power of the French king Louis XIV, who considered himself above the law, to the despotism of the *Grand Seigneur* (*Gran Signor*). For him the revocation of the Edict of Nantes (1685), which by decision of Henry IV in 1598 had granted the minority Protestants substantial rights in mainly Catholic France, illustrated the nature of the despotic, arbitrary power in France. The court of Louis XIV was equated with the tyranny of Turkey, acting against natural reason and claiming the lives and goods of his subjects. It had become "Turk and not Christian"; the king was trying "to turn us into Turks."

Thomas Hobbes (1588–1679) appears to have been the first theorist clearly to use the term *despotism* in political discussion, writing of "bodies patrimonial and despotical" and referring to "kingly despotical," the power of a master over servants.[9] Influenced by the current civil war in England and wanting order and stability, Hobbes defined *sovereignty*, in a clearer way than Bodin, as the command of an absolute, unlimited ruler exercising supreme power over subjects who were completely obedient to him and who had transferred their rights to him by contract or conquest. Like Bodin he argued that sovereignty was an essential characteristic of any regime. Because in all systems there was a final and uncontrollable rule-making power, despotic monarchy was normal, not barbarian, and no different from any other sovereign system. The rights and consequences of both paternal and despotical dominion were the same as those in a system set up by institution or choice of sovereign.

A generation later, John Locke (1632–1704), in *Two Treaties of Government*, provided a rebuttal to Hobbes's view of sovereign power. Government should not exercise all power and cause citizens to surrender all rights because of fear of a brutal state of nature as Hobbes had argued, but should secure those rights and produce certain benefits for citizens who had entered into a contract. A chapter in his second *Treatise*, echoing Hobbes's own chapter title, is headed "Paternal, Political, and Despotical Power, Considered Together."[10] Locke defined *despotical power* as "an absolute, arbitrary power one man has over another to take away his life wherever he pleases," and as a system where people "have no property at all." Despotical power was appropriate only for captives, taken in a just and lawful war, because that power did not arise from and was not capable of entering into any compact.

ENLIGHTENMENT PERCEPTIONS

Paul Hazard, in his classic work on the eighteenth-century Enlightenment, wrote, "there became apparent an effervescence and diffusion of ideas so remarkable in its nature, so far-reaching in its extent as to be without parallel in history."[11] Even if, in recent years, some scholars have argued that the Enlightenment should be regarded as a more complex phenomenon and a more diverse movement than a single, unified group, mostly of French intellectuals propounding similar arguments aiming to destroy the *ancien régime*, the central thrust of those intellectuals and like-minded European writers remains clear. They were advocates of rationalism and science and the use of empirical observation. They argued for emancipation from autocracy and despotic politics, for the equal dignity of people, and the elimination of intolerance in society and politics. If not always antitheological they did call for the reduction of the power of the church in social and political affairs. If the argument of Isaiah Berlin is correct, that the central dogma of the Enlightenment was the assertion of universal and unalterable principles, one such salient principle would be the call for freedom and emancipation from political and religious restraints.[12]

To some extent, Enlightenment writers praised the Oriental world for its past contributions to science, mathematics, medicine, and the arts. Some of the *philosophes* even uttered kind words about Ottoman society. More significant, some of their writing on Eastern systems and denunciations of Oriental despotism, identified in the eighteenth century as Eastern systems, can be considered, at least in part, as implicit criticism of their own regimes, autocracy in France, or the sexual peccadilloes of Charles II in England. However, this contention has perhaps been exaggerated as has the argument that the concept of Oriental despotism was formulated to justify Western control over the East.

That concept of Oriental despotism stems from criticism of the Orient by Enlightenment writers including, among others, Nicolas Boulanger (1722–59), the Marquis de Condorcet (1743–94), Claude-Adrien Helvétius (1715–71), Louis de Jaucourt (1704–79), and the Encyclopédie group, who were often influenced by Montesquieu. Their collective critical analyses and indictments of Oriental political systems, especially of the Ottoman Empire, constitute an intellectual anatomy and structure, going beyond the direct observation of the travelers discussed earlier, to interpret the nature of Oriental despotism.[13] That empire was now perceived to be the main example of Oriental despotism, a system of arbitrary, absolute power wielded by the sultan.

Nicolas Boulanger in his *The Origin and Progress of Despotism*, published posthumously in 1764, echoing Aristotle and Montesquieu, was another writer who suggested that climate was a factor that induced despotism. More importantly he also argued that in the early history of the world despotic authority was related to religion that was based on fear, the primeval terror of the heavens. He applied this general theory to Asia where the rulers were regarded as "visible gods." Boulanger held that in this distressful region, "man is seen to kiss his chains, without any certainty as to fortune and property, he adores his tyrant; and without any knowledge of humanity or reason, he is reduced to have no other virtue but fear."[14] Asia was plunged in sloth and servitude, while history shows us, he wrote, that Europe was ever jealous of her freedom. The Oriental monarch was sovereign arbiter of the faith of the subjects over whom he reigned. In Asia there was no law other than the will of the monarch, whose rule was that of the father, head of the family, theocratic god-king. Boulanger compared East and West: "every object impresses on the mind of a young Asiatic that he is a slave, and ought to be so: the European learns, from everything around him, that he is a rational being."

Not surprisingly the Marquis de Condorcet, a believer in universal and eternal principles – in the progress of mankind, rationalism, and liberalism – and in human diversity, saw Eastern systems as embodying the antithesis of his principles. They were characterized by single despots, by tyrannical rule that became more cowardly and cruel, and by religious intolerance. In his view, Islam led to slavery, stupidity, and despotism, a development that Condorcet, with his advocacy of the end of inequality among nations, the advance of equality within a single people, and the improvement of individuals, found offensive. Yet the sixth stage of his *The Progress of the Human Mind* presents a more balanced picture. The manners of the Arabs were gentle and dignified, but they suffered from religious fanaticism. With the Arabs the sciences were "free," but the people lived under a despotism sanctified by religion.

Claude-Adrien Helvétius, in his book *De l'Esprit* (1758), attacked the Catholic Church, the monarch, and traditional morality, and these views were the subject of considerable controversy. He was even more critical of Eastern systems, which he saw as tyrannies that imposed an unsupportable yoke. He compared the sultans of Asia, whom he described as stupid, to vampires who suck the blood of their subjects; control honors, riches, and punishments; and debase the minds of their subjects, who were forced through fear and hope, to accept the law and the visions of the prophet Muhammad. The sultan was the sole disposer of rewards and punishments. The Ottoman Empire was nothing more than an immense desert; Persia had twenty tyrants; and the inhabitants of India were a slothful people, debased by slavery. The article in the *Encyclopédie* on despotism, written by Louis de Jaucourt, had a similar thrust, describing it as a tyrannical, absolute, arbitrary government by one man. Typical examples of despotic rulers were the Turkish sultan, the Mughal emperor, rulers in Japan and Persia and in almost all of Asia. The ruler governed according to his will, granting authority to those he liked. The system was founded on fear, not glory or grandeur; women were regarded as slaves.

Other French writers followed in the footsteps of the *Encyclopédistes*. One of the most critical of the Orient was Count Volney. The ultimate objective of Volney (1757–1820), originally Constantin François de Chassaboeuf, French *philosophe* and politician who lived for two years in Egypt and the Levant and learned Arabic, was to unite all religions by recognizing their common truths. Nevertheless, he was critical of Eastern systems and of Islam.[15] In a sweeping generalization, Volney portrayed a lamentable state: all Asia was buried in the most profound darkness; the Chinese were subjected to an insolent despotism; the Indians vegetated in an incurable apathy; the Tartars lived in the barbarity of their ancestors; the Arabs endured anarchy of their tribes and jealousy of their families; and the Africans were in a condition of servitude.

The Turks had founded an empire, became wealthy, and then had fallen into despotism and ignorance.[16] They destroyed everything and repaired nothing. The barbarity of ignorant despotism (the Turkish government) never considered tomorrow. The sultan "intoxicated with his greatness" possessed all the vices of arbitrary power. He had become a depraved character, was weak and arrogant at the same time, lived in enormous luxury, and neglected his people.

Commenting on conditions in Egypt, Volney reiterated the argument that there was no noble class, no clergy, merchants, or landowners who could constitute an intermediate body between the common people and the government. In the Ottoman Empire, the sultan, with his absolute and arbitrary power, delegated authority to viziers and pashas who also acted as absolute despots. The entire country was regarded as the sultan's private property and all his subjects as his servants. Corruption was habitual and general. Sovereignty to these Eastern rulers meant, not the governmental art of directing to one common goal the various passions of a numerous society, but only the means of procuring more women, more boys, horses, and slaves, and satisfying all caprices.[17]

Volney saw "the spirit of Islamism" as the original source of the abuses of government and as a cause of people's ignorance and indolence. They became fatalistic through their acceptance of the Islamic concept of predestination, and thus Muslims would accept anything as the will of God. If the Koran had any coherent meaning it was "the force of an obstinate, impassioned fanaticism."[18] The consequence was the establishment of the most absolute despotism because Muhammad's objective was not to enlighten men but to rule over them; he wanted subjects, not disciples. Muslims submitted to "the most unexpected transition from opulence to poverty." In Volney's presentation of a dialogue between a Christian and a Muslim, the former says "your fanaticism has never ceased to spread desolation and carnage. Asia once flourishing, is now languishing in insignificance and barbarism because of Islam . . . it consecrates the most absolute despotism in him who commands and imposes the most blind and passive obedience in those who are governed."[19] Parenthetically interesting is the fact that Volney's work was internationally influential. In 1802, while President of the United States, Thomas Jefferson translated part of the *Ruins*, and Percy Bysshe Shelley drew on Volney in both his poetry, as in *Ozymandias*, and in his introduction to the English translation of Volney's writings.

Equally harsh criticism of Eastern systems appeared in the English popular press and in America in the eighteenth century. A striking example is the work by Cato, the pseudonym of John Trenchard and Thomas Gordon, two English Whig journalists who wrote 144 essays for papers between 1720 and 1723. They were subsequently published as Cato's *Letters or Essays on Liberty, Civil, and Religious.*[20] Writing on the merging of the roles of kings and priests in Eastern countries, Cato maintained, in a letter dated February 17, 1721, "There never lived more raging bigots or more furious and oppressive barbarians." The monarchs of Persia, a severe tyranny, had the priesthood annexed to it. The Turkish religion was founded on imposture, blended with outrageous and avowed violence. Muhammad was troubled that "common sense might get the better of violence" and forbad free discussion of the Koran. Cato amusingly drew a parallel; the imperial executioner was revered as the most sacred institution, after the Koran. In a later letter, dated July 7, 1722, Cato categorized the most despotic governments in the world as those "where the whole property is in the prince, as in the Eastern monarchies." Two weeks later on July 22, 1721, Cato regarded Turkey as an enslaved country, concluding that the private will, interest, and pleasure of the governors were the sole end and motives of their administration.

In America similar views of the religious and political tyranny in the Orient were expressed by a number of writers. William Eaton, American consul in Tunis (1799–1803), another individual influenced by Volney, commented on the religious system in North Africa, which favored indolence by relying on divine will. The Tunisians were slaves to their despotic government and, because they could not own property, had no ambition to cultivate the land. They were subject to a double tyranny, political rule and the despotism of priest craft, the worst of all tyrannies. Eaton was especially critical of the Prophet. The North Africans lived in more solemn fear of the frowns of a bigot who had been dead and rotten more than a thousand years than of the living despot whose frown could cost them their lives. The ignorance, superstitious tradition, and civil and religious tyranny depressed the human mind in Tunis and excluded improvement of every kind.

A decade later, the consul in Tunis, Mordecai Manuel Noah, often regarded as the first American Zionist, noting that the Moors in the past had introduced a prosperous and enlightened system in Spain, nevertheless believed that the system had not been maintained because of Islamic religious zeal, lack of disciplined troops, and overexpenditure. Perhaps the most interesting early American commentary on the Orient came from Alexander Hamilton in *Federalist* 30. Writing on December 28, 1787 about the issue of taxation for the contemplated federal government, he used the Ottoman Empire to bolster his argument. Hamilton wrote that in the empire, "the sovereign, though in other respects absolute master of the lives and fortunes of his subjects, has no right to impose a new tax." He therefore allowed the governors of provinces to pillage the people without mercy, and in turn squeezed out of them the sums he needed. In America the government of the Union had likewise dwindled into a state of decay. Hamilton concluded that the peoples in both countries would be happier if competent authorities in the proper hands provided the revenues that the people might require.

But not all the eighteenth-century commentary on Eastern systems was so critical. Some eighteenth-century writers were aware of the changes in the Ottoman Empire that led to restraints on power. Challenge to the dominant perception of these systems as Oriental despotism and sometimes objection to the validity of the concept came from various sources. They included some prominent eighteenth-century French Enlightenment writers such as Voltaire, Helvétius, Simon-Nicolas-Henri Linguet, and Abraham-Hyacinthe Anquetil-Duperron. Other figures more sympathetic to the empire were experienced diplomats such as Sir James Porter, English ambassador to Turkey; travelers such as Jean de Thévenot, who journeyed to Anatolia, Palestine, and Ottoman Egypt and praised Eastern religious rituals, kindness, and generosity; and the Chevalier d'Arvieux, a traveler, merchant, and diplomat who regarded the Bedouins – civil, hospitable, honest – as the best people in the world; keen observers such as Lady Mary Wortley Montagu, Adolphus Slade, and Richard Francis Burton, translator of *The Arabian Nights* and admirer of the East; scholars and historians such as David Hume and Thomas Carlyle, who touched on the issue with incidental remarks; and Robert Orme and Alexander Dow with mixed views on India.

These commentators who wrote more sympathetically about the Orient, particularly about the Ottoman Empire, based their arguments on observations that the power of the sultan was becoming restrained in various ways and that the empire tolerated other religions. They pointed out that, contrary to the perspectives of other writers, sultans now lacked power to dismiss Janissaries at will, alter the coinage, interfere with the harems, and were not likely in arbitrary fashion to declare war. The sultans in the eighteenth century, they believed, had no more power over the rights and inheritance of subjects than did European rulers. The rulers lived within a system of laws, in which private property was secure, and women were respected. Francis Osborn praised the Turkish system in which all honors and places of profit were determined without the least partiality shown to greatness of birth.

Lady Mary Wortley Montagu, wife of the British Ambassador in Turkey (1716–18) and renowned letter writer, thought that the information on Turkey available in Britain was biased, and complained that religious leaders had invented "a thousand ridiculous stories in order to decry the law of Muhammad." In her letter of April 1, 1717 to Lady Bristol, she wrote that the *Gran Signor* might have absolute power, but, because the government was entirely in the hands of the army, he was as much a slave as any of his subjects and "trembled at a Janissary's frown." Also, if, despite their professed unlimited adoration of the sultan, the people were displeased and threatened a minister, the sultan sat fearful in his apartment. Such was the "blessed" condition of the most absolute monarch on earth. Lady Montagu compared Turkey favorably with the Catholic countries, France and Spain, argued that Turkish subjects had more freedom than British subjects, that Turkish law was "better designed and better executed" than British law, and that the condition of women in

Turkey was not in practice what it seemed to be in theory.[21] In a letter to her sister, Lady Mar, she even wrote, "On the whole, I look on the Turkish woman as the only free people [*sic*] in the Empire."[22]

Less dramatically than Lady Montagu, a generation later the long-term English ambassador in Constantinople, Sir James Porter (1746–62) acknowledged that, although some abuses were evident, the Ottoman Empire was a kind of limited monarchy acting according to law. He praised the system's administrative efficiency: "There is no Christian power which can vie with the *Porte* (Turkey) for care and exactitude in the several offices; business is done with the greatest accuracy."[23] He suggested that the Turkish government was much less despotic than the government of some Christian states. Yet Porter's views on the religious character of the Turks were harsh: "The Turks hold all who are not of their belief and embrace not the doctrines of their Prophet, to be objects of divine vengeance, and consequently of their detestation, and against whom they are to exercise violence, fraud, and rapine." Moreover, Porter argued that "Muhammetans are ever ready to demonstrate their zeal by spurning and ill treating the persons, plundering the property, and even destroying the very existence of those who profess a different religion." He believed that they were commanded and convinced that this behavior was "most meritorious in the sight of God and his Prophet."[24]

Linguet and Anquetil-Duperron were the most articulate among the French critics of the concept of Oriental despotism in general and Montesquieu in particular. Linguet, lawyer and journalist, who attacked the "fanaticism of the *philosophes*" of the Enlightenment, but was to be guillotined in 1794, argued that Montesquieu's classification of regimes, discussed in Chapter 4, was arbitrary. Critical of the absolute French monarchy and the institutions and corporate bodies in England that could limit power, Linguet praised "Asiatic" autocracy and the Ottoman Empire where the inhabitants passed their days in the most peaceful and happy security if they observed the laws. Asiatic authoritarianism was superior to British constitutionalism: its beauty was its simplicity. Linguet believed the sultan only rarely confiscated the estates of private persons, and Eastern rulers might be overthrown if they abused their power.[25]

The most sustained criticism of Montesquieu's theory, discussed in Chapter 4, was that by Anquetil-Duperron (1731–1805), antiquarian, armchair philosopher and historian, researcher learned in Hebrew, Persian, and Sanskrit, fascinated by Zoroastrian texts and most celebrated for making them known, who left France in 1755 for India where he spent seven years. He identified errors or misunderstandings in Montesquieu's work and criticized the latter's reliance on the dubious evidence of the early travelers. Anquetil-Duperron's challenging premise was that Oriental despotism was an intellectual hypothesis, and that it did not really exist in Turkey, Persia, and Hindustan. He spoke of "the phantom of despotism"; accusations of pure arbitrary power were not justified.

Anquetil-Duperron admitted the existence of tyranny and abuses of power in those three countries, but this should not be described as despotism because all systems in the world experienced abuses. He wrote, anticipating some present-day arguments, that the concept of Oriental despotism was "an imaginary and phantasmatically pure power," a cautionary fiction used to justify European colonial rule, particularly British rule in India, and oppression practiced in Asia.[26] For him, Eastern systems were unjustly condemned as the embodiment of evil. The Turkish system did not entail rule by simple arbitrary decree but was more complex and more public than Montesquieu related. The sultan conducted state affairs and received petitions openly. In Persia where there were hereditary offices, the king was partly elected and took an oath of office. Anquetil-Duperron admitted that slavery existed in Asia, but he held that not everyone was a slave there.

Moreover, he argued, some restraints resulted from the Koran and Islam, which had a code of law and moral precepts that regulated life, and the sultan took an oath to uphold Islamic law and felt bound by that law. Central power was limited by what Anquetil-Duperron called "natural equity" and political circumstances.[27] He also challenged the thesis of Bernier, which had influenced so many later writers, that private property in the Orient did not exist. On the contrary, he argued that private property and commercial rights did exist as laws and contracts proved. The sultan had scarcely any more rights over inheritances than did the sovereigns of Europe.[28] Some lands did constitute the royal domain, and the ruler was viewed as "the sovereign lord," but private owners enjoyed stable possession of their lands.

Another challenge to the general critical view of Oriental despotism came from the well-informed French ambassador, the Comte de Choiseul-Gouffier, at Constantinople in 1786. Referring to the changing situation in Turkey, in the context of the centralization of authority and growing royal autocracy in France, he wrote in a letter that "[t]hings here are not as in France, where the king is sole master; here it is necessary to persuade the ulema, the men of law, the holders of high offices, and those who no longer hold them."[29] Choiseul-Gouffier's comparison was a specific contradiction of Machiavelli's comparison of the powers of "the Turk and the king of France." He was reflecting the attempts at major changes in the realities of life in Turkey, especially the efforts at decentralization of power.

Mixed or critical messages emanated from the philosopher David Hume, Robert Orme, who joined the East India Company as a writer in 1743,

Alexander Dow, the Scottish employee of the East India Company, and Adolphus Slade, a naval officer. At one point, Hume thought the government of Persia was despotic yet did not eliminate all nobility.[30] In another reference, he remarked that it was a fundamental maxim of the Turkish government that the *Gran Signor*, though absolute master of the lives and fortunes of all the individuals, had no authority to impose a new tax.[31] Robert Orme, in his *General Idea of the Government and People of Indostan* (1753), wrote of the fear that reigned throughout Eastern systems. Though in theory despotism was absolute in those countries, nevertheless in practice certain constraints, such as religion and custom, existed on the exercise of power.

A favorite correspondent of David Hume was Alexander Dow (1735–79), who had spent four years in the Bengal infantry division of the East India Company and was the author of the *History of Hindustan* (1770). His analysis was ambivalent. If his analysis of the Mughal regime and Indian society cannot be described as laudatory in character, he did make some admiring and positive remarks about them. Like others who wrote about the Orient, Dow spoke of the languor in India, occasioned by the hot climate, humidity, and fertile soil, which inclined "the native to indolence and ease" and to think the evils of despotism were less severe than the labor of being free. This had reduced Hindus to a state of slavery and accustomed an indolent and ignorant race of men to the simplicity of despotism.[32] In addition, the seeds of despotism resulting from the Indian climate and soil had reached "perfect growth by the Muhammadan religion." The faith of Muhammad was particularly calculated to produce despotism: characteristics of the behavior of adherents of Islam were obedience, acceptance of a regime of arbitrary power, belief in predestination, polygamy, laziness, voluptuousness, unlimited power over wives and family, and ignorance.[33] To some extent, Dow mitigated this critical perception of Islam by arguing that the Hindu caste system was also one of despotic order, though it was tempered by the virtuous principles inculcated by the Hindu religion. Yet in his collection of tales in Persian, a language in which he was proficient, Dow was critical of the sexual and moral corruption of Muslim rule in India, even suggesting at one point an alliance between Christian governors and Hindu priests to strengthen British authority in India to counter Muslim influence.

Politically, Dow saw the Mughal emperor as the absolute and sole arbiter, controlled by no law. All lands, except some hereditary districts, were considered to be his property. The emperor's arbitrary and cruel behavior was displayed when he pronounced the death sentence by simply waving his hand or saying "take him away." Justice was executed in privacy.[34] Yet Dow was critical of British colonialism. Somewhat surprisingly after his other thoughts about Muslim Oriental despotism, Dow, like Robert Orme, suggested the Mughal rule and other Asian systems, though despotic, were in practice benevolent, moderate, and limited; they respected privileges, titles, and private property, and could protect their subjects. Dow even suggested that despotism was bound by the ideas of mankind with regard to right and wrong. India had once been wealthy and prosperous. The decline of India began when "Bengal fell under the dominion of foreigners . . . who were anxious to secure a permanent advantage to the British nation." Though a former employee, Dow was critical of the "barbarous conquerors" of the East India Company.

A nuanced view of Oriental systems was portrayed by Adolphus Slade (1802–77), a British naval officer who traveled to Turkey in 1829 and then traveled elsewhere in the East. In a number of books, he defended the existing Ottoman Empire, though with some critical remarks, and opposed those who would reform it. Unlike those whose criticism was unreserved, he viewed the sultan's power as checked by various factors: the hereditary nobility; provincial and urban officials; the peerage of Turkey; the Islamic hierarchy; the ulema; and the Janissaries.[35] Though he did write of the "leaden hand of Eastern despotism," his position was that the Ottoman system was not an Oriental despotism but an absolute government limited by those factors.

At the same time Slade wrote of the cruelty, ingratitude, unbending obstinacy, and increase in personal power in the Ottoman Empire and held that it existed for the personal enjoyment of the Sultan Mahmud. The ruler was regarded by subjects as the vice-regent of the Prophet, as superior to ordinary mortals. He was resolved there should be no power that did not emanate from, or depend on, his will. Slade observed the authority and increase in central control was becoming more efficient thanks to the modernization taking place in the Ottoman Empire.

The most influential early-nineteenth-century commentary on the Orient came from Hegel. In oracular language he described the historical process of government as going through four stages: the Oriental world, the Greek world, the Roman world, and finally the German world in which freedom at last was embodied in the state. History had traveled from East to West, and Europe was the end of history.[36] Hegel concluded that in the Eastern world only one person – the ruler – was free; in the Greek and Roman worlds some people were free; and in the German world all were free. For Hegel the first political form in history was despotism, which typified the East; "the glory of Oriental conception is the One Individual as that substantial being to which all belongs, so that no other individual has a separate existence, or mirrors himself in his subjective freedom." Oriental history was "unhistorical." Hegel saw only duration and stability; "Empires belonging to mere space, as it were." Asia was the first area to attain "substantive freedom" embodied in the state, but it had not progressed to the principle of subjectivity: only the despot was free through his will.

Discussing the question of church and state and the distinction between their separate modes of existence, Hegel remarked that the unity of the two was found in Oriental despotism.[37] He continued, "[A]n Oriental despotism is not a state, or at any rate not the self-conscious form of state which is alone worthy of mind, the form which is organically developed and where there are rights and a full ethical life." Hegel was critical of Asian societies: China and India remained in the "childhood" stage of history; Hindus were characterized by cunning and deceit, cheating, stealing, robbing, and murdering; and Persians were weak slaves to sensuality.[38] Hegel contrasted the Eastern form of despotism with monarchy as it had developed in his own era. He commented that the old patriarchal principle of monarchy had now reached a new point because the monarch "was the absolute apex of an organically developed state . . . this was of the utmost importance for public freedom and for rationality in the constitution."[39]

THE CONCEPT OF ORIENTAL DESPOTISM

Perceptions of Oriental despotism, if sometimes based on stereotypes or misunderstandings, did not stem from ignorance about Oriental societies or from racial attitudes inherited from Aristotle. The "Orient" was a reality, not a fiction devised by the West. Nor was the concept of Oriental despotism simply a metaphor, a warning about the possibility of absolute government in European systems. Early writers on despotism did not focus entirely on Asian or Islamic countries: they also made references to African, Russian, and even pre-Columbian American systems. They did concentrate on Asia, recognizing that Eastern countries had political structures, religions, and social behaviors, especially treatment of women, markedly different from those in the West. As discussed earlier, the distinction was clearly made by Machiavelli between Western systems, imperfect though they might be, in which people were reasonably free, and those in Eastern systems in which people lived in a slavish condition or in a barbarous country.

The postmodern view, as discussed in the introduction, is the premise that the concept of Oriental despotism has been used less for understanding and analyzing the realities of Eastern societies and politics objectively than for buttressing arguments for colonial or imperialist control by the West over those societies, or for internal Western political purposes. Certainly some of the writing on the Orient stemmed from agents or officials of Western governments and commercial companies, but most of the valuable writing came from political theorists, engaged in comparative analysis, and from travelers who had no official positions: "Travelers never did lie, though fools at home condemn them," Shakespeare wrote. One cannot discount the sympathetic portrayals of some aspects of Eastern societies not only by writers discussed in the preceding text but also by others, including those Jesuits who spoke of India and China in positive terms, such as Father Catrou about the Mughal emperors, and wrote of Confucianism as a secular morality, or Athanasius Kircher in the seventeenth century, who provided a laudatory picture of Chinese civilization.[40]

Even if some travelers to the Orient had mixed motives in writing their narratives they did provide empirical information and acute direct observations, which were valid and also helpful for political scientists developing comparative concepts of political structures.[41] This was noticeable in French writings of the late seventeenth and eighteenth centuries in which authors, because of concern about the arbitrary rule of Louis XIV and internal religious dissent, used the despotic East, as stated in preceding text, to warn against excessive power in their own country and to call for restraints and limits on European monarchical power.[42] Admitting inaccurate observations to some degree, and a number of self-serving motivations for negative presentations of the Orient, nevertheless Oriental despotism was not a fantasy but rather a style of politics and society embodying certain characteristics, such as arbitrary autocracy, opulence, and lack of political and economic development.

ARBITRARY

A cardinal feature of Eastern systems for almost all commentators was the arbitrary, autocratic behavior of rulers. Diplomats and merchants alike, critical of the political and domestic autocracy and tyranny in the Ottoman Empire, also drew attention to the discrepancy between the words and promises made by Ottoman rulers and their actions or, usually, nonactions. The views of Edward Gibbon, Charles Eliot, and William Hunter may be taken as illustrative of many others. Gibbon, writing of Persia but alluding to other Oriental societies, indicated the nature of their political systems with the "ruler's fatal word," the monarch's frown, the master who could take back what he had bestowed, the sultan who was the descendent of the Prophet and the vice-regent of heaven, the unlimited obedience of the subjects, the intolerance of other religions, and the theocratic values of Islam.

Eliot considered every sultan as an autocrat, but the reality depended on how much he chose to exert his powers.[43] The Turkish regime he described was a real autocracy, a state where everything was directed by the pleasure of the ruler. No distinction existed between church and state in Islam, and the sultan, also as caliph, was pope as well as emperor. Hunter traveled in the Ottoman Empire and saw the sultan regarded as omnipotent.[44] The system disclaimed the law of nature, equity, and reason and exhibited an augmentation of injustice, tyranny, and vice. It trampled on the most sacred rights and privileges of humanity and perpetuated horrors of cruelty and desolation.

OPULENCE

All the travelers and most observers of the Orient, particularly on Turkey and Persia, waxed over the opulence displayed in those countries. Ralph Fitch at the court of the Great Mughal in the 1580s wrote of the "great market of diamonds, rubies, sapphires, and many other soft stones." Bernier informed Colbert in Paris of the spectacle of the Mughal entourage with its two to three thousand fine horses, always ready in case of emergency, eight or nine hundred elephants, and the enormous expenses of the seraglio. William Hawkins (1585–1613), the first envoy of the East India Company to the Mughal court in 1609, remarked, in a whole chapter devoted to the subject, that the emperor was exceedingly rich in diamonds and all other precious stones including pearls, emeralds, and rubies, and clothes and bestiary. Sir Thomas Roe, English ambassador in 1616, saw the wealth of the Mughal emperor of his day as "far above the Turk." In jewels he was the treasury of the world, and yet all this greatness was "like a play, that serves more for delight and to entertain the vulgar than for any use."[45] Roe's chaplain, Edward Terry, similarly saw the emperor as possessing "unknown treasure, with silver . . . like stones in the streets."

SENSUALITY

Connected with and part of the opulent display was the extravagant sensuality of Ottoman society, of which the seraglio and the harem are the most well-known features. Bodin was one of the few who did not subscribe to this characterization of Turkish society. The prevalence of this view, however, is evident in European literature. Shakespeare, for instance, in many of his plays, often alluded to the sensuality of the Orient: one particular example is in *King Lear* when Edgar, among other boasts, claimed he had "in woman, out-paramoured the Turk." The Koran appeared to confirm sensuality, with the acceptance of polygamy, and the attitude to women as servants rather than as companions. The emphasis of so many Western writers on the sensuality in

Islamic societies may have been a consequence of the Christian prohibition of polygamy and concubinage.

LACK OF DEVELOPMENT

A frequent theme in Western commentaries on Eastern societies, if not articulated as vigorously as those of opulence and sensuality, was the lack of political and economic development and progress for which Oriental despotism and Islamic societies were held responsible. This lack of development was contrasted sharply with the West, in which the scientific method and rationality were significant. The early travelers to the Orient were conscious of this backwardness. Bernier believed that most Asian peoples were infatuated with astrology, whereas in Europe, where science flourished, professors in astrology were considered little better than cheats or jugglers.[46] Chardin held that, unlike the rational inquiry in Europe, the knowledge of Asians was so restricted that it consisted only in learning and repeating what was contained in the books of the ancients.[47] Among the more prominent of later thinkers who made similar arguments about development were Montesquieu, Anne Robert Jacques Turgot, William Robertson, William Jones, Herder, Hegel, James Mill, Karl Marx, and Richard Jones. The last can be used as an illustration of this view.

Richard Jones (1790–1855), British economist and teacher at Haileybury College, was interested in the different forms that ownership and cultivation of land and conditions of production and distribution in the world assumed at different places and times in the world. Influenced by Bernier's view that Oriental despotism resulted from the ruler's ownership of land and revenue, Jones argued that the Turkish economic and political system rested on the assumption that the ruler was the legitimate proprietor of conquered land and was the sole source not merely of protection but also of subsistence. Throughout Asia the sovereigns had always had exclusive title to the soil of their dominions and kept it unimpaired. People were dependent on the sovereign for their livelihood, because of the ruler's sole ownership of the land that was the real foundation of "the unbroken despotism of the Eastern world." Jones held that taxation like the excessive *ryot* rents paid by peasants in Asia led to stagnation.[48] Asian despotism was destructive of the industry and wealth of its subjects and of all the arts of peace. Moreover, Jones argued that the form of government in Asian empires was pure unlimited despotism.[49] The nature of those despotisms, however, differed depending on the climate, soil, and even government of countries. He regarded Persia as perhaps the greediest and the most wantonly unprincipled of all the despotic governments of the Orient.[50] He adopted Montesquieu's view that Eastern systems lacked intermediary bodies between the sovereign and producers. Nevertheless, Jones did add a caveat. Though no really independent bodies had political influence in the despotism systems, the governments, in their own interests, limited their actions and had "considerable forbearance."

CONCLUSION

Political thought at its best stems from analysis of real behavior present in societies and of problems faced by those societies. Acknowledging that political and social terms may lack the rigor and precision of mathematical modeling, analysts must still use models or typologies in order to understand fully the nature of political structures. Reading the accounts of Oriental societies by scholars, political thinkers, diplomats, and travelers, it is reasonable to conclude that the concept of Oriental despotism is not an arbitrary exegesis, the result of prejudiced observation, having little relation to Eastern systems, but rather reflects perceptions of real processes and behavior in those systems.

In this chapter a general history of the development of the concept of Oriental despotism has been laid out. In the following chapters the perceptions of the Orient of several key thinkers on political and social issues are discussed in detail. They were not disengaged theorists but commentators using arguments based on the political reality they observed or studied in their own original fashion. Collectively, they illustrate a syndrome of the characteristics of a regime that can validly be termed *Oriental despotism*. The axiomatic starting point is Montesquieu, not only because of the brilliance of *L'Esprit des Lois* but also for the insight implicit in it that Western Europe was not only geographically but also politically and culturally different from the Orient, and that the political liberty and restraints on the exercise of power in the West starkly contrasted with the restrictions on political and personal liberty in the Orient.

4

The Oriental Despotic Universe of Montesquieu

A truth almost universally acknowledged, reiterated in Chapter 3, is that Aristotle's *Politics* has profoundly influenced all political thinkers engaged in comparative analysis. Using multifarious political and social empirical data and differentiating the systems and societies he examined, Aristotle postulated a number of concepts, including those of tyranny and despotism. He was the first major thinker to compare his West, the land of the Greeks, with the East, that of the Persians and non-Hellenes. Building on Aristotle's theories, Western European writers increasingly went beyond treating the concepts of tyranny and despotism as abstractions, and attempted to relate those concepts more specifically to the real political structures, rules, and social and cultural behavior in Western and non-Western, essentially Oriental regimes.

Gradually, a concept, if unsystematic, of Oriental despotism, usually in Islamic societies, emerged to depict a specific type of political system and a set of relationships between the ruling power and the ruled that was distinguishable from concepts of tyranny or autocracy, forms of government long familiar in Europe.[1] Niccolo Machiavelli contrasted the Ottoman state with West European monarchies, Jean Bodin differentiated Western monarchies from Eastern despotism, Francis Bacon wrote of the different kind of aristocracies in Western and Eastern systems, Algernon Sidney discussed the idea of *virtu* in Eastern systems, and James Harrington analyzed and compared, in general, the economic foundations of political systems. Much of this analysis derived from empirical observation of the role of three great autocrats in Eastern countries – the Ottoman sultan, the Persian Shah, and the Mughal of India, all Muslim potentates, by early travelers and scholar-diplomats. Among the more influential, and most frequently quoted, of these observers up to the mid-eighteenth century were the travelers, Ogier Ghiselin de Busbecq, Jean-Baptiste Tavernier, François Bernier, Paul Rycaut, John Chardin, and Constantin Volney, discussed in Chapter 3.

This chapter looks at the work of Montesquieu, Charles de Secondat, Baron de la Brède et de Montesquieu, the first writer to formulate in detail the concept of Oriental despotism as a particular form of government structure. His work influenced all subsequent discussion of the subject, including those by Karl Marx and Max Weber. Born in the family castle in 1689, Montesquieu studied law in Bordeaux and practiced in Paris before inheriting land, income, and the office of the *président à mortier* – a chief officer of a district *parlement* or court of justice whose chief function was to record edicts of the King – in the *parlement* of Guyenne in 1716. Personal experience of this kind no doubt influenced his later political reflections about power when he generalized that monarchies "are corrupted when the prince insensibly deprives societies or cities of their privileges" and were destroyed when the prince "deprives some of his subjects of their hereditary employments to bestow them arbitrarily upon others."[2]

Montesquieu helped to found and delivered a number of philosophical papers to the Academy of Sciences in Bordeaux. In 1721 he published, anonymously in Amsterdam, his first significant work, *Lettres Persanes (Persian Letters)*, "a sort of novel" as he called it, in which two Persian travelers to Europe correspond with each other and with friends, with wives in the seraglio, and with the eunuchs who guard them.[3] Montesquieu, like so many other European travelers did not seem to appreciate that the Italian "seraglio" and the French "serial" versions of the Perso-Turkish "saray," which simply meant royal palace, mistakenly limited the meaning of the word to the gynaeceum of the palace, a purely European definition, which perhaps showed what really interested some people in the West. A rare exception was the Venetian, Ottaviano Bon, whose early seventeenth-century book, *A Description of the Grand Signior's Seraglio*, showed a greater understanding of the saray.[4] Montesquieu occupies a prominent place in the list of those Western European writers and painters who engaged in a kind of genteel pornography in their depiction of the "unbridled passions" of the seraglio in the Orient.

Montesquieu was not the first to use the device of the outside observer to comment on the political and social affairs of a society, especially Oriental countries. The most prominent of these other early European writers was the Genovese, Giovanni Paolo Marana, whose *Letters Writ by a Turkish Spy* was published in Italian in 1684, and then in French and English. These letters, supposed to have been translated from Arabic and written by a man named Mahmoud who had been a secret agent of the Ottoman sultan in Paris, have usually been seen as the direct inspiration for the *Lettres Persanes*.[5] At the outset it is fair to acknowledge that Montesquieu's historical criticism and his understanding of the Middle East is not completely accurate. Montesquieu's use of *Asia* and *the South* must not be taken too literally because he situated the Ottoman Empire in Asia at a period when its capital and central provinces were in mainland Europe. There are other factual errors as well, especially about the powers of the sultan of the empire and other rulers, and the features of their governments.

Although not directly imitative of Montaigne or La Bruyère, *Persian Letters* is written in a French literary style associated with those two great authors, essentially political reflections and aphorisms, ironic comments, and rococo disorderliness and decorativeness in its juxtaposition of events in France and in Persia.[6] What is the "novel" about? Montesquieu spoke of "the invisible chain" of the letters, but the search for the link has proved as elusive as that for the Holy Grail.[7] Parts of the story, reflections and comments, often based on specific events, are witty, sometimes flippant. It contains commentaries on social behavior in France and pointed criticisms of what Montesquieu thought was the excessive monarchical power of Louis XIV and the privileges of the French Church. These observations have led many commentators to see the *Letters* and other of Montesquieu's works as primarily concerned with necessary correctives and constitutional controls over French absolutism lest it become arbitrary.[8] Starobinski, for example, commenting on eighteenth-century literature in which sensuality appears in the guise of exotic ornamentation and background, argues that exoticism was used to disguise social satire and allow denunciations of Paris "under a thin veil of fiction that situated them in Laputa, or exposed them to the wonderment of a Persian."[9] However valid this point of view, it cannot ignore the fact that the most interesting and original aspect of *Persian Letters* is the mildly titillating and erotic story of the nature and growing disorder of the seraglio and the relations of its ruler, Uzbek, to his women and eunuchs, thus providing a striking small-scale portrait of the essence of despotic government. Perhaps anticipating modern feminism, the Persian visitor to France commented on the influential role of women there: "these women constitute a sort of republic. It is like a new state within the state."

The *Letters* rapidly established Montesquieu's reputation in the literary and cultural world of France in which he soon became a familiar and active figure. With his early election to the French Academy in 1728, he sold his inherited political office of *président*, thus ending any overt participation in public affairs. He went on a period of travel abroad, including two crucial years during 1730 and 1731 in England whose political institutions he admired. In 1734 he published *Considérations sur les causes de la grandeur des Romains et de leur decadence (Considerations on the Causes of the Greatness of the Romans and Their Decline)*, a brilliant work now unduly neglected, and in 1748 he published *L'Esprit des Lois*, usually translated in English as *The Spirit of the Laws*. Montesquieu died in 1755.

Montesquieu was not a prolific writer; his place in intellectual history rests on one very long, major work written during a twenty-year period, and two shorter, less well-known but important books. Interpretation and assessment of that output, especially of his major work, have varied widely. Some of the ambivalence toward his writings stems from the fact that *The Spirit of the Laws* is less a systematic political treatise than an accumulation of brilliant and original thoughts, sometimes haphazardly arranged and disparate in parts, which many readers have found intellectually indigestible.[10] Among the many topics on which Montesquieu reflects are Italian and English opera, the burning of Jews, black slavery, and the nature of citizens of Moscow.

If Montesquieu has earned a significant place in Western thought, that place is not readily located because he does not fit into a narrow, disciplinary slot. He is first a political theorist in the classical line that runs from the Greeks to the present day, though less concerned than many with direct and open advocacy of a particular argument. He also contributed to or lead the way in other fields of intellectual inquiry: political science, comparative politics in his identification and classification of whole societies and political systems; innovative approaches in cultural and political history, which drew praise from Gibbon; cultural anthropology, political culture, and socialization in his concern with the interrelationship of laws, customs, manners, and forms of government; political behavior in his examination of the effect of external and internal factors on patterns of behavior; and political pluralism in his recognition of the variety of laws and societies and the ends they sought.[11]

It is also not easy to assess Montesquieu's methodological approach with assurance. Was he primarily an objective social scientist collecting empirical data and then framing general principles or an advocate of an *a priori* rational approach working deductively?[12] Was he a determinist in his analysis of the effect of "the nature of things" (such as climate, customs, religion, principles on laws and politics), or did he believe that human laws might overcome these things and contribute to customs and morals? He was both a relativist and an eighteenth-century humanist and moralist.[13] Montesquieu warned that "to apply the idea of the present time to distant ages is the most fruitful source of error." His leading figure in *Lettres Persanes*, Usbek, whose views can probably often be taken to be those of the author, recognizes that "things in themselves are neither pure nor impure . . . objects do not affect all men in the same way, since what produces a pleasant sensation in some men produces a feeling of disgust in others." In his own voice, Montesquieu argued that laws differ in societies, because of the various tempers of the mind and the passions of people in different climates, and laws are formulated in relation to the variety of those passions and tempers.

Yet at the same time, Montesquieu qualified this relativistic position. He spoke from time to time of natural laws: peace, self-preservation, sex, sociability, "the first principles of justice," and reason. Moreover, Montesquieu was an enlightened, liberal aristocrat; he was not averse to moral denunciation of iniquities such as the Inquisition.[14] In a fashion similar to that of Tocqueville a century later there was no relativism in his views about slavery. Montesquieu explained in his chapter on the subject, "I do not know whether this article be dictated by my understanding or by my heart." The state of slavery is "in its own nature bad. It is neither useful to the master nor to the slave."[15] Equally passionate was his judgment on despotism as "monstrous governments" that cannot be mentioned without horror.[16]

Montesquieu's method of inquiry is undogmatic, devoid of transcendental disposition or teleological direction.[17] He wrote that he was "obliged to wander to the right and to the left, that I may investigate and discover the 'truth.' " But that "truth" is not devoid of ambiguity on matters such as causation of events, interrelationship between or primacy of the factors affecting behavior, the interaction of physical and moral causes, or even the definition of "law." Montesquieu's reasoning is sometimes circular. At one moment, climate is the first, the most powerful factor in formation of a society. At another, climate may have produced "a great part of the laws, manners, and customs of this nation (Britain); but I maintain that its manners and customs have a close connection with its laws."

One might well conclude that Montesquieu derived his laws of politics and society from historical inquiry, and that the accumulation of observations about France, Britain, and the Orient led to generalizations about political relationships, conclusions that have more of a rococo than a neoclassical character, more ornate than linear.[18] Yet he did write in his preface that "I have laid down the first principles, and have found that the particular cases follow naturally from them; that the histories of all nations are only consequences of them." He stressed a number of times that the world is not a theater of chance events. In a frequently quoted passage in *Considerations* (Chapter 18), he wrote that "It is not chance that rules the world. ... There are general causes, moral and physical, which act in every monarchy, elevating it, maintaining it, or hurling it to the ground. All accidents are controlled by these causes." The infinite diversity of laws and manners are not solely conducted through caprice or fancy. Events incessantly arise from the nature of things; "it was not the affair of Pultowa that ruined Charles XII (defeat of Charles XII of Sweden by Peter the Great in 1709). Had he not been destroyed at that place, he would have been in another."

Thus, Montesquieu was a relativist and a political realist. He recognized that political systems and institutions stemmed from and were appropriate to a variety of factors; the complexity and diversity of human affairs did not lend themselves to a one-dimensional approach. Montesquieu was, as Harold Laski called him, the supreme realist of the age in his revolt from the abstract; he approved Solon's reply about the laws he had given to the Athenians, "I have given them the best they were able to bear."[19]

Unlike other seventeenth- and eighteenth-century political theorists, Montesquieu was little concerned with the problem of the origin of society, "which seems to me absurd," but rather with the concrete different types of political systems and the laws found in different societies.[20] Montesquieu challenged his readers to search for "the design" of *L'Esprit des Lois* and spoke of the "chain which connects" a great many truths with others.[21] A useful starting point in the chain, following the title of his major book, is the "general spirit" of laws and nations, formed out of various factors or causes: "climate, religion, laws, maxims of government, precedents, morals, and customs." Each of these causes has a different impact in time and space thus explaining the diversity of laws and political systems. Laws, for example, are strongly related to the different manner in which nations procure their subsistence. A nation engaged in trade and navigation requires more laws than those who lived by agriculture; even fewer laws were needed for those who lived by flocks or herds or by hunting.

But even more, laws were related to the "nature" and "principle" of governments.[22] The nature of government is that by "which it is constituted," or the basic structure of its institutions and power relationships. The principle refers to the motive force in the character of subjects, the basic attitudes or "the human passions which set a government in motion" and make it act. Any government ought to be directed by a principle, or it is imperfect. Corruption of every government generally begins with that of its principle. Once the principle is corrupted, the very best laws become bad; when the principle is sound, even bad laws have the same effect as good ones. Some legislators have "confounded the principles which govern mankind."

Montesquieu's formulas of principles of government have to be seen in three ways; as "ideal" types, as ways of explaining political and historical phenomena, and as attempts to make order of the diversity of empirical reality.[23] Perhaps his major contribution to political theory was to formulate a typology of whole governmental systems.[24] At the same time, he anticipated criticism that regimes did not embody all the characteristics of his "ideal" types in a consistent way. In an aphorism, Usbek says of European monarchies that "it would have been difficult for them to have existed for long in a pure form." In his *Considerations*, Montesquieu writes that "it is an error to believe that any human authority exists in the world which is despotic in all respects. There never has been one, and never will be, for the most immense power is always confined in some ways." He admits the possibility of variation; "though despotic governments are of their own natures everywhere the same, yet from circumstances (of varied kinds) . . . it is possible they may admit of a considerable difference."

Even disregarding Montesquieu's own qualifications of his starting premise, a broad typology of the kind he proposed is obviously open to criticism. Voltaire quickly recognized that Montesquieu's generalizations sometimes rested on misquotations and on faulty or selective information.[25] Anquetil-Duperron, the great Orientalist scholar discussed in Chapter 3, devoted most of his 1778 book *Législation Orientale* to Montesquieu's factual inaccuracies and argued that Montesquieu's analysis lacked clarity in organization, was sometimes imprecise, and was occasionally contradictory.[26]

Yet Montesquieu did try to avoid "the bold flights" or "sallies of imagination" to be found in contemporary writings of his time.[27] Intellectual history is a flowing river fed by many streams. Internal evidence such as the contents of his library, and the authors he quotes in his own writings, reveal Montesquieu's erudition and wide reading, and his impressive knowledge of a host of subjects not pertinent to this book and of the political theorists who may have influenced him.[28] Montesquieu did not engage in intellectual dialogue with past political philosophers, except at rare points and mostly with Thomas Hobbes and Pierre Bayle. However, the typologies he used to explain differences of political systems reflect the intellectual political analysis of his predecessors, starting with Aristotle whose views of forms of government he challenged. At the same time they also rest on the use of empirical information, contemporary political activity, political history, and travel books.[29] His theory of three main types of government may be "metaphysical and Aristotelian" as Isaiah Berlin suggests,[30] but it also reflects Montesquieu's understanding of historical and contemporary systems, including ancient city republics, seventeenth- and eighteenth-century Western European monarchies, and Middle Eastern and Asian empires.

It is well to start with Montesquieu's distinction between three ideal "natures" or "species" of governmental form: republic, monarchy, and despotism. In a republic, the body of the people or a part of it has supreme power. In monarchy a single person governs but does so by fixed and established laws. In despotic government a single person directs everything by his own will or caprice. This tripartite distinction is immediately qualified by a division of the republican type of government into two categories: a democracy where the body of the people has supreme power and an aristocracy where the supreme power is in the hands of a part of the people.[31] Montesquieu warns that corruption of one type of government may change it into something approximating another type. For example, if the principle of aristocracy is corrupted because the nobles do not observe the laws, the system becomes "a despotic state swayed by a great many despotic princes."

Most significant in Montesquieu's typology is his distinction between moderate governments, which include both republics and monarchies, and despotic governments. It is this fundamental distinction that allows Montesquieu to make generalizations about politics throughout *L'Esprit des Lois* and to envisage despotism as a distinctive and qualitatively different kind of political type in his taxonomy of systems. One can appreciate this classification as both an abstract system and as relevant to certain historical moments. His concept of despotism is useful to comprehend Islamic fundamentalism much as one would use the twentieth-century concept of totalitarianism, another distinctive type, to understand the regimes of the Soviet Union, Nazi Germany, and Fascist Italy.

With his love of political liberty and belief in a spirit of moderation in politics Montesquieu was deeply concerned with and feared the grievous dangers of political systems that were based on discretionary or arbitrary use of power and were ruled by individuals without constraints and in which power was not limited by fundamental law or checked by powerful social groups, such as nobility, that could act as a bulwark against actual or potential unbridled authority. He feared his own France might be moving in that direction. Accordingly, his whole work has to be seen not simply as an analytical construct, but also as advocacy, sometimes polemical, for institutional and social restraints on the exercise of power. This is especially so in his eleventh book of *Esprit des Lois* with its argument for a separation of powers and legal checks and balances in the political system. Parenthetically, it is worth remembering that the Founding Fathers of the United States frequently referred to that eleventh book in their deliberations about a constitution.

Corresponding to each of Montesquieu's three types of government were "principles" or human passions that set the structure of government in motion.[32] For republics, the principle was virtue or, more specifically, political virtue; for a democracy the principle was equality, and for aristocracy it was moderation ("a spirit of moderation"). In monarchies, the principle was honor; in despotic government it was fear. These principles or spirits provide the key to Montesquieu's analysis of the differences between the three political systems, to his reflections on education, laws that uphold the systems, civil and criminal law, amount of luxury, condition of women, corruption, safety, and liberty.

THE NATURE AND PRINCIPLE OF DESPOTIC GOVERNMENT

Montesquieu is the first theorist to distinguish in a full way a despotic type of government that is different from monarchy, even absolute monarchy, systems that had some form of constitution, some law of succession to the throne, and some intermediary bodies), and to describe despotism as a system natural to the Orient.[33] Many earlier writers differentiated between systems based on consent and law, and those that were arbitrary or absolute. Going back to the Greeks, Xenophon distinguished between a regal government, in which submission to the ruler was voluntary and authority conformed to law, and a tyranny in which people were compelled to obey.[34] A generation before Montesquieu, Giovanni Vicenzo Gravina compared a pure empire ruled by an absolute prince and a mixed empire with limited rule by a magistrate.[35] Bodin, also proposed a tripartite model, using his idiosyncratic terminology: a royal government where the prince obeys the laws of God and the subjects obey the prince; a despotic government stemming from the right of conquest in a just war; and a tyranny in which the laws of nature are defied, subjects are oppressed, and property regarded as belonging to the tyrant.[36]

Other writers anticipated Montesquieu's concept of despotic government, though not as definitively. Immediate predecessors of Montesquieu, who may have influenced him, include Paolo Doria who in 1710 divided governmental forms into republics, monarchies, and despotisms, and attributed to each a particular principle; and Thomas Gordon who discussed the nature of despotism and the character of the despot.[37] Gordon described the despot as a man without experience, a savage bursting with brutal passions and following stupid fantasies. He associated these despots with Asia, and particularly with Turkey and Persia. This anticipates Montesquieu's reference to "the princes of the Orient," who, once they had chosen a subordinate, a vizier, abandoned "themselves in their seraglio to the most brutal passions, pursuing . . . ever capricious extravagance." In the same way, one can trace other intellectual influences on some of Montesquieu's other ideas: John Arbuthnot on climate, John Mandeville and William Warburton on religion, and Henry St. John Bolingbroke, who also influenced Thomas Jefferson, on "the general spirit."[38]

In addition to his drawing on earlier political theorists in his formulation of the nature of Oriental despotic government, Montesquieu relied even more on the works of travelers and on the prevalent imaginative literature about the East. Between 1660 and 1700, more than forty works on travels in the Orient appeared, as well as others on the Far East by the Jesuit fathers, Dr. Kaempfer on Japan, and Father Du Halde on China.[39] These latter Jesuit missionaries wrote positively about the area; Du Halde in his work on the Chinese Empire wrote there was "no monarchy more absolute than that of China . . . but no people in the world have better laws of government." Increasingly in the seventeenth century, a literature appeared partly of imaginary voyages of different kinds, and partly of writings on little-known countries such as those by Pierre Bergeron in 1648 on Madagascar, "land of the noble savage," and Denis Vairasse d'Alais in 1677 on Australia.

Yet if Montesquieu drew on the work of other theorists, on travel and imaginative works, he was wholly original in his comprehensive presentation of the distinctive political system of despotic government.[40] The distinction between despotic and other, more moderate, types of government was crucial for him from a number of points of view. Under despotism, "man is a creature that blindly submits to the absolute will of the sovereign." In monarchical, moderate states power was limited by restrictions. A monarch may have as much power as a despot but in a moderate, monarchical system the prince "receives instruction," and he chooses ministers who are more competent than in despotic systems.[41]

Montesquieu argues that nondespotic systems have varying complex laws controlling the distribution of property, inheritance, the conduct of commerce, and civil and criminal crimes. Despotic governments are simpler. Unlike moderate systems where it is "necessary to combine the several powers" and to counterpoise them against each other, a despotic government has no need of laws to balance various interests because there is only one interest, that of the ruler. Thus despotic government "offers itself, as it were, at first sight; it is uniform throughout; and as passions only are requisite to establish it, this is what every capacity may reach."[42] Punishments are more extreme in a despotic government, where the driving basic force is fear (though Montesquieu sometimes speaks of "terror"), than in a monarchies or republics whose spring, or source, is honor or virtue.[43] This principle of fear means despotic governments "neither grant not receive" pardons. By comparison, in monarchies clemency is characteristic and in republics it is not necessary.

The regimes also differ in degree of corruption. In all regimes, the basic principle can be corrupted, thus corrupting the nature of government, but "the principle of despotic government is subject to a continual corruption, because it is even in its nature corrupt" and has "intrinsic imperfections." The central distinction between despotic and moderate regimes lies in the nature of the ruling process. In republics, citizens participate in the governing process. Monarchies differ; in some, a sovereign may exert the full extent of his power, in others, his power may be restrained within narrower limits. Though occasionally despotic government may appear to be only a corruption of monarchy, it is clearly distinguishable, marked by absolute power without laws.

Montesquieu's advocacy of political moderation, especially in contemporary France, was the counterpart of his detestation of despotic government. He confessed when talking of liberty that "even the highest refinement of reason is not always desirable, and that mankind generally finds their account better in mediums than in extremes." Even liberty can go too far. He preferred the liberty found in London, "the liberty of gentlemen" to the "license" in Venice or "the liberty of the rabble" in Holland. He even suggested that *L'Esprit des Lois* was written to prove that the spirit of a legislator ought to be one of moderation; political like moral good always lies between two extremes. Political liberty is found only in moderate governments, and sometimes not even there if power is abused. Anticipating Lord Acton's famous, if much misquoted dictum, Montesquieu states that "every man invested with power is apt to abuse it, and to carry his authority as far as it will go." It is essential that "power should be a check to power." Because political liberty is "a tranquility of mind arising from the opinion each person has of his safety," it is requisite that government be so constituted that "one man need not be afraid of another."

Montesquieu is troubled by any extreme forms of social and political behavior. To survive, democracy must avoid two excesses: the spirit of inequality, which leads to aristocracy or monarchy, and the spirit of extreme equality, which leads to despotic power. Moderate systems have a system of law that is prudent and perfectly well-known, so "even the pettiest magistrates are capable of following it." But law is the momentary will of the prince in a despotic government, and those who will for him, as subordinates, follow his "sudden manner of willing." Furthermore, because a despotic government has no moderating influence and the people are "without tribunes," the population, carried away by passions, may revolt, thus leading to chaos and violence. A moderate government may, without danger, "relax its springs" because it supports itself by the law and by its own internal strength, but the despotic prince cannot dare do so.

In the following pages Montesquieu's theory of Oriental despotism is discussed sequentially starting with his explanation of the causes for its existence. As much as possible the postulates are presented in Montesquieu's own words because not only his concepts but also his language became the basis for subsequent writing on the subject. As mentioned earlier his concept of despotic or Oriental government, and of the factors that account for it, are not presented in one continuous text. They emerge from the scattered references to it in his writings as he compares and contrasts despotism with moderate regimes.[44] Montesquieu may be imprecise and unclear from time to time, and his methodology may lack rigor and consistency. Nevertheless, he painted a revealing portrait of the particular type of political system called *Oriental despotism.*

CLIMATE

Since Aristotle, writers have discussed, although sketchily, the effect of climate on politics and social affairs. A long list would include many important Western European authors, such as Machiavelli, Bodin, Adam Ferguson, Chardin, and also several medieval Muslim authors, notably Ibn Khaldun. Some no doubt influenced the generalizations Montesquieu made about the nature and consequence of three different climates – hot, temperate, and cold – in the world. His originality lay in going much further than his predecessors in integrating views on climate with those on religion, manners, customs, laws, and political systems.

Montesquieu considered that patterns of life in hot climates coincided with those found in despotic systems.[45] From his discussion of the climatic factor in hot countries, he drew broad conclusions on Oriental society and politics, focusing on sexual passion and the seraglio, polygamy, sexual inequality, and the Islamic religion, all found in despotic systems. Statements on these issues are present both in the *Persian Letters* and the *Pensées*, in aphoristic form, and in *The Spirit of the Laws* in more scholarly argument. He applies his conclusions to the individual seraglio, as a system of power, and to despotic systems as a whole.

His general starting point was that the temper of the mind and the passions of the heart diverge sharply in different climates and that the laws of countries in different climates are related to the variety of those passions and tempers. In cold and temperate climates, the air has physiological effects that make people more vigorous, sincere, courageous, franker, active, and less suspicious, with few vices and little sensibility for pleasure. In Northern climates peoples have a spirit that leads to a sense of liberty and an independence lacking in the South. In contrast, hot climates enervate the body, make people so slothful and dispirited that nothing but the fear of chastisement can oblige them to perform any laborious duty. The hot climate produces an indolence of mind, naturally connected with that of the body, timidity, and "an imagination so lively that every object makes the strongest impression on them." Great heat also exhausts the body; rest is delicious and motion painful. Montesquieu believed that Indians (he was speaking of Mughal Indians) consider entire inaction as the most perfect of all states, and the object of their desires. In the Orient, because of the hot climate, laws, manners, and customs remain the same as a thousand years ago.

Montesquieu locates despotism in the Orient, or Asia or the South as he calls it from time to time. He argues that the wants of people in the South differ from those in the North. The first have every convenience of life and few wants; they are lazy, subject to slavery, in a state of violence. Despotic government is appropriate for them.[46] By contrast, Northern nations have many wants, few conveniences, and people who are active, industrious, and free; despotism is therefore unnecessary. Despotism thrives in Asia because it has no temperate zone, in comparison with Europe where the temperate zone is quite extensive. In a curious geopolitical explanation, Montesquieu asserts that in Asia the strong nations are "opposed to the weak; the warlike, brave and active people touch immediately on those who are indolent, effeminate, and timorous." Asia is therefore weak and enslaved; referring to what he calls "Upper Asia," Montesquieu says it has been subdued thirteen times in history. In Europe, there have been only four great changes because strong nations are opposed to other strong ones. The consequence is a balance of power and liberty in Europe, and slavery and despotic government in Asia.

Montesquieu gives various reasons why the Islamic religion is appropriate for hot climates. People in the warm countries of the Orient are less inclined to action than to speculation; Islamic ritual lends itself to passivity. In Asia the number of dervishes or monks seems to increase with the warmth of the climate. The law of Muhammad, which prohibits the drinking of wine, is fitted to the climate of Arabia, where people perspire and need water. The domestic order required by polygamy renders necessary the separation of wives from men and their close confinement.

People, Montesquieu says, have "exquisite sensibility in hot climates, exhibiting strong passion and sexuality. Love there is liked for its own sake; it is the only cause of happiness, it is life itself." People in these countries fancy themselves entirely removed from the constraints of morality; their strong passions produce all manner of crimes. Usbek, the master in *Persian Letters*, is troubled by secret jealousy and fear of infidelity of his wives.[47] Two men are killed for merely looking at the wives of the master.

WOMEN

Opinions differ on whether Montesquieu should be regarded as an eighteenth-century feminist or as a misogynist. What is clear is that he connects Oriental despotic power with the servitude of women and the more open monarchial system with freedom for women.[48] Women are at the disposal of the Oriental master and subservient to his pleasure. They are objects of luxury, and generally constitute part of the master's property. Women are confined, spied on, subjected to terror and to propaganda; "how fortunate" writes Usbek to his favorite wife, "you are to be in the sweet land of Persia."[49]

The parallel of the seraglio to the despotic state is specifically drawn in some of the *Persian Letters*.[50] In the ninth letter the First Eunuch says that "the seraglio for me is like a little empire, and my desire for power, the only emotion which remains to me, is to some extent satisfied." The seraglio is the despotic society writ small in a number of ways: it is based on fear, it subjects the inhabitants to the will of the ruler, it is a simple institution, it is isolated, it is a place of indolence, it is an unhappy place, it is a prison in which inmates have as their prime function keeping their master satisfied.[51]

The seraglio is based on subordination and duty. The First Eunuch tells his master: "You temper fear with hope, and are more completely dominant when you make love than when you threaten." He had already written, "I never forget that I was born to command over (women) and it is as if I became a man again on the occasions when I now give them orders." The slavery of women conforms to the spirit of despotic government, which manages all subjects through discipline. In Asia, Montesquieu argues, domestic despotic slavery and despotic government walk hand in hand. Individual men follow the spirit of the government and treat women as slaves in their own families.

In hot countries of the South, there is a natural inequality between the two sexes, and polygamy is "extremely natural." Passions are stronger and appear earlier than in colder climates. In hot countries, women marry at eight, nine, or ten; often childhood and marriage go together. Monogamy is appropriate for the climate of Europe but not to that of Asia because women in hot areas lose their beauty quickly. Continuing even further, Montesquieu believes that Islam, because it permitted polygamy, was easily established in Asia; by contrast Islam found more difficulty in being accepted in Europe, which was by nature monogamous. Moreover, in Islamic states not only the life and goods of female slaves but also what Montesquieu calls their virtue or honor is at their master's disposal.

SLAVERY

One consequence of hot climates is that slavery is more tolerated in despotic regimes than in other countries. Montesquieu does not believe that Aristotle proved there were "natural slaves," though he does admit that in some countries slavery is "founded on natural reason" and that natural slavery is "to be limited to some particular parts of the world." Among those parts is certainly

Asia where "there reigns a servile spirit which they have never been able to shake off, and it is impossible to find in all the histories of that country a single passage which discovers a freedom of spirit."[52] Coming from a man who knew none of the languages of the "Orient" or of "Asia," and little of the real history of the region, Montesquieu's statement is somewhat rash.

In general, Montesquieu declared that hot climates and the resulting effeminacy have led to slavery. By contrast, the courage of people in cold climates has enabled them to preserve their liberties. Despotic countries are already in a state of political servitude, and therefore "civil" slavery is more tolerable than in other governments because the condition of a slave is hardly more burdensome than that of a subject. Despotic power has always considered subjects as slaves: the political servitude of the whole body takes away the sense of civil slavery.

SIZE OF THE STATE

Political systems have a territorial imperative, so size and location are factors in determining the form of rule. Montesquieu argues the spirit of a state will alter proportionally as it contracts or extends its territory. He correlates the three types of government with size in a simple way. A republic must have a small territory to survive. In an extensive republic, the public good is sacrificed to a thousand private views; in small states the interest of the public is more obvious. A monarchy must be of moderate size. If small, it will become a republic; if too large, the nobility will become too rich and independent. The latter situation would lead to despotism. In a picturesque phrase, he concluded that "The rivers hasten to mingle their waters with the sea; and monarchies lose themselves in despotic power." A despotic government can be large because a single individual determines all laws. He can act quickly because he needs no consent from others, and he can rule through fear.[53]

TERRAIN

Asia, where despotic regimes are located, does not have easily defensible mountainous areas and islands. Countries in Europe therefore are not as vulnerable as Asian countries, and so can have and maintain moderate governments. In Europe, natural physical division leads to the existence of many nations of moderate extent, and thus to rule based on law, and the presence of liberty. With the exception of a few places, Asia and Africa have always been crushed under despotism. In Asia, absolute power was in some measure "naturalized," and therefore one would expect it to be always found in the Orient.[54]

ISLAM AND DESPOTISM

Montesquieu made clear that he was "not a divine but a political writer" and did not deal in his work with "truths of a more sublime nature" or doctrinal issues from a theological point of view. His interest in religions is limited to their influence on laws and political systems. He equated Christianity with nondespotic politics. The mildness preached in the Gospels is incompatible with the rage and cruelty of despotic princes. He gives a rather curious example. He postulates that the Christian religion hindered despotic power from being established in Ethiopia, in spite of its extent and hot climate. Montesquieu maintained that internal and external political actions are more humane in Christian than in Islamic countries, and Christian princes are less cruel than Islamic princes, who incessantly condemn others to death or are killed themselves.

Montesquieu asserts that despotic government is the result of the "inundation" of Muslims.[55] Islam, which speaks only by the sword, still acts on men with the same destructive spirit with which it was founded. Through despotic rule, which deprives people of their will, Islam induces laziness. In a circular argument, Montesquieu writes that from the inactivity of the soul springs the Islamic doctrine of predestination, and from this doctrine springs the inactivity of the soul. The frequent daily praying, the doctrine of unalterable fate, and the habit of "speculation" lead to "indifference for all things," to apathy, political obedience, and economic backwardness. Usbek writes of Islamic beliefs, "there seems to be something unjustifiable about doing useful, durable work . . . we live in a state of general apathy, leaving everything to be done by Providence." In despotic countries, Montesquieu maintains, religion has more influence than anywhere else; it is fear added to fear. In Islamic countries, it is partly from religion that people derive the unquestioning veneration they have for the prince. One can compare the eunuchs in the seraglio – a place of order, silence, isolation, and submission, exerting domestic despotism on behalf of the master and adhering to the "stern laws of duty" – with Islamic mullahs.

In the Islamic world because the doctrine of a rigid fate directs all conduct, justice by the magistrate is passive and uncaring; "he thinks that everything comes from the hand of God, and that man has nothing more to do than to submit." In European countries says Montesquieu, justice is an active process ordinarily regulated by rules of prudence; good or bad outcomes are the result of wisdom. In the Orient "you see men incessantly led by blind fate and rigid destiny."[56] Montesquieu is continually uncomplimentary and often caustic about Islam. He saw it as a religion characterized by ritualism and taboos, predestination, laziness of the soul, fatalism, apathy, lack of concern for the future, intolerance, economic underdevelopment, polygamy, and demographic depopulation. He constantly links Islam to despotic government, upheavals, and war. It is the Islamic world, not China, Russia, or the France of Louis XIV, that is the setting for and logically connected with Oriental despotism, as Christianity is logically linked with moderate governments.[57] Unaware of past Islamic glories, Montesquieu argues that, except for a few large towns, the Islamic world is one of ruins and deserts, devoid of industry or commerce. It is also a cruel and arbitrary world where sultans have the "habit of having anyone who displeases them executed, at a wave of the hand."

In an interesting digression Montesquieu decries the fact that the Turks cannot regulate disease and the plague as can Christians. Beginning in the fourteenth century, Western European seaports began to protect themselves against the plague. The system of quarantine, the waiting period of forty days imposed by Venice in the fifteenth century on outsiders from Ottoman lands, became more widespread, which resulted in a growing disparity in standards of public health between Europe and its Eastern neighbors.[58] At the same time, the picture was not as bleak as Montesquieu says. In a letter from Adrianople on April 1, 1717, Lady Mary Wortley Montagu described to her friend the successful process every year of vaccination against small pox of thousands of Turkish women, which "will make you wish yourself here."[59]

DESPOTISM AND FRANCE

Much of the wit and ironic commentary in *Persian Letters* is subtle criticism of the French regime. Montesquieu continues the aristocratic tradition from Fénelon to Boulainvilliers of criticizing monarchical aggrandizement, centralization, control over the *Parlements*, and neglect of provincial estates. In similar fashion to other contemporary French commentators, Montesquieu alluded to struggles between the crown, the clergy, aristocracy, and magistracy. He associated Louis XIV's policies with "Turkish style monarchy." By comparing him to Oriental despots Montesquieu criticized Louis XIV's incompetence, ostentation, love of glory, fear of clever men, choice of bad generals, and his mediocre qualities as a king. Assuming that Montesquieu's leading character, Usbek, is often making comments that reflect his own views on France, it is evident that he finds Louis XIV "a figure of contradictions I am unable to resolve." He describes Louis's great talent as the ability to command obedience; Louis's favorite type of government in the world is that of the Turks, or the sultan, "such is his esteem for Oriental policies." The French King is the most powerful ruler in Europe, exerting authority even over the minds of his subjects; he makes them think what he wants. Yet it seems excessive to argue, as does

Althusser, that Montesquieu used the concept of despotism to oppose absolute monarchy in France and to support the case for particular liberties and security to ensure the survival of the feudal nobility.[60]

Montesquieu was preoccupied with need for stability in monarchies. In those systems the state is more fixed, the constitution is more unshakable, and the persons who govern are more assured than in despotic systems. His fear of the corruption of monarchy that might deteriorate into despotism is constantly present in his thinking about politics in general and France in particular. His character Usbek expresses this view: "monarchy is a state of tension, which always degenerates into despotism or republicanism." Montesquieu states that despotic states and moderate and monarchical ones exercise power. The difference is that in a monarchy the prince gets advice and has more gifted ministers, versed in public affairs, than despots have. He also does not act counter to people's customs and religious beliefs.

One of Montesquieu's major political assertions is that in moderate governments this deterioration is prevented by institutional and cultural controls over the exercise of power. These governments have a great advantage over despotic governments because they have fundamental laws and because they have "several orders or ranks of subjects."[61] In monarchical government the prince was the source of political and civil power but intermediate, subordinate, and dependent powers exist. They prevent the monarch from becoming a despot, as does the principle of honor. The monarch governs in accordance with the law and cannot put to death nobles who have offended him.

At the core of nondespotic government is limitation of power and moderation in its use. The most significant, most natural intermediate, subordinate power for Montesquieu is the nobility. He provides a simple aphorism: no monarch, no nobility; no nobility, no monarch. If the privileges of the nobility, the clergy, and the cities were to be abolished, the monarchy would become either a "popular state or else a despotic government." Intermediate powers restrain monarchs as physical obstacles, weeds and pebbles on the shore that stem the ocean tide.

Montesquieu's concern about France stems from what he saw as a threat to the intermediate powers. He observed that Cardinal Richelieu was a man in love with despotic power who advised monarchs against allowing people to raise difficulties on every trifle. Usbek sees that the French *Parlements* can still dispense justice but "are like a ruin which can be trodden underfoot." Together with the intermediate powers in moderate systems are the bodies responsible for the depository of the laws (*dépôt des lois*). This depository would consist of judges of a supreme court who promulgate the new laws and revise the obsolete. The presence or absence of these checks on power is crucial. Despotic governments have no fundamental laws, no "depository," and no intermediate groups.[62] They are hostile to a hereditary aristocracy.

Nor is Montesquieu enamored of the power and privileges of the clergy; he is especially caustic about the Inquisition of Spain and Portugal and regards ecclesiastical power as dangerous in a republic. In a different context the clergy is another serviceable barrier against the intrusion of arbitrary power. Even though he is so critical of Islam and its role in despotic governments, Montesquieu recognized that religion is politically useful. He examines it mainly in relation to the good it produces in civil society and whether or not it renders men good citizens. All political systems have some underlying religious code, and some sacred book serves for a rule. The religious code "supplies" the civil code and acts to contain political power; it is "a restraining motive" even if it does not always restrain.[63] In spite of possible abuses, religion is a lesser evil than atheism, which might not restrain a ruler. Even in Islamic societies, religious laws are of a superior nature because they bind the sovereign as well as the subject. People there may slay a parent if the prince commands, but they cannot be forced to drink wine.

CHARACTERISTICS OF DESPOTIC REGIMES

From the various writings of Montesquieu one can assemble a set of characteristics – all of them negative – of despotic government. It is unstable; as instability is natural to a despotic government, so insecurity is interwoven with the nature of rule by one person. It is arbitrary; it is a system in which honors, posts, and ranks are all abused. Despotic governments indiscriminately make a prince a scullion and a scullion a prince.[64] For Montesquieu a defining characteristic of despotic governments is the absence of fundamental law. With the momentary and capricious will of a single person governing the state, nothing can be fixed, and there is no fundamental law. Monarchs who live under the fundamental laws of their country, which impose a limit on power, are far happier than despotic princes who govern by caprice and have nothing to regulate, neither their own passions nor those of their subjects.

Neither is there, in Montesquieu's view of these despotic systems, any settled or fixed manner by which judgments are made. For him, in despotic governments there are no laws. He wrote that a timid, ignorant, and faint-spirited people have no occasion for a great number of laws; no new notions need be added. As described earlier he concludes that, because all the lands belong to the prince who controls monopolies, marriages, and slaves, it follows there is little need for civil laws regarding landed property, inheritance, credit, commerce, or dowries. This view, greatly influenced by Bernier, about laws in Islamic states was, however, incorrect by Montesquieu's time.

Montesquieu also states that in a regime without fundamental laws there is no fixed law of succession to the throne. The successor is declared by the prince or by a civil war. A despotic state is therefore, for another reason, more liable than a monarchical government to dissolution. In the Orient, Montesquieu believes the consequence of this selection process is that the new prince, afraid for his position, often immediately strangles his brothers as in Turkey, or puts out their eyes as in Persia, or eliminates their ability to comprehend as in India. Montesquieu was not aware that the resort to fratricide, at least on paper, was discontinued in early-seventeenth-century Turkey.

Regarding law, the judge decides by just carrying out the law of Islam. Despotic governments may seem to have an advantage in the speed with which all legal matters are decided, as in Turkey, "the most ignorant of all nations." The price paid is little regard for the honor, life, or estate of the subject. The legal process is haphazard; the method of determining legal cases is a matter of indifference, provided that they are determined. It is inflexible; unlike moderate systems where monarchs formulate different laws for different areas of the country when necessary, the despot establishes general measures. In nondespotic systems, laws may be interpreted in different ways by judges, a problem that is redressed by a legislator from time to time. In despotic countries, there is nothing that the legislator is able to decree, or the magistrate to judge, because, on the one hand, there are few civil or commercial laws and, on the other, a large number of slaves in the population who have no will of their own.

A despotic regime is corrupt by nature. It wastes the talents of its subjects. It is defensively weak; contrary to his assertion that a despot can act quickly, Montesquieu argues that when a vast empire, like Persia, is attacked, it is several months before the troops are assembled in a body, and then they are not able to make such forced marches. It suffers from a poor economy. It is not a happy system; monarchs are far happier than despotic princes. The prince knows nothing and can attend to nothing. He is naturally lazy, voluptuous, and ignorant. Both ruler and ruled are ignorant; excessive obedience supposes ignorance in the person that obeys and in him who commands. On this point Montesquieu seemed unaware that Ottoman sultans were well educated and that some of them were poets. He is more accurate when stating that Oriental despotism is hedonistic; the prince throws himself into pleasures, lives only for pleasure, does not govern, and leaves administration to his ministers. The system is also cruel; the cruelty of the sultans "makes us shudder at the thought of the miseries of human nature." It is inhumane. It is ruined by its own imperfections.

Montesquieu, influenced by Chardin and other travelers, assumes that the whole system of despotic government is wholly corrupt. No one in a system of this kind comes to a superior without a gift. The Mughal never receives the petitions of his subjects if they come with empty hands. In despotic governments, people can rarely petition or complain to the ruler. In Europe, magistrates may shelter merchants from confiscation and taxations, but in Asia the magistrates are the greatest oppressors. Unlike nondespotic governments, where honor and public virtue are rewards in themselves, despotic governments can only reward people with money. The ruler cannot pay people sufficiently well; hence his subordinates grasp for themselves, embezzle public money, and despoil the country for their own advantage.

THE QUESTION OF DEVELOPMENT

Contemporary political scientists have recognized that all states contain a mix of traditional and modern elements and are at varying stages of political development. Though development is not easy to define or to assess in practice, it is associated with certain institutional and behavioral patterns: a complex governmental structure in which different institutions and people perform different functions, an increase in political participation, integration of the community, ability to manage tensions within the system, and a rational basis for the authority to exercise power. On this scale, despotic governments in Montesquieu's version register low. They are "simple" systems lacking any real institutional structure, political, economic, or military; have a concentration of power at the top; are unlimited or with few restraints on the exercise of power; are unpredictable; have no fundamental law; are based on the principle of fear; are economically undeveloped; are based on an apathetic and obedient subject people who have no part in the governing process; are essentially static; and are Oriental.

Moderate governments are likely to have a complex political structure, a form more admired by Montesquieu than a simple one. A moderate government, combining different powers that counterpoise each other, is a masterpiece of legislation, rarely produced by chance, and seldom attained by "prudence." Inherent in it is balance and regulation of the several powers it contains. In a brief description of the evolution of monarchies, Montesquieu praised the emergence of "Gothic government" after the conquest of the Roman Empire by the German nations.[65] This complex system, consisting of at first mixed and then representative government, led to a perfect balance among the civil liberty of the people, the privileges of nobility and clergy, and the prerogative of the prince, and could be viewed as a well-tempered government. By contrast, in a despotic government in Asia, says Montesquieu's Usbek, "the rules of politics are the same everywhere."[66]

The differences between the complexity of moderate government, and the simplicity of despotic government are apparent in many ways: in the ties that unite people; existence or suppression of differences; presence or absence of intermediate groups; immediacy or delay of obedience to commands; attitudes to customary law; existence of fixed and established laws or of will and caprice; and political goals. Despotic government in modern political terminology is neither a developed nor a modernized system. It is monolithic. Power is concentrated in the ruler and virtually unlimited, with the ruler being his own judge. The regime lacks magnanimity and glory and does not have the "true dignity and greatness" that adorn monarchies. It also rests on forced unanimity. In moderate systems, all the parts of the body politic cooperate for the general good, but in Asiatic despotism concord is to be seen not in united citizens of the country but in dead bodies buried next to each other.[67]

In despotic government, the single person invested with despotic power delegates the execution of that power. Montesquieu generalizes from the aphorism of John Chardin that Eastern kings are never without viziers. The immense power of the prince devolves entirely on those to whom he entrusts the administration. The master similarly entrusts power in the seraglio to his agents. Usbek tells the Chief Eunuch: "I am putting the sword into your hands" ... for vengeance; "I must rely on you to restore my happiness and peace of mind." His wives are told that "the whole seraglio will kneel before" the Chief Eunuch.

All political systems have the same general end, self-preservation. A despotic state has only a single real political goal or objective: the preservation of the prince or the palace where he is confined. Whatever does not directly threaten the palace makes no impression, and little thought is given to events in general. The political government is as simple as the civil administration. Montesquieu writes that "[t]he whole is reduced to reconciling the political and civil administration to the domestic government, the officers of state to those of the seraglio." Despotic power is a political vacuum. No one is a citizen.

In a despotic state, the prince's will is law. In moderate governments, Montesquieu thought, the law is prudent and well-known, so all to whom power is delegated can follow it. Courts and civil service are independent to a considerable degree. By contrast despotic power is unsystematic, highly personal, and marked by unstructured administrative discontinuity.

Monarchies are corrupted when the prince insensibly deprives societies or cities of their privileges, and usurps power; when, among other things, a prince deprives some of his subjects of their hereditary employment to bestow it arbitrarily on others; when he is fonder of being guided by fancy than by judgment; or when a prince directs everything to himself.

Once the will of the despotic prince is made known, it infallibly produces its effect. There are no limitations or restrictions, no mediums, terms, equivalents, or remonstrances. Only religion may sometimes oppose the prince's will. Yet even religion may not be a limitation on the ruler. Montesquieu argues that "it is religion that amends in some measures the Turkish constitution . . . subjects are connected with (the state) by the force and principle of religion." As mentioned earlier, at the same time he asserts that "in Islamic countries, it is partly from their religion that people derive the surprising veneration they have for their prince."

SEPARATION OF POWERS

The real checks on power, on excessive use or abuse, are institutional.[68] Moderate governments need the "counterpoising" of the several powers. To achieve this balance requires a masterpiece of legislation, rarely produced by hazard, and seldom attained by prudence. Through this legislation a constitutional system, balanced and tolerant, which respected individual liberties, can come into existence. Such a system is concerned for legality, defending aristocratic privileges and property rights, and creating power that is "a check to power." The most complex and, for Montesquieu, admirable institutional mechanisms to prevent despotism are systems of separation of powers and mixed government. Discussion of these two topics had been continuous in political theory from Plato and Aristotle to Locke, each writer analyzing the powers of government in different terminology. Montesquieu's version of the two concepts, logically and analytically distinguishable from each other, has been particularly influential. It was Montesquieu, wrote Robert Shackleton, "who dignified and rationalized the concept of the separation of powers, linked it to a theory of liberty, and handed it to posterity as a doctrine far more practical than its proponents had known."[69]

The theory of the separation of powers, partly descriptive and partly prescriptive, is based on two elements: analysis of governmental activity into different functions or powers, and advocacy that separate institutions or personnel should be responsible for each function. Though Montesquieu did not always use the same terminology in his analysis, his contribution was to define them in a way now familiar to us: legislative, executive, and judicial powers. From his understanding or, as some scholars think, misunderstanding of the British Constitution, Montesquieu analyzed not only the idea of separation of powers but also that of mixed government, the governmental structure that contains differing elements of monarchy, aristocracy, and democracy, and in which different individuals or groups, sometimes jointly, exercise power.[70] Critics of Montesquieu, especially those who argue that he misunderstood the British system, have not acknowledged that Montesquieu did not suggest that powers were completely separated. Because there must be movement in human affairs, the three powers "are forced to move, but still in concert." This harmonious cooperation, appropriate for limited government, helps guarantee liberty and is a bulwark against tyranny.[71] He gives a number of examples, obviously drawn from British experience, of ways in which those primarily exercising one of the three functions sometimes intruded on another function.

Yet Montesquieu's main argument, in spite of qualifications and perhaps some misunderstanding, is clear. When the legislative and executive powers are united in the same person, or in the same body of magistrates, there is no liberty. Again, there is no liberty if the judicial power is not separated from the legislative and executive power. The ruler must not judge cases himself. If this is not the case, as in the Orient, the result is arbitrary control, violence, and oppression. His example is Turkey, "where the three powers are united in the Sultan's person, the subjects groan under the most dreadful oppression." Montesquieu was, of course, concerned about the power of the nobility, "the most natural, intermediate, and subordinate power." But Montesquieu, although far from being a democrat himself, realized the need in a country of liberty "for every man to be his own governor." In theory, the legislative power should reside in the whole body of the people; in practice, for reasons of convenience, it should be in the hands of representatives. He does not dwell on this point, but inherent in it is the view that the distributions of political power among different social groups – king, nobility, and people – or in mixed government is a key to political liberty and an obstacle to despotic government.

Montesquieu argues that no rational administrative system exists in a despotic government. Official positions and honors depend wholly on the monarch's whim. A man can never be sure that he will not be dishonored tomorrow. Today, writes Usbek rather hyperbolically, a man is the general of an army; the monarch is perhaps about to make him the royal cook. In Persia, a man is a great lord only if the monarch declares him as such and gives him some share in the government. If those people who are not actually employed by the ruler were still invested with privileges and titles, the consequence would be to create a class of men who might be great in themselves, a circumstance that would be contradictory to the nature of despotic government.

In the same way the seraglio is marked by unpredictability and caprice. The First Eunuch worries that "I am never certain of remaining in my master's favor for an instant." In the despotic worlds, political and domestic, all are equal in their nothingness and are slaves. Despotism has no fixed rule of direction, and its caprices are subversive of all others. The insuperable problem with this system is that subordinates will not be men of ability. Persons invested with self-worth are likely to create disturbances; therefore, fear must extinguish even the least sense of ambition. Montesquieu's thoughts here closely resemble the views of Plato in the *Laws* and Aristotle in *The Politics* in that the tyrant dislikes everyone who has dignity or independence. Despotic rulers, Montesquieu states, remain suspicious of their army. A monarchical system has fortresses to defend its frontiers and troops to garrison those fortresses. However, despots are afraid of their troops. They dare not entrust their officers with command at the frontiers, as none of their officers have any affection for the prince or his government. In these countries there must always be a body of faithful troops near the prince, ready to fall instantly on any part of the empire that may chance to waver. This military corps must awe the rest of the military and strike terror into those who, through necessity, have been entrusted with any authority in the empire.

FEAR IS THE PRINCIPLE

Fear is the principle, the spring or source of despotic government, in the political world and in the seraglio. A moderate government may, without danger to itself, relax; it supports itself by laws and by its own internal strength. However, a despotic prince dare not cease for one single moment "to uplift his arm." All men are restrained by examples of severe punishment. Commenting on the difference between European and Asian habits, Rica writes to his friend Usbek that in Persia "everyone's character is uniformly the same, because they are forced." Because of the enslavement of heart and mind, nothing is heard but the voice of fear, which has only one language. In a series of letters at the moment of crisis in the seraglio, Usbek instructs his eunuchs to exercise unlimited powers on his behalf over the entire seraglio. "Let fear and terror be your companions; go with all speed to punish and chastise . . . everyone must live in dread."[72] In the wider world, fear is a more simple principle than the honor of republics or the political virtue of republics. It therefore requires fewer laws to be implemented. The consequence of fear is a society marked by strict obedience, silence, isolation, apathy, and tranquility.

Despotic government requires "the most passive obedience." Man's life, like that of beasts, is instinct, compliance, and punishment. It is enough that an order is given; in Persia, when the king has condemned a person, it is no longer lawful to mention his name or to intercede in his favor. The mark of obedience is silence. In despotic states tranquility is not peace; it resembles the silence of those towns that the enemy is about to invade.[73] In a free nation it is often a matter of indifference whether individuals reason well or badly. It is sufficient that they do reason, and from this comes liberty. In a despotic government, it is of no consequence whether they reason well or badly. Reasoning in itself is sufficient to undermine the principle of that government.

Again, Montesquieu draws the parallel between a despotic regime and the seraglio. Usbek tells his wives that the task of the Chief Eunuch is "not to guard but to punish you. ... The whole seraglio will kneel before him." One slave, Pharan, in the seraglio writes to Usbek: "I kiss your feet, sublime lord, in deepest humility." In the seraglio where submission is both sexual and political, Usbek tells his favorite wife Roxana that "I cannot imagine you have any other purpose than to please me." Similarly in the Islamic world, Montesquieu says, female slaves are at the master's disposal; "the greatest part of the nation are born only to be subservient to the pleasures of the other." Subjects are used instrumentally: the women in the seraglio are to be made aware of their absolute dependence. The eunuchs are "mere tools" whom the master can break at will, and of whom Usbek will take "no more notice than of the insects that I tread beneath my feet" if they fail in their duty.

EDUCATION AND IGNORANCE

Obedience, Montesquieu asserts, is even more deeply ingrained by education or, more strictly speaking, indoctrination in the system. Unlike moderate systems where education tends to raise and ennoble the mind, the only aim of education in despotic regimes is to debase the mind. It is quite limited, strikes the heart with fear, imprints a very simple notion of a few principles of religion, is confined in a very narrow compass, and is really needless. People are ignorant of the "natural stupidity" of the prince, hidden in his palace. The prince is lucky; the people need only his name for him to govern them. Even this may not be necessary. Asian kings hide themselves. The result is that "this invisible ruling power always remains identical for the people. Even if a dozen kings . . . were to slaughter each other in turn, they would not be aware of any difference: it would be as if they had been governed by a succession of phantoms."

Montesquieu views people in despotic nations as ignorant of the world outside. Despotic countries are closed and isolated internally and externally.[74] In *Persian Letters*, Rhedi, writing of his interest in the origin and history of republics since his arrival in Europe, says that "most Asians have no ideas [*sic*] that this type of government exists; their imaginations have not stretched far enough to make them realize that there can be any other sort on earth except despotism." External isolation has been deliberate. Montesquieu argues although republics provide for their security by uniting, despotic governments do it by separating, and by keeping themselves . . . single . . . by ravaging and desolating the frontiers they render the heart of the empire inaccessible. A despotic system preserves itself by putting the most distant provinces into the hands of a great vassal. The Mughal emperor, the king of Persia, the sultan of the Turks, and the emperors of China have all done this. Montesquieu concludes that a despotic state is happiest when it can look on itself as the only one in the world, when it is surrounded by deserts, and when it is separated from those people regarded as barbarians. Because such a state cannot depend on its militia, it is proper it should destroy a part of itself.

Internally, isolation has the appearance of a prison, politically and domestically, for the prince as well as the subjects. Every tyrant is at the same time a slave. There is less communication in a country where each, either as superior or inferior, exercises or is oppressed by arbitrary power, than there is in those where liberty reigns in every station. Fixed and established customs "have a near resemblance" to laws. In despotic states, each house is a separate government; as education is largely social converse, it is very much limited. Usbek is worried by the "Asiatic seriousness" in Persia and Turkey that comes from the little contact people have. They see each other only when social conventions demand. Otherwise, they withdraw to their houses . . . each family is, so to speak, isolated.

Inside the seraglio, in Montesquieu's depiction, all are aware of their isolation and see it as a prison. The wives grumble that they are prevented from being seen by anyone except the master. The First Eunuch complains of being "shut inside this dreadful prison, always surrounded by the same things, and devoured by the same anxieties." Usbek asks one wife: "What would you do if you could get out of that holy place, which seems to you a harsh prison?" But the master is also chained. Another wife writes to Usbek: "Although you keep me imprisoned, I am freer than you . . . your suspicion, jealousy, and vexation are so many signs of your dependence." Usbek is worried if he returns to the seraglio that "I shall be surrounded by walls more horrible for me than for the women they enclose." Less metaphorically, his favorite wife tells him of each of the wives being shut up in her apartment and, though alone, forced to wear veils. "We are no longer allowed to speak to each other; it would be a crime to write; the only freedom we are allowed is to weep."

UNDERDEVELOPED SOCIETIES

Montesquieu regards Oriental societies as economically undeveloped, poor, dependent on usury, and bereft of every resource, even the capacity to borrow.

Merchants cannot carry on an extensive commerce but live from hand to mouth. These societies do not obtain the beneficial effects of commerce found in moderate systems: raising the level of agreeable manners, diffusing knowledge, and creating peace between nations.

The worst society for Montesquieu is the one in which the prince declares himself owner of all the land and heir to all his subjects. Like many previous and subsequent writers on the Ottoman Empire, Montesquieu oversimplified and misunderstood the complex system of land tenure, as Marx and Engels were to do more than a century later. In Montesquieu's view the results of the land ownership system in the Ottoman Empire were agricultural neglect and industrial ruin. Under a despotic government, nothing is repaired or improved. No ditches are dug or trees planted. Everything is drawn from, but nothing restored to, the earth. The ground lies untilled, and the whole country becomes a desert. The image of immediate consumption: "when the savages of Louisiana are desirous of fruit, they cut the tree to the root, and gather the fruit" is an emblem of despotic government and the need to satisfy the despot. Unlike moderate governments, despotic systems have little trade. A slave nation labors more to preserve than to acquire. Poverty and the precariousness of property make usury natural and misery is widespread.

DANGER OF REVOLUTION

Politics in despotic systems is unpredictable. As mentioned earlier, a monarchical system has several orders of subjects, a permanent state, a steady constitution, and a person who governs securely. Despotic regimes, in Montesquieu's words, are subject to popular revolutions and sudden and unforeseen riots. The people, lacking representatives, are carried away by their passions, apt to push things as far as they can go, and engage in extreme disruption. Western European histories are full of civil wars without revolutions, while the histories of despotic governments abound in revolutions without civil wars. Monarchs who live under the fundamental laws of their country are far happier than despotic princes who have nothing to regulate, neither their own passions nor those of their subjects.

ISLAM, THE ORIENT, AND DESPOTISM

Montesquieu's concept of despotism is essentially Oriental in nature. Scattered throughout his work are occasional examples of despotic behavior drawn from outside the Middle East; he discusses the excesses of the Roman Empire with "the horrid cruelties of Domitian," the Papacy with the pope who assigned the administration entirely to his nephew, Russia where "the Czar may choose whom he has in mind for his successor," Sweden where Charles XII, while abroad, wrote home that "he would send one of his boots to command his people," or China where some princes "governed by the force of punishments." Almost all the factual illustrations of Montesquieu's general remarks on his model of despotic government came from Turkey, Persia, or Mughal India. He talks of these countries in a critical or pejorative fashion. Turkey, for example, is "the most ignorant of all nations . . . where little regard is shown to the honor, life, or estate of the subject." No one is free in Turkey, not even the prince. Usbek writes of "the weakness of the Ottoman Empire. It is a diseased body, preserved not by gentle and moderate treatment, but by violent remedies which ceaselessly fatigue and undermine it." Commerce is in the hands of foreigners and minorities, and the empire is doomed. Pashas despoil the provinces like a conquered country. The military is unruly, the towns are deserted, the countryside laid waste, and agriculture and trade are completely abandoned. Possession of land cannot be guaranteed, and thus any eagerness to develop it is reduced. With this view of the Ottoman Empire, Montesquieu could wittily criticize Louis XIV as a monarch who "has often been heard to say that of all the types of government in the world, he would most favor either that of the Turks or that of our own august Sultan, such is his esteem for Oriental policies."

Montesquieu sees Eastern countries as embodying social and political immutability. In them, the hot climate, Islamic religion, and despotic government, with its cruelty and intolerance, are all interrelated. They are a stage for indolence of mind and body, the incapacity to exert any effort, and with laws, manners, and customs the same as they were a thousand years ago. People do not seem what they are, but what they are obliged to be. Eastern countries have crueler penalties and harsher punishments than do European states, but public order, justice, and equity are not better preserved in Turkey, Persia, or under the Mughal, than in Holland, Venice, or England.

Montesquieu compares the use of power in East and West. The power of European kings, writes Usbek, is very great, but they do not use it to the same extent as our sultans, because they do not want to go against their peoples' customs and religious beliefs and it is not in their interest to carry it so far. Oriental despots have a habit of having anyone who displeases them executed, thus destroying the proper relationship between crime and punishment. Consequently, subjects are naturally inclined to subvert the state and conspire against the sovereign. If eastern princes, with their unbounded authority, did not take so many precautions to preserve their lives, they would not survive for a day.

Oriental systems have a static quality that is reinforced by a quietistic Islam that encourages veneration of the prince. There is scarcely any change in the methods of government used by Oriental sovereigns: "what other reason can there be except their methods are tyrannical and atrocious?" The despots have no desire to make changes because they already have everything they want. The subjects can only obtain change by assassination of the despot.

CONCLUSION

In a powerful attack on Montesquieu's work, Macaulay said he had ransacked history, carelessly collected materials, and was indifferent to truth in his eagerness to build a system.[75] It is undeniable that Montesquieu's images of despotic government were less historically accurate than his analysis of the European countries with which he was familiar.[76] Montesquieu never understood some aspects of the reality of the Ottoman Empire as well as did the French Ambassador, Count de Choiseul-Gouffier, quoted in Chapter 3, reporting from his post in Istanbul in a letter in 1786 that "things here are not as in France where the king is sole master; here it is necessary to persuade people."[77]

All specialists in Middle Eastern affairs can readily perceive that Montesquieu had somewhat imperfect knowledge of the Middle East, Persia, or India. Furthermore, Montesquieu was not aware that in the eighteenth century some changes of the Ottoman state and society had already occurred. The power of the ruler had noticeably declined, the ruler did not own all the land, part of which was private property, nor did he automatically inherit from his subjects, other than from those with heirless property. The ruler could rarely exercise personal central control over his entire kingdom. Montesquieu did not have firsthand knowledge of the Islamic religion or of the role of the *sharia* or the interrelation between the Koran and the law of the prince.

Yet his construction of a model type of Oriental despotic government is logically compelling and became the archetype of all forms of absolute power.[78] In Montesquieu's perception it exists in hot climates, large countries, and usually Islamic nations. Its essential characteristic is rule by the will and caprice of a single person who communicates his power to subordinates. It is arbitrary and cruel. It resembles in the public sphere what the seraglio is in the private one. It is in essence corrupt. It has no real political objective other than to preserve the prince. It is dominated by fear, and subjects obey passively. It has no real institutional structure, fundamental law, or process of succession. Power is concentrated in the ruler who possesses all property rights, and there are few checks on power other than religion. It is economically weak and static in every way. It is less stable than nondespotic systems. With this intellectual construction of Oriental despotism, Montesquieu could rightfully say at the end of the preface to *L'Esprit des Lois*, quoting the words of Correggio after first seeing the work of Raphael, "*ed io anche son pittore*, I am also a painter."

5

Edmund Burke and Despotism in India

Unlike Montesquieu, whom he regarded as "the greatest genius who has enlightened this age" and "a genius not born in every country or every time, a man gifted by Nature with a judgement prepared with the most extensive erudition, with a Herculean robustness of mind . . . a man who could spend twenty years in one pursuit," Edmund Burke was an active politician, a formidable parliamentarian in the House of Commons, a government minister for a short time, and a loyal and prominent member of his political party, as well as a speculative political thinker.[1] That speculation did not take the form of a grandiose political philosophy nor is it to be found in a systematic treatise in traditional fashion. On the contrary, Burke's thoughts on politics stem from direct involvement in the major issues of his day, in countries as diverse as Britain, Ireland, the American colonies, France, and India, and constitute an intriguing mixture of philosophical generalizations, aphoristic wisdom, polemical advocacy, passionate and often extreme rhetoric, and a vast amount of empirical information. His wide interests, shown in speeches in the House of Commons, ranged from local affairs in Britain, relief to Roman Catholics in Ireland, the Irish penal code, poor law reform, the Corn Laws, free trade, divorce, lotteries, international trade, the House of Lords, the British Museum, copyright legislation, political party loyalty, abolition of slavery, opposition to the rights of dissenters, and the East India Company. Dr. Johnson, according to Boswell, spoke of Burke as an extraordinary man, of "his great variety of knowledge, store of imagery, and copiousness of language."

During a long parliamentary career from 1765 to 1794, speaking and writing on a variety of issues with majestic eloquence but with varying success and often at inordinate length in what John Morley called his "ornate style . . . overlaid with Asiatic ornament," Burke was not always consistent in the political positions he took.[2] Sensitive to this charge of inconsistency on specific political issues, Burke replied by distinguishing between "difference in conduct under a variation of circumstances, and an inconsistency in principle."[3] In this connection Burke also wrote of the need for sound, well-understood priciples without which all reasoning in politics, as in everything else, would be only a confused jumble of facts and details. Burke did make influential contributions to the facts and details in the political discourse of his time, though his verbose and embroidered rhetoric, his exaggerated argument, and his occasional resort to scatological passages, zoological metaphors, and sexual images did not make him a successful House of Commons man.[4] Moreover, his fate was to be in almost permanent political opposition. Of the twenty-nine years he was a member of the House of Commons, his own party was in power for less than two years.

Few will argue that any single theme dominated Burke's writings and speeches or lay at the center of his political outlook during a thirty-year period. He was a man for all seasons as well as being intellectually incorruptible. Whether to define him as primarily a defender of the social order and the fount of contemporary conservatism, an advocate of constitutional principles in political systems, a premature anticolonialist because of his defense of the rights of the American colonies against British rule or because of his support for Catholic emancipation against Protestant ascendancy in Ireland, a cold war warrior against revolutionary influence coming from France, a pluralistic liberal concerned about abuse of power wherever it occurred, or simply as a pliable paid spokesman for his Whig patrons and friends, has perplexed political analysts who have tried to label him in some clear or unilateral way.[5]

Here we are concerned with analyzing Burke's participation in Indian affairs from which one can conclude that detestation of despotism or arbitrary power was a major motif in his attitude to India as it was toward other issues in the different countries with which he was concerned.[6] The overwhelming factor in that attitude was his criticism of Warren Hastings, who was Governor of Bengal in 1772 and then in 1773 the first Governor-General of India, a position created together with a four-person governing Supreme Council by Lord North's Regulating Act of the same year. At the core of Burke's accusations against Hastings was that he was despotic; he rejected what he thought was Hastings's claim that Asia was despotic and therefore had to be governed in that fashion. Burke repudiated Hasting's argument that he had an arbitrary power to exercise and had done so. He held in his remarkable speech of February 15, 1788 that arbitrary power was a thing that neither any man can hold or can give, Burke was deeply concerned about what he perceived as despotic modes of governance, which were contrary to moral principles of eternal justice or even to the law of nature, developed by British officials in India. He was also troubled by the same problem that concerned Tocqueville. The latter was worried about the ill effect of actions and experiences of French troops when they returned from Algeria to France. Burke was concerned that similar pernicious modes of behavior and corruption might creep from India into Britain and alter the constitution and the existing political system, which was based on "a nice equipoise" and was "placed in a just correspondence and symmetry with the order of the world."

Burke's concerns were most completely expressed during the impeachment trial of Hastings, which provided the occasion for a dialogue between him and the lawyers who defended Hastings. At that trial, acute differences of opinion emerged about the character of Mughal Islamic rule in the latter part of the eighteenth century, the existence and exercise of despotic rule in India, and the appropriateness of the nature of British rule in that country.

BURKE AND THE EAST INDIA COMPANY

Burke's concern about the use of arbitrary or despotic power in India gradually developed as his interest in and knowledge of British rule, some of it gathered as a member of the House of Commons Select Committee (1781–3), and of the role and behavior of the East India Company (hereinafter referred to as, the Company) grew. That Company was a remarkable and changing mixture of commerce and governance. It had been founded by British Royal Charter in 1600 and derived its powers from that charter and other statutes of the British parliament that delegated considerable authority to it. In addition, it obtained some authority from the Mughal Emperor. At first its powers were confined to commercial and trade affairs. Gradually these were extended to civil and criminal jurisdiction and to military control and a private force, with the Company becoming, in Burke's phrase of February 15, 1788, "in reality a delegation of the whole power and sovereignty" of Britain sent into the East. From a trading company the Company had been transformed into a great empire "carrying on subordinately, under the public authority, a great commerce." A commercial venture had become a political system, administering an annual revenue of several million pounds, commanding an army of sixty thousand men, and disposing of the lives of millions.

Burke was concerned with the conduct of British rule. He never clearly stated a political or moral position on the desirability of that rule or of British colonial experience in India. The closest he came was in his speech of February 16, 1788, during the impeachment of Hastings, which began in 1787, in which he took a position that might be called benign colonialism: "if in that part of

India whose native regular government had [in 1756] broken up . . . a star had risen from the West that would have prognosticated order, peace, happiness, and security to the natives of that country . . . it would have been glorious to this country . . . (and) had done honor to Europe, to our cause, to our religion."[7] In any case Burke did not appear to be troubled by the question. In words reminiscent of what Montesquieu had said about China, Burke stated "there is a secret veil to be drawn over the beginnings of all governments."[8] British rule in India had an origin like those that time had "sanctified by obscurity." Earlier in 1782 Burke explained that the Select Committee of the House of Commons on the administration of justice in Bengal which he had joined in 1781 would report on "how the British possessions in the East Indies may be governed with the greatest security and advantage to this country, and by what means the happiness of the natives may be best promoted."[9]

British rule was taken for granted by Burke if it was appropriate rule: "if we are not able to contrive some method of governing India *well*, which will not of necessity become the means of governing Great Britain *ill*, a ground is laid for their eternal separation."[10] Britain should remain in Bengal, but should use power with restraint and not shake "ancient establishments" or lightly "adopt new projects."[11] In April 1782 he was still arguing that the Company, if reformed and under some form of British parliamentary control, was preferable to direct official government in India.[12] He did not call for British withdrawal from India nor did he denigrate it. Burke was aware of the need for reform. Because of the diversity of people, manners, religion, and hereditary employment in India, he concluded that the handling of the country was a matter that was critical and delicate. Discussing the governing of India in the debate on December 1, 1783, on the East India Bill, Burke declared "there we are; there we are placed by the Sovereign Disposer, and we must do the best we can in our situation. The situation of man is the preceptor of his duty."[13] He freely admitted the claim of the Company to exercise power and carry out its functions, but he also argued that all political power ought in some way or another be exercised ultimately for the benefit of the ruled. In an interesting formulation Burke declared that "duties were not voluntary: indeed duty and will were contradictory terms."

Certainly, Burke had no consistent position on the role of the Company and its relationship to the British government. The question of that unusual and complex relationship preoccupied, and even bedeviled, British politics in the quarter century from 1772 to 1795. Rapid developments in the subcontinent outdistanced the efforts of Parliament to understand and deal with them and gave rise to difficult questions. Could the quasisovereignty of the Company be reconciled with its necessary subordination to Parliament? Should the state, the

British government, leave the Company's privileges and powers untouched and hope for a practical resolution of problems? Or should it take over the Indian territories then under the Company's control, if not possession? Or should there be a partnership between the two with the state being the controlling partner on governmental issues but leaving trade matters to the Company, which habitually paid the state an annual sum for permission to trade, raise revenue, and control part of India.[14] These problems arose because of the imprecise relationship between the British public authorities and what was in essence a private body.

In a debate in the House of Commons at the end of 1766 regarding the creation of a parliamentary committee to inquire into the revenues of the Company, Burke, at the time relatively uninformed on the issue, argued that the government and the Company were "as equal dealers on the footing of mutual advantage." He was shocked that the Company "was to be covered with infamy and disgrace."[15] For the most part, from 1767 to 1773 Burke opposed government proposals to control the Company. Close to 1773 Burke warned that "the pretense of rectifying abuses of nourishing, fostering, and protecting the Company was only made with a design of fleecing the Company."[16] He spoke of the 1773 Regulating Act, the first important attempt to assert parliamentary control over the Company as an "infringement of national right, national faith, and national justice."[17] At this stage Burke accepted and agreed with the position of his Whig party leaders, the group based on Lord Rockingham, who opposed government regulation partly because they thought it would entail control of the patronage and resources of the Company and thereby strengthen the power of the British monarch and the government, which was in the hands of their political opponents.[18] This view always overstated the dangers of state control and minimized the problems caused by the Company.

Burke in principle loyally defended the "great and glorious Company" in parliamentary speeches. Yet a certain ambiguity began to appear in those speeches. In the recently created East India Select Committee on April 13, 1772, he spoke of the "unlimited authority that fell necessarily into the hands of (the Company's) governors"; they had a discretionary power, and their chief executive was "forced occasionally to act the despot, and to terrify the refractory by the arm of power or violence."[19] Again, on April 5, 1773, criticizing the government of Lord North, Burke warned of the effect of the Company on British politics: "this cursed Company would at last, viper, be the destruction of the country which fostered it in her bosom."[20] This early argument would reappear in his last speech that began on May 28, 1794 when he reminded the House of Lords that "the manners learned in an Asiatic absolutism . . . threaten English ways."[21] Burke had always feared that the power and style of the Company might endanger British rule in India.[22]

In the 1770s Burke wavered in his attitude to the role and power of the Company. The enthusiasm of Burke and the Rockingham group for the Company waned after the deposition and arrest of their associate Lord Pigot, the recent Governor of Madras, by his colleagues in the Madras Council in 1777, and his later death. Burke attacked the Company's policies in Madras and the Carnatic, criticized the Company's "masterful servants," called for inquiry into abuses, and began his assault on the leading British official, Warren Hastings.[23] Beginning his intensive study of the Company in 1781, Burke became its most active and passionate critic, pulling his party with him. From 1782 he urged that the Company be brought under parliamentary control, that its political power be reduced, and that Hastings be impeached by the House of Commons for high crimes and misdemeanors.

For the rest of his life India became the main preoccupation of Burke until the French Revolution in 1789 and consequent events absorbed much of his energies and passion. He spoke in the debate on Fox's East India Bill on December 1, 1783, of the "infinite mass of materials which have passed under my eye" on Indian affairs, and a few months later, on July 28, 1784, said he had looked at everything that could throw a light on the subject. Though he never visited the country nor knew any of its languages, Burke mastered a remarkable mass of detail on the complex history and affairs of India. He became expert on arcane issues, in which few others were knowledgeable or interested: the Nawob of Arcot's debts, the invasion of Tangore, Hyder Ali of Mysore, Cheyt Singh, the Rajah of Benares, and the Begums of Oude (also sometimes spelled Awadh). By 1794 he was "as conversant with the manners and customs of the East as most persons whose business has not directly led them into the country."[24] If his understanding and formulation of that history was somewhat distorted for polemical purposes and by his strong emotion and stubbornness, his raising of significant problems was to have a formative influence on British policy in India.[25] Among the issues he raised or stimulated was the nature of empire, corruption of power, despotic or arbitrary rule, Indian culture and society, trusteeship over occupied territory, and the relevance of natural law.

It remains a mystery why Burke, between 1781 and 1795, became so passionately absorbed by Indian affairs compared with his interest in other political issues, except the Revolution in France; why he worked so hard in the Select Committee, preparing at least two of its reports; and why he pursued the impeachment of Hastings, whom he did not know, with such determination and venom. Certain explanations appear more plausible than others. Most objective analysts reject the view that Burke's interest was sustained for personal or family reasons, even if the financial problems of the Burke family, not so much his own but rather those of his cousin William and brother Richard, in speculation on the Company's stock, which collapsed in 1769, may have sparked some early interest.[26] In one of his last letters, to French Laurence on February 10, 1797, talking about the labor and expense of the impeachment proceedings, Burke wrote, "a sober and reflecting man" he did not have the excuse "of acting from personal resentment or from the sense of private injury, never having received any."[27] Though his friend and colleague Charles James Fox spoke of Burke's temper and deficiency in political tact, personality characteristics are unlikely to be the answer for the campaign against Hastings.

To some extent the motive may have been his admiration of Indian society and Hindu civilization that, with its stability, harmony, antiquity, and what he called "great effects," must have appealed to his conservative disposition. That admiration was apparent in his description of the Indians, "a people for ages civilized and cultivated . . . cultivated by all the arts of polished life, whilst we were yet in the woods."[28] He appealed, in the opening speech on impeachment of Hastings, to the House of Lords "to respect a people as respectable as yourselves . . . a people who knows as well as you what is rank, what is law, what is property, equity, reason, proportion in punishments, security of property."[29] Burke could not pass judgment on people "who had framed their laws and institutions prior to our insect origin of yesterday." Above all, in his attitude to India as on other issues, Burke was a conservative, desirous of maintaining custom and calling for change only when necessary to protect traditional values, social hierarchy, and constitutional balance.

Clearly Burke also feared that the experience of British officials in India would have a corrupting effect on British politics in general and on his own party in particular.[30] He mentioned this on many occasions. As early as April 1773 in criticizing Lord North's East India Resolutions he foresaw that the Company "would be the destruction of this country," and preferred the ruin of the Company rather "than have the base of the English Constitution undermined."[31] In particular, Burke regarded the nabobs, those who had made fortunes in India before returning to England and then purchased titles, membership of Parliament, and respectability, as "birds of prey" that he believed blocked attempts to limit the privileges of the Company. To Lord Rockingham he wrote on April 27, 1782, imploring him, regarding political intrigues on India, to act "to prevent an evil that will not be confined to the mismanagement of India, but will subvert all your present power in the House of Commons."[32] Speaking on December 1, 1783, he said "every means, effectual to preserve India from oppression, is a guard to preserve the British constitution from its worst corruption."[33] During the impeachment of Hastings, Burke declared it was not only meant to punish a delinquent but also to preserve the manners, characters, and virtues of the people of England. Burke feared the use of "all the corrupt wealth of India, acquired by the oppression of that country, for the corruption of all the liberties" of Britain.[34] Burke was troubled that the representatives of the Company in the House of Commons were a threat to the British system, concerned as they were with their own selfish interests rather than with the rule of law and constitutional behavior. In his very last speech, on June 16, 1794, Burke spoke of the "enormous and overpowering influence of Eastern corruption," and feared the "corrupt principles of Hastings" might become principles of the British system.[35] Earlier, on May 28, 1794, he spoke of the problem that would arise in Britain when "persons [presumably Company officials] who came from that school of pride, insolence, corruption and tyranny, came to mix themselves with the pure morals of this country."[36] At the very end of his life, writing to French Laurence on July 28, 1796, and referring after the impeachment to "this cruel, daring, unexampled act of public corruption, guilt, and meanness," he asked his friend, "Let my endeavors to save the nation from that shame and guilt be my monument, the only one I ever will have."[37]

Undoubtedly Burke was influenced and encouraged by Sir Philip Francis who was appointed a member of the newly constituted Supreme Council in Bengal after the 1773 Regulating Act and soon became an implacable opponent and professional rival of Hastings with whom he fought a duel as a result of the latter calling him devoid of truth and honor. Francis was, as Macaulay put it, a man prone to "mistake malevolence for virtue . . . which he paraded with Pharisaical ostentation."[38] He not only objected to specific actions such as Hastings's policy on property in Bengal. He also went further in mounting a strong attack on the Company, which he regarded as a trading concern that had gained important executive powers and was engaging in peculation.[39] Francis began supplying Burke with information and ideas on India, especially after his return to England in 1782. His influence is clear in the Ninth and Eleventh Reports of the Commons Select Committee, which Burke wrote.[40]

Francis has to be seen as a major figure, if not the moving spirit behind the impeachment, though he may have inflated his own importance.[41] His influence is clear from Burke's letters to Francis. On December 10, 1785, Burke wondered if the "extreme remedies" of impeachment were appropriate for "some wrong actions during many years continuance in an arduous command." We ought together, "to be very careful not to charge what we are unable to prove."[42] By December 23, 1785, however, Burke was discussing the strategy of the proceedings against Hastings: "I have sent you the first scene of the first act, the Rohilla War. You will make it what it ought to be . . . our Resolutions or Articles of Impeachment as they may turn out will convey a tolerable clear historical state of the delinquencies."[43] Burke was to compare this action with that of Cicero who impeached Verres, the corrupt governor of Sicily, in 70 BC.

The most persuasive explanation for Burke's obsession with the Company and Hastings is his zeal to remedy another example of arbitrary power by a ruling group. Abuse and oppression were, he thought, to be found everywhere in the Company's rule. In his opening impeachment speech in February 1788, which lasted four days, Burke spoke "on behalf of all the people of India, all victims of an oppressive system." In a letter, circa March 17, 1796, to Lord Loughborough, after the acquittal of Hastings on all counts, Burke bitterly wrote, "We cry out against their (Indians') oppression, and we end our process (the impeachment) by rewarding the person whom we have fixed on as the author of it."[44]

Even when reforms in the Company were introduced to get greater administrative efficiency, Burke was suspicious that they would lead to oppression. Burke believed two reasons were advanced to increase the power of the Governor-General and the Council in Bengal. One is that the Company had succeeded to the authority of the ruler of Bengal, who was a prince exercising arbitrary powers, unlimited by any law, and it could rule in the same manner. The second was the right that came from conquest, an argument Burke found "dark and arduous."[45] Conquest entailed duties to preserve the people in all their rights, laws, and liberties, to protect the people, and to observe the laws, rights, usages, and customs of the natives. Those who "give and those who receive arbitrary power are alike criminal."[46]

In 1786 a bill was introduced in the House of Commons to amend the 1784 India Act by strengthening the powers of the Governor-General of Bengal. Burke opposed the proposed change, arguing that "[t]he principle of the bill was to introduce an arbitrary and despotic government in India" on the false pretence that it would give energy, vigor, and dispatch to the executive government. As the examples of the Turkish and every arbitrary government could show, "arbitrary and despotic government produced weakness, debility and delay."[47] Burke attacked arbitrary power in principle: "it is blasphemy in religion, it is wickedness in politics, to say that any man can have arbitrary power" (February 16, 1788). In one of his last speeches in May 1794 Burke emphasized the dire consequences of arbitrary power, "always a miserable creature." No one dared to tell any disagreeable truth to the ruler because one's "life and fortune depended on his caprice." The ruler was thus condemned to ignorance and consequently acted unwisely.[48] Arbitrary power was also contradictory to higher law. Making his most general philosophical point, Burke, in criticizing Lord North's 1773 Regulating Bill, thought it was "contrary to the eternal laws of right and wrong . . . laws that ought to bind men and legislative assemblies."

Whether his concern for the oppressed people of India was, as Conor Cruise O'Brien suggests, partly the result of his transferred concern and feeling of guilt as a Protestant Irishman who had spent the first twenty years of his life in Ireland for the oppressed Catholics there who, unlike him, were subject to the Penal Laws, or whether it was the product of his sense of duty imposed by his situation, his passion about the arbitrary power in India led him to a single-minded devotion to the interests of that country as he saw them for a fifteen-year period.[49] Whatever his real motive for his criticism of the abuses by the Company, Burke spoke of his involvement in India in a letter to John Bowles circa March 12, 1796, as "that public act which is to be the glory or the shame of my whole public life."[50] It was the "greatest and longest labor of a very laborious life."[51]

The initial problem Burke faced was how to explain his change of attitude from nonintervention to public control over the Company. In January 1781 a Select Committee of the House of Commons was set up to consider petitions from Bengal against the Company, and Burke became a member of it. Growing familiarity with conditions in India led him to believe that the Company should be limited to commercial functions and that public control over it was necessary. This he expressed in rhetoric that sometimes took on a physical coloration. Corruption and disease had "burst into eruptions"; "the real seat of the disease, which is in the blood, [is] from corruption" (April 30, 1781).[52] In milder language he spoke on June 27, 1781, of the judges in Bengal who had extended British law there, saying "they were arbitrary in the extreme" and had made "encroachments on the most sacred privileges of the people, whose dearest rights had been violated."[53]

In 1783, Burke, in ministerial office for a short time as Paymaster-General, drafted the legislation, known to history as Charles James Fox's East India Bill, which provided for stricter governmental control over the Company, including punishing abuses and observing Indian rights and customs. In his great speech of December 1, 1783, on the bill that he saw as "the Magna Carta of Hindustan," Burke justified intervention against a chartered company by differentiating between two kinds of rights.[54] He distinguished between "chartered rights of man," and the rights given by charter to private bodies such as the Company. The natural rights of mankind, an issue on which Burke was ambivalent, he regarded here as "sacred things" that cannot be subverted except by tearing up the roots of the principles of government and even of society.

On this last point controversy still continues regarding whether Burke can truly be considered an advocate of natural law and natural rights as Peter Stanlis and Father Francis Canavan argue. For them natural law is fundamental to Burke's conception of man and society. Certainly some of the phrases he used suggest that this was the case. At different times Burke spoke of natural law, the law of nations, eternal laws of justice, the great and fundamental axioms on which every form of society was built, the law of our Creator, and the law of humanity, justice, and equity. Specifically, Britain should govern India according to the natural law that was pertinent to it.

An important example of the "chartered rights of men" was Magna Carta, "a charter to restrain power and to destroy monopoly." A different kind was the East Indian Charter "to establish monopoly and to create power."[55] Its charter from Parliament, Burke held, allowed the Company to govern: it did not give the Company arbitrary power. Because rights and privileges are a trust they must be rendered accountable. The Company must therefore be accountable to Parliament from whom the trust is derived and which can interfere with the Company's rights if they were abused as Burke thought they were. It must be judged by the standard of what is good for the Indian people. No charter should survive if it had become the means of destroying an empire and of cruelly oppressing and tyrannizing millions of people. The Company had violated its "subordinate derivative trust." Parliament should therefore control it and provide a real chartered security for the rights of men who were cruelly violated under the Company's charter.[56]

Burke compared the Company unfavorably with the former Asian rulers of India, "the Arabs, Tartars, and Persians . . . for the greater part, ferocious, bloody, and wasteful in the extreme."[57] But the Asiatic conquerors "very soon abated of their ferocity, because they made the conquered country their own." It was the British "protection that destroys India . . . young men govern there, without society and without sympathy with the natives," extracting money from the inhabitants, and controlling the whole revenue of the country by a spoils system. For Burke, on December 1, 1783, the government of the Company was "absolutely incorrigible" both in conduct and constitution: he spoke of its peculation, oppression, and tyranny.[58] He could not, however, persuade the House of Commons, which defeated the East India Bill and with it the government. With William Pitt as the new prime minister, Burke's party was out of power for a generation.

In opposition once again after 1783, Burke's rhetoric on British policy in Indian affairs increased in ferocity and extremism in parliamentary debates. In his speech of July 30, 1784, on Almas Ali Khan, Burke claimed to speak on behalf of those Indians "whom our barbarous policy had ruined and made desperate" and whose grievances "were unparalleled in history."[59] The Company's treatment of Khan, the largest revenue administrator in Oudh, was an "exercise of a ferocity, the foulest and the most atrocious, that ever blackened the use of usurped authority." Burke continued this severe criticism of British rule in another of his great speeches on February 28, 1785, regarding the Nabob of Arcot's debts, an issue he regarded as a corrupt bargain between Pitt's government and the Nabob's creditors, involving "fraud, injustice, oppression, [and] peculation."[60] Again, he spoke of that rule as shameless, corrupt, totally perverted from its purposes, "a bloated, putrid, noisome carcass, full of stench and poison."

THE IMPEACHMENT OF HASTINGS

From 1786 Burke made clear his intention to impeach Warren Hastings, whom he saw as the personification of the evils in India, for high crimes and misdemeanors. On April 25, 1787, he brought the first seven articles of impeachment, which he regarded as an act of imperial justice to protect the rights of the dependent people in the empire. These seven articles were reduced to four during the course of the trial. The House of Commons agreed to impeach on December 10, 1787, and trial began in the House of Lords on February 13, 1788, with Burke as the manager and leading figure. Burke, playing the most central role in his political career, put the whole system of British rule on trial through Hastings, "the first man of India, in rank, authority, and station."[61] The impeachment dragged on until April 29, 1795, partly because Pitt shrewdly recognized it was absorbing the time and talents of Opposition leaders, especially Burke. Though the trial lasted more than seven years, different members of the Lords actually sat only on 149 days for a few hours each time. Only forty peers attended more than half the sittings, and only twenty-nine peers took part in the verdict of acquittal on all charges.[62] The disappointed Burke, in his final parliamentary speech spread over two weeks, May 28 to June 12, 1794, a few weeks before resigning his seat in the House of Commons, using the metaphor of a stage production wondered "by what secret movement the master of the mechanism has conducted the great Indian opera, an opera of grand deceptions, and harlequin tricks."[63] Burke sadly confessed that on the Indian issue he had labored with the most assuity and met with the least success.

Even recognizing, as did Macaulay, that Burke's imagination and passion went, in extravagant fashion, "beyond the bounds of justice and good sense," and aware of the scatological, and sometimes sexual, images in his prose, how can one account for the intensity and vehemence of his attack on Hastings?[64]

Writing to Sir Thomas Rumbold on March 23, 1781, Burke remarked, while disagreeing with the policy of Hastings that led to war against the Rohillas, that he did not speak "from the smallest degree of prejudice or animosity" against him; Burke confessed "I was always an admirer of his talents."[65] He agreed that Hastings had performed a valuable service in printing the code of Indian jurisprudence. In letters at the end of his life Burke maintained there was nothing personal in the attack. To Lord Loughborough, circa March 17, 1796, "What motive could I have for personal animosity to a man, whose face I never remember to have seen till he came to make his defense in the House of Commons? A man with whom I never had any intercourse whatever, a man with whom I never had any personal, or any party quarrel?"[66] He made the same point on December 14, 1784, to Lord Thurlow that Hastings "never gave me cause directly or indirectly."[67] Burke explained that India "under his care is sacked and pillaged, and I know he is the government."

In his opening impeachment speech, on February 15, 1788, Burke refers to Hastings as "the chief of the tribe, the head of the whole body of Eastern offenders, a captain-general of iniquity, under whom all the frauds, all the peculations, all the tyranny in India are embodied, disciplined, and arrayed." He referred to "Mr. Hastings' government (as) one whole system of oppression, of robbery of individuals, of destruction of the public, and of supersession of the whole system of the English government."[68] Burke would not accept the argument of the Hastings defense that the "Moorish dominion" was more inhumane and perfidious than the English rule and any crimes of Hastings.[69]

Among those crimes were actions contrary to "those eternal laws of justice which are our rule and our birthright." Burke's campaign against the crimes continued to the end. On December 18, 1790, he wrote to John Hely Hutchinson that he was going to Parliament "to recommence my tenth year's warfare against the most dangerous enemy to the justice, honor, law, morals and constitution of this country, by which they have ever been attacked."[70] At the very end, after Hastings's acquittal, writing on December 28, 1796 to Dudley Long North, one of the managers of the impeachment, Burke said, "As to the nation, God of his mercy grant they may not suffer the penalties of the greatest and most shameful crime that ever was committed by any people."[71]

What could possibly be that crime about which he was so passionate? Burke's language, temperate for the most part but also often violent, extreme, relentless, and sometimes bordering on paranoia, increasingly took on a tone of a holy crusade. By historical coincidence the impeachment process overlapped with the events of the French Revolution and Burke linked them together. In a number of letters in his last years (1794–6), Burke spoke of the "two great evils of our time," "the different enemies which are sapping (our government and our laws), Indianism and Jacobinism." He explained he had been combating both of them for similar reasons; they were destroying the traditional order, they were corrupt, and they exercised power in arbitrary fasion. Not unexpectedly he held that the first "is the worst by far and the hardest to deal with."[72] Though he never defined "Indianism," one assumes from the context that it meant corrupt and oppressive power, arbitrary rule, in India.[73] The other enemy, Jacobinism, was indirectly alluded to in Burke's *Reflections on the French Revolution* in which he wrote that although the monarchy in pre-Revolution France was full of abuses, reforms were being considered and corrective checks on power were present, and "to hear some men speak of the late monarchy of France, you would imagine that they were talking of Persia bleeding under the ferocious sword of Tahmas Kouli Khan or at least describing the barbarous anarchic despotism of Turkey."

In the cases of both France and India, abuse of or uncontrolled power was his main concern. In the latter case, the Company was "one of the most corrupt and destructive tyrannies that probably ever existed in the world." Its crimes and those of Hastings "have their rise . . . in everything that manifests a heart blackened to the very blackest . . . a heart corrupted, vitiated, and gangrened to the very core."[74] Hastings was not only personally corrupt, in accepting "presents" (bribes) and improperly awarding contracts but also was responsible for "systematic, premeditated corruption of the whole service from the time he was appointed."[75] By the end of the impeachment trial Hastings had become "the most daring criminal that ever existed" (February 15, 1788), a "mere bullock contractor" (May 30, 1794), a Macbeth (June 3, 1794), a "bad scribbler of absurd papers" (May 30, 1794), a swindling Mecaenas, the head of a gang of plunderers and robbers, a tyrant, oppressor, and murderer.[76]

The extravagant and excessive rhetoric was present from the start of Burke's campaign against both the Company and its head. On February 13, 1786, informing the Commons of his future campaign against Hastings, he said that this business "of great national importance" was "the greatest and most important inquiry that ever appeared before a human tribunal."[77] Similarly, in his speech on Almas Ali Khan on July 30, 1784, he swore "that the wrongs done to humanity in the Eastern world shall be avenged on those who have inflicted them."[78] By the end of the trial, the Company and Hastings had been responsible for a "great encyclopedia of crimes," the "enormous and overpowering influence of Eastern corruption, the greatest moral earthquake that ever convulsed and shattered this globe of ours."[79]

Burke was the manager of the impeachment proceedings and the formulator of the charges against Hastings. Those original charges, attempting to cover the whole of Hastings's administration, consisted of twenty-two articles concerning violation of treaties made with the Nawab of Oudh, interference in internal affairs in Oudh, cruelty in the cases of Chait Singh and the Begams of Oudh, arbitrary settlement of the land revenues of Bengal, fraudulent deals in contracts and commissions, and acceptance of presents and bribes. Some charges against Hastings concerned policy issues, internal administration, revenue, and foreign policy; others involved allegations of personal corruption, which included acquiring money for himself or for rewarding adherents.[80]

Historians still differ about the validity of Burke's charges. Certainly some of them had merit, even if impeachment proceedings were not the most appropriate venue for their discussion.[81] The most convincing were the injustice in 1780 to Chait Singh, the rajah of Benares who was forced to contribute money or to offer a bribe, depending on interpretation; the treatment of the Begams of Oudh in 1782; and some other questionable activity. Yet almost all commentators agree that Burke's charges and condemnations were excessive and that his vituperation against Hastings went far beyond the bounds of acceptable discourse.

At the same time there was little unqualified praise of Hastings. For one objective analyst the career of Hastings "has always been and probably always will be a subject of controversy."[82] Even some of his allies could not defend all of his financial administration. Macaulay, who praised Hastings's "singular equanimity and fertile mind," recognized he had committed some crimes yet regarded him as a great public servant, "one of the most remarkable men in our history," who had produced in India order – a system for dispensing justice, collecting revenue, and maintaining peace.[83] A recent writer holds that Hastings rewarded his friends extravagantly even if he was personally not corrupt.[84] If one commentator sees Hastings as an authoritarian person, ready to justify his conduct by the argument of state necessity, and as the controller of Bengal who performed arbitrary and ruthless acts, another scholar concludes he was a good administrator in a difficult period, though less competent on revenue problems.[85] In a long letter to David Anderson on September 13, 1786, Hastings pointed out his own best features: "integrity and zeal; affection for my fellow servants, and regard for the country which I governed; [various other administrative qualities]; and patience, long suffering, confidence, and decision."[86]

Part of the problem in assessing the role and character of Hastings is that he acted in a country where, as Smith remarked, "power was uncertain, jurisdiction undefined, and successions disputed all over India. . . . The emperor had nearly all the rights and hardly any of the powers of government."[87] But also, Hastings rarely enunciated the major premises on which he would act. Disappointingly, Hastings, in his review of the state of Bengal written in 1786, did not explain "those principles which are necessary to the preservation" (of the

Company) in India. In his memoirs written at sea during his passage from India to England in 1786, he wrote "I am sure that the Company possessed a political character . . . before the period in which I was appointed to the principal administration of their affairs." Hastings stated he was not the author of the changes in the system of rule, which were "sown by the hand of calamity . . . nourished by fortune and cultivated and shaped . . . by necessity." At first the system was commercial; it obtained "in its growth, the sudden accession of military strength and territorial dominion, to which its political adjunct was inevitable." It was a mistake to think of the Company "still as a body of merchants, and consider commerce as their only object."[88]

Hastings was aware of the criticisms aroused by the Company's military operations and other activities, and the burdens, inconveniences, and sufferings they produced. He also knew that accusations of party adherents who "exaggerate the temporary evil that exists" were added to the complaints of individuals. In response Hastings argued that these critics ignored the fact that the territories under Company control were not only better cultivated than any other area of India but also were superior to their condition before Company rule.[89] In his major statement in 1786 in defense of his administration Hastings dealt almost entirely with the details of the charges made against him. But in a short passage he did offer an explanation of the basis of his powers in Bengal. Sovereignty there "fell to his lot" quite unexpectedly; he was "too little of a lawyer" to know if his sovereign powers were delegated to him by any act of Parliament. The Company, however, clearly and indisputably did possess sovereignty, ceded by the vizier, and its rights were those established by "the law, custom, and usage of the Mughal Empire" and not by an act of the British parliament. It was those rights that Hastings was "the involuntary instrument of enforcing." Any future British statute that aimed at limiting those rights would result in sovereignty becoming a "burden instead of a benefit, a heavy clog rather than a precious gem." Only a "uniform compact body" could control the problems arising from the variety of arrangements of landed property and feudal jurisdiction, the divided and unsettled state of society, and the anarchy and confusion of different laws, religions, and prejudices, moral, civil, and political, all jumbled together.[90]

In his 1786 *Memoirs*, Hastings did argue for strong rule by the governor in India, but he added to prevent any misunderstanding that he meant only "such powers as appertain to the nature of government, not to such as might affect the lives, persons, or property of individuals."[91] But no such limitation was apparent in his letter to Pitt of December 11, 1784 that it "is necessary that the Governor, or first executive member [of the Company], should possess a power absolute and complete within himself and independent of actual control."[92]

Hastings recognized that this might be an "unpopular doctrine, and repugnant to our domestic constitution, and may therefore be rejected." Nevertheless, other arrangements "cannot be too despotic for the rule of a province so remote of a free state like that of Great Britain." Perhaps Hastings envisaged a kind of benevolent despotism because he was always conscious of the need to take account of local sentiment and fellow officials.

In a letter of March 26, 1772, to Mr. Colebrooke, chairman of the Company Court of Directors, Hastings, discussing possible administrative and financial changes, remarked that though many regulations would be necessary, they would exclude those "perhaps which the original constitution of the Mughal Empire hath not before established and adopted and thereby rendered familiar to the people."[93] He also disclaimed that he acted unilaterally or as a despot. Hastings explained in a letter of August 3, 1773 to the Revenue Board that he had "cautiously abstained from every act of authority" over the new Calcutta Court of Justice, "which have always [been left] at full liberty to follow the unbiased dictates of their own judgments."[94] He also, in 1786, defended himself as "sometimes availing myself of the transitory moments of power which the hand of God afforded me, at others using the resistance which the influence of possession or opinion enabled me to make or the caution of opposition permitted . . . never possessing the allowance of authority but always charged with responsibility."[95]

Whatever differences of interpretation of his administrative, judicial, and financial actions and changes in Bengal, and on his extension of British power in the subcontinent, there is no doubt Hastings was a man of scholarship and a linguist in Persian, the diplomatic language, Bengali, the local language, Urdu, and some Arabic. Burke entirely neglected Hastings's interest in and encouragement of Oriental studies, generally sympathetic attitude toward Hinduism and Indian culture, conviction that British officials should be knowledgeable about Indian law and customs, and encouragement of the study of Sanskrit.[96] Equally, he ignored Hastings's desire to preserve Indian society and its institutions, to impose rules of conduct or standards for property on Indians, and to adhere to traditional Indian methods and forms of government where possible.[97] Despite Burke's charges against him Hastings can be regarded as the real founder of British Orientalism in India and of a British civil service elite there that was acculturated to the society, could communicate in native languages, and was concerned with the welfare of the people.[98]

MUGHAL INDIAN HISTORY AND CULTURE

The case presented by Burke against Hastings, and indirectly against the Company, can be looked at in two ways: the factual accuracy of the charges of impeachment and the analysis of Indian history and thoughts about arbitrary or despotic power. Few have been willing to follow Burke in detail when assessing Hastings's guilt or innocence, and conclusions on the matter are disputed. More important for our purpose is assessment of Burke's analysis of the key players and the nature of Indian history, including the role of the Company. The discussion of Indian history by Burke and the Hastings defense are almost wholly concerned with the rulers of the Mughal Empire, with only perfunctory attention given to the majority Hindu population and political regimes that had been supplanted. The Muslim invaders, including Tamerlane and Genghis Khan, had come from central Asia, defeated the Afghans who had ruled part of North India since the eleventh century, and maintained uneasy relations with the Hindu majority. The Mughal Empire was founded by Babar in 1526, but its first important ruler was Akhbar, who in 1556 took the throne at age fourteen and ruled for forty-nine years, subjugating some parts of the country and annexing others, and creating a viable administrative structure.[99] Most of his successors were less gifted.

By the eighteenth century the Mughal Empire had begun to decline, though the emperor, the Great Mughal, in nominal fashion continued his supposed great authority. In effect, the great nobles, governors, and princes controlled their individual areas. Quasi-independent kingdoms were carved out of the ruins of the empire by native governors, often freeing themselves of real obligations to Delhi or to the Great Mughal's viceroy in Hyderabad.[100] In addition to civil war that raged intermittently, further disintegration resulted from the rise of the Marathas, guerrilla armies, in the seventeenth century, and from the invasion by the Persian King, Nadir Shah, who sacked Delhi in 1739.

In theory, the Mughal emperor had absolute power, unlimited by restrictions except Islamic law, but in practice he was assisted by ministers in daily administration.[101] No code of criminal or civil law existed other than judgments by individuals following Koranic precepts. The character of the Mughal regime, whether or not it is characterized as Oriental despotism, depended on the capacity and temperament of the ruler, his personal wishes, and his military power to maintain internal order and wage war or preserve peace.[102] The Hindu majority was at first treated with tolerance, but the later rulers were less congenial with orders to destroy unfinished and some established Hindu temples and to construct mosques in their place. For Hindus the system appeared even more alien with, at least at first, senior positions being filled by Persians and Afghans. The Mughal Empire declined in the eighteenth century as a result of various factors: self-indulgent and inefficient rulers, widespread poverty amid imperial splendor and lavish expenditure on magnificent monuments, inability to fulfill police functions, deterioration of the army, civil wars over the imperial succession and political positions, and military humiliation and widespread corruption.

The political vacuum caused by the Mughal disintegration was filled by European trading companies and rivalries between the major West European countries from which Britain emerged as the dominant power. The Company had become a political and military power employing soldiers and governors. British authority in India derived partly from the British crown and parliament and partly from the Great Mughal and other native rulers. The exercise of power was even more complex because Britain had different arrangements in different parts of the country. In Bombay the Company, by grant under the British crown, had sovereign powers over issues such as military troops, justice, levying taxes, and coining money. In Madras and Calcutta it operated by grants from Indian rulers.[103]

After the victory of Robert Clive, who established the military and political supremacy of the Company in Southern India and Bengal by his victory at Plassy in 1757 over the last fully independent Nawab of Bengal, the Company in reality had become the sovereign power in Bengal. In 1772 Warren Hastings, who had first served in India between 1750 and 1764 as a Company official, returned as governor of Bengal and later governor-general of India. Hastings was adept at raising money and increased his range of activities in territories beyond Bengal, including Benares. He wielded power over the territories through his control over the nominal sovereign, the Nawab of Oudh, leasing out the Company's troops to the nawab at a high price, extorting money for the Company, and allowing Company officials to engage in individual extortion for their private purposes. Sometimes this practice of extortion and bribery led to improper pressure or torture.[104]

Two of the most notorious cases of this practice, which were prominently featured in the impeachment process, concerned the two eunuchs of the Begams of Oudh and the Brahmin businessman Maharaja Nandakumar, usually referred to as Nuncomar. In the first case the eunuchs were tortured to reveal the location of the large sums of money received by the Begams (the mother and grandmother of the young prince who inherited the position of Nawab of Oudh in 1774) from the deceased nawab. In the second case, Nuncomar, who had alleged that Hastings had accepted a bribe from the former chief minister of the nawab to allow him to get out of prison by dropping charges against him, was arrested on charges of felony and found guilty by the Bengal Supreme Court, presided over by a friend of Hastings. Because British law at that time allowed capital punishment for forgery, Nuncomar was put to death.[105]

In making his case, Burke differed sharply from the Hastings argument about Mughal emperors and the character of their rule. He changed his mind on the issue, after some ambivalence when he first dealt with it. Though, on March 30, 1772, he held that Mughal government was not arbitrary because "there is an equitable government by the Koran," in general he was at first critical of Mughal power. In notes for a speech in 1779 Burke spoke of "the cruel tyranny and usurpation of the Muhammads over Tanjore" and felt that the Hindus were suffering under Muslim tyranny.[106] Burke may have been influenced on this point by his friend William Fullarton, former commander of one of the British armies in Southern India, who wrote of Tanjore, "so wanton and iniquitous is the sway of despotism there that the goods of the merchant or carrier are frequently seized by order of the ruler, the Durbar."[107]

Burke was at his most critical in the pamphlet written by William Burke and himself, *Policy of Making Conquests for the Mahometans*, in 1779 in reply to one written by James Macpherson on behalf of the Nawab of the Carnatic. In it, Burke, assuming that he had written most of the pamphlet, and writing in favor of the Rajah of Tangore, who had been deposed in 1773 and then restored in 1776, tried to portray the rajah as an independent, sovereign ruler by right. In doing so he was caustic about the bitter and implacable enemy of the rajah, Muhammadan despotism with its "ferocious rapacity." In nations ruled by Muhammadan government, "there is no settled law or construction, either to fix allegiance or restrain power."[108] Burke's generalizations refer not simply to the specific case of Tanjore but more widely to "the horrors of the Muhammadan government in India," its destruction of the eminent nobility, oppression of the industrious part of the Indian community, fierce and cruel nature, and imposition of "the intolerable burden of the Muhammadan yoke."

Similarly, in one of his speeches on the Bengal Judicature Bill of June 1781 he compared the "free system of Great Britain" to the "system of rule more despotic" with which Indians were familiar and that had become congenial to them. The British, Burke argued, in their rule of India must be guided "as we ought to have been with respect to America, by studying the genius, the temper, and the manners of the people, and adapting to them the laws that we establish."[109] He was to make a similar argument in his speech on the East India Bill. Even in his opening impeachment statement Burke spoke of the "era of great misfortune . . . the era of the Prophet Muhammad who has extended his dominion, influence, and religion over [India]."[110] Despotism was connected with his religion in this era of the Arabs, which lasted through a dynasty of thirty-three kings.

But this was only a prelude to a more tolerant attitude to "the ancient people" and their property and religion and to the "ancient sovereigns of the country possessed of an inferior sovereignty." At the same time, in the early years Burke also spoke more kindly of some Islamic people, the Rohillas, the

Oudh royal family, and the emperor Shah Alam, "amiable in his manners, respectable for his piety according to his mode, and accomplished in all the Oriental literature."[111] He also, in the *Observations* on the First Report of the House Select Committee, wrote in February 1782 that it was an error to regard the people in the areas ruled by Britain as living "without any fixed law before the British establishment." The Muhammadans were subject to the Muhammadan law, as it is found in the Koran and its authorized interpreters, and all persons, from the lowest slave to the most powerful prince, were bound by it.[112] By the time of Burke's opening speech of impeachment he was trying to show that Islamic governments were based on law. Even the sultan (the Grand Seignior) was not arbitrary because he did not even have "the supreme power" in the Ottoman Empire.[113] In his last impeachment speech he regarded Islamic law as "law interwoven into a system of the wisest, the most learned, the most enlightened jurisprudence that perhaps ever existed in the world."[114]

Burke's argument as it developed saw the Mughals as moderate and restrained by law, approved Islamic rule, and praised individual rulers. The Mughals, after trying to convert Hindus, had "suffered their religion to operate on them as it could." The emperors never destroyed the native nobility, gentry, or landholders. The rajahs were not in an abject state under Tamerlane. On the contrary, during his reign and that of his successors, "which we consider a despotism," the chief rajahs "were admitted to easy reconciliations" instead of being treated as wretches. Tamerlane was no barbarian, but an emperor who was just, prudent, and politic, different from "the ferocious, oppressive Muhammadans who had forced their sword into the country."[115]

For Burke the perusal of the Islamic laws as well as the Institutes of Genghis Khan and of Tamerlane did not show arbitrary power. Quoting the latter work, Burke concluded no other book "contains nobler, more just, more manly, more pious principles of government than this book." The Islamic laws are binding on everyone. It is an utter falsehood to argue that "the people have no laws, no rights, no usages, no distinction, no sense of honor, no property; and that they are nothing but a herd of slaves, to be governed by the arbitrary will of a master whose rights are everything and their rights nothing."[116] On the contrary, Burke argued, on May 30, 1794, "the sovereign is rather nothing, and the people are everything."[117]

Carried away by his passion, Burke exalted Indian history: "these people lived under the law which was formed even whilst we . . . were in the forest, before we knew what jurisprudence was." Hastings was wrong to have ransacked all Asia for principles of despotism and to have believed that this was the norm of Indian history in order to justify his own arbitrary rule.[118] The morality of the East was equal "to ours as regards the morality of governors, fathers, superiors." Hastings was not justified in claiming that despotism was the genuine constitution of India. Nor was the British governor-general "possessed of an arbitrary and despotic power, bound by no laws whatever but his own will" by any grant from the British parliament or the Company. India was not the seat of arbitrary power nor of "a government of misrule, productive of no happiness till subverted" by British rule. Burke contrasted the beneficent system of laws in India with the arbitrary power of Hastings.[119]

According to Burke neither Tamerlane nor Genghis Khan was an arbitrary monarch or despotic authority. Both were elected to their office, the latter calling "a great parliament" and getting its consent.[120] Genghis Khan was bound by laws and was responsible in turn for good and wise laws, even over conquered territory. Similarly, Tamerlane never claimed arbitrary power but considered the nobility his brethren and the people as his children. Burke even compared Hastings unfavorably to the two Mughal emperors; the British ruler was "bloated with corruption . . . insolence of undeserved and unmerited power . . . an arbitrary sovereign . . . declaring that the people have no rights, no property, no laws."[121] Neither the laws of the Mughals, the Hindus, or the Muhammadans could support the power of Hastings or sanction arbitrary power. Nor could the Mughals have given the Company despotic power when they gave charters to it.[122] The Company had only limited power by law, just as the Mughal emperors were obliged to govern by law and by compact.[123] Similarly, the Company had never bestowed arbitrary power on Hastings.[124] Burke was critical of Hastings on two grounds. Hastings had violated British law in claiming "that high, supreme, legislative sovereignty which the law attributes, with the consent of both Houses of Parliament, to the King, and the King only." Also, Hastings had abrogated "the refined, enlightened curious, elaborate technical jurisprudence of Islamic law."[125]

DISPUTING BURKE'S VIEWS OF MUGHAL RULE

Burke's picture of an ideal Indian past also included, through all the revolutions and changes in the Mughal era, "a Hindu policy and Hindu government . . . until finally to be destroyed by Mr. Hastings." In the sixteenth century the Hindus "were a favored, protected, gently treated people," and this continued in the era of Tamerlane.[126] Even under the cruel tyrants (the Muslim rulers, the virtually autonomous subahdars in Bengal in the "troubled and vexatious" era of the eighteenth century), the Hindus "were everywhere in possession of the country . . . and still preserved their rank, their dignity, their castles, their houses, their seignories."[127] Quoting a work by John Holwell, Burke painted an idyllic picture of the old Hindu system in which the property as well as the liberty of people was inviolate and where "no robberies are heard of, either public or private."[128] This state of affairs, with a Hindu policy and government, was disturbed by the "barbarism of foreign conquests" until they were destroyed by Hastings in 1756.

Burke's picture of an idyllic period, however, does not coincide with general historical analysis; the more acceptable view is that of Macaulay's portrait showing "no known and definite constitution in India" after Tamerlane, but rather a condition of transition, confusion, and obscurity.[129] Many other historians are even more critical, pointing out the cruelty, fanaticism, and profligacy of the rulers.[130] It was the very inability of native administration in the mid-eighteenth century to act competently that led first to the system of dual government, by which the British under Clive were granted land revenue and administered civil justice, and then to the expansion of the powers of the Company as the native system withered.[131]

Against Burke's version of Indian history, Edward Law, the main defense lawyer for Hastings and destined to become Lord Chief Justice, argued on February 14, 1792, for "a fair, plain, candid representation of the actual situation" in India, devoid of Burke's "high-wrought colorings, with ideal representations of an unreal and imaginary state of things . . . made up of dream and fiction."[132] Basic to the defense argument was that arbitrary or despotic power was the norm in Islamic India. Even the early history, pre-Islamic under the Brahmans, was not a sort of golden age in which the lamb and the tiger laid down together; rather it was a history of bloody wars, in which millions of men and thousands of elephants were involved. For Law, "the Muhammadan era was a system not of government but of cruelty and rapine . . . nothing but the spoilation of the miserable people considered by the Muhammadans as idolators, and carried by destruction of the country and massacre." In his panegyric on the arts and civilization of the Rohilla Afghans, Burke had called them "the most honorable nation on earth" and referred to their land as "the garden of Eden"; for Hastings, the Rohillas were a military tribe "who quartered themselves on the people."[133]

The general Western perception of India and the nature of its governmental system came largely from information gathered by individuals discussed in earlier chapters, such as travelers, merchants, ambassadors, and missionaries, among the most important of whom were Sir Thomas Roe, ambassador of James I to the Mughal court, and François Bernier, who visited India in 1668.[134] Montesquieu, as we have seen, was one of those who derived information from these same sources. Not surprisingly, Burke, aware of the impact of the travelers, said on May 13, 1794, "I mean to prove that every word which

Montesquieu has taken from idle and inconsiderate travelers is absolutely false."[135] Not until the late eighteenth century did scholarly studies emerge on the subcontinent, largely because the Company wanted its officials to be familiar with the law and history of the area. Others studied classical Sanskrit literature and the Asian religions. The doyen of these studies, Sir William Jones, the early scholar who had mastered Middle Eastern as well as Western European and classical languages, wrote as his first book a *Grammar of the Persian Language*. In 1784 the Asiatic Society was founded. With the help of Hastings the College of Arabic Studies was founded in Calcutta in 1781.

Edward Law, knowing little of Indian history and society, relied heavily on the seventeenth- and eighteenth-century writers who had influenced Western perceptions of the Orient; among others he used Gibbon, Alexander Dow, Major James Rennell, D'Herbelot, Edward Terry, Jean de Mandelslo, Jean-Baptiste Tavernier, François Bernier, and Montesquieu to reply to Burke's eulogy of the Mughal era, especially about Tamerlane.[136] D'Herbelot ascribed to the Tartar leader Tamerlane the sayings that a prince should always have his sword in motion, and that a monarch was never safe on his throne except when a great deal of blood was shed around him.[137] From Gibbon, Law took the aphorism that Tamerlane "erected on the ruins of Baghdad a pyramid of 90,000 heads." Alexander Dow, author of the *History of Hindustan*, is quoted on the consequences of a military victory of Tamerlane, who gave orders to put everyone above the age of fifteen to the sword; "100,000 men were massacred in cold blood." Major Rennell called Tamerlane an "inhuman monster . . . who obtained in Hindustan the title of the Destroying Prince." Law contrasted this record of cruelty with the absence of any well-authenticated instance of personal cruelty under British rule.[138]

To meet Burke's defense of pre-British rule, Law sought to establish that, with some few exceptions, the history of Islamic India was one of intemperate power. Even Akhbar, "a prince of great generosity and liberality" who reigned forty-nine years, "permitted himself the use of the base arts of assassination and poison." Ironically he mistakenly took poison intended for another and died. After this long reign, the country suffered from continual turbulence, civil wars, assassination of sons of the prince, and from the exercise of arbitrary power, defined as a governmental system dependent entirely on the discretion of the sovereign. After his recital of the vices and iniquities of the Mughal rulers, assassinations, fratricide, poisonings, brutish pleasures, brutal extraction of revenue, religious persecution, and despotic disposing of lives and fortunes, Law argued that "the government of Asia, before it was supplanted by the free government of Britain was a government of misrule . . . no benefit to the governed . . . every species of vexation, cruelty, and oppression."

The group of writers on whom Law relied all indicated the existence of arbitrary power. Edward Terry, chaplain to the British ambassador to Emperor Jehan Ghyr quoted Aristotle, rather inaccurately, to describe the Mughal system as "despotic, arbitrary, unlimited, tyrannical, such as a most severe master uses to servants, not that which a good king administers to subjects." The king measured his power by his sword in making his will his guide. In language similar to that to be used by Montesquieu, Terry thought no laws regulated governors (in the empire) in the administration of justice except what was written in the breast of the king and his substitutes. In addition, making a point that would be important for later writers, including Marx in his work on India, Terry believed "there is never a subject in that empire who has land of inheritance which he may call his own, but they are tenants at the will of their king."

Three others can be quoted on this point. Mandelslo, with ambassadorial experience in Moscow and Persia, wrote, "The authority of the Mughal is so great, and his sovereignty so absolute that he is master of the whole property of all his subjects . . . he disposes despotically of all their lives and fortunes . . . the greatest lords are executed at his mere command." Similarly, Tavernier believed that "The Great Mughal is surely the most rich and powerful monarch of Asia, the territories which he possesses being his own hereditary possessions, and being absolute master of all the territories when he receives his revenues."[139] François Bernier said, "All the lands of the kingdom [are] the emperor's property," an argument repeated by F. E. Catrou. Quoting from Catrou and John Ogilby on the simple form of government in which "the emperor alone is the soul of it," Law also relied on Montesquieu's assertion that "the people of Asia are governed by the cudgel and the inhabitants of Tartary by whips."[140]

Law took the House of Lords through a brief assessment of the different Mughal rulers. He spoke of the cruelty of Jaffier Khan who controlled the provinces of Bengal, Behar, and Orissa under Aurungzebe, and whose character could be summed up in rigid exaction of the revenue, in merciless and undistinguishing punishment of all offenders, and a zealous, persecuting attachment to the faith of Muhammad. A later prince, Jehander Shah, degraded the Mughal throne of Delhi with brutish and low vices and scenes in the capital "that were fit for the times of Heliogabalus and Caracalla."[141] His successor, Farouksir, was blinded and deposed. Under Mohammed Shah the Mughal Empire crumbled to pieces in 1717. But the cruelties in India continued under other rulers in an increasingly complex situation in which power was exercised at different times and in different places by the Sikhs, the Mahrattas along the west coast, the Jats, the Rohillas, the governments of Oude, Arcot, and the Deccan under Nawabs and the Nizam. Into this complex and unsettled set of conditions British power was introduced and forced to defend itself from attacks, especially in Calcutta, and from destruction. For Law, in view of these conditions, the British Empire in India was founded on a just cause and in self-defense.

In May 1794 Burke objected, in his long-delayed reply to Law, to the whole argument of the defense that he said was based on "an extended series of quotations from books of travelers, for the purpose of showing that despotism was the only principle of government acknowledged in India." This he tried to do by his historical survey of Indian laws and customs. On the fourth day of the trial Burke challenged "the whole race of man to show me any of the Oriental governors claiming to themselves a right to act by arbitrary will."[142] In manuscript fragments of notes containing some material not included in Burke's final speeches, he succinctly presented the case he would have to oppose. Hastings, in what Burke called his "system of principles of maxims of government" invented to justify his misdemeanors, laid it down as a rule that despotism is the genuine constitution of India, that a disposition to rebellion in the subject, or dependent prince, is the necessary effect of this despotism, and that jealousy and its consequences naturally arise on the part of the sovereign.[143] Burke answered these "principles" in equally epigrammatic fashion. Nothing was more false than that despotism was the constitution of any country in Asia he knew. Despotism was not part of any Muhammadan constitution. Despotism did not abrogate duties or "weaken the force and obligation of engagements or contracts." Despotism may not have a written law to bind it, but this did not cancel the "primeval, indefeasible, unalterable law of nature and of nations."[144] Earlier in 1786, Burke had asserted that though Magna Carta was not present in India, the people there had the law of nature and nations, the great and fundamental axioms on which every form of society was built.

PERCEPTIONS OF ORIENTAL DESPOTISM

At the core of the whole dispute between Burke and the Hastings defense was the question of Oriental despotism, or arbitrary power, as it was termed by both sides. A number of general issues were confronted. Was arbitrary power the norm of Asian governments, especially Islamic regimes, and the habitual form of rule accepted for centuries in India? If so, did British rule have the right to exercise arbitrary power or to act in accordance with what it conceived to be standard practices and local standards, even if those standards were morally different from those applicable in British politics, or were the laws of morality the same everywhere? Did British rule have to govern on the basis of what it considered to be existing reality in India or were moral obligations imposed on the British occupiers? Even if they concurred that British rule should follow Indian precedents as much as possible, Burke and Hastings did not agree on what those precedents were, nor on the nature of Mughal government, nor on the interpretation of customs, nor even on specific questions such as property rights and the status of the *zamindar*, landholder, whose precise legal position and rights were controversial.[145] At the same time it is not easy, as Marshall observes, to see fundamental differences between the two adversaries on the aims and methods of British rule in India.[146]

Burke's view of despotism, whenever he mentioned the subject in earlier writings, derived from Montesquieu.[147] Despotic governments were founded on the passions of men and principally on the passion of fear. Despotism abhorred "power held by any means but its own momentary pleasure." Its nature was to "annihilate all intermediate situations between boundless strength on its own part, and total debility on the part of the people."

With this definition in mind, Burke, in his opening impeachment speech of February 16, 1788, first tried to state the essence of Hastings's position on arbitrary power before refuting it. British rule and arbitrary power in Bengal, ceded by the vizier of Benares, in Burke's version of Hastings, stemmed from the law, custom, and usage of the Mughal Empire, not from the British parliament. The differing assessments by the two of the nature of the empire therefore became crucial. The secondary question was whether the British parliament hindered Hastings from exercising "this despotic authority." Burke tried to dispose of what he conceived to be the basic view that Asian governments had been arbitrary and therefore Hastings was entitled to act in the same way. This was a travesty of Hastings's position that, never expounded in any complete fashion, seemed to limit the use of arbitrary power to emergency situations or to discretionary power. "I never," said Hastings in the House of Lords on June 2, 1791, "considered that my will or caprice was to be the guide of my conduct."[148] He believed he had acted on the basis of political necessity or *raison d'état*. At one point on May 28, 1794, Burke did acknowledge, guardedly, that there had previously been arbitrary power in India, tyrants had usurped it, and sometimes meritorious princes had violated the liberties of the people and had been deposed for it.[149] He also acknowledged that Hastings was invested with discretionary power, but that power had to be used according to the established rules of political morality, humanity, and equity, and "in regard to foreign powers, he was bound to act under the law of nature, and under the law of nations."[150]

However, Burke created, in slightly different language at the beginning and at the end of the impeachment process, the intellectual structure that he would answer. Burke articulated Hastings views. Every part of Hindustan had been exposed to a variety of disadvantages ever since the Muhammadan conquests. The Hindus were kept in order only by the strong hand of power. Sovereignty in India implied nothing else but despotism. The whole history of Asia was nothing more than precedents to prove the invariable exercise of arbitrary power. That history, and the very nature of mankind, demonstrated that the subjects of a despotic empire were always vigilant for the moment to rebel, and the sovereign was always aware of rebellious intentions. As a result, Hastings had declared he was a despotic prince, that he could use arbitrary power, and that "all his acts are covered by that shield."[151] But his assertion that he knew the constitution of Asia only from its practices implied that the corrupt practices of mankind were to become the principles of government.

Burke on February 16, 1788, declared that Hastings thought the condition of the country made him govern "upon arbitrary and despotic, and, as he supposes, Oriental principles." The Hastings claim that arbitrary power was normal in Asia implied for Burke that there was no universal norm of morality in politics.[152] In that February 16, 1788, speech Burke insisted that Oriental governments knew nothing of arbitrary power. Most of Asia was under Muhammadan governments, and these were governments by law. "To name a Muhammadan government is to name a government by law."[153] Moreover, that law was more binding than in the case of European sovereigns because it was "given by God, and it has the double sanction of law and of religion," and no prince is able to dispense with it. Based on his reading of the Koran, Burke argued it did not authorize arbitrary power, and its exponents, "the great priesthood" or men of the law who are conservators of the law, were secured from the resentment of the sovereign.[154]

Burke challenged what he regarded as Hastings's explicit comparison of his power with that of the Ottoman sultan, the Grand Seignior, exalted in titles. Burke replied that the Grand Seignior could not tax his people, dispose of the life, property, or liberty of any subject, or declare peace or war except by a *fatwa*, a sentence of the law. Burke thought that the sultan, even more than European sovereigns, was a subject of strict law and might be deposed by that law. Muhammadan rulers could not exercise "any arbitrary power at all agreeably to their constitution."[155] Burke did admit the existence of corruption, murder, and false imprisonment in Asia, but this did not justify the actions of Warren Hastings. Burke also admitted the custom throughout Asia by which presents were given to rulers. Yet he also argued, without evidence, that the constitution of Asian countries disavowed them. Equally, Burke rejected the supposed Western perception that the people of Asia had no laws, rights, or liberties. On the contrary, every Muhammadan government was one of law founded on the Koran, the *fatwa*, cases adjudged by proper authority, the written interpretation of the principles of jurisprudence, the *Kanun* – the equivalent of acts of Parliament, and the common law of the kingdom.[156]

Among Burke's original charges of impeachment was one concerning the subverting of Indian laws, rights, and liberties and destruction of property, in the name of the people of India, the House of Commons, the eternal laws of justice, and in the name of human nature, which Hastings "had cruelly outraged, injured, and oppressed, in both sexes, in every age, rank, situation, and condition of life."[157] It was this appeal to a higher law that Burke employed to undermine Hastings's claim, or supposed claim, that use of arbitrary power in India was justified. Earlier in this chapter the controversial question was raised as to whether Burke is to be considered an exponent of natural rights theory and whether his political viewpoint was based primarily on natural law. It is manifest that Burke frequently attacked the concept of "metaphysical" or "abstract" rights – the "specious folly" of the rights of men he called it – as meaningless political argument. He was more likely to rely on prudence and Utilitarian expediency for the operation of government and also to maintain that wisdom was embodied in existing institutions and in traditions.[158] In one of his most well-known aphorisms, Burke proclaimed that "prudence is not only the first in rank of the virtues political and moral, but she is the director, the regulator, the standard of them all."[159]

Yet, from time to time in the various political issues that concerned him, Burke also appealed to the "natural rights of mankind," which were "sacred," or to moral natural law as political anchors.[160] In his great speech on the East India Bill on December 1, 1783, Burke based his case for control of the Company to some extent on the need to provide for the people of India "a real chartered security for the rights of men, cruelly violated" under the existing Company charter. Though he did not fully develop his argument, Burke implied that legal rights, to be valid, must correspond to natural rights.

Underlying this argument is Burke's assumption of some form of natural law that was the basis of human justice. Already in his speech on Almas Ali Khan on July 20, 1784, Burke had spoken of the one standard by which "the judge of all the earth would try" people and of "the prior rights of humanity, of substantial justice, with those rights which were paramount to all others."[161] Again, in the speech on February 28, 1785, regarding the Nabob of Arcot's debts, he argued, "The benefits of heaven to any community ought never to be connected with political arrangements, or made to depend on the personal conduct of princes."[162] The reliance on natural law became more pronounced in the impeachment speeches. "Will you ever," he asked the Lords on February 16, 1788, "hear the rights of mankind made subservient to the practice of government?"[163] He continued, in one of his most majestic passages, "We are all born . . . in subjection to one great, immutable, pre-existent law, a law prior to all our devices and all our contrivances . . . by which we are connected in the eternal frame of the universe, and out of which we cannot stir." For Burke, law and arbitrary power were eternally hostile. The person who would substitute will in the place of law is "an enemy to God."

In Burke's view Hastings would come in this category. Burke vehemently opposed the Hastings defense argument that actions in Asia did not bear the same moral qualities that the same actions would bear in Western Europe. He opposed this argument as "geographical morality" that is related to "climate, degrees of longitude and latitude"; he did not accept the view that moral standards for Europeans were not appropriate for others. On the contrary, the laws of morality are the same everywhere, and actions should be governed by relation "to the great Governor of the Universe" or to mankind. The rights of men, Burke considered, were sacred things. Britain should not suspend the universal moral and political norms that were applicable everywhere. The case against Hastings and his arbitrary power is not simply empirical, but it is based on a more fundamental foundation. All power, argues Burke, comes from God and "is bound by the eternal laws of Him that gave it which no human authority can dispense," neither ruler nor subject.[164]

The appeal to natural law, to eternal laws of justice, to final justice emanating from the Divinity, all phrases used by Burke, may have been a rhetorical device to convince the House of Lords that Hastings's actions were immoral and illegitimate or may have been deeply felt.[165] Whatever the motive, by making the appeal Burke could counter the arguments that India should not be regarded or British rule there be judged by the moral criteria and code appropriate in Western Europe. The laws of morality are the same everywhere.[166] For Burke, not to oppose despotism was a crime against the law of God, and only "absolute impotence" could justify such lack of opposition.[167] In the same way, anyone substituting will in the place of law was an enemy of God.

Yet, in spite of this recourse to eternal laws, Burke recognized that "custom" or "opinion" in India, as elsewhere, was important. We know, he said on February 15, 1788, and repeated on a number of occasions, "that if we govern such a country, we must govern them upon their own principles and maxims and not upon ours . . . we know that the empire of opinion is, I had almost said, human nature itself."[168] In his evidence on the Begams of Oudh on April 22, 1788, Burke argued that local customs "are stronger where they prevail than the customs of general nature . . . and that (they may be) the strongest influences that govern their minds."[169]

Hastings could not base his practical policy on such an elevated concept of natural law or eternal laws, but he did in fact accept a position similar to that of

Burke's that power should be limited, that British rule should conform as closely as possible to Indian models, respecting local culture, leaving local administration to Indians, and allowing his new courts to use traditional Hindu and Muslim law.[170] The Hastings defense rested on contemporary reality, not lofty rhetoric. Against Burke's intransigent argument that law should never give way to the "immediate momentary purpose of the day," Hastings responded that the actions for which he was criticized were taken in times of difficulty, distress and imminent danger.[171] He had always stated he did not want Hindu and Muslim law to be displaced by British law.

Sometimes Hastings used necessary powers to perform his task: "the dominion of an extensive kingdom, collection of vast revenue, command of armies, direction of a great political system."[172] In a letter to Lord North on January 20, 1776, Hastings, while discussing proposals for changes in the judicial system, also pointed out what he termed "an inherent prerogative of government," the power of using extraordinary force in cases of danger or insecurity or of an "unlicensed authority over the inhabitants, which may call for the sudden interposition of government."[173] This was a discretionary power in the hands of the governor, where it should remain.

In his final impeachment speech, starting May 28, 1794, Burke again stated the principles on which Hastings had acted and the essence of his argument. Hastings was possessed of an arbitrary and despotic power, restrained only by his own will.[174] For Hastings the rights of the people in India were nothing, and the rights of the government were everything. The people for Hastings "had no liberty, no laws, no inheritance, no fixed property . . . no subordinations in society, no sense of honor or of shame." The people are only affected by punishment if it is a "corporal infliction."

He asked the Lords to look at "the whole nature of the principles" of Hastings. The defense appealed to the custom and usage of the Mughal Empire, and the constitution of that empire was arbitrary power. Further, Hastings pretended that no present parliamentary statute restricted his exercise of arbitrary power, and also thought any future restraint would be undesirable if it hindered his exercising "this despotic authority."[175] Burke denied that any statute of the British parliament gave Hastings any such despotic power, nor did or could the Company give it. Burke denied that there exists anywhere a power to make the government of any state dependent on an individual will.

Similarly, the claim to arbitrary power was not supported by the laws of the Mughals, the Hindus, or the Muhammadans, or by any law, custom, or usage that has ever been recognized as legal and valid.[176] The Company never received the right to use despotic power in India or to overturn the existing Muhammadan political arrangements.[177] As in the case of the British parliament the Mughal who gave the Company their charters could not and did not give them such a power. If Hastings exercised despotic power, or his "darling arbitrary power" as Burke once called it, he usurped it.[178]

Hastings explained the maxims he had laid down for his conduct and by which it was invariably guided.[179] First, he wanted to implant the authority of the Company and the sovereignty of Britain in the constitution of India. But also, among his other maxims, he wanted to abolish all secret influence and make the government responsible for all measures, allow all complaints to reach him, relieve oppressive taxes, and introduce a regular system of justice and protection into the country. Hastings reviewed the nature of his administration in 1777.[180] He had tried to restore the authority of government, act directly instead of by indirect influence, manage the public revenue, establish regular courts, and transfer a share of wealth to Britain. He also explained that his discretionary power did not mean that will or caprice was to be the guide of his conduct.

Hastings took a more realistic view of pre-British rule than Burke said he did. Writing to Lord Chief Justice Mansfield on March 21, 1774, he explained he wanted to dispel the misperception about local law.[181] It was not true that written laws were totally unknown to the Hindus; rather they had laws since antiquity. These laws remained even under the bigotry of the Muhammadan government and should remain under British rule. To this end Hastings began a project to compile these laws, written in Sanskrit, and to translate them into Persian and English. The Muhammadan law was as comprehensive and as well defined as that of most states in Europe. Hastings informed Dr. Johnson, in a letter of August 7, 1775, that for different reasons he had employed "some of the most learned Muhammadan and Hindu inhabitants" to compile their respective laws.[182]

The dispute between Burke and Hastings on practical and philosophical matters had a significant effect on the intellectual controversy about the nature of rule in India, the ability of Westerners to understand non-Western societies, the morality of colonial rule, and the concept of stages of civilization, as well as on administrative behavior by British officials in India and the indirect effects of that behavior on British life and politics. Burke's onslaught against Hastings and his appeals to higher authority, the laws of local areas and principles of English law to justify his case did not end the perception that Oriental despotism was normal in India, especially because of the Mughals, nor did it prevent practical activity from being based on that perception. The successors to Hastings as governors-general of Bengal, Charles Cornwallis (1786–93) and Richard Wellesley (1798–1805), tended to think of the Indian past as one of the despotic native rulers, uniting legislative, executive, and judicial powers of the states, and exercising them according to their own discretion. They saw their task as limiting government power and preventing abuse.[183]

Later British administrators in the 1820s and the 1830s, such as Thomas Munro and Mountstuart Elphinstone, tended to believe that India had to be governed on the basis of native institutions and customs.[184] This view of governance differed from that proposed by Jeremy Bentham and James Mill and their fellow Utilitarians discussed in Chapter 7. For them the primary need was good government, sound revenue, and judicial systems, which would overcome the problems created by past despotic governments. This meant direct British, not indirect, rule because it would be efficient and eliminate the evils of despotic rule. The Utilitarian concepts of scientific administration would be applied to India. Those concepts also implied replacing personal discretion by the rule of law.

What is apparent in the continuing discussions on Indian affairs is an inherent relativism based on what was supposed to be appropriate for societies at different stages of development. Those principles appropriate to the American colonies or Canada were not seen by most interested British parties as relevant to India, where British rule would modify the past Oriental despotism by introducing changes where necessary in local laws and paying heed to local custom. This entailed authoritarian government, unfamiliar in Britain, tempered by "benevolence" and "improvement," which was to be appropriate for this particular society.

The whole question of different stages of development for different societies stems to a considerable degree from the idea of progress as it developed in the late eighteenth century and became a guide by which to evaluate stages of civilization.[185] Not surprisingly, the European thinkers who used the idea for the understanding of history, as did Condorcet, tended to be less admiring of the non-European world than had the *philosophes* of the earlier part of the eighteenth century. In this essentially Eurocentric view, the Orient would rank low in the hierarchy of civilizations.

To some extent this view was countered or qualified by those sympathetic to Indian concerns or by scholarly Orientalists concerned, among other matters, with the relationship between Sanskrit and certain European languages. One such prominent figure was Sir William Jones, both as an Orientalist and as a Supreme Court judge in Calcutta, whose importance in the understanding of India came not only from his study of Sanskrit but more from his project for a digest of Hindu and Muslim law that would allow British administrators to be more aware of native laws and customs.[186] Jones implicitly rejected the idea of an Oriental despotism in which no private property existed in India before British rule, a rejection already made by Anquetil-Duperron in his *Législation*

Orientale (1778) and followed by Charles Rous in his dissertation on *Landed Property of Bengal* (1791).[187] Jones held that in Muslim law the ruler had no claim on the property of the people. Nor did Indian princes have, or pretend to have, an unlimited legislative authority, but rather they were under the control of laws believed to be divine. At the same time Jones held British democracy was "wholly inapplicable" to India with its "inveterate prejudices and habits"; British liberty, if forced on them, would make Indians "as miserable as the cruelest despotism." Indians are "incapable of civil liberty" and must be ruled by absolute power.[188] For Jones this meant British rule on the basis of the old Indian system and on his digest of laws based on indigenous Indian codes of law.

Jones, admired for his Oriental scholarship and his humane concern for a just British rule in India, unwittingly became the starting point for an important ensuing intellectual dialogue on Indian history and society. The chief reason was that his ideas and his approach to the subject were subjected to severe criticism by James Mill, particularly in his multivolume *History of British India* (1818), who was in turn criticized for his inaccuracies by a later editor of his book, H. H. Wilson, who defended Jones against the author. The discussion took on special significance because the *History*, regarded by Macaulay as the greatest historical work in English since that of Gibbon, became the standard work for officials of the Company and the text for candidates for the Indian Civil service.[189]

Parenthetically, one aspect of the exchanges between Jones, Mill, and their various critics that has contemporary relevance because of the influence of Foucault on modern intellectuals, was the difference in the role of European observers, especially those with imperfect knowledge and ignorant of local languages and of other cultures. On one side, Mill, who had never visited India, took the view that more knowledge could be acquired by reading in a closet in England everything of importance on India than by long residence there.[190] Proper perspective on Indian culture depended on a critical distance from and an objective assessment of it, rather than from too much sympathy with it. By contrast the Orientalist Jones argued, "no man ever became a historian in his closet." India could only be understood by personal observation, local knowledge, and reading primary sources in Persian and Sanskrit.

James Mill, and his friend and mentor Jeremy Bentham, already had criticized Burke's philosophy for being "absurd and mischievous" and for its "artificial admiration of the bare fact of existence, especially ancient existence." In an 1810 essay, Mill castigated Jones's "susceptible imagination" that led him to be impressed by "the idea of Eastern wonders."[191] In his *History*, Mill disparaged the "fond credulity," which Jones shared with others, in presenting inaccurate portrayals of the advanced level of civilization of the

Hindus, and his "panegyrics on the wild, comfortless, predatory, and ferocious state of the wandering Arabs."[192] Instead, Mill sought the true state of the Hindus in the scale of civilization and wanted to counter the favorable view of India presented by the Orientalists.

In his lengthy *History*, discussed more fully in Chapter 7, James Mill, dividing Indian history into three parts – Hindu, Muslim, and British – believed that the country had mainly been ruled by despots and tyrants until the British arrived. This view of a static society, unchanged from the time of its origin, dominated by despots who owned the land, and a culture that did not contribute to individualism or rationalism, allowed Mill to allocate India a place inferior to Europe in the scale of civilization. By his classification "the relative positions of nations may be accurately marked."[193] Mill thought it untrue that the Hindus were once in a state of high civilization and had fallen because of foreign conquest and subjugation. On the contrary, "the hideous state of society" of the Hindus, with its "degrading and pernicious" caste system, was the result of despotism and priest craft that made Hindus the "most enslaved portion of the human race."[194] Despotism in one of its "simplest and least artificial shapes" was established in Hindustan; the government was monarchical and, with the usual exception of religion, absolute.

Like the later Burke, Mill was less critical of Muslim rule, enormous as its defects were. His essential reason was the absence of caste in Muslim despotisms, which treated all men as equal and had no nobility, privileged class, or hereditary property. Mill recognized the simplicity of Oriental despotism in which there was little room for diversity of form. Yet even here the Muslim form of despotism was preferable to the Hindu for at least two reasons. One was the regular distribution of functions of government to known officials compared with Hindu "confusion of all things together in one heterogeneous mass." The second, a more surprising argument, was the closer identification of the power of the priests with that of the sovereign among the Hindus compared with the "much less complete" alliance under Muhammadan sovereigns between the church and state.

Mill's arguments of a static Indian society, an inferior level of character and civilization compared with "the gothic nations," and political despotism as the norm in India were to affect the Western perception. Certainly Hegel's views of the Orient coincided with Mill's in the depiction of a stationary history, an unchanging Indian village as the key to its society, despots ruling over a powerless people, continual conquests and subjugations, and an inherent passivity; all led him to conclude that India was outside the mainstream of world history.

The continuing dialogue from Burke through Mill to nineteenth-century thinkers touched on other contentious questions related directly or indirectly to the issue of the existence and normality of Oriental despotism. Foremost was the question of the justification of colonial rule. In principle, Mill, Bentham, and other liberals of the early nineteenth century were critical of colonization, the settlement of areas by people from another country, and consequent inefficient and corrupt government. These areas might justifiably claim self-government. But the Utilitarians were more ambivalent about India, where most Europeans were not settlers but were employed by official civil and military bodies. Here colonial government might be, as Mill said, a financial burden, but also it might embody liberal values, free trade, reduced government expenditure, and productive enterprises through correct policies and legislation. In a country used to despotism and "if it is determined that they [the Indians] must have masters," wrote Jeremy Bentham, "look out for the least bad ones . . . our English company." To some degree the British liberals saw British rule in India as a mild version of what in France would become *la mission civilisatrice.*

6

Alexis de Tocqueville and Colonization

The stature of Alexis de Tocqueville (1805–59) as a political thinker has varied during the last century and a half. The rapid acknowledgment of the importance of his writings immediately on their publication, and the warmth and extent of his voluminous correspondence with both French and foreign, especially British, distinguished individuals, including John Stuart Mill and Nassau Senior, testify to the admiration for his intellectual brilliance and appreciation of his acumen and even prophetic insight on political affairs. That admiration was officially and explicitly shown by his election in 1838 to the Académie des Sciences Morales et Politiques and in 1841 to the illustrious French Academy after the second of his volumes on *Democracy in America* had been published the previous year.

If that admiration and high regard seemed to have ebbed, as all literary reputations do from time to time, for a while in the early twentieth century, it has in recent years swelled in full flood as analysts of different points of view and with diverging interpretations have seen him as an astute observer of politics or discussed his relevance for understanding the nature and problems of democracy and of social and political development.[1] His works have not only been considered in scholarly fashion; they have also been used for ideological reinforcement, or ransacked by politicians for polemical purposes or by those seeking aphoristic nuggets for verbal impact.

Tocqueville's ambition was not confined to brilliantly written, influential original publications on political and social issues, now regarded as masterpieces.[2] He was not and did not see himself as an isolated, aloof academic observer of public affairs. The successful writer on the subjects of politics, society, and history intersected with the active public figure, a nineteenth-century public intellectual. From an early age he was ambitious, eager to participate in political affairs and anxious to gain "political glory." He confessed to Louis de Kergorlay, a cousin and close friend, in a letter of July 23, 1827, that he had a craving to excel that would make his life a torment. Similarly, in a letter of October 18, 1831, to Eugene Stoffels, the young Tocqueville confessed his need for bodily or mental excitement, indicated his irresistible desire for strong emotions, and announced his susceptibility to violent passion. High among those emotions was the passion for liberty. To the same correspondent he wrote, on July 24, 1836, that he had always loved liberty instinctively, was as tenaciously attached to liberty as to morality, and was ready to sacrifice some of his tranquility to obtain it.

On a number of occasions Tocqueville revealed to friends his inherent temperament. For him fame was the spur. Typical examples of his self-analysis are letters of June 29, 1837, and August 15, 1840, to Pierre-Paul Royer-Collard, the philosopher and statesman.[3] In the first, he wrote that "Great esteem, won by honorable means, always appeared to me the most worthy good in the world and the only one worth the sacrifice of time, strength, and the pleasures of life." In the second, he confessed his "weak side," a love of success in public affairs: "I have never known how to rest peacefully and steadily on myself, and this noise which rises from the crowd has always seemed to me the most beautiful music." Near the end of his life, in a revealing letter of February 11, 1857, to Sophie Swetchine, Tocqueville wrote of his restlessness and incoherent agitation of desires that had always been a chronic malady.[4] In other letters Tocqueville wrote of storms, floods, anxiety, and dread in his life. In a highly personal letter of July 6, 1835, to Louis de Kergorlay, Tocqueville wished that "Providence would present me with an opportunity to act in order to accomplish good and great things."[5] In a similar letter of September 27, 1841, he wrote of his active and ambitious nature and of his liking of power if it could be honorably acquired and kept. Later, discussing the forthcoming election to the Constituent Assembly in 1848, for which he and his correspondent were both candidates, Tocqueville wrote to his friend Gustave de Beaumont on April 22, 1848, that "perhaps a moment will come in which the action we will undertake can be glorious."[6] The moment of glory never came for him in that fashion.

Though it was not Tocqueville's destiny to implement important political policies or good and great events or to set causes in motion, he had an honorable, if limited, public career. Appointed as a result of his good connections at the age of twenty one as a minor judge (*juge auditeur*) in the law courts at Versailles (1827–30), he ran unsuccessfully for election to the Chamber of Deputies in 1837. Elected to the Chamber in 1839 from Valognes (Normandy), near the family home, he was reelected until the end of the July monarchy in 1848, and his speeches there were invariably treated as significant pronouncements.[7] His fellow deputies recognized his disciplined mind and intellectual capacity and chose him to be the rapporteur of parliamentary committees considering bills on slavery, prison reform, and Algeria. Tocqueville was also elected in 1842 to the departmental General Council of La Manche, of which he later became president. After the fall of the July monarchy in February 1848, he was elected to the Constituent Assembly of the short-lived Second Republic. A year later he was elected to the new Legislative Assembly and was appointed Minister of Foreign Affairs, a position he held for four months. Opposing Louis Napoleon's *coup d'état* of December 2, 1851, Tocqueville was imprisoned for one day. His public political life was over, and he died of tuberculosis at the age of fifty-four while in retirement in 1859.

In *Democracy in America* Tocqueville talked of a new science of politics, which was needed for a new world, but he never formulated any grand schema or proposed a systematic theory of society and politics. In his writings, highly original and forthright, if sometimes changing in emphasis, he did not seek to build a comprehensive intellectual structure nor did he uncritically accept the validity of general ideas for explanatory purposes. Such ideas were always incomplete and "always cause the mind to lose as much in accuracy as it gains in comprehensiveness." He was critical of abstract terms, which were "like a box with a false bottom; you may put in it what ideas you please, and take them out again without being observed."[8] On most things rather than certainties, he wrote to his friend Charles Stoffels on October 22, 1831, "we have only probabilities. To despair that this is so is to despair of being a man, for that is one of the most inflexible laws of our nature."[9] He noted that men grasped fragments of truth but never truth itself.

Though possessing and advocating strong convictions of his own, Tocqueville, tolerant, open-minded, and undogmatic, held that to judge men's conduct one should place oneself at their point of view, not take the position of absolute truth.[10] Opposing simplistic theories, such as Count Arthur de Gobineau's theory of racial differences as a major explanatory factor of behavior by different peoples, which concluded that the white, Aryan race was superior to others, Tocqueville believed that differences among individuals and peoples sprang from a variety of factors: political, national, economic, "civilizational," as well as race. Without specifically mentioning Marx, Tocqueville in his *Recollections* written between November 1850 and March 1851, wrote that "for my part I hate all those absolute systems that make all the events of history depend on great first causes linked together by the chain of fate and thus succeed . . . in banishing men from the history of the human race . . . I believe that many important historical facts can be explained only by accidental circumstances, while many others are inexplicable . . . Chance is a very important element . . . but chance can do nothing unless the ground has been prepared in advance."[11] One of Tocqueville's most perceptive aphorisms was that history was a gallery of pictures in which there were few originals and many copies.

An aristocrat from old nobility, Tocqueville was always conscious that his immediate family had suffered during the French Revolution. Ten of his family were imprisoned, six including his grandparents were guillotined, and his parents were only saved from death by the downfall of Robespierre. As a result of the ordeal his father's hair had turned white at the age of twenty-one. The political realist Tocqueville recognized the implacable changes in social relations and in political regimes and institutions. These changes and the end of the feudal society were a providential fact. In a sense Tocqueville can be seen as a singular mélange of Cavalier and Roundhead. He confessed he had an intellectual preference for democratic institutions but was aristocratic by instinct, despising and fearing the crowd. In his own words he was an "aristocrat of the heart" and "a democrat of the mind." He wrote on January 1, 1839, to Paul Clamorgan, his friend and local political adviser, that no one not only in France but in Europe "has endeavored harder than I to prove that the aristocracy had lost its grand prerogatives forever."[12] This acceptance of political reality is apparent in his writings and his political career. A democratic age was replacing one of aristocracy: it was marked by "the prevalence of the bourgeois classes and the industrial element over the aristocratic classes and landed property."[13] In a letter of March 22, 1837, to Henry Reeve, his English friend and translator, Tocqueville explained he was not susceptible to political illusions, and neither hated nor loved the aristocracy: "I was so thoroughly in equilibrium between the past and the future that I felt naturally and instinctively attracted to neither the one nor the other."[14] He accepted the reality that politics meant compromise and conciliating different interests, and that a democratic government could bring real benefits but that an ideal democracy is "a glowing dream." Similarly, in international affairs it was necessary to be concerned not "with what has been, or will be, but with what is."

In an early undated letter of June 1835 to John Stuart Mill, Tocqueville attempted a political self-definition. "I love liberty by taste, equality by instinct and reason.[15] These two passions I am convinced that I really feel in myself, and I am prepared to make great sacrifices for them." Comparing the French and English concepts of democracy, he favored the latter, because the objective should be to put the "majority of citizens in a fit state for governing and to make it capable of governing." That was the only way to save them from barbarism or slavery. He did not regard the current great democratic revolution "in the same light as the Israelites saw The Promised Land," but it was useful and necessary. To attempt to check democracy "would be to resist the will of God."

Tocqueville in the introduction to *Democracy in America* (vol. I), said that the book favored no particular views, nor had he any design to serve or attack any party. In active politics he acted on this principle. According to remarks by Beaumont who discussed Tocqueville's political career with Nassau Senior on August 18, 1861, Tocqueville thought from the beginning that he ought to be an independent member of the Chamber of Deputies and vote according to his conscience, untrammeled by party connections.[16] Characteristically he chose his seat in the Chamber of Deputies to be slightly left of center; in letters to Francisque de Corcelle on September 26, 1840, and to Henry Reeve on November 7, 1840, he wrote that party attachment was foreign to him, and that national interest was more important than party. This may have been making virtue out of necessity. Independence from party and faction may have resulted from what some other politicians saw as his uneven temperament, his aloof and cold personality. Though he was ambitious and wished for power throughout his career, he remained unattached to either of the main political groups and thus was not supported by any party for ministerial office. Politically, Tocqueville cannot be easily classified, and both the political left and the right have drawn ideas and themes from him on sociological and political issues. He has influenced discussion on a host of issues: the dangers of big government, voluntary associations, civil engagement, limits of political power, the need for decentralization, prison reform (on which he co-wrote his first work), the tension between liberty and egalitarianism, the general apathy of people in democracies, the use of religion for self-discipline, problems of modernity, liberal democratic values, comparative sociology, and probable tendencies in democratic systems. In view of Tocqueville's subtle prose, lacking in doctrinaire certitude and sometimes in metallic precision, no sect, movement, or party can rightfully claim the mantle of his inheritance.[17] There is no "Tocquevillism."

Tocqueville is world renowned and best known for his books on the United States and on the history and politics of France. The two volumes of *Democracy in America* (published in 1835 and 1840), written after his journey at the age of twenty six to the United States during 1831 and 1832, purportedly to study the penitentiary system but really to study the customs and institutions of American society, received enormous acclaim on their appearance. After the end of his political career in 1849, Tocqueville wrote his *Souvenirs* (Recollections) during 1850 and 1851, his version of the politics of 1848 to 1851, and the *L'Ancien Régime et la Révolution* (The Old Regime and the French Revolution) in 1856.

Many political scientists and historians in the post–World War II period have tried to diagnose and interpret Tocqueville's analysis of democratic societies and their problems. A considerable part of that diagnosis has focused on Tocqueville's changing emphasis from the concept in the first volume of *Democracy in America* of "tyranny of the majority" to that of "democratic despotism" in the second volume. The latter he saw as a new form of despotism different from that of the past, and more extensive and mild in character. It resulted from the continually "increasing taste of individuals for worldly welfare" while governments acquired more and more possession of the sources of that welfare. That taste, and the tendency of individuals to be isolated, prevented them from taking part in public affairs, while their love of well-being forced them to closer and closer dependence on those who governed. Tocqueville's conception of the psychological isolation of people in mass society is a striking anticipation of David Riesman's *The Lonely Crowd*. Tocqueville postulated a startling image, which many commentators have seen as prophetic of modern times. Above the innumerable multitude of men, he argued, all equal and alike, each living apart, stood "an immense and tutelary power, which takes on itself alone the responsibility to secure their gratifications and to watch over their fate. This power is absolute, minute, regular, provident and mild . . . the supreme power extends its arm over the whole community . . . it does not tyrannize but it compresses, enervates, extinguishes, and stupefies a people." People, with contradictory propensities, wanting to be led and wishing to be free, devise a sole, tutelary, and all-powerful form of government, but unlike despotisms in previous historical periods it is elected by the people.

Much less well-known than these thoughts and his books on the United States and France, and only in recent years a subject for serious commentary, is Tocqueville's long interest in and his writings, speeches, and letters on French foreign policy, the French role in Algeria, and the desirability and benefits of European colonization.[18] From the character of that interest and his views, changing during the twelve-year period from 1837 to 1849, on French policy toward Algeria and the Mediterranean area, the Levant, emerges a political portrait of Tocqueville quite different from the familiar one of the tolerant liberal who was concerned about the future of democratic societies and the dignity of the human race. That portrait, surprising and troubling for many analysts and admirers of Tocqueville, illustrates a trenchant patriot, nationalist, even imperialist, and an advocate of the French control of Algeria and a sympathetic if dispassionate commentator on British rule in India. The partisan for liberty, the astute sociologist, the advocate of the abolition of slavery, was also the defender of colonial domination by France in North Africa.

That French domination began in the 1830s. As discussed in the introduction, in 1816 a British fleet had bombarded Algiers to discourage piracy coming from Algerian ports. France sought the same outcome. After a minor dispute with the governor of Algiers in 1827 France conducted a blockade of the city, and in 1830 invaded Algeria ostensibly to reduce piracy in the area. Four years later France formally annexed Algeria, thus raising the questions of French control over it and the structural, military, economic, and international dimensions of that control, a problem that lasted until 1962.

That Tocqueville was an ardent patriot and nationalist eager for France to retain a prominent role in international affairs, and for that to be generally acknowledged by foreign powers, is readily apparent in many of his writings, letters, and speeches. His nationalism and patriotism lasted throughout his life; his ardent advocacy of this position was to be a bone of contention between him and John Stuart Mill. In *Democracy in America* he remarked that instinctive patriotism arose from affections for birthplace and that patriotism and religion were the only two sources that could urge everyone toward the same end. During his retirement in 1856, he commented that the interests of the human species were better served by giving each person only one particular country to love rather than by actions aimed at an amorphous "humanity." Troubled by his perception of the weakness and lack of will, and the lack of interest in political affairs, of fellow French citizens, he wrote to Royer-Collard on August 15, 1840, "the best thing our country has left is national pride . . . the greatest sentiment that we have and the strongest tie that holds this nation together."[19] Though he was no admirer of Napoleon he commented that this great man understood that some kind of strong passion was needed to stir the human spirit, which otherwise would decay and rot. Tocqueville constantly spoke of and appealed to the pride, perhaps the most solid and strong link among French people, that they had in their past. That pride was based on ideological as well as material factors. France since the Revolution had influenced other countries in advancing its principles of equality, civil liberties, right to property, and the end of exclusive privilege. In his speech of November 30, 1840, he declared that the chief interest and permanent mission of France was the replacement of despotic institutions by liberal ones; "what is France if not the heart and head of democracy?"

At that time Tocqueville was delighted that his constituents in Valognes, after hearing the rumors of war in 1839, firmly supported the idea of possible hostilities against Britain, which had attacked Egyptian territory. He worried that this readiness to go to war in what he saw as national interest was not universally embraced in France. Referring to the struggle in Algeria in strong language, he was disturbed that "if France were to shrink from an enterprise in which she was faced with no more than the natural difficulties of the terrain and the opposition of little tribes of barbarians, in the eyes of the world she would appear to be yielding to her own powerlessness and succumbing because of her lack of courage. Any nation that readily lets go of what it has taken and withdraws peacefully of its own accord back inside its old boundaries proclaims that the golden age of its history is past. It visibly enters the period of its decline."[20] It was important to maintain in a nation the feeling that leads to great actions; the people must not be taught to submit quietly to being treated with indifference. This emphasis on pride was still manifested when at the end of his career, during his brief tenure as foreign minister, he remarked on the French expeditionary force sent to Italy in 1848 after Italian republicans had driven Pope Pius IX from Rome; to be defeated by the same men (the republicans) who had been defeated by the Austrians in battle after battle would be a frightful disaster. While foreign minister he was unhappy that the French people, who remembered the past great strength of their country and aspired to everything though they were aware of its limited power, still essentially neither wished nor possibly could do anything.

Tocqueville made clear in *Democracy in America* that he understood the power of public opinion, which could influence the government against acting energetically and continuously. He envisaged that power affecting current affairs in France. In the discussion on July 2, 1839, in the Chamber of Deputies regarding the Orleans monarchy, which he had not supported in 1830 when it came to power but now accepted, he was convinced that the monarchy would not last if this nation, once "so strong, so grand, which had done such great deeds, which has interested herself in all things in the world, will no longer take an interest in anything, that she no longer has a hand in anything, that all is done without her."[21] Underlying Tocqueville's writings on politics runs a perception that imagery of French power was important for external consumption as well as internally for French citizens. The good opinion people had of France would keep her in the front rank of nations. It was important to obtain this good opinion from European countries because France had nothing to put in its place. The power of France, and its image in the world in international affairs was crucial for Tocqueville and should be demonstrated, in extreme form if necessary. In a speech in the Chamber on November 30, 1840, Tocqueville spoke of his liking for peace but, disagreeing with some fellow Deputies, not to the point of appeasement or weakness in a conflict. A government that could not make war was contemptible; this would entail a peace without glory.[22] Tocqueville in this resembled a French Winston Churchill, not a Neville Chamberlain.

This interrelationship of internal and external factors was a constant factor in Tocqueville's writings. French demonstration of national strength and striving for glory in foreign adventures were desirable both to achieve internal political and social unity, thus reducing the possibility of disharmony or revolt, and for the nation to play an important role in international affairs. As early as the second volume of *Democracy in America*, in the midst of his ambivalent discussion of peace and war, Tocqueville remarked that "I do not wish to speak ill of war; war almost always enlarges the mind of a people and raises their character." Colonization of Algeria would increase the prestige of France, and this would be done through "the principles and the enlightenment the French Revolution spread throughout the world."

On the international stage, France, with its special interest in the area, had to maintain a strong presence in the Mediterranean, and North Africa, which meant among other things attempting to prevent Britain from controlling Egypt. In opposition to some government ministers in Paris, he was prepared to see France go to war over the Eastern Question at a moment when European armies were fighting in the Middle East in 1840 and the European world was rising up. France had not been a party to the London Agreement of July 15, 1840, for the cease-fire of the fighting. "Do you think," he challenged, in the Chamber in the November 30, 1840, speech, "that a nation that wishes to remain great ought to be present at such an event without taking part in it? Do you think we ought to permit two peoples of Europe [Russia and England] to take possession of this immense heritage with impunity? Rather than allow that, I shall say to my country with energy and with a firm belief, let us rather have war."

Tocqueville answered his own questions by urging that, during the 1839 and 1840 Syrian-Egyptian crisis facing European countries, France must play a strong role, even be prepared to go to war, an action that the French government was reluctant to undertake, and do so in spite of the fact that the country was unprepared. An assertive role would be understood by foreign powers: "Europe knows that if the material strength of France has been diminished, there remains to her that extraordinary power that waits upon extraordinary moments, and also an energy without equal, whose impetuous, passionate, fierce, proud, movements can baffle all the combinations of the great powers and wrest victory from them at a single stroke and make it pass to her side." Interestingly, Tocqueville was admonished for this apparent belligerence by his friend and admirer Nassau Senior, the British economist, in a letter of February 27, 1841, who contrasted Tocqueville's contentious language in the Chamber with the more measured utterances by statesmen in the British parliament. It would be utterly ruinous, Senior wrote, for a British politician to argue a case for war merely "to prevent our being excluded from taking part in the affairs of Syria or Egypt."[23]

There was a new development in the 1830s in the Eastern Question, the debate and diplomatic maneuvering by European countries as the Ottoman

Empire was dwindling in importance in Eastern Europe and North Africa; this was the increasing power and ambition of Muhammad Ali Pasha (1769–1849) who had been appointed Ottoman viceroy in Egypt in 1805 and founded Egypt's final royal dynasty, which lasted until 1953. He not only became virtually independent of his nominal superior, the sultan, but also was seemingly challenging the Ottoman regime for leadership. In June 1839 Muhmmad Ali had defeated the Ottoman army at Nizip, and the Ottoman fleet had surrendered at Alexandria. Speaking on July 2, 1839, about the actions of Muhammad Ali in Egypt, Tocqueville in his first speech in the Chamber, on a bill to appropriate extra money for French maritime forces in the Levant, discussed the role of the great powers in the Middle East. Russia's main interest was the destruction of the Ottoman Empire, and therefore it supported the rule in Egypt of Muhammad Ali, who challenged the empire. By contrast, Britain was opposed to Muhammad Ali; it wanted the empire, and the sultan, to survive but did not want Egypt to head it. France, which like Britain wanted to curb Russian expansion, had a double interest. It also did not want the empire to end and thus opposed Muhammad Ali, but at the same time it disapproved of British control of Egypt.[24]

Without an ally in this complex imbroglio, France, in Tocqueville's view, had to depend on itself and participate in resolving the international crisis in an energetic and prudent fashion. In undated notes, probably written in mid-1840, he stressed the need for France to play a role in the questions of the Orient, which he saw as the question of the century. In particular he wanted France to challenge the British attempts to control maritime shipping. If it did not, France would be reduced to the level of a second-rank power and would be obliged to acquiesce in the expansion of the power of Russia and Britain. A similar argument was made in Tocqueville's speech on November 5, 1840, regarding the same crisis when he rejected "the honorable and sincere but incorrect" opinion that France could not act in the current crisis. Not acting would, in the eyes of foreigners, illustrate weakness. The French regime, he wrote in his letter of August 15, 1840, to Royer-Collard, might fall as a result of "the sight of Europe dividing up the Ottoman Empire with arms in hand and without us." France should persuade the European powers calmly but firmly that disregarding France "would bring on a general war that everyone dreads."[25] Tocqueville argued for France to play a role, even risk war, over the international Middle East crisis of 1840 and more generally for a clear foreign policy on issues such as the Orient, British control of maritime shipping, and the drama of European activity in fostering development in Asia. He regretted that the crisis was resolved by the London Treaty signed on July 15, 1840, by concerned European powers, England, Russia, Austria, and Prussia, but without the presence of France.

The opportunity for France to play a prominent international role, to gain conquest and glory, was provided by Algeria. The writer who revealed in his letters his personal desire for action and glory supported French policy in Algeria, which would embody those desires on behalf of the nation.[26] Such a policy and action might also lead individual citizens of France to overcome what he found troubling in the country, the "gradual softening of mores, abasement of the mind, the mediocrity of tastes."[27] One could not let France take up the habit of sacrificing what it believed to be its grandeur to its repose. He was still concerned with the question of liberty, so crucial in *Democracy in America*, and with "an enthusiasm for liberty" and also for the dignity of the human race. But more important were his intense, compelling advocacy of French domination over Algeria and colonization there and his ardent, sometimes belligerent, patriotism.[28]

As early as 1828 Tocqueville approved the French expedition in Algeria in which his friend Kergorlay participated. He also approved the French invasion and capture of Algiers in 1830, originally intended to restore French honor after a trivial affront in 1827 when the Dey, the governor of Algiers, hit the French consul with a fly whisk during an argument. Tocqueville had a personal as well as political interest in Algeria. In 1833 he thought of buying, together with Kergorlay, an estate in the Sahel in the country and considered learning Arabic.[29] He told Beaumont, in a letter of August 9, 1840, that he was studying the large government blue books on Algeria. He first visited the country in May 1841, as a member of the Chamber of Deputies, but became ill with dysentery and thus limited his stay. He paid a second visit, accompanied by wife and some colleagues in 1846.

Tocqueville's political interest in the issue of Algeria began early and continued through most of his life. Between the times of the publication of the two volumes of *Democracy in America*, he wrote *Two Letters on Algeria* on June 23, 1837, and August 22, 1837, as articles in *La Presse de Seine-et-Oise*, a rather obscure Versailles paper in which he was a shareholder.[30] Tocqueville studied the Koran and published some notes on the first eighteen *suras* of it in March 1838. After his first visit to Algeria, and while recuperating from his illness, he wrote an *Essay on Algeria* in October 1841. As a member of the Chamber of Deputies he spoke on the Algerian question on many occasions including contributions to the debate on special funding appropriations on June 9, 1846. He was chosen to be the *rapporteur*, the person who drafts parliamentary reports, for bills considering special funds and extraordinary credits for activities and agricultural camps in Algeria. In addition, Tocqueville also served as *rapporteur* of parliamentary commissions on the abolition of slavery and on prison reform. He, and his friend Beaumont, withdrew from an extraparliamentary commission set up in 1842 under the Duc Decazes when they realized the government was not taking it seriously. For a brief time, he was involved in a committee deciding whether to consider the Didier proposal for a legal framework for the administration of Algeria. Tocqueville's preoccupation with Algeria was such that he wrote on June 6, 1847, to his English friend and translator Henry Reeve that he could write a big book on Africa, but he never did.[31]

Even in the latter part of his parliamentary career Tocqueville intervened in discussions of Algeria on three occasions in 1848 and 1849: regarding the general budget of Algeria, the discussion of credits for colonization, and in a general debate in December 1849. It should be acknowledged that during the period of his interest in the subject Tocqueville changed his mind and positions on Algeria, the nature and justification of the war, colonial policy and colonization, and the desirability of empire. His overall opinion, on French foreign policy in the area, especially as expressed in his speeches of July 2, 1839, and November 30, 1840, was that France should maintain its position in the Mediterranean and in North Africa. By 1847 he was advocating the extension of France in the area. He propounded the case for French control over North Africa, not out of any conviction of racial superiority, but because it was important for France to maintain its stature as a formidable international power, which would stimulate the energy that he saw lacking in contemporary France and would allow it to help elevate less developed countries such as Algeria.

His writings on Algeria and on French policy were direct, controversial, and contentious. While working on *Democracy in America* (vol. II), Tocqueville had written on September 19, 1836, to John Stuart Mill that he had "never taken up my pen to support a system or to draw . . . certain conclusions. I give myself up to the natural flow of my ideas . . . therefore until my work is finished, I never know exactly what result I shall reach, or if I shall arrive at any."[32] In marked contrast to this disinterested attitude were his conclusions and definite opinions about Algeria and his commentaries on French foreign policy. Even though he acknowledged that in 1830 France was profoundly ignorant of everything concerning Algeria and should be more informed, he was convinced that France should control the country and establish settlements there. In a revealing remark in his speech in the parliamentary debate on June 9, 1846, Tocqueville said the "immense African question" must not sink back into oblivion. Moreover, he believed, as one who had studied "questions of this order closely, perhaps more closely than anything else, who had visited new countries" that the problems in Africa were like those that had arisen, and still arose, in every new country.

While finishing the second volume of *Democracy in America*, Tocqueville was also absorbed in a wide reading that included the Koran as well as the great European writers, Rabelais, Plutarch, Cervantes, Machiavelli, Fontenelle, and Saint-Evremond. Unlike his friend Beaumont who he thought, not unkindly, could not "do two things at once. Your mind is indivisible," Tocqueville confessed he had "an insatiable, ardent curiosity" and that a "thousand strange ideas" crossed his mind. Among those ideas, surprising to many, were his views on Algeria and French policy toward it, views that evolved during a twelve-year period from 1837 to 1849, especially on the possibility of harmonious arrangements with the Arabs, though his perception of Islam remained constant. His formal publications on the subject began with the *Two Letters on Algeria* in 1837 in which he discussed the composition of the Algerian population and the desirable French policy toward it.

In the *First Letter* of June 23, 1837, Tocqueville wrote of the indigenous, sedentary Kabyles (Berbers) living in the Atlas Mountains and cultivating the soil. They did not form one great people subject to a single government but were divided into small tribes, living separately, often at war with each other and with independent governments and uncomplicated legislation. By contrast, the Arabs who lived in the valleys, both in the coastal area and in the interior, were partly sedentary and partly nomadic. The two groups posed different problems for France.[33] The Kabyles had pride, a sense of honor and were civil toward foreigners they respected. They were indifferent to religion and worried far more about this world than a future world, and thus could be won over peacefully, more by French "luxuries than with cannon." Here Tocqueville appears as a premature Keynesian, believing that change could come not through violence but through demand for consumer goods.

The Arabs, cultivators and herdsmen in the north and more nomadic in the south, were more heterogeneous. They were divided into small tribes more or less independent of each other as they were 1200 years ago, electing their own leaders (sheikhs) and discussing their own affairs, but contrary to the Kabyles the tribes formed a single people with a shared identity. Though Arab family leaders formed a sort of military aristocracy, the Arab aristocracy was primarily based on religion. The men with a reputation for extraordinary holiness, the *marabouts*, men of religion and scholarship who felt or affected great detachment from the world, were the most influential members of Arab society.[34] Tocqueville saw the Arabs of the coastal plains as having certain general traits: brilliant and sensual imagination, shrewd wit, courage, inconstancy. They adored physical delights but put "freedom" above all pleasures. They loved war, pomp, noise and, "like all half-savage peoples," honored power and force. They were sometimes subject to an unreflective enthusiasm and an exaggerated despondency. They were often excessive in their actions and always more willing to feel than to think.

In his *Second Letter*, of August 22, 1837, Tocqueville continued to contrast the two main groups in Algeria and the relevance of the differences between them for decisions about French conquest and occupation of that country. Military conquest or colonization of the Kabyles was not a possibility because of the impenetrable mountains in which they lived and their "inhospitable humor." He argued that unlike the Arabs, they had remained fairly independent during the long occupation by the Turks and were therefore largely unaffected by the collapse of that rule. However, Tocqueville believed that following that collapse they had become more unapproachable, hating foreigners and Christians. Nevertheless, he thought France could establish closer commercial relations with the Kabyles. It could manipulate the Kabyles through their love of material pleasures. They were far less inclined than were the Arabs to go to war with France, which ought to subdue them by its arts, not by its arms, altering the customs and ideas of the Kabyles without their perceiving the change. The "soul" of the Kabyles could be penetrated by France. When the Kabyles no longer feared French ambition and felt protected by French law, France would perceive "the almost invincible attraction that draws savages toward civilized man at the moment they no longer fear for their freedom." For Tocqueville, the Kabyles appeared to be more advanced along the scale of social progress than the Arabs.

The question of the Arabs was more complex. They were different from the Kabyles. They held their sparsely populated land but cultivated only a very small part of it. They sold land readily and cheaply, and a foreign population could easily establish itself next to their communities without their suffering. Tocqueville argued it would be easy for the French to occupy a large part of the soil without violence and to establish themselves peacefully and in large numbers in the midst of the surrounding tribes. In this early work, Tocqueville envisaged a peaceful intermixture of Arab and French settlers in the near future, and even the amalgamation of the two races.[35] "God is not stopping it; only human deficiencies can stand in its way." Within four years he would change his mind on the possibility of assimilation and conclude that the idea of fusion of the two peoples was a chimera.

Tocqueville explained the Arab lack of political development by the fact that for three centuries in North Africa the Arabs had been subject to the Turks and had lost the habit of governing themselves. The rule of the Ottoman Empire was one of violent exploitation of the conquered by the conqueror. The Turkish government was detestable, but it did maintain a certain order, and though it tacitly allowed continuing wars among Arab tribes, it provided security by curbing theft and ensuring safe roads, and providing the only link between the diverse tribes. After the Turkish rule had ended no substitute countrywide government existed over the Arab territories. The Arab tribes began to fight each other; the result was frightful anarchy, brigandage, lack of justice, and resort to force by everyone. In his *Notes* on May 7, 1841, Tocqueville depicted the social and political state of Muslim and Oriental populations: polygamy, sequestration of women, absence of any public life, and a tyrannical and suspicious government that forced one to conceal one's life and keep all affections within the family.

Tocqueville envisaged France having different relations with the two main groups. With the Kabyles, France must focus above all on questions of civil and commercial equity; with the Arabs it should be on political and religious questions. Some Arab tribes could be directly governed by France, but the majority of them could be ruled only indirectly and through influence. Because of its superior knowledge, and as a powerful and civilized people, France could exercise an almost invincible influence on small and fairly barbarous peoples. France's concern should be to live in peace with the Arabs because it could not at that time hope to govern and organize them without danger. Where French people and Arabs lived in proximity, security required direct rule by France.

Tocqueville's argument was that France should not let the Arabs in Algeria establish a single, powerful ruler. The French conquest had restored the authority of the *marabouts* who "took up the scimitar of Muhammad" to battle the infidels and govern their fellow citizens. France must make use of the Arab military and religious aristocracy to rule, but it had to draw on the Arabs' own political customs and only gradually modify the rules of their civil law, most of which could be traced to the Koran, because civil and religious law were always mixed together without distinction. France had to respect the need for diversity, giving up its taste for uniformity, and should propose different laws for the two peoples.

Tocqueville was optimistic at the end of his *Second Letter on Algeria* (1837) that though the majority of the Arabs retained a lively faith in the Islamic religion, in Algeria "religious beliefs are continually losing their vigor and becoming more powerless." Religion, he thought at that time, was only a secondary cause of war between France and the Arabs; the French were opposed much more as foreigners and as conquerors than as Christians. He believed that if France could demonstrate that Islam was in no danger under French administration of Algeria, religious passions would end, and France would have only political, not religious, enemies in Africa.

Yet Tocqueville remained troubled by the character and thrust of Islam. In a passage in *Democracy in America* (vol. II), Tocqueville generalized that "at times of general culture and equality," religions ought more cautiously than at any other times "to confine themselves to their proper sphere . . . if they wish to extend their power beyond spiritual matters they run the risk of not being believed at all." From this point of view he compared Islam and Christianity. Muhammad professed to derive his mission and laws from heaven. He had inserted in the Koran not only religious doctrines but also political maxims, civil and criminal laws, and theories of science. In contrast, the Christian Gospels spoke only of the general relations of men to God and to each other and imposed no point of faith. This alone, besides a thousand other reasons, sufficed to prove that Islam could never long predominate in an enlightened and democratic age, while Christianity was destined to retain its sway in these as in all other eras. In Tocqueville's letter of March 21, 1838, to Kergorlay, he wrote he was reading about the life of Muhammad and Islam, and could not understand how General Juchault de Lamorcière, a friend of Kergorlay, could say that the Koran was an improvement over the Gospels (L'Evangile).[36]

On the contrary, as Tocqueville expostulated in a letter of October 2, 1843, to Gobineau, "I cannot understand how, when you read the Gospels, your soul does not soar with that higher sense of inner freedom that their pure and stately morality evokes in my own." It seemed to him that Christianity "accomplished a revolution, you may prefer the term considerable change, in all the ideas connected with rights and duties: ideas that are, after all, the basic matter of all sound morality. . . . The magnificent achievement of Christianity is to have constructed a human community beyond all national societies." Christianity was the great source of modern morality. Almost all, he wrote in 1843, of what was called modern principles should be considered as new consequences drawn from the old Christian principles because of our present political and social condition. Christianity had given new form to two principles: the equal rights of every man to the goods of this world; and the duty of those with more to help those with less. Christianity made charity a personal virtue and responsibility. One cannot doubt the sincerity of Tocqueville's argument, though it is surprising coming from a man who confessed he had at an early age lost all belief in Catholic dogma.

In the *Letters on Algeria* (1837) Tocqueville discussed two factors that led him to support the French conquest of Algeria, an event that would raise "a great monument to our country's glory on the African coast."[37] One was the heritage of the Ottoman regime, the Oriental despotism that kept Arab tribes in an inferior position and that was, in effect, a "continuation of conquest, a violent exploitation of the conquered by the conquerors" that Tocqueville had mentioned. The other was the Islamic religion. Although, as mentioned in the preceding text, Tocqueville studied the Koran he was no expert on

Islamic law and wrote an analysis of only the first eighteen *suras* of the Koran. He saw the Koran as "the source of the laws, ideas and customs of all this Muslim population with whom we have to deal."[38] It was important that France spend money to provide a good translation of it and textual commentary. Tocqueville's views on Islam are revealed in fragmentary discussion, letters, and in the *Notes on the Koran*, written in March 1838. In *Notes*, written before his visit to Algeria in 1841, Tocqueville outlined his thoughts. Muhammad preached his religion to peoples "peu avancés," nomads and warriors; at that time his religion had few rituals and a simple cult with a priest hardly necessary. Even the word *clergy* did not exist in Arabic. Islam grew into a religion that commingled religious and secular power: religious leadership and political rule were invested in the same person, and civil and political acts were more or less regulated by religious law. This concentration of power was the main cause of despotism and above all of social immobility, characteristics that made Islamic nations succumb to nations whose political systems separated spiritual and temporal control.

Islam, Tocqueville thought, exercised immense power that was more detrimental than salutary. Religion and justice were fused in Islamic countries, similar to what Christian ecclesiastics had tried to do in the Middle Ages.[39] Justice was rendered in the name of God rather than by royal decree; its rules were not contained in civil laws but in the Koran and its commentaries. The basic aim of Islam was to wage wars of conquest and expansion. Tocqueville wrote that Muhammad, the Prophet, was more preoccupied with making himself believed through the use of violence and force than with promoting rules of morality. Tocqueville repeated this view in his letter of March 21, 1838, to Kergorlay: the first of all the religious duties in Islam was to obey blindly the Prophet, and the first of all the good works was holy war.[40] These concepts, he said, were to be found in every page and almost every word in the Koran. The violent and sensual tendencies in the Koran were striking. Tocqueville characterized *jihad* as sacred war, obligatory for all believers, the natural state of relations with infidels with whom one could only declare a truce. For believers, Tocqueville suggested, the message promoted was fanaticism and greed.[41]

Tocqueville was consistent in his critical view of Islam and in contrasting it negatively with Christianity. In a striking passage, in his letter of October 22, 1843, to Gobineau, Tocqueville wrote he had "often studied the Koran when concerned with our relations with the Muslim populations of Algiers and the Orient . . . I emerged convinced that there are in the entire world few religions with such morbid consequences as that of Muhammad. To me it is the primary cause of the now so visible decadence of the Islamic world. . . . I still regard it as decadent compared to ancient paganism."[42] By contrast, Christianity had been able to advance civilization toward liberty and democracy and was the necessary condition for social progress and elevated duties, while Islam was responsible for political and cultural decay in the world. In one late letter, including Hinduism as well as Islam in his generalization, Tocqueville wrote of the inequalities promulgated by the religions of Asia and Africa that had led to cultural stagnation.

He touched on a similar point in a letter of November 13, 1855, to Gobineau who had visited the Middle East and who was "in the heart of the Asiatic and Islamic world." He asked Gobineau, "to what do you attribute the rapid and seemingly inevitable decadence of the races you have seen, a decadence which, as it has already delivered some, may deliver all of them to the domination of our little Europe which so often trembled before them in the past?" Tocqueville asked, where was the "maggot eating this large Asiatic body," and what was the "irredeemable decadence dragging it down through the centuries?" He went on to elevate European civilization. In his letter to Gobineau he commented that a few million men who, a few centuries ago, lived nearly shelterless in the forests and in the marshes of Europe would, within a hundred years, transform the globe and dominate other races. The European races were often the greatest rogues, but at least they were rogues to whom God had given will and power and whom He seemed to have destined for some time to be at the head of mankind. This argument was amplified in his speech in the Chamber of Deputies on November 30, 1840, about the events in Syria and Egypt in that year that showed "all societies tottering, all religions weakened, all nationalities disappearing, all enlightenment extinguished, the Asiatic world disappearing and in its place the European world ascending."[43]

Yet Tocqueville's criticism of Islam was not unlimited. In his *First Report on Algeria* (1847), he wrote that "Islam is not entirely impenetrable to enlightenment: it has often admitted certain sciences and certain arts within itself. Why don't we try to make them flourish under our rule?" He held that Muslim society in Africa was not uncivilized; it was merely a backward and imperfect civilization. He frankly discussed the relevance of Islam to his image of the new colony in Algeria. He criticized French authorities for diverting the use of the large number of Islamic pious foundations that provided charity or public instruction. Surprisingly, Tocqueville added that "we have made Muslim society much more miserable, more disordered, more ignorant, and more barbarous than it had been before knowing us."

Part of Tocqueville's approval of French control of Africa stemmed from his conviction that the Orient was less developed than was Europe, and that European control would improve living conditions. In the *Essay on Algeria* (October 1841), referring to changes brought about by Abd-el-Kadar, the person who had emerged as the main Arab leader, he remarked that "these half-savage African countries are undergoing a social development very much like that which took place in Europe at the end of the Middle Ages." In the *Notes on the Voyage to Algeria*, he wondered on May 29, 1841, why peoples, like the Kabyles, who had reached the first stage of civilization, had not gone further. In his explanation he cited their situation as a mountain people, the proximity of the Arabs, their religion, and especially their division into small tribes.

Tocqueville's theory that a more developed Europe could help modernize less developed countries was a major factor in his assessment and general support of French policy toward Africa and the Orient. Tocqueville addressed the issue in different ways, partly because French policy from 1828 to 1847 kept changing, from the original intention to control ports in North Africa to prevent piracy to increasingly bitter warfare and to proposals for colonization. An additional problem was that during this period the French military authorities in Algeria were not fully under political control by the government in Paris and often acted independently.

The issue of maintaining international prestige and power for France was crucial for Tocqueville. France had to protect its position in the Mediterranean and in North Africa, control the port of Mers el-Kebir and Algiers, and should prevent Britain from controlling Egypt. As the Ottoman Empire was faltering Tocqueville was prepared to see France go to war over the Eastern Question. In various writings, Tocqueville expressed the view that war was no more of a threat to a nation than was decadence. In *Democracy in America*, he held that war almost always enlarged the mind of a people and raised their character, and that it was well to expose a community from time to time to matters of difficulty and danger in order to raise ambition and give the people and the country a field for action.[44] However, would the French people be firm in the presence of dangers, and above all in the discomfiture that war brought? The best thing for the country was national pride. Colonies would help provide that pride. Tocqueville was troubled by the effect on that pride if other European countries were seen to be dividing up the Ottoman Empire by military activity and without France. The rapid colonization and peaceful rule of Algeria, he thought, was the most important business France had before her. French preponderance in Europe, the order of its finances, the lives of part of its citizenry, and its natural honor were engaged here in the most compelling manner. France, he wrote in October 1841, could not think seriously of leaving Algeria. The abandonment of Algeria would denote decline of France and the end of its greatness. Not only would it allow other European countries to control North Africa, but also it would also mean France had given up its attempt to ensure that Africa had entered into "the movement of the civilized world."

The emphasis on strength and action was consonant with Tocqueville's general attitude to the use of force as well as to French politics and life at this point. Leaders of modern society, he wrote in *Democracy in America*, would be wrong to seek to lull the community into a state of a too uniform and too peaceful happiness. Tocqueville was no pacifist; it was pacifism not war that weakened the country. Strength, he wrote in a letter to Jean-Jacques Ampère on August 10, 1841, "appears at its best in the midst of the universal weakness that surrounds us." In a letter of September 27, 1841, to the philosopher and statesman Pierre-Paul Royer-Collard, he was caustic about the political ineptness and weakness of Louis Adolphe Thiers, prime minister in 1836 and 1840, and François Guizot, the eminent historian who replaced Thiers in 1840 and remained prime minister until 1848. There was no French action, and what was politics without action? Tocqueville saw himself as almost alone in the Chamber of Deputies and he wanted to be active. The best he saw for himself was to be regarded in the country as a moral force, a power that had become rare. Yet Tocqueville always added to moral force his version of political realism, arguing for an energetic foreign policy to contravene the weakness of the French political leaders. His position on this interrelationship of morality and power in international politics interestingly anticipates the mid- and late-twentieth-century writings of authors such as Hans Morgenthau, George Kennan, Reinhold Niebuhr, and Raymond Aron. Tocqueville continually warned of the dangers both of the passivity of French leaders who desired political tranquility and also of the decline in the country of those passions for freedom, love of country, dedication to glory, and national grandeur, concepts that he held stemmed from the French Revolution. In a speech in the Chamber of Deputies on January 17, 1844, he cautioned that the nation was asleep: its awakening should be feared by the whole world because new revolutions would occur from that awakening. The Arabs, if backward, were not all nomads; they were more mobile than the Europeans. They could be used as agents of the government, but only if guided by the notions of civilized men and with French maxims. At the same time, as Tocqueville wrote in his *First Report on Algeria*, the Muslim subjects must not get exaggerated ideas of their own importance, nor believe they should always be treated as equal fellow French citizens.

However, France should study the Islamic way of life in order to govern Arabs intelligently and not destroy their culture or Moorish architecture. At this point Tocqueville's thoughts on Islam were relevant to those on political and military actions.[45] Even in his *Democracy in America*, Tocqueville had touched on the question, comparing the decline of the Turkish tribes in his day with their past glory. They had accomplished great things as long as the victories were triumphs of the Muslim faith. In the present age they were in rapid decay because their religion was declining and only despotism remained. French domination did not imply neglect of the interests of Arab inhabitants. They were owed good government, and actions appropriate to them were carried out "with zeal for the continued development of their imperfect civilization." Arabs could not at that moment be pushed along the road to European civilization. France should not force Arabs to go to French schools; they should be encouraged to reestablish their own schools and teachers and to increase those institutions that train lawyers or men of religion that Muslim civilization needs. Tocqueville called for the French parliament to be more concerned about the governing and administering of Algeria. A good government, he thought, could lead to real pacification and a notable diminution in the French army.

Tocqueville realized from the beginning the difficulties and problems arising from the invasion and conquest of Algeria. Replying in the Chamber on June 9, 1846, to those who believed that the African question could be solved by an administrative stroke of luck or informed curiosity, he dismissed the view that "somewhere in the world there was an idea, an institution, a system, which if sought for and found, would someday provide a very simple solution for the problem."[46] He understood that France would never be able to do all the great things it set out to do in Algeria, and that "we have quite a sad possession there." Yet domination by France of the area was necessary and practicable, though troublesome. On one hand, Western conquest was desirable; on the other, the violence involved was regrettable. Realistic factors affected the balance between the positions.[47] In his letter of October 10, 1846, to Corcelle, Tocqueville indicated the dilemma; the need to create and secure a French colony in Africa and a concern for the native Arabs.

Tocqueville exhibited this balance in his analyses of events in Algeria. He believed that at first France did not intend, unlike the barbarians who invaded the Roman Empire, to take possession of the territory of the conquered Algerians. The only goal was to seize the government. France must try to persuade the Muslim subjects that it would not take away any of their patrimony without payment or by dishonest transactions. Although supporting occupation of the country, he did not want the natives to be crushed or exterminated, but also he believed that "trusting to the good will of the natives in order to maintain our presence in Africa is a pure illusion that it would be folly to cherish." At the same time Tocqueville warned that France must not allow a great Arab powerful figure or Arab princes to establish rule in the Algerian interior and unite the tribes. Their passions for religion and depredation would always lead the Arab tribes to wage war on the French. Those tribes were deeply divided by old hatreds: their common link was religion and their common sentiment was xenophobia and hatred of the invading infidel. The assurance and strength of rule by Arab princes were related to the degree of their fanaticism and hate against the French. Historically, Tocqueville suggested, that kind of fanaticism had been shown by Muhammad, the first caliphs, and the different regimes on the coast of Africa. The French had to be aware of the Arab prince Abd-el-Kader, "a sort of Muslim Cromwell," a prince parading with the image of a saint, constantly hiding behind the religion for which he said he acted. It was as an interpreter of the Koran, with it in hand, that Abd-el-Kader ordered and condemned, using religious hatred against the French to bolster his power. To this end he cleverly exploited the only feeling common to all Arabs, hatred of Christians.

Abd-el-Kader's power had to be destroyed.[48] He was preparing to create a confederation of Arab tribes. He had crushed the armies of opposing Arab tribes and had centralized government, formed his own large army, levied regular taxes, and was making war not only on the French but also on the hereditary aristocracy of his own country. Drawing a historical parallel Tocqueville held that Abd-el-Kader's rule of the people through enthusiasm and fear was not new in the world. If Abd-el-Kader was to be destroyed it would only be with the help of some of the tribes subjugated by him. To create a schism among the Arabs would be profitable for France, which could win over some Arab leaders by promises of largesse, or could dishearten and exhaust the tribes through war, making the position of the tribes who supported him so intolerable that they would abandon Abd-el-Kader. The most effective way to subjugate the tribes was by interdiction of commerce; ravishing the country was second in importance. Personal ambition and greed had animated the Arabs even more powerfully than fanaticism and national spirit, a motivation that always occurred among half-civilized men.[49]

Tocqueville made a strong case for French domination of Algeria. His two *Reports* of 1847 put forward a program of French control, without any substantial increase of French troops. He proposed organizational changes, simplifying the administrative process, and decentralizing the powers in the hands of the governor-general. He recognized the inconsistencies in French conduct toward the indigenous people, "from benevolence to rigor." French policy had been benevolent and harsh. On one side, there was forbearance, protection, and justice. On the other, there was destruction or confiscation of Arab property, and the misuse of Muslim pious foundations and their revenues. In his speech on July 9, 1847, regarding the proposed 1848 budget for Algeria, Tocqueville commented that the French government was mistaken in removing administration of the Islamic pious foundations from the Islamic authorities, partly because of the implication that the funds were being misused. Exact but rigorous justice should be the French principle of conduct at all times. French domination did not imply neglect of the interests of Arab inhabitants.

On a number of occasions Tocqueville stated that good government meant being attentive to the needs of the natives, respecting their property rights, and sincerely trying to provide for their well-being and their civil rights. Natives should not be pushed along the road toward European civilization and its mores, ideas, and customs but in the directions proper for them. Tocqueville remained convinced that French colonization would improve the condition of life of the Arab population as well as being the mechanism for development by France. The two peoples needed each other: the European needed the Arab to make his lands productive; the Arab needed the European to gain a higher income. If the condition of the natives was not improved, "the two races would fight each other without mercy, and . . . one of the two would die." It was important for French security and honor to respect indigenous property as well as to strengthen the ties of Arab tribes to their territory rather than transport them elsewhere. France, Tocqueville thought, had to try to reduce the hostile sentiments of the natives and to persuade them that a foreign and Christian power could be useful to them. A good government could lead to real pacification. France must not push aside or trample the natives. He drew an interesting parallel: "let us not in the middle of the nineteenth century begin the conquest of America over again . . . let us not repeat the bloody deeds that the whole of humanity condemns." The consequence might be that Algeria would become a closed field, a walled arena, where the two peoples would have to fight without mercy, and where one of the two would have to die.

Tocqueville recognized a perfect solution was not at hand.[50] In the 1847 *Report* he stated that "What we may hope for is not the suppression of the hostile feelings that our dominion inspire, but their softening. . . . It would be unwise to believe that we will succeed in forming between us a bond based on the community of ideas and of customs, but we can hope to form such a bond out of the community of interests." At one point, in 1837, Tocqueville believed that assimilation of Arabs in Algeria would occur; only human deficiencies stood in its way. He considered the possibilities of the mixture of the two peoples that were growing ever closer, of intermarriage between French and Arab people, and common laws and religious toleration. However, four years later in 1841 he was no longer persuaded of "the possibility of a mixture of the two races." The fusion of the two populations was a chimera. In 1846 he was even more emphatic. In a letter to Corcelle on December 1, 1846, he comments on the hatred between the races, which was painful to see. In his speech in the Chamber on June 9, 1846, he dispelled, at least for the present, "the illusion of noble and generous hearts" that the goodwill of the indigenous people would aid and support France in keeping Africa under French law. It was an illusion to expect this from an Arab population "with their customs, habits, social state, passions, antipathies, and mobility.[51]

The dedicated colonialist was apparent in 1847 when Tocqueville presented the two *Reports* of the parliamentary commission of the Chamber of Deputies examining two government draft bills on Algeria. In them Tocqueville discussed alternative points of view, but one can assume that the conclusions incorporated his own personal views on the war, the relations between the French and the Arabs, and the necessity and requirements of colonization. The former believer in assimilation in Algeria now recognized that France faced in Algeria not a real army but the population itself. It was less a matter of defeating an Arab government than of subjugating a people, especially the tribes in the hinterlands who were hostile to the French presence. The resistance of the Arabs indicated that France could not "easily and in a short time succeed in eradicating the silent hate, nourished by foreign domination in the heart of the native." Unfortunately, the Islamic and Christian societies had no links; they formed two juxtaposed but completely separate bodies.

A new tone entered Tocqueville's discourse. France had conquered Algeria, even before knowing the Arabs. Now they could be known: "one can study barbarous people only with arms in hand." The European population had arrived in Algeria: civilized and Christian society had been founded. It was now necessary to deal with the issues of domination of the conquered country and with the administration of the French settlers. Tocqueville ended his *First Report on Algeria* (1847) emphasizing the need for French officials to deal with the problem of North Africa and arguing that those in power were not devoting themselves to this "overwhelming problem with anything like constant preoccupation."

Tocqueville had addressed the broader issue of colonialism in his *Notes on the Voyage to Algeria in* 1841 (May 7–30) and in the *Essay on Algeria* (October 1841).[52] In the *Notes* he commented on the feverish activity in the town of Algiers with its mix of races, customs, and languages: "it is Cincinnati transported onto the soil of Africa." At this point Tocqueville had no fixed position on the different possible goals in Algeria and was aware of the dilemma for France. If France tried to make use of its holdings in the province of Constantine to colonize, peace would end and French domination would be challenged. Since, he wrote in May 1841, war was probable "as soon as we seriously try to colonize with Europeans . . . it would be better to use the land in the Egyptian manner, to have the natives farm it, but to the government's profit." However, where would a domination that did not result in colonization lead France?

Though he approved of the war in Algeria, Tocqueville was critical of both the French military conduct, and the administration of the areas controlled by France. During his voyage to Algeria in May 1841, Tocqueville became aware, as a result of his conversations with officials and military officers in Algeria, of the violence of the colonial warfare and its effect on both Arabs and French settlers. He objected to the coarseness of military power and its arbitrary rule, and to the ardent and unintelligent hatred of the soldier for the civilian, personified by the Commander General, soon to be Marshal, Thomas-Robert Bugeaud who had been appointed military leader in October 1840 and governor-general in December 1840. He found it inconceivable that "a nation that calls itself liberal should have established, close to France and in the name of France, a government so disordered, so tyrannical, so meddlesome, so profoundly illiberal . . . and so alien, indeed, to the most elementary notions of a good colonial regime." In his *First Report* (1847) he recommended, among other things, an institution on the lines of Haileybury College, which trained individuals for the British civil service in India. He also suggested simplification of governmental authority in Algeria and the creation of a ministry for Algeria in Paris.

Tocqueville discussed alternative military strategies for France. He rejected two contrary arguments: one was fighting the Arabs with the utmost violence and "in the Turkish manner" by killing everyone the French troops met, a strategy that was unintelligent and cruel; the other was avoiding strong conflict. The war had become more brutal. After French blockades of Algeria in 1827, the bombardment of Algiers in 1829 and the capture of the city in 1830, and the official annexation of Algeria in 1834, more French troops were sent into the country. Under Bugeaud, whom Tocqueville had at first defended but then criticized for his increasing belligerence toward the Arabs, the troops engaged in brutal behavior, destroying agricultural fields and villages and carrying out the so-called *razzias*, ruthless raids that seized men and herds. These actions, which had rendered Arab society more miserable, continued until Bugeaud resigned in 1847.

It is on this last point, on the use of violence, that Tocqueville has been most open to criticism. Yet on many occasions Tocqueville expressed his perturbation at the use of military means in Algeria, which he thought should not be unlimited. Tocqueville was actually ambivalent about the degree of force and the brutality that French forces should use in their efforts to dominate. He was at times very critical, for both moral and pragmatic reasons, of the use of extreme violence. His internal turmoil is shown in a letter of December 1, 1846, to Claude-François (Francisque) de Corcelle: "it was not only cruel but also absurd and impractical to want to repress or exterminate the natives, but by what means could the two races really be in contact? The hatred between the two races was painful to see; contempt and anger was felt by French officers, in whose eyes the Arabs are like malevolent [*malfaisantes*] animals."[53] Tocqueville did not doubt that in Algiers the Arabs and the Kabyles were more irritated by the presence of French settlers than by French soldiers. The question in Algeria was no longer between governments but between races. In order to colonize to any extent, France had to use violent measures and visibly iniquitous ones. Rapid colonization was not impractical; the greatest obstacles were "less in the country than in ourselves."

The question Tocqueville asked himself, in a letter of October 11, 1846, to Corcelle, was how to raise a French population in Algeria with French laws, manners, and civilization, and at the same time treat the natives with the consideration to which France was bound by honor, justice, humanity, and its real interests.[54] He accepted as "unfortunate necessities," to which one had to submit and that in any case were less violent than what occurred in European wars, the burning of harvests, the emptying of silos, and the seizing of unarmed men, women, and children, and the rapid and brutal incursions, the *razzias* whose purpose was to seize people and steal herds. He expressed this strongly in a later letter of April 5, 1846 to General Lamoricière: "Once we have countenanced the great violence of conquest, I believe we must not recoil before the specific acts of violence that are absolutely necessary to consolidate it." He believed that the effect of the *razzias* might be to cause Abd-el-Kader to sue for peace or might induce some Arab tribes to desert him.

Tocqueville was troubled that French forces were fighting far more barbarously than the Arabs.[55] He was also concerned about the effect of the Algerian war on soldiers, especially officers, who might contract habits, ways of thinking and acting that were dangerous everywhere but especially in a free country, and would pick up the practices and tastes of a hard, violent, arbitrary, and coarse government. In language almost prophetic of events in France in the 1950s he feared that one day soldiers from Algeria would appear on the domestic stage with the force of opinion they acquired abroad: "God save France from ever being led by officers from the army in Algeria."

Tocqueville opened his *Essay* of October 1841, probably the most extreme of his writings on the subject with a stark statement: "I do not think that France can think seriously of leaving Algeria." In the eyes of the world this abandonment would be the clear indication of French decline.[56] Though now conscious and critical of brutality by the army, he still defended some of the violence used in Algeria, considering it necessary in order that France maintain its position in North Africa and be seen as an international power. France, he argued, should leave Algeria only if she were undertaking "great things in Europe" at the same time but not at the present time when she appeared as a second-rank power. France must act quickly, or "our action in the world will be suspended." Its influence in the world would be greatly enhanced if it held the coast of Africa, especially Algiers and the port of Mers-el-Kebir, firmly and peacefully. The chief merit of French colonies for Tocqueville was not in their markets but in the position they occupied on the globe; this made several of them the most precious possessions that France could have.

The conquest and control of Algeria was taken for granted. However, it was necessary but not sufficient. Tocqueville pondered the manner in which it should be done. Conquest could be either by the English method of subordinating inhabitants and governing them directly or indirectly or by replacing the former inhabitants with the conquering race, the European style. French colonization had to accompany the military domination of Algeria.[57] Domination without colonization would be easier to establish, but it would not be worth the time, money, or loss of men. It was only a means to achieve colonization. Similarly, colonization without domination would always be incomplete and precarious. It would require force, for a century if not forever. Tocqueville was troubled, as other French people were to be a century later, by the dilemmas posed by colonialism in Algeria, and the tension between moral behavior and political necessity. His troubled mind is apparent in another letter, of December 1, 1846, to Corcelle: "What means should be used in order for the two races truly to come into contact? I confess with sorrow that here my mind is troubled and hesitates."

In his first *Report* of 1847 Tocqueville opposed those who argued that the Arabs were merely an obstacle to be pushed aside or trampled underfoot. In that case, the issue between the two races would be that of life or death. However, the reality was that colonization and war had to proceed together. The main thing to do to preserve Africa was not to defeat the natives, who were already defeated, but to import into Africa a European population. Domination over semibarbarous nomadic tribes, as in Algeria, could never be so complete as to allow a French civilized, sedentary population to settle nearby without any fear or precaution. The settlers must be protected, and they in turn would make the war easier, less costly, and more decisive.

In his speech in the debate over the appropriation of special funding for Algeria on June 9, 1846, Tocqueville tried to deal with the real state of affairs in the country. He was optimistic: "the war is still troublesome, still a burden, but it is no longer a danger." He made clear he did not want to "expel" or "exterminate" the natives. Tocqueville did not want "the natives to be exterminated . . . but to trust in their good will in order to maintain our position in Africa is pure illusion, one to which it would be madness to subscribe." That position in Africa, and French domination, depended on the arrival on African territory of a European population, a population engaged in agriculture, and on the establishment of good government.Those colonists must be good people, introduce a free market system, and organize an efficient administrative system. The great objective for France was setting up a European society in Africa, but Marshal Bugeaud, the governor-general in Algeria, whose "great military qualities" Tocqueville recognized, had not done that and did not believe in it. In his article in *Le Siècle* of October 23, 1843, Tocqueville declared that the preservation of colonies was essential for the greatness of France. In his *First Report* (1847) he stated that the European population had arrived; a civilized and Christian society had been founded. The task was to know under what laws it must live and what must be done to hasten its development. In his *Second Report* (1847) he now thought that France should create in Algeria not a colony properly speaking but rather the extension of France across the Mediterranean, implanting a population that resembled France in everything.

Tocqueville devoted considerable thought to the conditions for that society. They included agricultural development by the settlers and agricultural camps, building or expanding towns, favorable economic conditions to allow settlers to produce goods cheaply, financial assistance, light taxes, freedom of commerce, and transfer of land. The settlers must have civil and religious liberty and the same judicial guarantees, civil as well as criminal, that they possessed in France. An administrative court would establish principles of administrative justice and would ensure guarantees on property. Algeria was partly occupied but not fully or even actually owned. The public domain was large and its lands, the best in the country, could be distributed to European farmers without injuring anyone's rights. Transactions for land must be set by the state, which would grant property titles, and the state should not subsidize or give capital for the agricultural enterprises. Tocqueville thought the best settlements were rural communities. The principal issue was how to attract and retain in Algeria a great European population of farmers. Presently, there were some one hundred thousand Christians in Africa, but they were almost all in large towns, and the countryside was empty. France had to take an example from the early United States and populate the land.

Tocqueville, however, recognized that the rules regarding the right of property in Africa were obscure, and they were further obscured by the attempt to impose a single, common solution. In his *Second Letter* (1837), he thought that the Arabs sold land readily and cheaply and that a foreign population could easily establish itself next to them without causing them harm. Yet in 1841 he recognized that what most worried and irritated the natives was to see the French settlers take and cultivate their lands. In this complex problem of land ownership he suggested to the Chamber that it was easier to introduce a new population to a territory that was owned communally than on to land that was protected by individual right and a particular interest.

Tocqueville expressed the view that to be successful, colonization required efficient administration.[58] He was disturbed by the sluggishness and uniformity of the French central government to which "the children of the desert" had to submit and complained of the tyrannical and arbitrary but weak and impotent character of the government of Algeria. He recognized in his *Notes* on May 24, 1841, that there was no government in Algeria "at least such as we mean by that word in the civilized countries of Europe." He indicated the "extreme abuses" of centralization, lack of settled property and of independent justice, press, and local assemblies. He provided various general and specific suggestions for overcoming these deficiencies. He called, in 1841 and again in 1847, for municipal councils, and for transferring to them some of the functions of the central authorities. The machinery of all administrative authorities should be under the direction or surveillance and control of the political power. Most urgently needed were institutions similar to those in France and the establishment of a municipal authority. France must move quickly to attach the settlers to their new land by giving them "collective interests and action." There must be more municipal functions in Algeria: they were necessary in order to create a social life that did not yet exist, and there was no need to fear that municipal liberty would degenerate into political license.

In his *First Report on Algeria* in 1847, Tocqueville argued that France should create in Africa a governmental machine simpler and more prompt to act than the one in place in France. The opposite was now the case in Algeria and municipal and departmental life did not exist at all. Everything was controlled by the central authority, and all the actions of public authorities in Africa were settled by offices in Paris. It was impossible to calculate the loss of time and money, the social suffering, and the individual miseries that had been caused by the absence of municipal power. Tocqueville held that although the government of the country must be centralized in Paris, the centralization of administration must be in the hands of a single official in charge of giving a common direction to all the departmental heads. Conscious as he always was of the dangers of centralization, and though calling for local autonomy and local councils for the settlers in Algeria, Tocqueville still thought that the colonists must be compelled to obey certain military controls.

THE ISSUE OF SLAVERY

Though he did not provide generalizations on the issue, still confronting the world in the twenty-first century, Tocqueville touched on the problem of the moral and political relations of advanced and less developed societies, and the extent to which the former countries should help advance or modernize the latter. Tocqueville never formulated any concept of historical stages nor posited any hierarchy of the peoples of the world, nor any concept of racial superiority, which he regarded as false and odious, though he sometimes wrote of "half-civilized" or "barbarous" peoples. Notwithstanding his advocacy of colonization and his emphatic assertions of French patriotism and nationalism, Tocqueville was not a racist. No trace of this appears in his public and private writings or in his speeches. This is very apparent in his correspondence with Gobineau, who had been his research assistant for a time in 1843 and his secretary when Tocqueville became foreign minister in 1849. During a three-year period of that correspondence, from 1853 to 1856, Tocqueville expressed increasingly critical opinions of Gobineau's self-professed racist theory, particularly in relation to Gobineau's four-volume *Essay on the Inequality of the Human Races*, which sees race as the main determinant of social and political life and propounds the biological superiority of the white race. For Tocqueville this was "a sort of fatalism or predestination." It promoted spiritual lassitude, removed any significant role for the individual in influencing social affairs, and led to weakness and self-pity and to the belief that nations were bound to obey some insuperable and unthinking power, the product of preexisting facts regarding race, soil, or climate. For Tocqueville it had never been proved that certain human tendencies and characteristics were insuperable in the different families of people making up the world.

In a particularly frank letter of November 17, 1853, Tocqueville, though using the term "lesser peoples," could not accept Gobineau's argument of races "that are regenerating or deteriorating, which take up or lay aside social capacities by an infusion of different blood." Tocqueville was forthright: "there is an intellectual world between your doctrine and mine." Gobineau's doctrines "at the opposite extreme" of Tocqueville's, resulted in a great contraction, if not a complete abolition, of human liberty. The doctrines were probably wrong and certainly pernicious. Tocqueville asked his "dear friend" what interest could there be in persuading people who lived in barbarism, in indolence, or in servitude, that, because they existed in such a condition by virtue of the nature of their race, could do nothing to ameliorate their condition, change their mores, or modify their government? Tocqueville repeated similar points in further letters to Gobineau, though discussion was now embarrassing to the two friends. On December 20, he referred to Gobineau's thesis as the most dangerous that could be maintained at that time. Finally, on January 8, 1856, Tocqueville wrote that Gobineau had written a book "which tries to prove that men in this world are merely obeying their physical constitutions and that their will power can do almost nothing to influence their destinies . . . [this] is like opium given to a patient whose blood has already weakened."[59]

Equally forthright as his denunciation of racist theory was Tocqueville's activity advocating, intellectually and politically, the abolition of slavery in the French colonies. Discussing the three races in the United States in *Democracy in America* (vol. I), Tocqueville commented that "among the moderns, the abstract and transient fact of slavery is fatally united with the physical and permanent fact of color." On the issue Tocqueville's essential position was clear: "man has never had the right to possess man, and the fact of possession always has been and still is illegitimate." Slavery, "the odious institution," was contrary to all the natural rights of humanity. The question was not whether slavery was or was not pernicious, but only when and how it was sensible to end it.[60]

Tocqueville was a constant proponent of emancipation from slavery, writing on the subject, speaking about it in the Chamber of Deputies, and joining in 1835 the Association for the Abolition of Slavery, founded the previous year and chaired by the duc de Broglie. Soon after he entered the Chamber, Tocqueville was, in 1839, appointed rapporteur of a committee studying a proposal for emancipation. Tocqueville's report, going further than the original proposal, advocated the immediate and simultaneous emancipation of all the slaves, then about 250,000, in the French colonies and financial indemnification of former slaveholders.[61] He was aware that gradual, rather than complete, emancipation could lead to psychological, social, and economic problems. To prevent problems after emancipation the government, for a time, should be the sole guardian of the emancipated. The report was shelved by the government; instead, another committee of peers, deputies, admirals, and former colonial governors was appointed with the duc de Broglie as chair and rapporteur. In the divided committee a majority proposed a compromise in 1843, approving emancipation in ten years time and recommending a waiting period before complete emancipation, during which slaves would be educated and prepared for freedom. Though Tocqueville still favored immediate emancipation, he voted for the 1843 compromise in order to obtain some government action. In a debate in May 1845, he was again critical of the policy of gradualism and political inactivity on abolition.[62]

Yet, if he saw the issue of the abolition of slavery as one of justice, he was always conscious of its relevance to France's economic and political interests, to the success of French colonization, and also to the competition of France with Britain as international leader of the cause of emancipation. He insisted that though Britain in 1834 had abolished slavery first, it was France that had spread throughout the world the notions of freedom and equality, which was not only France's glory but also its strength. It was France that had given a determined and practical meaning to the Christian idea that all men were born equal and had applied that to the realities of this world. France was, therefore, the true author of the abolition of slavery. Again, for Tocqueville morality and political interest interrelated. Humanity and morality had often, sometimes imprudently, called for the abolition of slavery, but now political necessity imposed it. In the same year he wrote six articles, published anonymously in *Le Siècle* on October 22 and 28, November 8 and 21, December 6 and 14, 1843, on the subject of emancipation. He recognized that maintaining the status quo would be the ruin of the colonies: if there was a way for France to keep her colonies it would come only from the abolition of slavery. The need for abolition resulted from the general movement of the century, from the spirit of the times. Slavery in the colonies must be ended; this would come when France was convinced that keeping the colonies was necessary for the strength and greatness of France. Unless slavery was abolished in the French colonies, they would bring France nothing but costs.

Tocqueville was troubled that France had not yet appreciated this need to abolish slavery though it was the country that propagated ideas of freedom and equality, ideas that were weakening or destroying servitude everywhere. He was chagrined that it was Britain that was applying French principles in their colonies and was acting in accordance with French sentiment. Britain, after banning the slave trade in 1808 and adopting the principle of abolition of slavery in 1823, passed a law in 1833 to end slavery in the British colonies the next year. Emancipation was successful in all the nineteen British colonies. Tocqueville asked the question: would France, the democratic country par excellence, remain the sole European nation to countenance slavery? If so, she would be renouncing the great role – the standard of modern civilization – that she "had the pride to take up, but that she does not have the courage to fulfill."

Although Tocqueville took the moral high road on the question of slavery realistically he recognized that moral, political, and economic problems would remain.[63] Even if slavery was in retreat "the prejudice from which it sprang remains unshaken." Its abolition would also create practical economic problems in the French colonies. These problems could be alleviated by colonization and settlers: "France works to create civilized societies, not hordes of savages." Yet France must also ensure that colonists not be ruined by the freedom of the slaves.[64]

ON BRITISH RULE IN INDIA

Tocqueville's argument, implicit or otherwise, of the superiority of Western values and civilization is clear not only in his later writings on Algeria but also in his general, if sometimes equivocal, approval of British control of India. He admired the rapidity with which that control had been established as well as its nature.[65] Tocqueville had been interested in Britain's activity in India since 1840, and at one point wanted to write a book on the British establishment there. Only a fragment of that projected book was written, and Tocqueville only touched on the subject in correspondence with British and French friends. Tocqueville was eager to examine "the causes that produces and sustained the astonishing greatness of the English in India. . . . It is particularly [interesting] now we have the colony in Algeria." A country almost as vast as Europe had been conquered in sixty years by a few thousand Europeans who landed on its shores as merchants. The British conquest was "an inexplicable and almost marvelous event." Even more, he admired the balance in the administration of India between the East India Company and the state.

Tocqueville sought to draw lessons from the conquest of India by Britain, his "second intellectual homeland" and the homeland of his wife. Yet he was ambivalent, neither fully defending nor disapproving of the conquest.[66] On one hand he wrote, "Nothing under the sun is so wonderful as the conquest and still more the government of India by the British." Britain should not withdraw from India. The country cost more than it brought in, but the loss of India would greatly lower the position of England. British control there brought a feeling of greatness and power to the British people. Yet on the other hand he was aware of the dilemma of colonialism for Britain as it was for France. In uncharacteristically harsh remarks he wrote about the British tactics in putting down the Sepoy Mutiny (1857–58): "Your title to govern these savages is that you are better than they are. You ought to punish them, not act like them." To Lord Hatherton he wrote on November 27, 1857 that in India he had never doubted "your triumph which is that of Christianity and of civilization." He defended the British role in India as a civilizing one, though he was concerned about the violence involved. In a letter of August 6, 1857 to Nassau Senior during the Sepoy revolt, he said, "there is not one civilized nation in the world that ought to rejoice in seeing India escape from the hands of Europeans in order to fall back into a state of anarchy and barbarism worse than before its conquest." A few months later on November 15, 1857, after the revolt had been ended, he remarked to Senior that though there was little sympathy for England abroad, "Your loss of India could have served no cause but that of barbarism." Again, he wrote on August 2, 1857 to Reeve that "to see the English domination in India reversed and nothing replace it and leaving the indigenous people to barbarism would be sad."[67]

Yet on the other hand, in the same letter of November 27, 1857 to Lord Hatherton, he rebuked the English who "had not in a century done anything for the Indian populations that might have been expected from their enlightenment and their institutions." In the unfinished work on India he wrote that in spite of British accomplishments there, such as the end of cruel customs and the creation of a sense of law, "nevertheless the primary effects of their domination have been to augment destitution, unrest, crimes." Britain had plundered and oppressed India. In his terse, unfinished notes on India, Tocqueville tried to explain why the country was not at a very advanced state before the British arrival. The laws were inadequate. Civil society was immobilized by religious law. The caste system, in which each caste formed a small, distinct nation that had its own spirit, customs, laws, and government, held back the formation of an advanced society and national unity. Indian development stopped at some medium level. Hinduism was ruled by superstition and enslaved the mind. Hindu knowledge of arts and sciences was imperfect; the Hindu people had not learned the secret of defending itself or struggling against tyranny. Buddhism, absorbent and tolerant, nevertheless maintained the caste system, so contrary to nature, and Buddhists were a privileged group.

Tocqueville painted a critical picture of Indian society and politics. It once had great despots but never strong governments. Power always resided in the man, rather than in the institution. The Hindu princes never had the idea of delegating power. The science of government, like all other sciences, had stopped at an imperfect stage. The Muslims in general seemed at first to have been tolerant, but they became intolerant under Aurengzeb. The immense empire of the Great Mughal had never been homogeneous or centralized. It had never had a proper central administration. The Great Mughal never spoke of subjects but of tributaries that conducted war among each other or with him. By the eighteenth century, the Mughal Empire was in full disintegration: the emperor had only nominal authority over the provinces where there were perpetual struggles between the different princes. Tocqueville saw India as in a stationary state, with no evidence of progress being made in the arts and sciences and no trace of amelioration of conditions. The country, because of its caste system, decadent and corrupt society, and privileged groups, was not at an advanced stage of development.[68]

Yet regarding the question of the British presence in India, Tocqueville, recognizing the political, financial, and military difficulties in the country, politely but affirmatively expressed "great doubts about introducing a European population" in the country. Without referring specifically to Algeria he remarked that the introduction of a European population "in the midst of the imperfectly civilized populations of the rest of the world" would result in more anger from that than from any political oppression because of the harm to individual interests and to the self-respect of the indigenous people caused by their feelings about the real and pretended superiority of the Europeans. In this regard Tocqueville was not in favor of either colonialism or colonization.[69]

ON COLONIZATION

Tocqueville also commented on Europe's mission in other areas. Expressing, in a letter to Henry Reeve of April 12, 1840, anxiety about the planned British expedition against China, he rejoiced in the thought of "an invasion of the Celestial Empire by a European army . . . at last the mobility of Europe has come to grips with Chinese immobility! . . . a great event [and] . . . only the continuation, the last in a multitude of events of the same nature all of which are pushing the European race out of its home and are successively submitting all the other races to its empire or its influence."[70]

This view was related to his position on Algeria. In the second volume of *Democracy in America*, Tocqueville had written of the "strange immobility" in the minds of the Chinese, that science no longer existed as it had in the past, and that they had lost the power of change and for them improvement was impossible. Tocqueville's advocacy of a civilizing mission for Europeans in general and France in particular accompanied the insistence on the need for France to play a role in Asia, the Mediterranean, and Algeria, and was combined with the need for heightened French nationalism. Tocqueville was at his most nationalistic point: "Any nation that readily lets go [in Algeria] of what it has taken and withdraws peacefully of its own accord back inside its old boundaries proclaims that the golden age of its history is past."[71] Colonization of Algeria was thus a manifestation of French power and national interest for Tocqueville. He started his *Essay* of October 1841 with his thought that France could not think seriously of leaving Algeria. The world would see this as a clear indication of French decadence (decline) and as yielding to her impotence and lack of courage.

Tocqueville argued that colonization was also in the interests of the colonial power. This was true in India: the brilliance of the British conquest "reflects on all the nation." It was also true of the French in Algeria, where their presence would create "on the African coast a great monument to the glory of our country." If France could manage to hold the coast of North Africa firmly and peacefully, its influence in the world's general affairs would be strongly enhanced. The two points in Algeria, Mers-el-Kebir and Algiers, would certainly add a great deal to France's strength. That strength was associated with national passion and pride. Writing to John Stuart Mill on October 18, 1840, Tocqueville, touching on Anglo-French differences and specifically that France not be treated by Britain with indifference, wrote "the most elevated feeling now left to us is national pride . . . we ought to try to regulate and moderate it but we must beware not to diminish it." In his long letter of March 18, 1841, to John Stuart Mill, discussing the two equally extreme parties, in favor of war and of peace, Tocqueville could not approve of either side. He argued that France should not lightly adopt the "habit of sacrificing what it believes to be its grandeur to its repose, great matters to petty ones." France should not believe that its prestige in the world was based only on constructing railroads or making private individuals prosper. Political leaders must maintain "a proud attitude," adopt language that "sustains the nation's heart," and try to limit the enervating taste of the nation it has for material enjoyments and small pleasures.

On this point Mill was more cautious and temperate. In his reply of August 9, 1842, Mill was aware of Tocqueville's arguments of the importance of national pride and of the need to encourage the desire to shine in the eyes of foreigners and to be highly esteemed by them. But Mill also advised that, in the name of France and civilization, men like Tocqueville should teach their countrymen better ideas than the low and groveling ones they seemed to have presently, of what constituted national glory and national importance. For him it really depended not on loud and boisterous assertion of a nation's importance or on its defiance of foreigners but on its industry, education, morality, and good government.

Tocqueville continued to assert that the nation's heart would be sustained by colonization.[72] In his letter of October 28, 1846, to Beaumont, he wrote that "however important the question of the Arabs and the war is to the government, I can consider it only as accessory to my concern. For me, above all, with no desire to leave the region of Algiers, the highest priority is the administration and establishment of the European society." That meant implanting in Africa a population that resembled French people in everything; it would not mean giving rise to a new people in Algeria.

Yet Tocqueville continued also to emphasize that the African question was complicated and important.[73] For him the dilemma was how to raise a French population (in Algeria) with French laws, manners, and civilization, and at the same time treat the natives with the "consideration to which we are bound by honor, justice, humanity, and our real interests." For Tocqueville the balance between idealism and humanity, on one hand, and concern for French national interests, on the other, vacillated. Bringing the European and Arab populations together, and destroying in the hearts of Arabs the blind hatred created and sustained by foreign domination, was not easy. Yet France must remain strong; it could not suppress, but it could weaken hostile sentiments. It could not expect a community of ideas and customs. It could try to persuade the Arabs of their community of interests with France through trade and agricultural help. Europeans needed the natives to increase the value of their land; the Arabs needed the Europeans to obtain a higher salary. Common interest might bring them together.

In a short manuscript, *Some Ideas about What Prevents the French from Having Good Colonies*, part of a longer manuscript written with his friend Beaumont in 1833 on prison reform, Tocqueville explained that the French genius did not appear to be favorable to colonization. France had always been in the first rank of continental powers, but maritime enterprises would never attract attention in France. The mix in the French character of domestic tension and passion for adventure was, for different reasons, equally bad for colonization. France would find it hard to find talented men to run colonial enterprises. For France to found a colony would be to give itself up to an enterprise full of perils and uncertain success.

However before long Tocqueville saw colonization in a different light. Preoccupied as he was with the greatness of France and the place of France in the world, he disregarded what he viewed in 1833 as the French taste for quiet pleasures, on the one hand, and the violent emotions if French people were uprooted on the other. Tocqueville became an unwavering voice advocating French settlement in Algeria. About the goal he was unambiguous: to implant in Africa a population that "resembles us in everything. If this goal cannot be attained immediately, it is at least the only one for which we should constantly and actively strive." Tocqueville, the constant and ardent proponent of universal freedom, cannot easily be reconciled with the advocate of colonization in North Africa. Throughout his life until the end Tocqueville stressed the value of liberty. In one of his last letters, that of February 27, 1858, to Beaumont, he wrote that "I have never been more profoundly convinced that [liberty] alone can give to human societies in general, to the individuals who compose them in particular, all the prosperity and all the grandeur of which our species is capable." Yet he was equally convinced of the importance of colonization for France. In his writings and public activity on Algeria the question was not whether to colonize Africa but what method of colonization France should follow.

Tocqueville can more rightly be considered a patriot and a nationalist than as an imperialist or irrevocable colonialist. He did not call, as did Napoleon and Talleyrand, for France to establish a colony in Egypt in order to aid the French struggle against Britain. Tocqueville, typically tentative rather than declarative, acknowledged that patriotism had been viewed as a false and narrow passion and that Christian moralists were more inclined to care more for humanity than for their fatherland. Rejecting this view, Tocqueville believed that people were more attached to particular passions, limited objects, and individual nations than to the entire human species.

Unlike a typical imperialist or colonialist, Tocqueville did not endorse the general principle of commanding or subjugating one people by another. He did believe, in the case of Algeria, that France could encourage a civilizing mission in a less developed country that had for centuries been under a type of Oriental despotism. He also believed, at one stage, that the Arabs would adopt the French style of life, if given an incentive to do so. This view was part of his general argument, especially in his strong advocacy for the emancipation of slaves, that France had spread the ideas of freedom and equality that were weakening or destroying servitude everywhere. For Tocqueville, France had given practical meaning to the idea that all people were born equal and should be guaranteed an equal right to freedom. Yet, Tocqueville was not, as were others such as Victor Hugo at times, an advocate of France's general missionary role as educator of humanity. Though troubled by "calculating patriotism founded on interest," as well as by a fear of possible decadence of the French population, Tocqueville, perhaps inherently a nostalgic aristocrat in spite of denials, was a patriot conscious of the past glory of France and anxious for it to play a prominent role in the international arena and impress international opinion. He hoped that a great French project might relieve what he viewed as the languor of fellow citizens. His thoughts, as his friend Beaumont suggested, always had a practical and definite object.

Can the liberal Tocqueville, the believer in freedom and equality, be reconciled with the proponent of colonization in Algeria? Perhaps the answer lies in Keats's concept of negative capability, the ability to live in uncertainties.

7

James Mill and John Stuart Mill: Despotism in India

One of the early English admirers of Alexis de Tocqueville was John Stuart Mill who immediately recognized the first volume of *Democracy in America* as "an excellent book, uniting considerable graphic power with the capacity of generalizing on the history of society."[1] After the publication of Tocqueville's second volume, Mill thought rather differently that the work was "really abstruse, by being so abstract and not sufficiently illustrating his propositions," thus making it difficult to review.[2] Nevertheless, Mill, in two, long admiring reviews, complimented Tocqueville on a great achievement that, he wrote, changed the face of political philosophy and the discussion on the tendencies of modern society.[3] Like his French friend, John Stuart Mill was another public intellectual, forwarding ideas to influence politics and culture. In his discussion of Tocqueville, Mill concluded that the Frenchman's definition of *democracy* was not a particular form of government but equality of conditions, the absence of all aristocracy, whether constituted by political privilege or by superiority in individual importance and social power.[4] More pointedly, in his May 11, 1840, letter, Mill praised one of Tocqueville's "great, general conclusions," that the real danger in democracy, the real evil to be struggled against, was not anarchy or love of change but "Chinese stagnation" and immobility.

John Stuart Mill in a number of his writings was to draw a similar conclusion on the issue of stagnation. He also took a similar position to that of Tocqueville about the possible tyranny of public opinion or collective mediocrity in democratic societies. However, in correspondence with Tocqueville between 1840 and 1842, Mill disagreed with him on a major issue, expressing his distaste for the Frenchman's emphasis on "*orgeuil national*" (national pride) and his concern that "the only appeal which really goes to the heart of France is one of defiance of foreigners."[5] Instead, Mill stated, Tocqueville and other French noble spirits should teach their countrymen "better ideas of what constitutes national glory and national importance": industry, instruction, morality, and good government. Later, in defending British policy, John Stuart Mill was to write that not only did Britain desire no benefit to itself at the expense of others, but also that it desired none in which all others did not freely participate.

Mill's critical remark about Tocqueville's nationalism virtually ended the correspondence between the two, apart from a final exchange of letters in 1856 and 1859. The ultimate irony in this first friendly and then uneasy relationship between the two thinkers was that John Stuart Mill's praise of the British role in India, if equivocal at times, was not too dissimilar from Tocqueville's approval of France's civilizing mission in Algeria, despite Mill's disagreement with Tocqueville's argument for colonization.

John Stuart Mill's father, James Mill, in an article of 1813, had anticipated his son's critique of Tocqueville.[6] He warned against the use of concepts such as national pride, glory, honor, and power. They were useful only for those whose interest was to keep nations involved in the expense of war. *Glory*, the most frequently used term, signified the exhibition or exercise of power over others, actions that were harmful to the mass of people in the nation. Instead of terms such as *glory* and *honor*, James Mill suggested *utility* and *justice*. On the question of conflict he suggested applying to it what he considered the principle of utility, "consider whether the evil which you have suffered is likely to be compensated by war." The calculus of relative ills or gains would be the rule to apply in determining whether or not to institute hostilities when a nation has suffered, or believed it has suffered, injury.

Just as Tocqueville's views on Algeria are much less familiar in general than his works on America and France, the writings of John Stuart Mill on Indian affairs have been given scant attention, even by his biographers, compared to the large output of commentary on his political, philosophical, and economic works, now collected in thirty-three volumes. Yet both John Stuart Mill and his father James spent a considerable part of their life dealing with India, and both were employees of the Company for long periods.

James Mill spent the last seventeen years of his life, and J. S. Mill the whole of his official working life, as officials of the Company. As described in Chapter 5, the Company was chartered in 1600 by Queen Elizabeth I. It started as a trading company that made calls at Indian ports, buying Indian cotton textiles. Then increasingly, it established coastal settlements. By the latter part of the eighteenth century it had gained various forms of control over large parts of India becoming the paramount power, though not the direct ruler because the rulers of the Native States, with whom the Company made alliances, had varying degrees of autonomy. An unusual dual arrangement for governing the country developed with the Company, a private company, administering territory and exercising political power. It conducted affairs in India on behalf of the British government, which exercised supervision through a Board of Control.

Because the Company needed protection in India it was given some power of government and was able to raise a military force. With the decline of Mughal power in the mid-eighteenth century, the Company increasingly intervened to establish stability. The Board of Control was created by Pitt's India Act of 1784 to regulate the activities of the Company.[7] Essentially, the directors sent proposals to the president of the Board of Control, usually a member of the British cabinet, who could reject or rewrite them, and sometimes lay down policy. The British government appointed the governor-general, based in Calcutta, and the governors of Bombay and Madras. The directors made other appointments. John Stuart Mill referred to the Company as the branch of government of India under the Crown.[8]

This unusual arrangement of a private company exercising political power had become increasingly important after the Company took over most of the administration in Bengal with Robert Clive's conquest of the area for it in 1757. The Nawab of Bengal remained, for a time, the nominal ruler, with the Company being the tutelary ruler, its officials and military force administering justice and supervising collection of taxes. In 1765 the nawab was deposed and the Company took over direct administration. Following that, the Company entered into treaties of subsidiary alliance with some of the Indian rulers and in the 1790s annexed other territories.

JAMES MILL AND THE HISTORY OF BRITISH INDIA

James Mill, the friend and disciple of Jeremy Bentham, the Utilitarian philosopher, was an important figure in Indian affairs, through his influential book *The History of British India*, published in 1817, and his official position with the Company in London. Following the publication of his book, in 1819 Mill was appointed assistant examiner of India correspondence in the Company and in 1830 was promoted to examiner of correspondence, the chief executive officer, responsible until his death in 1836 for preparing and overseeing the drafting of dispatches in all departments to India.

Paying assiduous attention to his job, which he found "highly interesting," James Mill became familiar with all aspects of Indian affairs and the conduct of British policy in relation to them. His son, John Stuart, complimented him on his dispatches in which he sought to improve India and to teach Indian officials to understand their tasks, and declared that his father's *History* had "contributed largely to my education in the best sense of the term."[9] John Stuart Mill paid a fulsome tribute to the literary and practical work of his father. He believed the *History* was a remarkable book, a guide to thoughts on society and civilization in India, and should be considered a valuable contribution to the history of the area. His father had set forth accurately, for the first time, many of the valid principles of Indian administration. Equally, John Stuart Mill held that his father, as an administrator of Indian interests under the Company, had effected a great deal of good, and laid the foundations of much more for millions of Asians, and had done much to promote the improvement of India and teach Indian officials to understand their business.

Born in Scotland in 1773, the son of a shoemaker, James Mill began his career as a journalist in London in 1802. After the failure of two journals with which he was associated, *The Literary Journal*, which he had edited for four years, and the *St. James's Chronicle*, he began his *History of British India*, taking eleven years to finish it. He acknowledged, in his preface, that he had never been in India and had only a slight acquaintance with the languages of the East, but nevertheless he believed he could still provide a useful work on the subject. Certainly, it contributed significantly to the dialogue of British officials and writers on India in the early part of the nineteenth century.

With the decay of the empire of Aurungzebe (1658–1707) and continuing wars among the princedoms in India, European respect for Indian civilization and the native way of life lessened and a view of India as a backward country became more pronounced.[10] Mill wrote his *History* as this change was occurring, combining a moral concern for India to become a more advanced civilization with a Utilitarian interest in efficiency and legal and administrative reform. Believing that the knowledge about India possessed by the British officials and community was singularly incorrect and inadequate, Mill made clear his book was a critical historical judgment.

History has to be put in the context of internal dispute in Britain about Indian society and politics and of the strong criticism of British administration in India by influential figures such as Charles James Fox and Edmund Burke who had expressed, a little earlier, some admiration for the Mughal Empire. James Mill, with his grounding in Utilitarian philosophy and Enlightenment radicalism, was aware of other British figures who, in different ways, were more critical of that empire and were advocating change, essentially modernization, for India.[11] Some were missionaries, including William Wilberforce and Charles Grant, anxious to overcome the defects of Hinduism through conversion to Christianity. Their missions began after the Charter Act of 1813, which also provided for the establishment of the first Anglican bishopric in India. Liberal reformers and those interested in increased free trade with India also called for change and a more open Indian society.

Mill's *History* may be little read today, but Thomas Macaulay paid it extravagant praise as "on the whole the greatest historical work which has appeared in our language since that of Gibbon."[12] It became the standard work for Company officials, a textbook for candidates for the Indian Civil Service and for the Company's college at Haileybury, which had been founded in 1805 as a training school for administrators. In *History*, James Mill was critical of that group of British officials who had political interests and of scholars, including Nathaniel Halhed, Sir Charles Wilkins, and Henry Thomas Colebrooke, who were more respectful than he of Hindu civilization. Colebrooke had called for the end of the Company's monopoly and had also compiled a study of Sanskrit and Indian law. For example, James Mill criticized Warren Hastings, the first governor-general of India, for respecting native Indian customs: "the custom of a country, where almost everything was corrupt affords but a sorry defense."[13]

However, Mill's main target was Sir William Jones, mentioned in earlier chapters, the distinguished lawyer, scholar, and authority on a number of Indian languages, who, for Mill, had provided a too favorable picture of Indian civilization and was overly enthusiastic about Sanskrit literature and poetic tradition. Jones was "actuated by the virtuous design of exalting the Hindus in the eyes of their European masters."[14] Jones on the subject "of a supposed ancient state of high civilization, riches and happiness among the Hindus, took everything for granted, not only without proof, but in opposition to almost everything . . . that could lead him to a different conclusion."[15]

James Mill's criticism of Jones is illustrative of the disagreement about the nature of Indian civilization and political history held by the so-called Anglicists and Orientalists. The two camps, though their views were qualified and sometimes overlapping, reflected differences not only on scholarly and intellectual questions but also on the manner and method by which British personnel should govern and try to promote change in India. They differed not only on the nature of the indigenous culture but also on the appropriate educational system and the language of instruction, and on relative merits of direct and indirect rule. The two groups differed on whether the native languages, Arabic, Persian, and Sanskrit, should be included in the curriculum as well as used as the medium of instruction. They differed on the training of the Indian elite: the Orientalists advocated the study of Indian philology, history, archeology, Hindu and Muhammedan law, and the native ways of life; the Anglicists wanted instruction in English – in English literature and science – and training of the elite for revenue and judicial administration.

The dispute took place in the context of the changing situation in India. The Company had conquered Bengal in 1757, and its officials studied Persian and Sanskrit, and others, such as Alexander Dow and N. B. Halhed, wrote texts.[16] The Asiatic Society of Bengal, founded by Sir William Jones in 1784, and a number of new journals fostered research on Indian culture, a subject that began to be studied in European universities. Warren Hastings thought that to communicate with the Indian people, it was necessary to acquire their languages. He was fluent in Persian and Hindi, sponsored translations of Islamic texts, and founded a Calcutta Madras. Such knowledge and communication, allowing "a domination founded on the right of conquest" was useful to the state and benefited the people. In 1800 under Governor-General of India Lord Wellesley, the College of Fort William was established as a training center in Calcutta for the Company with the ideal of educating an elite civil service to serve in India. The emphasis of the Orientalists changed from the concentration on the texts to greater concern for administering new knowledge while keeping traditional beliefs.[17] In the context of a culture in which the Brahmans were powerful and formed a hereditary class of priests, where the masses were ignorant, there was a low level of technological development, exactness in the legal code was absent, and despotic regimes existed, British officials had to deal with issues of revenue settlements, education, and administrative policies, and the charter for the Company.

Sir William Jones can be regarded as the most well-known exponent of the Orientalist point of view. Jones served as a Supreme Court judge between 1783 and 1794 and prompted a digest of Hindu and Islamic laws compiled by native lawyers, a digest that could provide for the people of Asia "stability to their property, real and personal, and security to their persons" and lead to improvement of "agricultural and mechanical arts."[18] Such a digest could help the establishment of a Hindu polity in which the authority of the religious groups in Bengal would be reduced and policy would be based on legal tradition.[19] Jones also advocated the study of Eastern languages and texts in India and the history and culture of India. A formidable philologist, who apparently knew more than twenty languages, Jones encouraged knowledge of Sanskrit and study of early Indian history through four media: languages and letters, philosophy and religion, the remains of old sculpture and architecture, and the written memorials of science and arts.[20] Jones translated the poetry of Arabia and Persia and nine hymns to Hindu deities into English. From these sources, literature, and legends, he believed a valid historical account of India could emerge.

Jones also believed that an authoritarian form of government was necessary in Asia and Africa, in the absence of virtuous nobility and in the presence of prejudices.[21] Though authoritarianism had been the mode, it was legal and restricted. "The Indian princes never had, nor pretended to have an unlimited legislative authority, but were always under the control of laws believed to be divine, with which they never claimed any power of dispensing."[22] The British, he thought, should allow the Indians to live according to their customs and laws while protected by an absolute but moderate ruler. British rules should take account of and be congenial "to the disposition and habits, to the religious prejudices, and approved immemorial usages of the people for whom they were enacted."[23] In court, where British subjects resident in India were protected and governed by British laws, the natives should be "indulged in their own prejudices, civil and religious, and suffered to enjoy their own customs unmolested."[24] The democratic system was not appropriate for India, where millions are "so wedded to inveterate prejudices and habits that if liberty could be forced on them by Britain, it would make them as miserable as the cruelest despotism."[25]

At this point perhaps two things should be clarified. The first is that the "Orientalist" group of scholars and administrators varied in their specific views and policies, and to see them as part of a unified discourse, as some modern-day critics of "Orientalism" allege, is intellectually simplistic and ignores the empirical evidence and concrete facts on which those views and policies were based.[26] Equally simplistic and strident as this first point is the argument that eighteenth- and nineteenth-century Orientalists were really only agents for the imposition of Western values on India, trade concessions, or ruling the East and delegitimizing non-Western forms of the state, or they were bigoted imperialists. Certainly, diffusion of Western ideas was urged by British liberal reformers, the opening of India to the West urged by those wanting to expand trade, and intrusion of Christian values urged by those believing that India had been held back by Hinduism.

Nevertheless, discussion in the British parliament of the activities of the Company in the early nineteenth century shows both the caution that British rule in India should not be too overbearing, and the concern that native society and politics be maintained. That rule should not exemplify a manifestation of imperial power. Above all that rule would aid India's cultural renewal; lead to political and social development and modernization, enlightenment of society, and creation of significant institutions; and prepare the country to overcome the historic despotisms that had dominated the country. One example of that aid to India renewal in the early nineteenth century was manifested by the work of James Prinsep, the secretary of the Asiatic Society of Bengal in 1832, who, among other things, was responsible for improved drainage in Calcutta, restoring the mosque of Aurangzeb, reforming Indian weights and measures, classifying the coinage system, fostering Indian archaeology, and above all deciphering and decoding the Gupta Brahmi script and contributing to knowledge of ancient Indian history. Another was the work of Alexander Cunningham, soldier and archaeologist, who in 1861 supervised the first professional excavations of Buddhist sites and helped found, and then direct, the Archaeological Survey of India.

James Mill for the most part exemplified the Anglicist perspective in the dialogue with the Orientalists. As a Utilitarian he believed the Orientalists concealed the backwardness of Indian culture, which preserved undesirable traditional institutions from which the country had to be emancipated through reforms based on the principle of utility. For him it was a mistake to view the Hindus as "a people of high civilization while they have in reality made but a few of the earliest steps in the progress to civilization." The actual condition of the Hindus, according to James Mill, was little beyond that of half-civilized nations. Mill challenged the view that they were once in a state of high civilization from which they had fallen through foreign conquest and subjugation.[27] On the contrary, everything "we know of the ancient state of Hindustan conspires to prove that it was rude." Wherever the Hindus have been exempt from foreign control their state of civilization was inferior to those who had long been subjects of a Muhammadan throne.[28]

For James Mill, the activity and writings of Jones was the product of an undisciplined imagination."[29] He contended it was unfortunate that a mind so pure, so warm in the pursuit of truth, and so devoted to Oriental learning, as that of Sir William Jones, should have adopted the hypothesis of a high state of civilization in the principal countries of Asia."[30] Jones was motivated by the virtuous design of exalting the Hindus in the eyes of their European masters. Jones had asserted that "we have certain proof that the people of Arabia . . . were eminently civilized for many ages before their conquest of Persia." Mill belittled Jones's "fond credulity" about the state of society among the Hindus, and his acceptance of the "loose and unmeaning" phraseology in the writings of the Brahmans.[31] He ridiculed Jones's "crude" ideas of Indian history: even Rousseau's rhapsodies on the virtue and happiness of the savage life did not surpass "the panegyrics of Sir William on the wild, comfortless, predatory, and ferocious state of the wandering Arabs."[32]

Though ignorant of Sanskrit, Mill refuted Jones's enthusiasm for the language and the claim that Oriental languages would provide a revitalized poetic tradition that would furnish a "new set of images and similitudes and a number of excellent compositions would be brought to light." Mill saw this as retrograde: "Poetry is the language of the passions, and men feel before they speculate. The earliest poetry is the expression of the feelings, by which the minds of rude men are most powerfully actuated."[33] Contrary to Jones, Mill was disparaging about Hindu literature; among other terms he called it extravagant, unnatural, and less ingenious and more immoderate about anything that could engage the affection, awaken sympathy, or excite admiration, reverence, or terror, and excessively prolix, insipid, trifling, childish, obscure, verbose, and incoherent. Only occasionally could one find, in Mill's words, a "vivid conception of a striking circumstance."[34] The Hindu legends presented a maze of unnatural fictions in which a series of real events could by no artifice be traced. Those legends marked the state of a "rude and credulous people," ascribing extravagant and unnatural events and independent and incredible fictions. In ancient Hindu literature, the legends, mixing the actions of men and those of deities, were more absurd and extravagant than those of any other nation. The Brahmans were the most audacious, and perhaps the most unskillful fabricators, "with whom the annals of fable have yet made us acquainted."

Certainly, Mill argued, the Brahmans played a major role in an India where "in rude and ignorant times" men were so overwhelmed with the power of superstition as to pay unbounded veneration and obedience to those who artfully clothed themselves with the terrors of religion.[35] The Brahmans had acquired and maintained a more exalted and extensive authority than priests elsewhere in the world. Yet these powerful Brahmans were holy men doing unnecessary penance, and engaging in useless and harmful ceremonies, rather than in urging morality and improvement. James Mill was equally scornful of the Hindu religion. He was severely critical not only of the literature and legends of the Hindus but also of their cosmology. Their view of the universe had "no coherence, wisdom or beauty: all is disorder, caprice, passion, contest, portents, prodigies, violence, and deformity."[36] They did not see the universe as a connected and perfect system, governed by general laws, and directed to benevolent ends. Their religion is only "primary worship . . . addressed to the designing and invisible beings who preside over the powers of nature, according to their own arbitrary will, and act only for some private and selfish gratification." No people, no matter how ignorant, had ever drawn a more gross and disgusting picture of the universe than what was presented in the writings of the Hindus.

Mill saw the endless ceremonies, the practical part of the Hindu religion, as mean and absurd, tedious, minute, and burdensome. He records the pollutions, penances, human sacrifices, and accounts of *suttee*. He links religion and political characteristics of Hinduism. In Mill's own language, "to the rude mind, no other rule suggests itself for paying court to the Divine, than that for paying court to the Human Majesty; and as among a barbarous people, the forms of address, of respect, and compliment, are generally multiplied into a great variety of grotesque and frivolous ceremonies, so it happens with regard to their religious service. An endless succession of observances, in compliment to the god, is supposed to afford him the most exquisite delight; while the common discharge of the beneficent duties of life is regarded as an object of comparative indifference."[37] How could, James Mill remarks, a religion that subjects its votaries to "the grossest images of sensual pleasure . . . [making] them even objects of worship" be regarded as favorable to chastity? In making these critical remarks on the Hindu religion James Mill referred to the Baptist William Ward who "above all others furnished superabundant evidence of the immoral influence of the Hindu religion, and the deep depravity which it is calculated to produce."[38]

According to James Mill, the Hindu people believed that the Divine Being had conveyed a complete and perfect system of instruction to regulate his public as well as his private affairs, and so he acknowledged no laws except those in the sacred books. Divine prescription had established everything: "the plan of society and government, the rights of persons and things, even the customs, arrangements and manners of private and domestic life." Their primary institutions of government were founded on divine authority. Nowhere among mankind had laws and ordinances been more exclusively ascribed to the Divinity than by those who instituted the theocracy of Hindustan. James Mill contended that the leading institutions of the Hindus were devised at a remote period, when society was in its crudest and simplest form. Those institutions continued into the present and Hindu society had remained in that condition resembling the most ancient times. This was true of their ideas of property. James Mill mentioned that the power of disposing of possessions, by testament, was altogether unknown to their laws.

James Mill was critical of all aspects of the Indian society and culture: the Hindu religion, the social arrangements, the "rude" civilization, its political ineptness, its backwardness, and its Oriental despotism. James Mill saw India as a backward and stationary society. The manners, institutions, and attainments of the Hindus had been stationary for so long that "in beholding the Hindus of the present day, we are beholding the Hindus of many years past, and are carried back . . . into the deepest recesses of antiquity." In an analogy, Mill took a surprisingly strong position: "By conversing with the Hindus of the present day, we, in some measure, converse with the Chaldeans and Babylonians of the time of Cyrus; with the Persians and Egyptians of the time of Alexander."[39]

James Mill saw Britain's task as overcoming the deficiencies he perceived so that India could progress toward a more civilized life and develop a higher moral and intellectual standard. Applying the concept of Utilitarianism, James

Mill commented on India's backwardness: "Exactly in proportion as Utility is the object of every pursuit, may we regard a nation as civilized. Exactly in proportion as its ingenuity is wasted on contemptible or mischievous objects, though it may be, in itself, an ingenuity of no ordinary kind, the nation may safely be denominated barbarous. According to this rule, the astronomical and mathematical sciences afford conclusive evidence against the Hindus. They have been cultivated exclusively for the purposes of astrology; one of the most irrational of all imaginable pursuits; one of those which most infallibly denote a nation barbarous; and one of those which it is the most sure to renounce, in proportion as knowledge and civilization are attained."[40]

James Mill criticized Hindu manners and behavior, attributing to them many unpleasant characteristics such as indolence, avarice, lack of cleanliness, ignorance, absence of rational thought, insincerity, mendacity, perfidy, and indifference to the feelings of others. The Hindus abounded in those frivolous refinements that were suited to the taste of an uncivilized people. They engaged in exaggeration and flattery. They exhibited habitual contempt for their women. India was marked by love of repose and physical indolence, characteristics due not to the climate but to absence of motives to work, subjection to a wretched government, and insecurity about the fruits of labor.[41]

Religion affected moral behavior and the nature of government. Alluding to Hindus as one of them, James Mill generalized that among "rude nations" religion had almost always served to degrade morality, by putting those external performances or those mental exercises regarding the Deity in the place of greatest honor. Because most of the life of Hindus was taken up by the performance of an infinite and burdensome ritual that extended throughout the day and was attached to every function, the Brahmans, the sole judges and directors in these complicated and endless duties, became masters over human life. The dominance of the Brahmans resulted from their primacy in the caste system, the social divisions on which the whole frame of Hindu society rested. In this system, the first and simplest form of the division of labor and employment, four orders existed: the military, husbandmen, the servants and laborers, and the elite group, the Brahmans or priests.

James Mill asserted that in India the priestly order controlled all the branches of government, the legislative, executive, and judicial functions. The Brahmans enjoyed the undisputed prerogative of interpreting the divine oracles. They had the exclusive power of legislation and also of interpreting the law. The king, though ostensibly supreme judge, always employed Brahmans as counselors and assistants in the administration of justice. The king was really the executive officer by whom the decisions of the Brahmans were carried into effect. Moreover, in "rude and ignorant times the uncontrollable sway of superstition confers on its ministers such extraordinary privileges that the king and the priest are generally the same person." James Mill was not altogether clear on the point. According to the original laws of the Hindus the king was little more than an instrument in the hands of the Brahmans; he performed the laborious part of government and sustained the responsibility, while they, whom the king was obliged to appoint as counselors and ministers, chiefly possessed the power. Yet Mill also says that the two roles, king and priest, were generally carried out by the same person.

Was the role of king therefore reduced to that of a dependent and secondary office? Mill suggests, by using evidence based on Hindu monuments, that the monarchy enjoyed authority and splendor. Monarchs were masters of the army and of the public revenue. They were a counterbalance to the legislative, judicial, and much of the executive power, "reinforced by all the authority of an overbearing superstition" held by the Brahmans. The sovereign had "an external lustre, with which the eyes of uncultivated men are easily dazzled." Moreover, in dangerous and disorderly times, the king as military commander exercised unlimited authority by universal consent. Because of the situation of "a rude and uncivilized people" surrounded by rapacious and turbulent neighbors, the king usually had unlimited authority. In addition, the Hindu king had the prerogative of the distribution of gifts and favors and patronage.

Though James Mill in his *History* stated there were circumstances that distinguished to a certain extent Muhammadan government from that of the Hindus, his general position was that, in the simplicity of a system of Oriental despotism, there was not much room for diversity of form. Despotism in one of its simplest and least artificial shapes "was established in Hindustan, and confirmed by laws of Divine authority." By the division of people into castes and by the prejudices of the detestable views of the Brahmans that fostered that division, a degrading and pernicious system of subordination was established among the Hindus. Through the power of priest craft, built on the most enormous and tormenting superstition, the minds of people were enchained more intolerably than their bodies. Mill declared that because of despotism and priest craft, the Hindus, in mind and body, were the most enslaved members of the human race. James Mill was critical of Sir William Jones's view that despotism and priest craft were limited by the Hindu code of law that provided for mutual checks. On the contrary, the two joined together in upholding their common tyranny over the people.

The Hindu form of government, the Asiatic model, was monarchical and absolute. Rule was the result of the will of a single person, with complete and uncontrollable authority. James Mill, using picturesque language, quoted the law of Menu: the king is "formed of particles from the chief guardian deities, and consequently surpasses all mortals in glory. Like the sun, he burns eyes and hearts; nor can any human creature on earth even gaze on him. He, fire and air; He, the god of criminal justice; He, the genius of wealth; He, the regent of waters; He, the lord of the firmament. A king, even if a child, must not be treated lightly, from an idea that he is a mere mortal: No; he is a powerful divinity, who appears in human shape. In his anger, death. He who shows hatred of the king, though delusion of mind, will certainly perish; for speedily will the king apply his heart to that man's destruction."[42]

James Mill contrasted "skillful governments of Europe" with Asian monarchies. In the first, officials are appointed for specific functions in different parts of the country, and all, coming together in the head of the government, act as "connected and subordinate wheels in one complicated and artful machine." In the "less instructed and less civilized inhabitants of Asia," the monarch divided his own power and authority into fragments to allow vice-regents to govern throughout the country, exercising absolute control. The king had wide powers: he presided over a powerful army, and he was responsible for justice and legislation on all occasions. Regal and judicial functions were united in the same person. Moreover, the judicial process was badly performed because it was not allowed to interfere with the business or pleasures of the king. A decision was more an exercise of arbitrary will than the result of an accurate investigation.

Yet according to James Mill, even in systems with absolute sovereigns, some checks were available to limit the exercise of power: they were religion, insurrection, and customs. Religious dignitaries, because of their authority resulting from their influence over the minds of men, might use their power to oppose the will of the sovereign. But realistically, in the Hindu system, the power of the priests was so associated with that of the sovereign that the priests had no motive to check sovereign powers but had every motive to support sovereign power. Thus, they were not likely to oppose misgovernment.

James Mill surprisingly argues that under Muslim sovereigns, the alliance between religion and the state was less complete than under the Hindus. Apart from the caliphs, who were leading magistrates and priests, the latter had little political power. Usually, the priests had neither sufficient influence nor inclination to protect the people from abuses of sovereign power, thus differing from the Hindu system of priesthood. Dread of insurrection was a possible second limit on the power of governments of the East. This fear of rebellion was the mainspring for any humane acts on the part of Oriental despots. The likelihood of rebellion depended on the character of the people. Recognition of the spirit, excitability, and courage of the Muhammadan part of the Indian population furnished a particular motive for good government.

A third limit on power could arise from the patterns of behavior and customs of the community. Using the language of Utilitarianism, a calculus of pleasures and pains, James Mill argued that only in a higher state of civilization than that of the Muhammadans or Hindus, did behavior or, in Mill's word, "manners" have any great influence in limiting the abuses of sovereign power. Limited though the influence was in India, it was more effective in the Muhammadan community than the Hindu one. In the former community were characteristics such as activity, manliness, and independence, making it more difficult for despotism to sink to the disgusting state of weak and profligate barbarism that was the natural condition of government among a passive people such as the Hindus. Even though the Muhammadan nations still retained the remains of barbarism that adhere to inhabitants of Asia, they were marked by considerable plain good sense, a quality in which the Hindus were deficient. This practical good sense influenced the mode of government.

James Mill made clear that Indian civilization had benefited from Mughal rulers: "human nature in India gained, and gained very considerably, by passing from a Hindu to a Mughal government."[43] This improvement could be assessed by improvements in four qualities: intelligence, temperance, justice, and generosity. The Mughals also brought social progress by bringing with them Persian civilization, its language, laws, religion, literature, arts, and knowledge. Hindu Indians who had not been subject to Mughal rule were at a less advanced level than those who were. However, James Mill made it clear that European rule was preferable to that of the Mughals. It would bring advantages to the country and increase its happiness.

Moreover, James Mill pointed out the dangerous nature of Oriental despotism in the Mughal Empire. That empire was founded by Babar who overthrew the Lodi Kingdom of Delhi in 1526, and it was consolidated by his grandson Akbar (1556–1605), who extended it and divided it for administrative purposes into fifteen provinces. Though concentrating on the activities and reign of Emperor Aurungzebe (1658 until his death in 1707), James Mill's account of the Mughal Empire is a dismal portrait of an unpleasant regime. Among its distinctive features were court intrigues, suspicion, treachery, deceit, removal of all danger of competition, jealous and revengeful passions, perpetual contests, crimes, and wars. Mill held that the experience of Oriental government told Aurungzebe that he was never safe while there was a man alive who had power to hurt him. Mill generalized: "To every brother under an Oriental despotism the sons of the reigning monarch look, as either a victim or a butcher, and see but one choice between the *musnud* (the seat for people of distinction) and the grave. The usual policy of Oriental fear is to educate the royal youths to effeminacy and imbecility in the harem."[44]

In the Muhammadan despotism of the East all men were treated as equals. There was no noble or privileged class and no legal hereditary property as the king was the heir of all of his subjects. The only form of distinction was in holding office, or exercising some of the powers of government, and people could rise to the highest levels in accordance with their qualities. Unlike Hindu government, there was, under the Muhammadan sovereigns, a regular distribution of the functions of government to certain fixed and regular officers. In comparing Muhammadan and Hindu law, James Mill concluded that the first may be defective if compared with any high standard of excellence, but that the latter originated in one of the weakest conditions of the human intellect, and the law was one of the least capable of producing the benefits that should be provided.

James Mill gives no full definition of the nature of Islamic law, but it was characteristic that it was unwritten, as law was in all less developed countries. The standard was the Koran, in which nothing beyond a few vague precepts could be found. To these were added the commentaries of the legal experts, some of whom were recognized as authorities. These commentaries were also vague. In the system of law, "in this barbarous state in which so little of anything was fixed or certain," a wide field was subject to the arbitrary will of the judge.[45]

Despite his generalization that "in the simplicity of Oriental despotism there is not much room for diversity of thought," James Mill recognized some differences between Muhammadan and Hindu governments. For him, the Mughals, at the time of their conquests in Asia, were prepared to take a step toward civilization. They were gifted in the sciences, astronomy, geography, mathematics; in paving streets; in conveying water; and in making silk paper. The defects of Muhammadan rule were less than those of Hindu rule; human nature in India benefited considerably from the change from a Hindu to a Muhammedan government. One important example of the superiority of the Muslim system was the absence of caste, that great barrier against the welfare of human nature.

Yet the Muslim system, like the Hindu system, had not led to an advanced civilization, and the task of Britain was to lead India in that advance and to modernize the country, economically and politically. Britain had to overcome the root cause of the "hideous state of society," the corruptive operation of the despotism to which the people of India had been subject for a long time.[46]

In James Mill's most well-known work, *An Essay on Government*, one can detect the influence of his great British predecessors, Locke and particularly Hobbes, in his views on good government and restraints on political power. In his views of India, its passive, indolent people, and despotic political regime, one perceives echoes of Montesquieu and even Aristotle. One can use the words of John Stuart Mill regarding his father in his *Autobiography* to relate to James Mill's formula to overcome the deficiencies he saw in India: "So complete was my father's reliance on the influence of reason over the minds of mankind, whenever it is allowed to reach them, that he felt as if all would be granted if the whole population were taught to read, if all sorts of opinion were allowed to be addressed to them by word and in writing, and if by means of the suffrage they could nominate a legislature to give effect to the opinions they adopted."

JOHN STUART MILL

Among political theorists and historians, John Stuart Mill, the philosopher of classical liberalism, occupies an eminent place in the roster of nineteenth-century writers who have shaped the literature on economics, logic, women's rights, and political science. As a public intellectual he was also a member of the House of Commons for three years (1865–8) as an independent and put the cause of women's suffrage on the parliamentary agenda, as well as championing Irish land reform. During the debate on the Reform Bill of 1867 he proposed an amendment that "person" be substituted for "man" in qualification for voting. As a young man he was an occasional political activist; at seventeen he was arrested for distributing literature on contraception. Regarding the condition of Ireland he wrote thirty-nine articles for the *Morning Chronicle* in 1846 alone. Mill was a participant in public affairs not a detached observer. When in 1865 Mill was making his first speech in Parliament, Benjamin Disraeli is said to have unkindly murmured about him, "Ah, the finishing governess," but Mill did want to use the House of Commons for didactic effect. As an activist, he advocated birth control, the end of slavery, and religious tolerance; argued for extension of the suffrage and equality for women, compulsory national education, and land reform in Ireland; and supported the North in the American Civil War. He campaigned against Governor Edward Eyre who had brutally suppressed a revolt in Jamaica. In his *Principles of Political Economy*, he was one of the first to warn of the environmental dangers of economic growth. Walter Bagehot, the influential economist and writer, praised the work for its originality and "eminent merit."[47] Mill's most well-known work, *On Liberty*, has stimulated countless discussions of liberalism, free speech, individuality, and concern regarding the nature of liberty and the increasing importance of public opinion and its possible tyranny in policy decisions. In contrast, Mill's work on Indian affairs has been relatively neglected.

Yet J. S. Mill spent most of his life as an employee of the East India Company in India House in London. He was first appointed, through his father's influence, in May 1823 at age seventeen as a junior clerk in the Examiner's

Office, working under his father without salary for three years. Two years later he was given a paid appointment in the correspondence branch of the Examiners Office. J. S. Mill began drafting dispatches on his own. In 1826 he was appointed as a clerk in that office, and then in 1828 was promoted to be an assistant to the examiner, in the Political or Diplomatic Department. Finally, in 1856 he was appointed examiner of Indian correspondence, where he supervised the drafting of dispatches by others. When the Company was dissolved in 1858 he was offered and declined a seat on the new Indian Council in the office of the secretary of state for India. "I had given," he explained in his *Autobiography*, "enough of my life to India."[48]

John Stuart Mill is purported to have spent few hours of his nominal 10 A.M. to 4 P.M. working day on official business and probably worked on it for some three hours a day. He used his office to entertain friends and the extensive intellectual network of his time, to write hundreds of his voluminous personal letters, many of which were on the paper of "India House," and to write all or part of some of his books, some on Company stationery, including *A System of Logic*, *Principles of Political Economy*, a draft of his *Autobiography*, and translations of parts of Plato's works.

John Stuart Mill benefited from a good secure income from the Company, generous paid vacations, and equally generous sick leave of which he took advantage on a number of occasions. Nevertheless, he complained to Thomas Carlyle in his earlier years in the office that his position in India House "hampers my freedom of action in a thousand ways." Similarly, he informed William Johnson Fox on June 17, 1834, that he could not be the editor of the *London Review* or be ostensibly connected with it in any way except as an occasional writer because of his position in India House. He did become editor of the *London Review* and of a new journal, *The London and Westminster Review* when the *London Review* merged with the *Westminster Review* in 1837.[49]

Whatever the truth of his work habits and the time devoted to his official job, his knowledge of and mastery of Indian affairs was deep, unmistakable, and long lasting. Near the end of his life in a letter to Charlotte Speir Manning of January 14, 1870, John Stuart Mill gave her information about ladies of the ruling families in India, explaining that the Native States were the responsibility of his department at the India House and he had opportunities of knowing everything about the manner in which the states were governed. An interesting example of this is shown in a letter of February 9, 1869, to C. W. Dilke, the author of *Great Britain: A Record of Travel in English-speaking Countries during 1866 and 1867*, in which John Stuart Mill politely pointed out errors Dilke had made on India, though he agreed with "its sound judgments and sustained tone of right and worthy feeling."[50]

During a thirty-five-year career as a professional administrator John Stuart Mill drafted more than 1,710 dispatches, on the average of one a week, on British policy on India, 1,523 of which were on political matters, including many regarding the relationship between the Company and the Native States. The question of the extent to which his own intellectual development was influenced by his experience in Indian affairs, and whether that experience affected his general political and social thought, is interesting to consider. It seems improbable that his thoughts and writings on other subjects would be unaffected by his years at the Company and his official experiences. Hints in his writings suggest that, to take a few examples, his views on land reform in Britain and in Ireland and his attitude toward landed aristocracy were affected by his experience of Indian conditions. Moreover, his position at the Company taught him lessons in practical politics; as he wrote, it made him aware of the difficulties of "moving bodies of men, the necessities of compromise, the art of sacrificing the non-essential to preserve the essential."

Besides his draft dispatches, John Stuart Mill performed many other duties for the Company. In 1852 he appeared in his official capacity before the House of Lords Select Committee on India as the representative of the Company. The charter of the Company was renewed every twenty years by Parliament after a committee had examined the record of the Company. John Stuart Mill appeared in 1852 to plead the case for renewal as his father had done twenty years earlier. He also wrote letters to the *Morning Chronicle* defending the Company, and wrote memos, especially the memorandum on *The Improvements in the Administration of India during the Last Thirty Years*, and reports on behalf of the Company during the difficult years of 1857 and 1858, trying to prevent its abolition and wanting to avoid more direct parliamentary control over it in the belief that it was the best system for India.

John Stuart Mill was bitter about the dissolution of the Company in 1858. "Parliament, in other words Lord Palmerston, put an end to the Company as a branch of the government of India under the Crown, and converted the administration of that country into a thing to be scrambled for by the second and third class of English parliamentary politicians."[51] Three years after the dissolution John Stuart Mill published his *Considerations on Representative Government*, commenting that it was not by attempting to rule directly a country like India, but by giving it good rulers that the English people could do their duty to that country; they could scarcely give it a worse form than an English cabinet minister who is thinking of English, not Indian, politics.

In considering John Stuart Mill's writings on India, three remarks are pertinent. It is not clear how many of the 1,710 drafts were written only by himself, how many were accepted by policy makers, and how many were changed or discarded in the chain of command up to higher officials and the Board of Control. Mill appreciated the bureaucratic dilemma as he admitted in June 1852 to the Select Committee on Indian Affairs: "chairs seldom send up a proposed dispatch which they know is contrary to the President's opinion." The question arises to what extent his dispatches reflected his own views.[52]

John Stuart Mill was deeply influenced by the work of his father whom he called "the last of the eighteenth century." His *Autobiography* starts with an unusual ring: "I was born in London, on May 20, 1806 and was the oldest son of James Mill, the author of the *History of British India*." On a number of occasions he paid fulsome tribute to the *History*. He pointed out in his preface to James Mill's *Analysis of the Human Mind* that his father was also the author of the *History*, and that most people would have thought the *History* was a sufficient achievement for a whole literary life. It could be regarded as the beginning of rational thinking of the subject of India and as one of the most valuable contributions to English history of the period it embraced. The son also praised his father's contribution to the Company: James Mill's dispatches did more than had ever been done to promote the improvement of India and to teach officials there to understand their business.

HOW INDEPENDENT WAS JOHN STUART MILL?

John Stuart Mill acknowledged his father's patronage: "In May 1823, my professional occupation and status for the next thirty five years of my life, was decided by my father's obtaining for me an appointment from the East India Company . . . immediately under himself." A fair conclusion would be that the young John Stuart Mill tended to reflect the views on India of James Mill, who had trained his son in the art of drafting dispatches. On the Indian educational question, for example, John Stuart Mill at first agreed with his father regarding the desirability of "useful learning," taught in English-language schools, not in those teaching in Sanskrit or Arabic. However, after the death of James in 1836, John Stuart Mill's dispatches reflected other influences on the nature of British rule and on educational questions, and he began putting more emphasis on traditional Indian centers of learning. That type of learning should not be denigrated because it was held by the people of India in "high estimation." Britain would benefit from the support of "those learned classes to whom Indians customarily looked for leadership in intellectual matters."

Among the major individuals who affected his outlook were a heterogeneous group: H. H. Wilson, an official in Bengal who became professor of Sanskrit at Oxford; Samuel Coleridge whose work *On the Constitution of the Church and*

State influenced John Stuart Mill on the need for an intellectual elite, "a clerisy" as Coleridge called it; other nineteenth-century romantics; Herder; the Saint-Simonians who were critical of Utilitarianism; and especially the high British officials in India, including Sir Thomas Munro (Governor of Madras), Mountstuart Elphinstone (Governor of Bombay, 1819–27), and John Malcolm (Governor of Bombay, 1827–30).[53] From this last group of those colonial administrators John Stuart Mill learned and understood the concern for security though for him security had to be accompanied by progress.

It is arguable that, in addition to John Stuart Mill's changes of opinion resulting from his rational appreciation of the various points of view of those who influenced him, he may have undergone an intellectual rebellion against his father after James Mill's death. John Stuart Mill never attended a university and never taught in one. Instead he was subjected to an extraordinary educational process imposed on him by his father. Not surprisingly, after learning Greek at age three, reading Plato in Greek at age seven and Demosthenes in the original at age eight, studying Latin in the same year and Aristotle at age eleven, working on the proofs of James Mill's *History* at age eleven, and editing the papers of Jeremy Bentham at nineteen – John Stuart Mill had a nervous breakdown at the age of twenty. He felt "a stifled, drowsy, unimpassioned grief." Paradoxically the education imposed by James Mill, whose Utilitarianism aimed at pleasure, ended in his son's unhappiness. From this education deficient in cultural interests and its neglect of sensibility and emotion, John Stuart Mill recovered by his reading of poetry, especially the romantic poets such as Wordsworth and Coleridge, and by his passionate love, which lasted for almost twenty-eight years, from the time he was twenty four, for the then married Harriet Taylor, who later became his wife in 1851. Through this, as he wrote to Thomas Carlyle, he was able to "remake all my opinions." One of those opinions was to give more weight to the sentiments of the Indian people and to their social customs and institutions.

Questions can fairly be raised about John Stuart Mill's official writings on the political, economic, and social issues concerning India. Are they consonant with his views on similar issues in his well-known published works, or were they the product of necessity? Early in his career he wrote to a friend: "We often find it necessary to write our dispatches first for effect here upon the Directors and the India Board, and afterwards shape them into something more suitable to the dignity of official authority exercised over gentlemen by gentlemen."[54] Was John Stuart Mill merely the conveyor of information along official channels rather than a more decisive player as James had been? Was he more Company man than enthusiastic reformer? At one point he referred to himself as "one wheel in a machine, the whole of which had to work together, doing his duty." Can he appropriately be put in the camp of British liberal imperialists?

ORIENTAL DESPOTISM

Unlike his father, John Stuart Mill never wrote any full analysis of Indian history, politics, or society. In his Company dispatches, which dealt with concrete issues facing British administrators, and in the fragmentary references in his published works, John Stuart Mill touched on the question of Oriental despotism obliquely rather than centrally. James Mill was clear on this issue. India suffered from despotism, morally and economically. For many generations it had been under the demoralizing influence of a bad government, under which its citizens found protection against oppression by cunning and fraud. The root of the bad state of society in Bengal was its corruptive despotism, which had kept India at a low level of development.[55]

John Stuart Mill pointed out that despotic monarchies had many problems. They might systematically organize the "best mental power in the country in some special direction to promote the grandeur of the despot," but the public at large remained uninformed and uninterested in political affairs. Members of the public suffered not only in their understanding but also in their moral capacities as "their sentiments are narrowed and dwarfed."[56] John Stuart Mill essentially approved the general principle Tocqueville enunciated in *Democracy in America* (vol. 2) that the widest dissemination of information about public affairs was the only means by which the public could be prepared for the exercise of any share of power and generally also the only means by which they could be led to desire it. In one of his last speeches, on an educational issue on April 4, 1870, Mill said, "What constituted the government a free and popular one was, not that the initiative was left to the general mass, but that statesmen and thinkers were obliged to carry the mind and will of the mass along with them; they could not impose these ideas by compulsion as despots do."[57]

Though John Stuart Mill held similar views as his father regarding the nature of native rule in India, he was less explicit. In occasional passages, he referred to "despotic governments of Asia," to "horrors of an Oriental despotism," to the "priest-led and despot-governed Asiatics," and to India where "a people inured from numberless generations to submission . . . were governed by their tyrannical or incapable native despots."[58] John Stuart Mill was more explicit in his comments on the backwardness, stagnation, and lower level of civilization he thought existed in India. In general remarks and in letters, he was critical of the stagnation, sometimes using the term "Chinese stagnation," and the immobility he observed in much of the world.

STAGNATION

The crucial concern of John Stuart Mill in *On Liberty* is focused on the nature and limits of the power that should be legitimately exercised by society over the individual. At the core of his concern is liberation from restraints and the self-development of character (an idea he may taken from the philosopher Wilhelm von Humboldt), which was the chief ingredient of individual and social progress and would become apparent when individuals expanded their moral and mental horizons. In his broad comparative concepts in the book, John Stuart Mill contrasted "the progressive principle," whether as the love of liberty or of improvement, with "the sway of custom"; the contrast between the two John Stuart Mill saw as the chief interest of the "history of mankind." Most of the world was under the sway of custom and "properly speaking [had] no history." This was true throughout the entire East, where custom was the final appeal and justice and rights were subordinate to it. As a warning example, Mill takes China, "a nation of much talent and . . . even wisdom" but that did not discover "the secret of human progressiveness."[59] He feared that the nations of Europe, where the "spirit of improvement" existed but that also were under the despotism of custom, might follow a similar path if they did not maintain individuality and singularity, diversity of character and culture. Europe owed its progressive and many-sided development to the plurality of paths it had followed. In contrast to Europe, China in its early history became stationary and remained so for thousands of years. Custom in the country had imposed an order that made people all alike, governing their thoughts and conduct by unchanging maxims and rules, "cramped and dwarfed," making them unable to develop fully and obliging them to obey unconditionally every mandate of persons in authority. John Stuart Mill believed that Eastern society was stationary and could only progress by outside help.

In Asia, India and China exemplified the stationary state, "in which no further addition will be made to capital, unless there takes place either some improvement in the arts of production or an increase in the strength of the desire to accumulate."[60] Any society, John Stuart Mill suggested, that is not improving is deteriorating. He had doubts about whether nations in the Orient could improve: if a nation never rose above the condition of an Oriental people, it would continue to stagnate. Even if "like Greece or Rome it had realized anything higher, it relapses in a few generations into the Oriental state."[61]

This view of the Orient is representative of John Stuart Mill's general concept, put forward in *Representative Government*, that there is an incessant and ever-flowing current pulling human affairs toward the worst; that current consists of all the follies, all the vices, and all the negligences, indolences, and "supinenesses" of mankind. The current is only controlled, and kept from sweeping all before it, by the exertions that some persons constantly, and others by fits, put forth in the direction of good and worthy goals.

In his discussion of the economic stagnation, low level of civilization, and widespread despotism in the East, John Stuart Mill never succumbed to racial theories in explaining diversity: "Of all the vulgar modes of escaping from the consideration of the effect of social and moral influences in the human mind, the most vulgar is that of attributing the diversities of conduct and character to inherent natural differences. What race would not be indolent and insouciant when things are so arranged, that they derive no advantage from forethought or exertion?"[62] Again, in a letter of April 6, 1860, John Stuart Mill did not agree "with the idea of attributing all variations in the character of peoples and individuals to indelible differences of nature, without asking whether the differences of education and the social and political milieu do not give a sufficient explanation."[63]

Commenting on the generalizations of Tocqueville and François Guizot on the "law of progress" as an inherent attribute of human nature, John Stuart Mill declared that the European family of nations was the only one in the world that had shown any capability for spontaneous improvement beyond a certain low level. This capability did not result from any superiority of nature but from "combinations of circumstances." Mill praised the spirit of commerce and industry as one of the "greatest instruments not only of civilization in the narrowest, but of improvement and culture in the widest sense."[64]

Among the generalizations in *The Principles of Political Economy*, John Stuart Mill points out the remarkable differences among states in regard to the production and distribution of wealth. He compared the progress of early Western societies with the lack of it in Asiatic countries. Like Montesquieu he contrasts Oriental systems in which a single monarch rules aided by a fluctuating body of favorites and employees with Western societies with their large, fixed class of great landholders and that exhibit far less splendor. Western societies had greater stability, fixed personal positions, growing security of persons and property, progress in the arts, and economic accumulation; they ripened into the commercial and manufacturing nations of present-day Europe. In contrast, Oriental society "is in essentials what it has always been; the great empire of Russia is even now, in many respects, the scarcely modified image of feudal Europe."[65]

Other differences also exist. The various nations of Asia are stationary states because there the principle of accumulation is weak. People do not save nor work to get savings; production is poor, partly because of lack of capital and insufficient use of technology (Mill uses the word *contrivances*). Oriental countries, including India, suffered, not only from insecurity of property and high interest rates but also from the fact that private property in land did not exist, a familiar argument from Bernier. In his writing on the economics of the despotic countries, John Stuart Mill concentrated on questions of land tenure, taxation, and rent, which were at the heart of Oriental despotism in politics and stagnation in economics. With stagnation came inactivity and absence of desire, which were fatal hindrances to improvement; the great majority of the human race was in this situation of a savage or semisavage state.[66]

Certain factors, helpful and necessary for progress to an advanced society, were lacking in all the Asiatic populations. Security was important if productive behavior and desirable conditions were to be established. Proper security meant protection by the government and, especially, against the government. If one's possessions could be torn away by tyrannical violence by the agents of a rapacious government, not many people were likely to produce much more than necessaries. In so many of the governments of Asia, property was in perpetual danger of spoliation from a tyrannical government or from its corrupt and ill-controlled officers. In a state of society like that in many parts of Asia, no security (except perhaps the actual pledge of gold or jewels) was good, and consequently people would accumulate less because of risk.[67] Lack of security handicapped development. Because of it, people bought those imperishable articles that were capable of being concealed or carried off, especially gold and silver. Many a rich Asiatic carried nearly his whole fortune on his person, or on those of the women of his harem. If the ruler felt secure, he would sometimes indulge a taste for durable edifices, such as the Pyramids, the Taj Mahal, or the Mausoleum at Sekundra.

Security was inextricably connected with the lack of private ownership of land. Both James and John Stuart were advocates for changing the existing system in India. James viewed the state as sole landlord, granting leases to cultivators, and exacting rent as land revenue. The revenue mainly was collected by the Bengal *zamindars*, the middlemen who often obtained a share of the produce and had some powers of government.[68] The sovereigns in India had not only the ownership but also all the benefit of the land. The *ryots*, the immediate cultivators, could use the soil, but the sovereign claimed a right to as much of the produce as he pleased and seldom left to the *ryot*s more than a scanty reward for their labor.

Because John Stuart Mill worked in the Political, not the Revenue, Department of the Company, he wrote little in his official capacity on social and economic matters in India, except on the problem of rent and on revenue policy. He took a similar view as his father about the land system and the role of the *zamindars*. John Stuart Mill argued that in most parts of India the landlord was generally the sovereign, except where he had conceded his rights to an individual who became his representative. Rents, paid by the *ryots*, the peasants, were based on custom, but the sovereign could change rents arbitrarily. Though some changes were made under Mughal rule, these were unimportant because they did not provide the *ryots* with any real protection against illegal extortions. British officials tried to put an end to the arbitrary character of the land revenue and the demands of the ruler. But John Stuart Mill thought those officials had blundered by supporting the *zamindars*, in the mistaken belief that they were the proprietors of the land and by inference the landed nobility and the gentry of India.[69]

John Stuart Mill was critical of the existing land system in India. The level of rent was set arbitrarily by the ruler because "the land is considered the property of the state . . . rent is confounded with taxation. . . . The despot may exact the utmost which the unfortunate cultivators have to give."[70] The level of rent was too high for capital accumulation or economic development to occur. Mill's conclusion on the appropriation engaged in by the extensive monarchies in Asia is harsh: "The government in these countries, though varying in its qualities according to the accidents of personal character, seldom leaves much to the cultivators beyond mere necessaries, and often strips them so bare even of these, that it finds itself obliged, after taking all they have, to lend part of it back to those from whom it has been taken, in order to provide them with seed, and enable them to support life until another harvest."[71] The consequence, among other things, was that the government's show of riches was quite out of proportion to the general condition of the society, leading to the universal impression of the great opulence of Oriental nations. The ruler, after taking care of his needs and of those of his inner circle, had a disposable residue that was used to exchange for luxury goods, elaborate and costly manufactured articles.

It would be desirable if land were to be leased in perpetuity at a reasonable level, but realistically John Stuart Mill appreciated this might not be possible. Therefore he advocated that rents should be "fixed by authority: thus changing the rent into a quit-rent, and the farmer into a peasant proprietor."[72] Linking private property to intellectual and moral development would, John Stuart Mill believed, stimulate economic growth, lead to social and moral progress, and increase security and expand cooperation. Economic independence would lead to responsible citizenship and active character, "the deeply-rooted conception which every individual . . . has of himself as a social being."[73] This change in turn would advance the community as a whole.

Letters by John Stuart Mill in 1869 show his concern about current British policy.[74] Although he preferred a system in which permanent rights of property were given to the actual cultivator, he realized that, unfortunately, many officials, especially young ones, favored a system of landlords. On January 1, 1869, he complained to Henry Maine that Britain was discrediting the ideas of protection of the interests of the great mass of the population by increasing the importance of the Taluqdars of Oudh, the feudal barons, the very men whose atrocities led the British to make the case for annexation of the country.[75] For John Stuart Mill it was a retrograde step.

A CIVILIZING MISSION

Even stronger than his concern about ownership of land in India by one man or by a small group, a practice that he saw as characteristic of an early stage of civilization, was John Stuart Mill's distaste for the despotic, arbitrary political structure in the country. James and John Stuart Mill recognized that contemporary European political systems were not the appropriate model for India. Even medieval European society, James Mill thought, was superior to Indian culture in economically efficient techniques of agriculture, art, and the intellectual and moral qualities of the people. In an 1810 essay, James wrote that "the stage of civilization, and the moral and political situation in which the people of India are placed, render the establishment of legislative assemblies impracticable. A simple form of arbitrary government, tempered by European honor and European intelligence, is the only form which is now fit for Hindustan."[76] What should Britain do about the existing despotisms? Should Britain rule directly or indirectly through the native princes? James Mill was critical of indirect rule and the subsidiary system by which the princes became allies, thus providing revenue for the maintenance of troops. He felt it would lead to a worse situation. Divided authority, he wrote, only leads to misgovernment, and in India misgovernment went to ultimate excess too often.

In his testimony to the Parliamentary Select Committee in 1832, James Mill said that "the best thing for the happiness of the people is that our government should be nominally, as well as really, extended over those territories; that our own modes of governing should be adopted, and our own people put in charge of the government." He held that for the mass of people it was of little concern who governed: "they are equally contented whether their comfort is under rulers with turbans or hats." James Mill's essential positions were opposition to Oriental despots and also the positive introduction of reforms.[77]

James Mill did not share the enthusiasm of Tocqueville for colonization. For James Mill, colonies were a handicap for various reasons, political and economic. They occasioned international conflicts: "that the colonies multiply exceedingly the causes and pretexts of war is a matter of history."[78] Only the rulers, or what he called "the Few," were interested in acquiring colonies to increase their power and wealth. From a general economic point of view, colonies were not beneficial, not "likely to yield any advantage to the countries that hold them."

Neither of the Mills encouraged British settlements for both political and economic reasons. They recognized that most of the British who went to India did so for a limited time and as employees of the government or the Company. They both realized that colonies were a drain on British resources and of little benefit to Britain: "a government always spends as much as it finds it possible or safe to extract from the people."[79] It was a moral, if not an absolute, impossibility that a colony could ever benefit the mother country. Furthermore, in India it was unlikely that trade would be increased because of Hindu adherence to traditional economic practices. Only occasionally did John Stuart Mill qualify his general position. In a remark, reminiscent of Tocqueville's argument, Mill, in a letter dated June 15, 1862, makes the point that "any separation [from the colonies] would greatly diminish the prestige of England, which prestige I believe to be, in the present state of the world, a very great advantage to mankind."[80]

Rather than advocating colonization, both the Mills saw the task for Britain as raising the "scale of civilization" and changing "the hideous state of society." One way, as John Stuart Mill argued in an early memorandum, was to ensure the rights and interests of Indians. Whether it can be construed as benign or tolerant imperialism or not, he proclaimed that the first and greatest principle was that Indians needed protection against the English, and that it was the duty of the British government in India to afford that protection. The British Empire in India would not exist for a day if Britain lost "the character of being more just and disinterested than the native rulers." Britain must ensure that Europeans and British personnel not commit acts that would "destroy the prestige of superior moral worth and justice in dealings which now attaches to the British name in India."[81]

In *A Few Words*, John Stuart Mill expressed pride that England was "incomparably the most conscientious of all nations . . . the only one whom mere scruples of conscience . . . would deter . . . and the power which of all in existence best understands liberty." He was particularly incensed by the "monstrous excesses committed and the brutal language" used during and after the repression of the Indian mutiny in 1857.[82] In a debate in the House of Commons on June 14, 1867, Mill expressed his disgust at the "inhuman and ferocious displays of feeling made by unmilitary persons" regarding the deeds in India, boasting about the inhuman and indiscriminate massacre and the seizing of people and putting them to death without trial. He said his eyes were first opened to the immoral condition of some of the English nation by the atrocities perpetrated in the Indian Mutiny and the expressions of approval that supported them in Britain.[83]

The essential question was how Britain was to perform its civilizing mission to end or reduce the inequities caused by Oriental despotism. Neither of the Mills advocated British control over the Indian way of life; native religious practices should continue unless they were "abhorrent to humanity." John Stuart Mill warned against "proselytism or acts, intentionally or unintentionally, offensive to the religious feelings of the people." At the same time John, the advocate of toleration and freedom of conscience, saw various practices, such as infanticide, as abhorrent, and others, such as the ban on the remarriage of Hindu widows, as unjust. He supported a new penal code, "the most thorough reform probably ever made in the judicial administration of a country." This would mean equality of the laws and protection for the Indians against those "who are naturally inclined to despise the natives and to seek to make themselves a privileged caste." The code should be simple and free from delay and expense.[84]

In this concern for a just law and a good administration of justice, John Stuart Mill had been anticipated by his father. James Mill called for law reform where necessary, and recognized the usefulness of a written code of law, without which there could be no good administration of justice. Sir William Jones and others had recognized this but were wrong, according to James, in employing natives to help formulate a new system. Employing the unenlightened and "perverted" intellects of a few Indian pundits would lead to undesirable consequences such as a disorderly compilation of loose, vague, stupid, or unintelligible quotations or maxims selected arbitrarily from books of law, books of devotion, and books of poetry, all of which provided little assistance in the distribution of justice. James Mill's concept of a simple, written, comprehensive penal code emanated from his Utilitarian philosophy. That concept influenced Thomas Macaulay, who was appointed a member of the Council of the Governor-General in 1833 and recommended legal reforms similar to those suggested by Mill.

A NEW EDUCATION

A crucial part of Britain's civilizing mission was the introduction of a suitable and appropriate educational system in India. On this question James and John Stuart differed from each other, the latter changing his opinions from time to time. The 1813 Charter Renewal Act required the Company to promote education in India. Differences among officials regarding educational policy in

India came to a height in the mid-1830s with the proposals on the subject by Thomas Macaulay in his February 2, 1835, *Minute on Education*, most of which were implemented. This *Minute* called for using government funds to promote teaching in India by using English rather than Sanskrit or Arabic: "the languages of Europe civilized Russia. I cannot doubt that they will do for the Hindu what they have done for the Tartar."[85] The use of the English language and educational system would produce a class of persons, Indian in blood and color, but English in taste, opinion, morals, and intellect. These persons might become emissaries promoting British values among the millions of Indians.

In his book *A System of Logic*, John Stuart Mill suggested the study of "ethology," character formation, the laws of human nature, and the ways in which circumstances affect people. Character, individual and collective, can be changed, leading to different forms of development. Education was one of the ways in which circumstances can be shaped in a manner favorable to the ends desired.[86] What was the most desirable educational system for India? Between 1825 and 1836 he prepared seventeen drafts on educational policy for the Company. On the issue he was not always consistent. At first he was essentially influenced by his father and praised the Hindu College in Calcutta where English was the medium for "useful" learning. Nothing, John Stuart Mill wrote in 1825, was of greater importance than the diffusion of the English language and of European arts and sciences, among the natives of India. As their dispatches show, both of the Mills at first did not support education through the Indian vernacular. However, by 1832 James, in testimony, expressed doubts about the use of English. He then stated that vernacular translations were the appropriate medium for change.[87]

John Stuart Mill came to favor a policy of only limited funding for the teaching of English to potential Indian government employees and to an Indian scholarly class, rather than the policy, proposed by Macaulay and Governor-General Bentinck, a strong supporter of English language instruction, for the general spreading of Western ideas and knowledge throughout the country to improve the intellectual and moral improvement of the people of India. Bentinck issued a resolution on March 7, 1835, that money should go for education in English and for the promotion of English literature and science through the use of English.

John Stuart Mill, in his new desire to revitalize traditional centers of learning and to ensure the emergence of educated Indians trained in native languages, was opposed to this policy of Bentinck. In the draft of his 1836 dispatch on the "Recent Changes in Native Education," John Stuart Mill wrote that "It is through the vernacular languages only that instruction can be diffused among the people; but the vernacular languages can only be rendered adequate to this purpose by persons who can introduce into them from the Sanskrit or the Arabic the requisite words and terms of expression. . . . What we may hope to do by means of English tuition is to teach the teachers; to raise up a class of persons who having derived from an intimate acquaintance with European literature the improved ideas and feelings which are derivable from that source will make it their occupation to spread those ideas and feelings among their countrymen." In a letter around the same time, John Stuart Mill was unusually waspish. His "cautious and deliberate measures for a great public end" had been upset by Macaulay, "a coxcombical dilettante litterateur who never did a thing for a practical object in his life."[88]

In taking this position on education, John Stuart Mill may have been influenced by H. H.Wilson who favored setting up new colleges devoted to traditional subjects to be taught to the elite castes. Mill now agreed that, in the traditional centers of learning, teaching subjects such as Sanskrit and Arabic to elite groups would be the best way to transfer Western ideas to India. He defended not only traditional learning and the use of native vernaculars but also the idea of endowments, which Coleridge had proposed to produce an educated elite in Britain, cultivated and diffusing their learning among the community. For John Stuart Mill, such an elite was crucial to foster knowledge in India as elsewhere.

Though John Stuart Mill's emphasis was on the use of native languages, he was suspicious of Indians who might want to study English not out of disinterested love of knowledge or desire for information but as a passport to public employment. English should be taught, but government funds should be used to ensure that the ancient learning and literature of India did not decline. This would foster the necessary intellectual elites in India. The essential thrust of John Stuart Mill's dispatch was that Oriental literature and learning should be promoted. The problem with the Macaulay-Bentinck policy was that it would not lead to intellectual development of Indians but rather to vocational goals where English would be useful. In such a case only a few Indians would learn English well enough to benefit, whereas many would benefit from education in the vernacular languages, including Sanskrit, Arabic, and Persian. Disappointed by the rejection of his dispatch, John Stuart Mill wrote little on Indian education after it.[89]

Less time was spent by the Mills on educational questions than on the nature of British rule in India and on British policy toward the native princes. James Mill strongly supported direct British rule of India in order to improve government and end the power of local despots, thus benefiting the people of the country. At first, John Stuart Mill appeared to see the Indian princes in similar fashion as despots, thus following the direction of his father. However, partly because he was aware of the considerable expense of British actions, John Stuart Mill was more cautious than his father in recommending rule over the Native States. On balance he preferred improvements in those states rather than dramatic innovations. In some of his dispatches he did suggest annexation of some areas, but in the complicated and changing British policies affecting different parts of India, John Stuart Mill also sometimes argued for preserving royal dynasties.[90] Much of his arguments centered on the need for security and tranquility: if security was threatened, the Company could intervene to restore order. John Stuart Mill felt his suggestions for preserving those monarchies were justified when, during the Sepoy Rebellion of 1857, which took place while he was the chief examiner of the Company, most of the princes were loyal to Britain.

NOT REPRESENTATIVE GOVERNMENT

Though their views on the most desirable form of British control of India varied from time to time, James and John Stuart Mill both took as a premise that India was not ready for self-government. At the abolition of the Company in 1858, John Stuart Mill was still pondering how Britain could best provide for the government, not of three or four millions of English colonists "but of 150 millions Asiatics, who cannot be trusted to govern themselves."[91]

In an important chapter in his *Considerations on Representative Government*, published in 1861, John Stuart Mill concluded that, because direct participation by people in public affairs was not possible except in a small town and on minor parts of public business, the best system must be representative government. Again, his father, in his *Essay on Government*, had anticipated his son by calling representative government "the grand discovery of modern times." Unfortunately, according to John Stuart Mill, representative government was not applicable in countries without a tradition of liberty or that were at a less advanced level of civilization such as Asia where a tradition of public discussion of affairs did not exist. In the tradition dating back to Aristotle, he contrasted the passive character found in Oriental societies with the "active ones required by representative institutions."[92] Political participation at the local level was important, fostered intellectual development, and led to more responsible citizenship. The public of India was not ready for a system of this kind because of "the passive and slavish character of the people in many parts of India."

In *Representative Government*, Mill had observed that progress was not automatic. The active character of responsible citizens in the West, who had a sense of duty and were disposed to act for the general good of humanity, was not present in the Orient. There, "Irresponsible rulers need the quiescence of the ruled, more than they need any activity but that which they can compel. Submissiveness to the prescriptions of men as necessities of nature is the lesson inculcated by all governments upon those who are wholly without participation in them. The will of superiors, and the law as the will of the superiors, must be passively yielded to. . . . Between subjection to the will of others, and the virtues of self-help and self-government, there is a natural incompatibility." Mill contrasted the passive type of character, favored by the government of one or a few, with the active, self-helping type, favored by government "of the many."[93]

John Stuart Mill felt that the Indian people were not able to make their circumstances, interests, and grievances known to the British people. Britain appreciated that government in India had to be adapted to the level of the capacities and qualities of such men as were available. Instead of representative government, India would benefit by a kind of enlightened benevolent despotism, rule by a superior people, or those lands at a more advanced stage of civilization. Ever the loyal employee, John Stuart Mill thought the Company brought good government, progress as well as order, through experts and professional bureaucrats.[94] At some future stage, India might take over responsibility for its own government. In the meantime, Mill's advice to the British officials was that "in seeking the good which is needed, no damage or as little as possible, be done." In praise of the Company Mill wrote "it has been the destiny of the government of the Company to suggest the true theory of the government of a semi-barbarous dependency by a civilized country, and after having done this, to perish."

John Stuart Mill was aware of the problems created by rule of one country over another. "It is next to impossible to form in one country an organ of government for another which shall have a strong interest in good government; but if that cannot be done, the next best thing is to form a body with the least possible interest in bad government; and I conceive that the present governing bodies in this country for the affairs of India have as little sinister interest of any kind as any government in the world." He applied to India the concept he enunciated in an article in April 1831: "there are states of society in which we must not seek for a good government, but for the least bad one."[95]

Slavery was one issue John Stuart Mill wanted the Company and the British government to address. He indicated the reforms fostered by the Company and his own concern about slavery and the slave market. Slavery in every form was an evil of great magnitude and peculiarly revolting to the moral feelings of Englishmen. He wondered to what extent it existed in the East. He realized that the British could not "interfere authoritatively" for the suppression of the slave traffic in the Native States but urged "exerting the influence of our friendly advice to discourage the practice."

WAS INTERVENTION NECESSARY OR DESIRABLE?

At the core of the debate regarding India was the wider problem of when is a nation justified in intervening in the internal affairs of another nation. John Stuart Mill's answer was clear. If a nation was not sufficiently advanced for representative government it had to be governed by the dominant country or by persons delegated by that country to lead the nation to development and eventual liberation.[96]

John Stuart Mill in his essay, *A Few Words on Non-Intervention*, talked of the Indian states as "barbarous," at a low level of social improvement. To India he applied his generalization that the need sometimes existed for despotic rule when a "rude people" was unprepared to take part in public affairs and to share in the benefits of civilized society. Despotism was a legitimate mode of government "in dealing with barbarians, provided the end be improvement, and the means justified by actually effecting that end. In *On Liberty* Mill argued that liberty as a principle had no application to any state of things anterior to the time when mankind had become capable of being improved by free and equal discussion. Until then, there was nothing for them but implicit obedience to Akbar or Charlemagne, if they were so fortunate to find one."[97] Liberty, John Stuart Mill argued, was meant to apply only to people with mature facilities.

John Stuart Mill had no qualms about this control by Britain. In *A Few Words* he argued that the same international customs and the same rules of international morality did not apply in all cases: they differed between one civilized nation and another, and between civilized nations and barbarians. Control over a barbarous people should not be construed as a violation of the laws of nations, because barbarians had no rights as a nation, except to get such treatment that might fit them to become an advanced nation at the earliest possible moment. Barbarians might benefit and progress if they were conquered and held in subjugation by foreigners, far better than if they were governed by "the precariousness of tenure attendant on barbarous despotisms."[98] In his *Civilization*, John Stuart Mill compared barbarous societies with civilized ones: in the former there was no commerce, no manufacturers; little or no law, or administration of justice; and no systematic employment of the collective strength of society to protect individuals against injury from one another.

Both of the Mills saw those barbarous despotisms, and their "corruptive operation" as responsible for the backwardness and stagnation in Eastern societies: one example was "the hideous state of society in Bengal." In what is perhaps one of his extreme remarks on the subject, John Stuart Mill confided to his diary on January 26, 1854, that "Perhaps the English are the fittest people to rule over barbarous or semi-barbarous nations like those of the East, precisely because they are the stiffest and most wedded to their own customs, of all civilized people."[99] Unlike other countries that have conquered the East and been absorbed into it and adopted its ways, Britain, if it "has one foot in India will always have another on the English shore."

Even if John Stuart Mill's views on the nature of that rule were less fixed and more subject to change, more complex and ambivalent, than those of his father, who favored extension of direct British rule and regarded most Indian princes as Oriental despots, he had no doubts about the validity and desirability of British rule in India. He expressed this emphatically: "In the more considerable native states, our influence is exerted on the side of good, in every mode permitted by positive engagement. Not only have the British representatives incessantly, and to great degree successfully, incited native princes to prohibit and suppress the barbarous usages which we have ceased to tolerate in our own territories; but defects have been pointed out, and improvements suggested, in their revenue and judicial administrations. Financial disorder and general misgovernment have been the subjects of grave remonstrance, followed up by such positive marks of displeasure as were consistent with the respective treaties."[100]

John Stuart Mill went on to give evidence of the success of British rule, of constant, if not rapid, improvements in prosperity and good administration. One example was the "enormous increase in the external commerce of India" and the increasing role of Indians in criminal and revenue administration. The Nawab of Rampur, who had worked for the Company had, on succeeding to the throne, introduced reforms he learned from it. Whatever the usefulness of Oriental despotisms in the past, they were now obstacles to further improvement. They lacked mental liberty and individuality, requisites of improvement.[101] John Stuart Mill's essential position was that British rule had to prepare the native population to have control of their own actions. "It was not by attempting to rule directly a country like India, but by giving it good rulers, that the English people can do their duty to that country."

However, John Stuart Mill's position cannot be simply defined. It was complex, varying between approval of direct and indirect British rule and taking account of the different circumstances in each political setting. At first, he seemed to follow the direction of direct rule, favored by his father. During the political crisis in the state of Mysore in 1831, both James, who wanted Britain to promote good and useful government, and John Stuart approved of the decision of Governor-General William Bentinck to set up an administrative structure in the state that would reduce the power of the Maharaja Krishnaraja. John Stuart Mill who wrote, between 1832 and 1834, three dispatches, parts of which were deleted by the Board of Control, on Mysore, referred to the absolute power of the maharaja and his defects, "love of ease and pleasure, which aggravated by habit and indulgence, has rendered him remiss in the duties of government, and prodigal in his expenditure . . . defects naturally generated by absolute power." Yet, in 1837 John Stuart Mill while writing about the Native State of Jaipur argued for British nonintervention. Earlier, in his first dispatch on Awadh in 1828, John Stuart Mill was critical of the British attempt to support the ruler and "the shortsightedness and rapacity of a semi-barbarous government."

In 1830 he wrote of the anarchy, the insubordination, the total disorganization of all the springs of social order, and all the sources of internal prosperity in the kingdom. John Stuart Mill was troubled by the British policy of using Indian rulers to implement British rule; this was tantamount to acquiescing in Indian despotism.[102] He was particularly concerned that troops led by British personnel were used to collect the revenue from the people demanded by the ruler: "The shortsightedness and rapacity of a semi-barbarous government is [thus] armed with the military strength of a civilized one." An Oriental despot should not be helped. His dispatch on Awadh drafted in 1834 urged Bentinck to take control of the area whose government had "become progressively more and more inefficient, and more and more oppressive." He argued for the British government to undertake the management of the country in the name of the king for as long as necessary for restoring order and establishing an efficient system of administration. Britain should improve administration for the good of the people not use its authority to preserve Oriental despots.

But within a few years, John Stuart Mill appeared to change his position on British direct or indirect rule in response to political developments in Indian states. In his 1837 dispatch on Jaipur, John Stuart Mill now supported in the state a "national government," an autonomous Indian ruler, and a policy of nonintervention by Britain, even though a British official had been murdered there. His virtual approval of the new policy of the acting Governor-General Charles Metcalfe to intervene as little as possible was a decisive shift for Mill.[103] His dispatches from 1838 on were less concerned with criticism of the native rulers and more concerned with stability and order, tantamount to approving a policy of upholding indirect rule. In 1838, for example, he changed his mind about Awadh, now stating his concern about the erosion of royal power there. He supported the raja, the ruler of Rajput, when his authority was threatened and the ruler of Jodhpur when local officials wanted to overthrow him. In 1846 he praised the chief *thakurs*, the nobility, of Jaipur for their public spirit and patriotism and hoped "the chiefs and influential classes in the Rajput States may be made willing agents for reforming the defects in the administration of those states."[104]

These statements, and others, by John Stuart Mill expressing general approval of indirect rule were consonant with the development of his idea that it was necessary to balance introduction of reform in India and retaining existing institutions. Unlike James's argument for better political institutions, John, influenced by the competent British rulers, such as Sir John Malcolm, governor of Bombay; Sir Thomas Munro; Mountstuart Elphinstone; and Bentinck, argued for gradual change by building on existing practices and through the political elites. For a time at least it seemed, Oriental despots would remain in place in this part of the British Empire.

Yet Mill again changed positions. In the 1840s, he challenged the policies of indirect rule, and favored intervention in despotic states, to stimulate modernization. In principle, though not without qualification, he approved a policy of taking over a state when there was no heir to the throne. At the same time, however, he thought that Britain ought to encourage native leaders to end social evils such as female infanticide and the custom of organized plundering raids. John Stuart Mill had no clear, totally consistent, position on this issue. He did try to explain that position in a letter of September 26, 1866, to John Morley. He approved of almost all the annexations taken by Lord Dalhousie (governor-general 1848–56), who extended British control both by conquest and by taking over Native States when their rulers died without natural heirs. He also explained that he did not approve of the dissolution of Native States without heirs if those states had distinctive nationality and historical traditions and feelings. However, in the modern states created by conquest, such as the Muhammedan and most of the Mahratta Kingdoms, which were not native, continuance of the dynasties in those states was not a right nor a general rule but a reward to be earned by good government.

JOHN STUART MILL: THE LOYAL EMPLOYEE OF THE EIC

John Stuart Mill argued that the Company could bring good government to India and could foster a trained group of Indian administrators. A beneficial form of despotism could result from the existing division of political control between the Company and the British parliament with inherent checks and balances. This control, devoid of party politics and based on the "personal qualities and capacities of the agents of government," could lead to progressive administration. In a somewhat surprising remark, made in a speech in

Parliament on August 12, 1867, John Stuart Mill argued that part of the great success of the British administration was due to the fact that the government had, to a large extent, been carried on in writing.[105]

On most occasions John Stuart Mill, the loyal employee, had nothing but praise for the Company. According to him this body, aloof from the party conflicts of English politics, devoted its whole time and energies to Indian affairs. He described the Company as a great corporation, which gained India for Britain, and had hitherto, before the change in 1858, been considered the best qualified to conduct its administration, under the authority of the Crown and subject when necessary to veto of the Board of Control. The government of which it had been a part was "not only one of the purest in intention, but one of the most beneficent in act, ever known among mankind."[106] The Company had made improvements and laid the foundations for further progress. In no government known to history had appointments to offices, and especially to high offices, been so rarely bestowed on any other considerations than those of personal fitness. Its administration had been disinterested and informed.

John Stuart was proud of the achievements of the Company in many fields. It had built canals, roads, irrigation systems, libraries, and medical facilities. It had established education programs and was perpetually striving toward improvement. He paid the Company a high compliment: few governments, even under far better circumstances, had attempted so much for the good of their subjects or had been so successful.[107] The Company had played an important role, together with the government, in promoting many reforms in Indian society. Mill outlined some of the reforms: suppression of crime, especially ridding India of the Thugs and Dacoitee; suppression of piracy; control of female infanticide; making *suttee*, the voluntary burning of widows on the funeral piles of their husbands, a criminal offense; punishing witchcraft and use of so-called supernatural powers for purposes of extortion, intimidation, and murder; suppressing *tragga*, a singular mode of extorting redress on the part of those who were, or believed themselves to be, injured; ending the *meriah* (human) sacrifices; abolishing slavery in 1843; abolishing forced labor, compulsory labor not only for building roads but also for personal services rendered to government officers and powerful individuals; extending civil rights to religious converts; and in 1856 legalizing the remarriage of widows.[108]

At the hearing of the Select Committee of the House of Lords in June 1852 regarding the renewal of the charter of the Company, John Stuart Mill made the case that the continuation of its authority was preferable to control of India by the British government and by Parliament, which did not have sufficient knowledge of India and its people and had not benefited, as had officials of the Company, from an apprenticeship in the study of India and its problems.[109] John

Stuart Mill praised the Company as the best governing body for India, a body of professionals who had acquired knowledge of the country, had been trained in place, and made its administration the main occupation of their lives. The Company had as much interest as possible in good government and the least possible interest in bad government, and had as little sinister interest as any government in the world. The Company had realized that its task was not to sweep away the rights they found established or to make them into something resembling those of England but rather to find out what they were; having ascertained them, to abolish only those that were absolutely mischievous; and otherwise to protect them, and use them as a starting point for further steps in improvement.[110]

JOHN STUART MILL THE PATERNALIST

In concluding *Representative Government* with some general remarks about theories of government, John Stuart Mill commented that "it has been the destiny of the East India Company to suggest the true theory of the government of a semi-barbarous dependency by a civilized country." Clearly, the British people, through the Company, had done its duty to India, introducing reforms in a number of areas, including health and education, and spurring progress in the country. In recent years John Stuart Mill has been the subject of severe criticism, for an alleged sense of superiority, seemingly contrary to his normal liberal thought, when addressing non-Western cultures, for his supposed Eurocentric outlook, and for distasteful, now politically incorrect, language used from time to time in referring to those cultures, including such egregious terms such as *barbarian*, *semibarbarous*, *nation of savages*, and *little-advanced civilization*.[111]

However unfortunate his choice of words, which understandingly grate on contemporary ears, John Stuart Mill was not a racist, as understood in our own age. Nor was he an individual who accepted the idea of inherent biological differences among peoples. He made this point in his letter to Thomas Carlyle, stating that it was not true that every difference among people was due to "an original difference in nature, and that even if that were true it did not grant any country the right to subdue another people." Furthermore, diversities of conduct and character should not be attributed to inherent natural differences. With this attitude in mind, it seems unreasonable to argue that Mill's writings on less developed societies illustrate "a missionary, ethnocentric, and narrow political vision" that dismisses nonliberal societies as primitive and in need of civilizing by liberal societies.

John Stuart Mill's language on this thorny issue of a possible hierarchy of different societies reflects the fact that he, like thinkers and organizations in our own day, was grappling with two interrelated problems: whether an advanced or developed country ought or should intervene in other countries for what it deemed desirable and humanitarian ends and whether advanced societies had an obligation to help less advanced ones, or those considered by nineteenth-century writers to be on a lower level of civilization, and to use methods and means to introduce social and economic modernization and political reforms.

John Stuart Mill's own answer, not devoid of contradiction and sometime changing in emphasis depending on the specific issue he was discussing, is found in a number of his works. He was not a dogmatic ideologue. He was troubled, as was Tocqueville in remarks on American society, by some characteristics of developed societies, especially the despotism of custom, which obliged everyone to conform to the approved current standard, the tyranny of public opinion, and the consequent possible loss of individual genius and energy, thus hindering further progress. Nevertheless, despite these problems, developed societies fostered desirable aspects of individual and social life through a commitment to toleration and self-determination. The features that John Stuart Mill admired in developed societies were adherence to the principle of individuality – for him the chief ingredient of individual and social progress, liberty, cultivation of character, activism, voluntary organizations, and local initiatives that would limit the power of the central state; continual striving toward material and cultural improvement; and maximizing happiness. For Mill those features were not likely to be present in less advanced societies.

John Stuart Mill was neither an imperialist nor a colonialist and was less dogmatic and less consistent than his father. Neither was he an isolationist; he had a deep interest in France, where he is buried, and in the United States. Unlike Tocqueville, in his thoughts on Algeria, John Stuart Mill did not call for British dominion or hegemony over India nor did he call for arbitrary controls. He ultimately concluded that the British attitude should be one of guidance not force. John Stuart Mill did not lack concern for the well-being of the inhabitants of India. Although he thought that regarding most issues Britain should respect Indian laws, customs, and religious practices, he was critical of and welcomed reform of those he thought were abhorrent to humanity, bad practices such as infanticide, *sati*, *thuggee*, *tragga*, witchcraft.

John Stuart envisioned a division in the world between "civilized" and "barbarian" societies. Civilized societies were on the road to perfection, happiness, and wisdom through moral improvement, education, cultivation of tastes, cooperation, and exposure to different modes of thought and action. In barbarian or uncivilized societies persons shifted for themselves and could not bear to sacrifice, for any purpose, the satisfaction of individual will. Those nations could not be depended on for any consistent observance of rules. In probably his most extreme statement, John Stuart Mill held that those societies had not gone beyond the period during which it was likely that, for their benefit, they should be conquered and held in subjection by foreigners. However, Mill immediately follows this statement by asserting that compulsion should be ended when those societies have attained the capacity of being guided to their own improvement.

John Stuart Mill conceived that a backward country like India was not ripe for a system of representative government, as the United States and Australia had been when they were new. How then could the melancholy fact of stagnation there and in other less developed countries be ended? The answer was either by an extraordinary genius in the country or through intervention by a culturally superior power. A stationary state was not merely "stupid tranquility with security against change for the worse." It also was often overrun, conquered, and reduced to domestic slavery, either by a stronger despot or by "the nearest barbarous people who retained along with their savage rudeness the energies of freedom."

John Stuart Mill was constantly concerned with this problem of stagnation. Europe had overcome stagnation because of various factors: the competition between religious and secular forces, the "contest of rival powers for dominion over society, the success in coordinating the rival powers naturally tending in different directions," and by toleration. In the backward countries improvement could not come from within, and therefore must come from outside. The point for which John Stuart Mill has been most criticized by some modern political theorists is his argument that despotism was a mode of government as legitimate as any other if it was the one that, in the existing state of civilization of the subject people, most facilitates the transition of backward countries to a higher state of improvement, and if the means were justified by the end. Those critics pay less attention to John Stuart Mill's statement that he was "not aware that any community has a right to force another to be civilized." John Stuart Mill may have been paternalistic, but he was not illiberal, colonialist, or imperialist, tolerant or otherwise.

8

Karl Marx: The Asiatic Mode of Production and Oriental Despotism

The search for the Asiatic mode of production (AMP) and its related political structure, Oriental despotism, in the writings of Karl Marx and Friedrich Engels may not have lasted as long as the quest for the Holy Grail, but it has had equally passionate devotees, heretics, and disbelievers disputing the nature and even the existence of the quarry. Marx, in the original preface to the first volume of *Capital* in 1859, conscious of the provocative character of his work, was aware that inquiry into the nature of political economy summoned as "foes into the field of battle the most violent, mean and malignant passions of the human breast, the furies of private interest."[1] The concept of the Asiatic mode has aroused even more emotional turmoil and heated polemical exchanges than is customary in the normally turbulent world of Marxist exegesis.[2]

Some of the heat engendered by the considerable debate about Oriental despotism and the AMP emanates from genuine differences in interpretation of the often opaque or contradictory writings of Marx and Engels. An unusually large variety of interpretations of the two concepts has been presented. They include the view of the AMP as a genuine socioeconomic formation unique to the Orient; a primitive society geographically widespread before the period of slavery; a variant of slavery or of feudalism; an "archaic formation"; a specific form of property ownership or of relations of production; a pseudoconcept that is really a hypothesis about the origins of modern bourgeois society; a society with a state but without private property; the most general form of the evolution of primitive communist society; the most primitive form of the state, a concept that could be applicable to precolonial black African systems; an imaginative sketch to help analyze capitalism; the only Marxist non-Western type of society; a political structure without a class system; a transitory formation between two kinds of class society; a stagnant variant of the ancient mode of production; and an important vehicle for Aesopian criticism of the despotic power of rulers. In light of the many different and contradictory interpretations, some analysts in despair have argued that the term *AMP* be dropped or buried.[3]

Even stronger has been the fervent hostility with which critics have attacked the concept of the AMP. For orthodox Marxists a theory such as the AMP, which implicitly argues that Western capitalist systems had been capable of positive benefit to colonies; a bureaucratic group, not defined in economic terms, might be the ruling class; no uniform pattern of historical development necessarily existed for all mankind; productive forces were not always the primary element in a society; progress was not inevitable; societies might become modernized by external forces; and geographical factors might limit the primacy of technology, was unacceptable. The concept of the AMP divided members of the Russian revolutionary movement at the end of the nineteenth and in the early twentieth century; it was condemned by the Chinese communists in Moscow in 1928 and by Soviet specialists in a celebrated meeting in Leningrad in 1931 and regarded as nonexistent by Stalin in 1938.[4]

One cannot point to any sustained, substantive, or systematic analysis of the Asiatic mode, Oriental societies, or Oriental despotism in the writings of Marx and Engels. Nor did they provide an account of any dialectical change from that mode to another in the process of historical development as they did for other economic and social systems. Compared with the thousands of pages by Marx and Engels on the history and societies of Western Europe, the stages of capitalist development, Roman history, the medieval origins of the bourgeoisie, feudal trade and finance, and the German Middle Ages, they wrote little about the Orient.[5] Their various commentaries and remarks regarding the AMP do not have the resonance or detail of their lengthy writings analyzing the system of capitalism.[6] Robert Tucker, the expert on Communist thought, has acutely observed that Marx spent thirty years writing and rewriting one book about capitalism under a number of different titles.[7]

Part of that book, in its various guises, was clarification of the preconditions for the emergence of capitalism. In the *Grundrisse*, part treatise, part inchoate notes for the writing of *Capital*, Marx asserted that bourgeois society was "the most developed and the most complex historic organization of production."[8] By understanding the relations and the structure of that society one could gain insights into "the structure and relations of production of all the vanished social formations out of whose ruins and elements it built itself up." The bourgeois economy thus supplied the key to the ancient one.

Yet even acknowledging the fact that their writings on European affairs far outweighed those on Asian affairs, it would be wrong to conclude that Marx and Engels were uninterested in Asia as such or that their study of Asian societies was merely instrumental for tracing the movement toward or the understanding of the political economy of capitalism. In the 1850s their interest in the Orient and their scholarly immersion in its history became serious as their correspondence and newspaper articles showed. One of the more amusing allusions to their growing interest was a note by Engels, in his letter to Marx of June 6, 1853, in which he informed his friend he had put off learning Arabic but had given himself a maximum of three weeks to learn Persian.[9] Engels later recognized that such economic science as "we possess up to the present is limited almost exclusively to the genesis and development of the capitalist mode of production," and that there was a need to study other systems.[10]

It is worth following chronologically the "study of other systems" by Marx and Engels as it relates to their development of the concept of the AMP. It is also worth remembering that the two writers were becoming influenced by the disciplines of archaeology and anthropology, which were becoming important in their time, and which they used for their own analyses. In the early writings of Marx and Engels the Orient is only mentioned a few times, in *The German Ideology* and by a reference in Engels's 1847 *Principles of Communism*. Marx first alluded to "Asiatic despotism" in his *Contribution to the Critique of Hegel's Philosophy of Right*, written in the spring/summer of 1843, where he argued that the political body in early history was either a real concern of citizens who participated in it as did the Greeks, or was nothing but "the private caprice of a single individual so that, as in Asian despotism, the political state was as much a slave as the material state."[11]

Their real, and continuing, interest in Asian affairs can be seen starting with the short articles in the *New York Daily Tribune* in 1853 and the correspondence between the two writers regarding India and China during that period. The articles were concerned with specific, empirical issues of the day: the renewal of the East India Company charter, discussed in Chapter 7, the social system in India, British rule and its future in that country, and the Taiping rebellion in China. These were written to inform serious newspaper readers of current events. But in these articles and in the letters that overlapped in subject matter, Marx and Engels put forward striking generalizations about the history and character of Oriental societies and suggested important differences between Western and Eastern styles of life. At this stage they depended on particular sources for their information and for some of their more general opinions about Asia; they made use of the work of writers like François Bernier, officials such as Sir Stamford Raffles, British government documents, and parliamentary debates. Later, their reading about the Orient and related matters became more extensive, especially on the history of Asia, including the work on Asiatic monarchies by Robert Patton and on early societies.[12]

Marx and Engels also absorbed and combined ideas from diverse nonspecialists on the Orient. They based their concept of Oriental despotism on Montesquieu whose writings Marx read in 1843; the absence of political participation and economic backwardness from Hegel; the stationary nature of the Orient from Voltaire; conflation of rent and tax from Adam Smith and Richard Jones; and the general belief that India was the cradle of languages and cultures from Jones.[13] Interestingly, Marx in an early letter of May 1843 to Ruge shows that he had not at first appreciated Montesquieu's differentiation of a despotic state from a monarchy.[14] At that time Marx saw the terms *monarchy*, *democracy*, and *tyranny* as referring to a single concept denoting, at best, different modes of the same principle.

Because the writings of the two never resulted in a concise treatise on Oriental societies, analysis of their work rests on a variety of sources: the newspaper articles; letters to each other and to the many individuals, mostly socialists, who sought their advice; passages from their economic analyses of precapitalist and capitalist societies; and, in their later years, ethnological studies and notes. Not surprisingly, writing at different times and in varying formats with different audiences in mind, they gave changing emphasis to the importance of specific factors in Oriental affairs. Also, these writings alternate between empirical remarks on historical and contemporary issues and current affairs, and theoretical and abstract analysis of the kind found in their major economic works, especially *Capital*.[15]

This is illustrated in the newspaper articles and letters as Marx and Engels grappled with the subject for the first time in earnest. In those writings their comments on Asian society emerged: the importance of separate village communities; the absence of private land ownership; and Oriental despotism, which meant, among other things, state ownership and control of water resources and other public works. Marx and Engels developed their ideas in a close symbiotic relationship. Marx on June 2, 1853, informed his colleague that he could answer the question: "Why does the history of the East appear as a history of religions?" Depending on "old Bernier," who Marx viewed as having correctly discovered the basic underlying cause of all social structures in the East, referring to Turkey, Persia, and Hindustan, the answer was the absence of private ownership of land. "This is the real key even to the Oriental heaven." Engels on June 6, 1853, quickly agreed that this absence of private ownership of land explained the political and religious history of the East. But why was it absent? Engels's first explanation is to say that its absence was mainly due to the climate and the nature of the soil in the East, which for him stretched from "Arabia to the highest Asiatic plateaus."[16]

Engels also introduced two important factors. He pointed out the need in Oriental countries for artificial irrigation He also analyzed Oriental governments as focused on only three goals: finance (plunder at home), war (plunder at home and abroad), and public works (provision for sustaining the society). Marx used Engels's description of government in Asia, adding that Oriental governments had existed in that form "generally, from immemorial times," in his article in the *New York Daily Tribune* of June 25, 1853, written on June 10.[17] He also repeated the assertions of Engels that climate and territory in the East meant that artificial irrigation was the basis of Oriental agriculture, and that government in Asia had to provide public works.

In this article, *The British Rule in India*, Marx discussed British colonial policy. In his view Britain had dealt with finance and war but not with public works. He was caustic about that policy, though even more about the Indian system of villages, each with a separate organization, each forming a world of its own. Explaining the reason for the stationary nature of Indian society, Marx gave two answers: the fact that public works were the business of the central government and the reality that the whole empire, except a few towns, was divided into villages. Drawing on the 1812 British report of the Select Committee of the House of Commons on the Affairs of the East Indian Company, Marx gave a picture of the organization of a typical village community with its top-heavy government of twelve different officials and its inefficient division of labor.

Both in the June 25 article, and in his letter to Engels of June 14, 1853, Marx made similar points about that village system. These village communities, "idyllic republics" in his ironic phrase, which still existed in parts of Northwest India, "had always been the solid foundation of Oriental despotism" or "the foundation for stagnant Asiatic despotism." He also remarked, in the letter of June 14, but without pursuing the matter, that "it seems to have been the Muhammedans who first established the principle of no property in land throughout the whole of Asia."

After a lull in their interest in Asia, Marx and Engels resumed writing on Indian and Chinese affairs between 1857 and 1862. They were now concerned with issues such as the Indian mutiny, the Anglo-Chinese war, changes in land ownership and confiscation of land, trade with China, and the opium trade. Allusions to Asia began to appear in Marx's major economic writings, especially as he compared precapitalist systems, including Oriental ones, with capitalism and the conditions necessary for the emergence of capitalism. References to Asia, Oriental economics, and to Asiatic societies were now put in the context of discussion of theoretical issues: production, distribution, commodity exchange, division of labor, levels of production, the relation of rent and taxation, state use of surplus labor, ownership of land, the relationship of town and countryside, the individual and the commune, and Oriental despotism. Oriental systems became part of his analysis of historical evolution when in 1859, Marx, in the *Preface to a Contribution to the Critique of Political Economy*, described for the first time the existence of an AMP.

Marx provided an initial explanation of the historical development of mankind in his letter of December 28, 1846, to Pavel Annenkov, a Russian liberal landowner. "If you assume given stages of development in production, commerce or consumption, you will have a corresponding form of social constitution, a corresponding organization, whether of the family, of the estates or of the classes a corresponding civil society, [and] a political system."[18] Economic forms, in which man produced, consumed, and exchanged goods, were transitory and historical. With the change in new productive faculties came changes in the mode of production. At other times, Marx argued that the economic process started with "socially determined individual production," and that production took place at a definite stage of social development.

Throughout their lives the two theorists were sometimes inconsistent in their presentation of historical materialism or the materialist conception of history and their concepts of modes of production and relations of production. The clarification of these views and concepts has given rise to a considerable cottage industry with diminishing intellectual reward. All might agree that Marx and Engels succumbed, as did other nineteenth-century thinkers, to what Ernest Gellner called "the charm of the world growth story; the image of a growing cosmos, of upward growth," and that they generally saw history as an "entelechy," as a series of successive and connected stages.[19] Engels, explaining Marx's work, acknowledged that Hegel was the first to demonstrate there was development, an intrinsic coherence in history.

It took Marx fourteen years from his first generalizations about historical development and categories of social and economic systems before he arrived at the AMP. Historical development, Engels explained in an essay in 1859, "proceeds by jumps and zigzags, and by and large from the simplest to the more complex relations."[20] He had joined Marx, in their first set of analytical categories to explain world history, in *The German Ideology* written during 1845 and 1846. Societies, they argued, differed most significantly according to their modes of production and the character of the social division of labor to which corresponded different forms of property. They outlined three forms of property ownership and social division of labor: tribal communal property ownership; the communal and state property ownership of antiquity; and feudal or rank property ownership.

In the first form, the undeveloped stage of production, people sustained themselves by hunting and fishing, by cattle raising or farming. Based on kinship groups, an elementary division of labor existed within the family, and the social hierarchy consisted of an extension of the family: patriarchal tribal chiefs, members of the tribes, and slaves. Slavery increased with the expansion of population, the growth of needs, and the result of wars or barter.

The second form, originating in cities formed by the union of tribal groups and exemplified by the Greek city states and by Rome, was based on slavery and communal ownership. Communal ownership would dissolve as private property became more important. The division of labor was more evident than previously; town and country were more differentiated; and a class system of free citizens and slaves existed.

The third form, feudal property ownership in the Middle Ages, had a social communal organization based on the countryside; small-scale cultivation of land owned by feudal lords using serf labor; handicraft manufacturing and the guild system; and an armed nobility. The feudal system led to a fourth system, the bourgeois form, with an increase in private property; the separation of town and country; growth of manufacturing; division of labor in the cities between production and trade; use of and greater concentration of capital; and the rise of a bourgeois class.

To help prepare for the *Communist Manifesto*, in 1847 Engels wrote the *Principles of Communism* in which he pointed out that one of the results of the industrial revolution was that the system of industry founded on manual labor was destroyed in all countries of the world. "All semi-barbarian countries, which until now had been more or less outside historical development and whose industry had until now been based on manufacture, were thus forcibly torn out of their isolation." Those countries, for example India, that for thousands of years had made no progress were revolutionized, and even China was marching toward revolution.[21]

The first well-known and widely used Marxist statement on historical stages came in the *Communist Manifesto* of 1848. It presented three stages, different from those in the 1845 formulation, which were characterized by types of relations of production and class society: slavery in antiquity, feudalism in the Middle Ages, and the modern bourgeois society from which socialism would emerge in the future. All the stages reflected class struggles: free men against slaves, feudal lords against serfs, and capitalists against the proletariat.

But the tribal or patriarchal societies of *The German Ideology* did not appear, nor did Asia, in this European-centered version of historical change. Interestingly, Marx, in analyzing the role of the bourgeoisie, praised it for having drawn "all, even the most barbarian nations into civilization."

The crucial passage relating to the non-European world was the conclusion: "Just as it has made the country dependent on the towns, so it has made barbarian and semi-barbarian countries dependent on the civilized ones, nations of peasants on nations of bourgeois, the East on the West."

The third version of historical change appeared in the *Grundrisse*, the lengthy first draft of *Capital*, written during 1857 and 1858 but not published until 1939. In the introduction Marx wrote of the problem inherent in categorization: "Since bourgeois society is itself only a contradictory form of development, relations derived from earlier forms will often be found within it only in an entirely stunted form, or even travestied. . . . The so-called historical presentation of development is founded, as a rule, on the fact that the latest form regards the previous ones as steps leading up to itself. . . . It would be unfeasible and wrong to let the economic categories follow one another in the same sequence as that in which they were historically decisive."[22]

In the *Grundrisse*, Marx compared precapitalist economic formations, the different forms of property ownership before capitalism, the development of private property, and the relations of production.[23] To this end he devised another set of categories to explain the alternative routes out of the primitive communal system, some favoring historical evolution and some not. Regarding slavery and serfdom as "secondary" forms of society, he concentrated on "primary" forms, which included a variety of tribal and other communities.[24] Marx started with the earliest form of landed property, that of the tribal community, the natural common body. This original community was modified depending on various external, climatic, geographical, and physical factors as well as on the character of the tribe. The community was, properly speaking, the real proprietor.[25] Politically, the emergence of the state power differentiated it from the primitive communal form of property. Economically, what existed was communal property and private individual possession.

This early kind of community existed in a variety of ways. Classifying them on the basis of different forms of communal and private property and the relations of production, Marx described four main forms: the Asiatic or Oriental, the Slavonic (which was not discussed but appeared to be a variant of the Asiatic), the ancient classical, and the Germanic. This was the first time that Marx presented Asiatic or Oriental society as a distinct category. That presentation is at a high level of generality and abstraction. As Eric Hobsbawm, the Marxist historian, acknowledged, the writing in the *Grundrisse* resembles a kind of "private intellectual shorthand which is sometimes impenetrable."[26] But the general meaning is clear. Asiatic or Oriental society is the starting point for Marx's analysis of relations of production.

The Asiatic society was based on tribal or common property, in most cases created through a combination of manufacturing and agriculture in small communities that were entirely self-sustaining and contained within themselves all the factors of production and surplus production. Above these communities was "the all-embracing unity," the higher or sole proprietor, while the people in the real communities were regarded only as hereditary and temporary possessors. The "unity" was the real owner of property and could appear as something separate and superior to the many individual communities. The individual was property-less, or property might be a grant from the total unity to the individual through the intermediary of the particular community. Property ownership was communal, stemming originally from group cohesion or tribal organization. More than one analyst has observed that Marx used the same term *Gemeinwesen* to denote different factors: common, tribal property, and membership in a tribal organization.[27] In his discussion Marx makes the interesting point that private property came later than communal property, not the other way round, as is commonly assumed.

The Oriental despot was "the father" of all the numerous lesser communities, thus embodying the common, higher unity. In Marx's general economic analysis a central feature of any socio-economic formation was the way that surplus value was appropriated from the direct producers. He held that the surplus product of those lesser communities in Oriental systems belonged to this highest unity. Oriental despotism therefore resulted in a legal absence of property. Surplus labor was rendered both as tribute and as common labor for the glory of the unity, symbolized by the despot, who was also the imagined tribal entity of the god. In Oriental societies, as in other precapitalist societies, surplus labor was not appropriated by purely economic means or by free exchange, but rather by other means such as force or sacred authority; it occurred through direct slavery, serfdom, or political dependence.[28]

Variations were evident in the Asiatic form of society. Labor in the communal property could appear in two ways. The small communities could "vegetate independently side by side"; within each one the individual worked independently with his family on the land, while a certain amount of labor was performed for the common store. Or the unity above the smaller communities could impose a common organization of labor, thus creating a formal system by which individuals had to perform labor on behalf of the whole community. Marx, somewhat confusingly, gave as examples of this latter system, countries and people as diverse as Mexico, Peru, the ancient Celts, and some tribes of India.[29]

Within the Asiatic form, the political character of the tribal bodies might also vary. The unity might be represented by a chief of the tribal group or by the patriarchs, the heads of the families. Therefore, the community could have a more despotic or a more democratic form. Above this was the higher unity, the despotic government that was poised above the lesser communities, responsible for the communal control of labor for irrigation systems, which was important among the Asian peoples, and the means of communication. Economically, the tribal community was the "hereditary possessor" of property, but it was subordinated to the state, the real owner.

Comparing the Asiatic or Oriental form with the other forms in his category, Marx asserted it "may appear as communal property which gives the individual only possession and no private property in the soil." The ancient classical form was characterized by a combination of state and private property. The Germanic form had private property supplemented by communal property.[30] The Asiatic form was not only the original form of direct communal property. It also "necessarily" survived longest and most stubbornly. Its survival resulted from its fundamental principles, that the individual did not become independent of the community and that the circle of production was self-sustaining. If the individual changed his relation to the community, he modified and undermined the community and its economic premise. Though Marx held the Asiatic or Oriental form to be the original one, "historically closest to man's origins," because of the survival of the primitive village community in the wider social system, that form did not necessarily lead to any other form nor did it become the starting point of the dialectical process of history.[31] The forms in the *Grundrisse* did not appear to represent successive chronological historical stages, denote any evolutionary process from one stage to another, or indicate a unilinear pattern of historical development, though they might represent changes in the evolution of private property.

In 1859, Marx again changed his categories of historical development in *A Contribution to the Critique of Political Economy*, the shorter, revised version of the *Grundrisse*. In the preface he briefly wrote: "In broad outlines, Asiatic, ancient, feudal, and modern bourgeois modes of production can be designated as progressive epochs in the economic formation of society." The German and Slavonic types had disappeared from his analysis. It was nowhere explicit that all societies had passed or would pass through these four epochs. Nor was it apparent why the Asiatic mode was a "progressive epoch" when Marx and Engels up to now had seen it as static and stagnant.

Marx's terse list in the preface was preceded by a sweeping generalization: "No social order ever perishes before all the productive forces for which there is room in it have developed; and new, higher relations of production never appeared before the material conditions of their existence have matured in the womb of the old society itself." As a result of class struggles and the developing tension in each mode of production a logical progression from the ancient mode to socialism was presumed. The Asiatic mode, however, did not logically appear to lead to the ancient stage nor to any other. Nor was it located in any particular time or clearly confined to Asiatic space. Moreover, the preface did not, as Georges Sorel pointed out, "aim to furnish the rules for studying a particular period in history. It deals with the succession of civilizations; thus the word 'class' is not even mentioned."[32]

After the 1859 *Preface to the Critique*, Marx did not formulate any further list of historical categories nor did he propose any other pattern of historical change. Marx and Engels, in a minor way, kept discussing aspects of Asiatic societies and Oriental despotism, and the destiny of the village community, partly because of their interest in the Russian *mir*, a form of early common ownership of land, which they addressed within the context of their general theoretical speculations in *Capital* and other works. In these works and in their unpublished statements and letters they often referred to terms such as "primitive communalism" or "primitive communal ownership" but the relationship between these socioeconomic forms and the AMP is not altogether clear. For instance, in the third of Marx's four drafts of his letter to Vera Zasulich the Russian Marxist living in Switzerland, in February and March 1881, he wrote that primitive communities were not all the same.[33] On the contrary, they constitute a "series of social groupings, differing both in type and in age, and marking successive phases of development." The general type, the "agricultural commune" included the Russian and German commune. The agrarian commune had developed from the more archaic type of community. The rural commune might also be found in Asia, among the Afghans, for example. But it appeared everywhere as the most recent type in the "archaic formation" of societies.

Marx and Engels began to use the terms "archaic formation" or "type," which appeared to include the four categories discussed in the *Grundrisse*, one of which was the AMP, the most primitive of the early socioeconomic formations. Thus, the AMP was still an inherent part of the Marxian historical outlook even if referred to in a more oblique fashion. Certainly Marx and Engels refused to regard the AMP as a variant of feudalism.[34] Marx rejected the argument of the Russian sociologist, M. M. Kovalevsky, that India be regarded as feudal because three of the four characteristics of Germano-Roman feudalism were present there. Engels, in *Anti-Dühring*, excluded the Orient from his discussion of feudalism.[35]

The change in terminology also reflected a change in intellectual interest. In *The German Ideology*, Marx and Engels had regarded the first form of ownership as tribal ownership. Influenced by Lewis Morgan and other anthropologists and ethnologists such as Henry Maine, John Phear, John Lubbock, and

M. M. Kovalevsky, whom they studied in the latter part of their lives, Marx and, especially, Engels became more concerned with tribal social organization that was based on the *gens*, a social group sharing a common ancestry, and with the evolution of the family from the stage of savagery through barbarism to civilization.[36] In the *Grundrisse*, early societies were said to be organized into clans or combinations of clans, communalities of blood, language, and customs. Membership of a naturally evolved society, a tribe, was a natural condition of production for individuals. Property meant belonging to a tribe.[37]

Engels went even further in his concern with ethnological issues, a subject on which both of them had been reading. Commenting in his letter to Marx of December 8, 1882, regarding the similarity between ancient Germans and American natives, he wrote that "at this stage, the method of production is less crucial than is the degree to which old blood ties and the ancient mutual community of the sexes within the tribe are being dissolved." In his introduction to the 1888 English edition of the *Communist Manifesto*, Engels proclaimed that Morgan discovered the nature of the clan and its relation to the tribe: "the inner organization of this primitive communistic society was laid bare in its typical form." In *The Mark* Engels declared that two fundamental facts that arose spontaneously governed the primitive history of all, or almost all, nations: the grouping of the people according to kindred and common property in the soil. This was the case with the Germans who had brought with them from Asia the method of grouping by tribes and *gentes*. By the 1880s Marx and Engels were seeing the *gens*, the clan, as the earliest form of social organization. For Marxist analysis the problem then arose of whether the structure of the family or of kinship developed in an independent way according to its own laws or whether it resulted from the mode of production.

As a result of Morgan's works, Marx and particularly Engels began to focus less on the Orient when dealing with early history. In his *The Origin of the Family, Private Property and the State*, published in 1884, a year after Marx's death, Engels argued that early history could better be understood through studying American Indian tribes than through studying India. The American Indian tribe was the original form of social organization, and the Greek and Roman forms were later and derivative. The Asiatic mode did not appear in this work, which discussed communal, antique, and feudal systems.

Engels, pursuing his revisionist opinion of the "pre-history of society," corrected, in his 1888 English edition of the *Manifesto*, Marx's original bold statement: "the history of all hitherto existing society is the history of class struggles." Marx really meant all *written* history.[38] Books by authorities such as August Haxthausen, who "discovered" common ownership of land in Russia, and G. L. von Maurer, who investigated the social foundation of all

Teutonic races, had, according to Engels, thrown light on prehistory, showing that village communities "were found to be, or to have been the primitive form of society everywhere from India to Ireland." Engels found communal ownership of the land among all Indo-Germanic peoples at a low level of development, from India to Ireland, and even among the Malays who were developing under Indian influence.[39]

These categories of the AMP and communal ownership, in different terminological formulations, have troubled those who adhere to or assume the main Marxist orthodox position of the relations of class, politics, and society. Discussion of the AMP has, as one contemporary Marxist analysis suggested, raised questions not simply about the relevance of orthodox Marxist concepts outside the European context but also about the entire set of Marxist views of class society, revolutionary change, and world history.[40] The implication of the AMP is that political power, Oriental despotism, is not the result of an exploitative class but rather results from the nature of the society and the performance of vital economic functions. Some fundamental tenets of Marxism appear to be challenged, if not contradicted, by analysis of the AMP and its related factors: the importance of geographical factors rather than the primacy of productive forces, the existence of social stagnation rather than progress in a historical setting, the argument that change in Asia had to be induced from outside, and the implication that social development from slavery to capitalism was essentially Western, and that there was no uniform pattern of development for all countries.[41]

That debate is parallel to, though not equivalent with, the broader study of Oriental societies or politics, and of all social and political systems that have for one reason or another lagged behind in economic modernization and political development. Discussion of this matter has become part of the contemporary controversy, examined earlier in the introduction, of whether Western commentators can objectively analyze and interpret non-Western systems, or whether that analysis can be anything other than a reflection of the imposition of power relationships. The charge of Eurocentrism in the writings of Marx and Engels would, for adherents of political correctness in this discussion, be accompanied by accusations of racism, cultural chauvinism, and Orientalism. The Marxist outlook would be seen as yet another manifestation of cultural hegemony; the belief in the innate superiority of European peoples and cultures; and a false ideological construction of the East, the Other.[42]

Without entering into the larger debate at this point, the terminology used by Marx and Engels can be discussed. Marx and Engels, like other nineteenth-century writers, made comparisons in terms of evolution and progress rather than race or ethnicity. A typical example might be the late preface in 1884 by Engels to *The Origins of the Family, Private Property, and the State*, where, following Lewis Morgan, he sketched the "picture of the evolution of mankind through savagery and barbarism to the beginnings of civilization." The use throughout their writings of concepts such as "primitive societies" is not to be taken as moral condemnation by Marx and Engels but simply as references to early history and to stages in the production process.

It must be admitted from the start that Marx and Engels, critical though they were of bourgeois society and its values, were, like other nineteenth-century thinkers, conscious of the prominence and dominance of that society among the nations of the world. Influenced by Hegel's philosophical analysis of world history and of the development of the world spirit, Marx and Engels accepted, at first, some of his empirical views about the Orient as well as his belief that the dialectic of historical change had been manifested in the progressive West. Hegel's concept of historical movement, rather than racism, was obviously in their minds when they spoke of "higher" or "lower" forms of society. Whether to regard these views as "Eurocentric" or unconsciously imbued with the conviction of Western superiority is open to question, but it does not necessarily follow that the theories of Marx and Engels were efforts to impose Western ideas on or to dominate the East. Moreover, they did not overtly echo Hegel's doctrine of a historical mission to be performed by the West, even if they sometimes indicated that only the Western nations were pursuing the road to industrialization in any significant way as well as dominating world trade. Besides, the two Marxists qualified their historical materialism on many occasions. "World history," Marx wrote to Kugelmann on April 17, 1871, "would be of a very mystical nature if 'accidents' played no part in it." In the first draft of his letter to Vera Zasulich he spoke of "historical twists and turns."[43]

Historical movement was also complex as well as unpredictable. What were the historical paths to be followed? One can extract from the writings of Marx both a unilinear and a multilinear model of historical change. In the unilinear model, the line of Western development would be the norm for all nations, and the capitalist system would be the culmination of that development before it was transformed into the final stage of socialism or communism.[44] This would suggest a given, universal sequence of historical stages and types, from tribal property or ancient mode of production to capitalism in all societies. Each stage would appear, develop, and then give rise to the next phase in the sequence. This law of social development, seen by some Marxists as scientific socialism and occasionally as "inevitable," could be the basis for decisions on revolutionary tactics in the transformation of societies.

But the AMP, if a distinctive socioeconomic form, did not fit into this universal perspective of social development. The AMP, if it were to be located anywhere in this schema, would probably be placed between primitive communism and the ancient (slave) mode of production. Historical change could also be seen as multilinear with separate lines of development for different countries. Those countries with the AMP might have a different history from those experiencing slave or feudal modes of production.[45] What preceded and what followed the AMP in the historical process? This remained unclear, but Marx asserted that "[a] more exact study of the Asiatic, more especially the Indian, forms of communal property would demonstrate how, out of the various forms of natural communal property, various forms of its dissolution are brought forth."[46]

This more sophisticated second model of multilateral change, with the AMP as a prominent feature, allowed a view of the history of societies as uneven; revealed the inadequacy of the unilinear model for historical analysis and for political tactics; promoted an interest in studying developing societies; brought about a revision in thinking about the role of peasantry in history; provided a base for revolutionary activity; and resulted in recognition of the state as not simply an inert part of the superstructure but as a factor that might have a decisive political role in developing societies.[47]

Where does history go? In his graveside eulogy of Marx on March 17, 1883, Engels said his friend had discovered the law of development of human history as Darwin had discovered the law of development of organic nature. He had also discovered the special law of motion governing the present-day capitalist mode of production and the bourgeois society that this mode of production had created.[48] In Engels's preface to the third German edition of Marx's *The Eighteenth Brumaire of Louis Bonaparte* he states that Marx's law – that all historical struggles were only struggles between social classes, and that these struggles in turn depended on the nature and mode of production and exchange – was the key to understanding the history of the French Second Republic.

Yet Marx and Engels realized that these laws have to be treated with caution. Engels in his preface to the 1888 English edition of the *Communist Manifesto* made a revealing statement implicitly suggesting that early societies were outside the scope of these laws: "the whole history of mankind [since the dissolution of primitive tribal society, holding land in common ownership] has been a history of class struggles." Marx and Engels were both anxious that their laws not be interpreted as historical inevitability for all societies, though the very concept of precapitalist societies, including the Oriental, may imply that change has occurred in a particular, if not inevitable, direction. Engels wrote a number of letters in the last years of his life trying to clarify the point: the Marxist materialist conception of history meant that the ultimately determining element in history was the history of real life, not that the economic element was the only determining one.[49]

Though Marx had proposed these various categories of historical development, he was conscious of the perils of intellectual generalizations about history. In the early *Poverty of Philosophy*, published in 1847, he objected to Proudhon's simplifications of history in his book *What Is Property*? Later, both Marx and Engels warned readers and correspondents on a number of occasions about wrong conclusions drawn from their theory of history.[50] Perhaps the clearest caution was given in the draft letter to the editors of *Otechestvenniye Zapiski*, written probably in November 1877 but not published until 1886. Written as a reply to his critic N. K. Mikhailovsky, Marx clarified his position, cautioning not "to metamorphose my historical sketch of the genesis of capitalism in Western Europe into a historico-philosophical theory of the general path every people is fated to tread." Marx denied he had sketched "a historico-philosophical theory of a Universal Progress, fatally imposed on all peoples, regardless of the historical circumstances in which they find themselves."

Again, in the first draft of his reply to Vera Zasulich, who on February 16, 1881, had asked his views on the commune in Russia and its likely historical path, Marx returned the question: "Does this mean that the development of the land commune must necessarily follow the same lines under all circumstances? Certainly not."[51] In the second draft of the letter, Marx wrote he had shown the metamorphosis of feudal production into capitalist production taking place in Western Europe, but "I expressly limited this 'historical inevitability' to the countries of Western Europe." By implication, Russia, as well as Asia, might take a different historical path.[52]

The discussion of historical development and of unilinear or multilinear change has been of more than academic interest in deciding on policy for developed countries, especially those that had colonies, toward those lands that had lagged behind in modernization and development. Not many would dare accuse Marx and Engels of being imperialists or colonialists. Their moral indictment of colonialism is evident.[53] Britain was waging an "unrighteous war" on China. Marx was caustic about the "Christianity-canting and civilization-mongering British government." He wrote of the "European despotism planted upon Asian despotism by the British East India Company, forming a more monstrous combination than any of the divine monsters startling us in the Temple of Salsette."[54] England had broken down the entire framework of Indian society. Marx criticized the history of English economic management in India as a history of futile and actually stupid economic experiments.[55] Near the end of his life, he wrote of the British in India: "the suppression of the communal ownership of land was only an act of English vandalism, which has brought not an advance, but a setback to the native peoples."[56] Similarly, in a letter to N. Danielson of February 19, 1881, Marx called the British appropriations from India "a bleeding process with a vengeance."

Yet both Marx and Engels also wrote on a number of occasions about the benefits of Western colonial rule in helping non-European peoples develop, especially countries such as India and China that for thousands of years had made no progress. In an article of January 22, 1848, regarding the revolt of Abd-el-Kader against France in Algeria, Engels argued, as de Tocqueville had also done as discussed in Chapter 6, that the French conquest was an "important and fortunate fact for the progress of civilization. . . . The modern bourgeois, with civilization, industry, order, and at least relative enlightenment following him, is preferable to the feudal lord or to the marauding robber, with the barbarian state of society to which they belong."[57]

Marx spoke of the progressive role of the British rule over India. Britain had brought more changes than had the French Revolution and had upset more property relations in India than were upset in the whole of Western Europe since the French Revolution. British political and economic power had disrupted the small economic village communities.[58] English steam and free trade, English commerce as a whole, had a revolutionary effect on those small, semi-barbarian, semicivilized communities as the low price of English goods destroyed the hand loom and the spinning wheel. Its intentions may have been vile, but by its actions and its introduction of private property, Britain was causing a social revolution in India, "the only social revolution ever heard of in Asia." "Whatever may have been the crimes of England it was the unconscious tool of history" in bringing change, "'the sine qua non' of Europeanization."

Summing up, Marx, in his important newspaper article of August 8, 1853, indicated the "superior" British double mission in India. One was destructive in breaking up the native communities and industries; the other was regenerating. Britain had laid the basis for a new society. It had brought the electric telegraph and communications, trained a native army and a native administrative class, set up a free press for the first time in India, established political unity, and begun the system of private property, "the great desideratum of Asiatic society."

Marx also appreciated that colonialism in India did not come cheap for Britain though he had mixed feelings about it. The colonial country had taken large sums from India. Yet, in articles in April 1859 about the financial crisis in India, Marx indicated the considerable British treasury deficit because of the greater permanent debt of Britain after the Indian mutiny, the high general military costs, more than 60 percent of aggregate regular income, and the negative effect on the British home market. About the same time, in a letter of April 9,1859, Marx argued, as he had done earlier on September 21, 1857, that only the British upper class and colonial administrators had benefited from

British rule. India had the "privilege of paying English capitalists five percent for their capital. But John Bull had cheated himself, or rather has been cheated by his capitalists." Similarly, Marx concluded after evaluating the pattern of Anglo-Chinese trade that Britain had a balance of trade deficit because Chinese imports of British manufactured goods had not increased whereas its exports to Britain had increased considerably.[59] "The consuming and paying powers of the Celestials have been greatly overestimated." In a number of articles Marx had the same explanation: the main obstacle to British imports into China, other than the opium trade, was "the combination of small scale agriculture with domestic industry," the same characteristics as in India.[60]

The second policy issue, the heated debate about the location of Oriental despotism and the AMP in the historical process, emanates from mixed motives. Some of the debate is the result of genuine differences in interpretation of the Marxist writings, especially of the more obscure passages, on these issues. Some also arises from the use or manipulation of those writings for political or ideological advantage, their possible relevance to commentary on past or existing social and political systems, or political tactics.[61] In the nineteenth and early twentieth centuries, the main controversy regarding the AMP centered on the *obshchina*, the Russian *mir* (commune). At the same time the very linking of Russia to the AMP meant emphasizing its non-European features, which affected the polemics of the Russian revolutionary movement, especially the internal disputes among the Marxists. In more contemporary times, discussion of the AMP has been in reference to the Soviet and Chinese communist regimes, especially to the years under the rule of Stalin and Mao. Criticism, and occasionally support, of those regimes has often been couched in Aesopian language, long familiar in such discussions, about the despotic power of the current rulers.[62]

In the latter part of their lives, from 1873 and for a decade, Marx and Engels read a great deal about the origin of the Russian village commune and Russian society, using the material for analyzing a noncapitalist system. They made ambivalent statements about that society, its history, and, especially, the destiny of the *mir*. They also occasionally interrelated Russian and Indian Oriental despotism. Both from time to time referred to Czarist Russia as "semi-Asiatic" or "semi-Eastern," in its condition, manners, traditions, and institutions, and as a country held together with great difficulty by Oriental despotism.[63] In his article, "What Is to Become of Turkey" (April 21, 1853), Engels wrote of the Russian autocratic system, accompanied with its concomitant corruption, half-military bureaucracy, and *pasha*-like extortion.

Marx found similarities between the Russian communal system and some Indian communities in the nondemocratic and patriarchal character of their communal management and in the collective responsibility for taxes to the state. Marx wrote of the Russian and Indian village communities suffering under the fiscal oppression of the despotic state, "the finest and broadest basis of exploitation and despotism."[64] In *The Frankish Period*, written in 1882, Engels wrote of the rise of despotic state power among the Aryan peoples of Asia and the Russians when the fields were still cultivated by the community for the common account and there was not yet private property in land.

On the question of the destiny of the *mir*, Marx and Engels could not give an unequivocal answer to their various interlocutors, despite their attention to the issue and their reading in the Russian language. Essentially the question was whether the *mir* could pass directly to the higher form of communist common ownership, or was it necessary for Russia to go through the same process of historical development as the West had done including capitalism.[65] Using a picturesque metaphor, Marx wrote that the Russian commune, the only one that had continued on a nationwide scale to his time, incorporated all the positive acquisitions devised by the capitalist system without passing through its Caudine Forks (the place of the humiliating defeat of the Roman army in 321 BC).[66] He also saw the commune as similar to the AMP, holding that the isolation of the commune, the lack of connection between the life of one commune and another, "the localized microcosm," caused a more or less centralized despotism to arise on top of the communes.

The uncertainty of the Marxists is best shown by Marx's inability to give a clear and quick answer to Vera Zasulich's letter of February 16, 1881. Perhaps the clue to his indecision can be found in the drafts of his letter, written before the final short, somewhat bland response of March 8. Marx explains the dualism in the commune between collectivism and common land ownership, on the one hand, and individual, peasant cultivation on his own plot, on the other.[67] The historical direction that followed, he said, would depend on the environment of the commune. Marx and Engels appear to have concluded that internal change in Russian society and economics would be dependent on external factors, "a sudden change of direction in Western Europe."[68] A proletarian revolution in the West, accompanying a Russian Revolution, might mean that Russian common ownership of land could serve as the starting point for communist development. The final remarks of Engels in January 1894 continue to be inconclusive; he could not say whether enough of the Russian commune existed for it to become, as he and Marx had hoped in 1882, "a point of departure for communist development in harmony with a sudden change of direction in Western Europe."[69]

The question of the future path of Russia and desirable revolutionary tactics led to fierce debates among the Russian Social Democrats. At the 1906 party congress the controversy centered on Lenin's proposal for the nationalization of land. George Plekhanov, who saw Russia as semi-Asiatic, argued that

Lenin's plan was likely to strengthen the existing absolute government and to lead to Oriental despotism. Lenin, who usually, though not always, viewed Russia as "partly Asiatic" and essentially feudal, declared that nationalization was appropriate for Russia's development if it took the road to capitalism. The debate among the Russian revolutionaries was closely tied to the perception of the AMP. Was it a mode unique to the Orient and to Russia, which also had communal property, or should it be regarded as the early stage in historical development as in the West?[70]

The implications of the question became clear in the Soviet Union when, for a twenty-year period from 1931 on, the Stalin regime prevented any publication about the AMP lest a comparison be made between that regime and Oriental despotism. In 1938 Stalin's own simplistic formula in his *Dialectical and Historical Materialism*, of five stages of modes of production, without reference to any Asiatic mode, became doctrinal truth for the whole communist world. Only after his death and with the process of de-Stalinization did the AMP emerge as a topic for intellectual dissection, especially regarding issues such as state control by a bureaucratic group that did not own the means of production, and therefore could not be considered a class in the classic Marxist sense, and on the question of the path of historical development.

A DISTINCTIVE MODE OF PRODUCTION

At this point it is useful to attempt a comprehensive summary of the AMP. Though Marx and Engels never presented their own systematic analysis of the AMP, and though the emphasis on particular features of the mode changed in different writings, as can be seen in the first part of this chapter, one can draw from the various references and passages devoted to Oriental affairs an interrelated syndrome of characteristic features that make it a distinctive economic and political system. One analyst has even argued that Marx's views on the AMP were well formulated and digested and had found their organic place in the Marxian political economy and theory of history. Marx and Engels used the Middle Eastern countries of Turkey and Persia, China, and, above all, Mughal India as the basis for their generalizations about the Orient, even if later they sometimes widened the geographical boundaries of the AMP to include Russia, American Indian tribes, and other countries or groups.[71]

The term *AMP* was first used by Marx in 1859 and rarely appeared again in that form. Engels usually spoke of Oriental despotism or Oriental society. In a number of places they made clear, either explicitly or by inference, differences between the Asiatic mode and other modes of production or property arrangements. One such difference concerned ownership of the surplus product of the society: in the antique mode it went to the slave owner, in feudalism to the feudal lord, and in the AMP to the state or Oriental despot. The social and political features of feudalism – seigniory, estates and corporations, its system of fiefs, and the personal dependence in relationships – all were absent from the AMP.[72]

Marx compared essential features of capitalism with those in early societies, including the AMP. Capitalist production rested on a complete separation of the producer from the means of production; the expropriation of the agricultural producer was the basis of the whole process.[73] In precapitalist forms, the laborer was tied to the community by patriarchal, tribal, or feudal bonds. Direct producers were not separated from the means of production. This unity between the worker and the conditions of labor had two main forms: the Asiatic communal system (primitive communism) and small-scale agriculture based on the family and linked with domestic industry.[74] Both were embryonic forms and equally unfitted to develop labor as social labor and the productive power of social labor. Also, in all precapitalist forms, it was the landed proprietor, not the capitalist, who directly appropriated the surplus labor of other people. Rent appeared historically as the general form of surplus labor, of labor performed without payment in return.[75]

It is, however, more difficult to differentiate clearly between the AMP and other earlier societies or even define the exact geographical contours of "Asia." These analytical problems arise because one of the essential features of the AMP, communal ownership of land, is said to exist in those other societies outside Asia to which Marx gave different names such as "old community communism," "primitive communal ownership or communism," or "tribal ownership."[76] Marx, in his discussion of the clan system in Scotland, even talks of "the ancient Asiatic family communities." At these times, and especially as the emphasis shifted to the discussion of tribal property and organization rather than state organization property in the later writings, the AMP may appear to be less a distinctive mode of production than a part of the category of primitive forms of society.

Yet for Marx the AMP was not a particular variant of the original communism at the beginning of history. It was different conceptually in at least two major ways: its villages were settled and engaged in agriculture and crafts unlike other societies that also engaged in hunting and gathering; and it had a political organization, the state, which was absent elsewhere.[77] In the four drafts of Marx's letter to Vera Zasulich, he discussed the differences between the various "archaic formations" of societies, the primitive communities and the agricultural commune, the most recent type. The primitive communities rested on natural kinship relations among members of the commune. The agricultural commune had emancipated itself from these relations, and thus could adapt and expand, and engage in contacts with strangers. In the agricultural commune the house and its complementary plot belonged to the individual farmer; in more primitive communities, communal housing and collective habitation was an economic base. In earlier societies work was done in common and the common product was distributed among the members according to needs; in the agrarian type, the arable land was periodically divided among the members of the commune.

First, the question of communal ownership, its origin, and its priority in property forms. Marx was always concerned to counter the view that private property was the natural form. Marx, in his letter to Engels of March 14, 1868, expressed enthusiasm that the German historian G. L. von Maurer had shown that private land ownership was of later origin than communal property: "The view I put forward that the Asiatic or Indian property forms everywhere mark the beginning of Europe receives new proof here."[78] Two years later he reminded Ludwig Kugelmann, the German socialist and member of the First International, on February 17, 1870, that common property was Indian, not Mongolian, in origin and "may therefore be found among all European peoples at the beginning of their development."[79]

Engels evaluated Maurer's work in similar fashion, as "devoted to proving the primitive common ownership of the land among all civilized peoples of Europe and Asia and to showing the various forms of its existence and dissolution." He sometimes appeared, however, to qualify this generalization. In *Anti-Duhring*, for example, private property had existed, though limited to certain objects, in the ancient, primitive communities of all civilized peoples.[80] Wherever private property evolved it was a result of altered relations of production and exchange in the interest of increased production.[81]

But the ancient communes "have also, for thousands of years, formed the basis of the most barbarous form of the state, Oriental despotism, from India to Russia."[82] Both Marx and Engels repeated the same point about communal ownership in slightly different ways. For Marx, at one point it existed among the Indians, Slavs, and ancient Celts.[83] At another time, he found it in various places, including the Russian and the German type of "primitive community" as well as in the village community in Asia.[84] In a late letter to Edward Bernstein, the German Social Democrat, of August 9, 1882, the peasant exploitation was extended in space and in time: "From Ireland to Russia, from Asia Minor to Egypt" and "since the time of the Assyrian and Persian Empires."[85]

Engels, in similar fashion to Marx, also ranged geographically.[86] He saw communal ownership, the primitive form of society, "among all Indo-Germanic peoples at a low level of development from India to Ireland." He also traced it historically among the Slavs, Germans, and the Celts.[87] He even, in two letters in 1884, wrote of the old community or primitive communism in Java and of the original tribal form among the American Indians. Engels, in the 1888 edition of the *Manifesto*, wrote that the primitive form of society from India to Ireland included Russia and all Teutonic races.[88]

What about China, from which fewer examples or illustrations were taken about the AMP? Did the Asiatic mode include China? In some twenty articles, mostly in *The New York Daily Tribune*, written between 1857 and 1862, Marx addressed current issues especially on British foreign policy and Anglo-Chinese trade. He did not designate it directly as an Oriental despotism nor as a society that depended on state controlled large-scale irrigation works. Appreciating that private landholding, "the combination of minute agriculture with domestic industry," existed in China, Marx could not completely fit it into the theory of a mode of production based on communal ownership.[89]

If Marx and Engels were not wholly consistent in their remarks about China, their characterization of it was similar to their view of India. Engels, in his 1847 *Principles of Communism*, wrote of "isolated, unchanging China" and, in a speech of November 30, 1847, commented on a country "which for more than a thousand years had defied progress and historical development" and was now being revolutionized by English machinery and drawn into the mainstream of European civilization.[90] Marx, in his July 7, 1862, article, saw China as "a living fossil" in which the unchanging social substructure was accompanied by "unceasing change in the persons and tribes who manage to ascribe to themselves the political super-structure." In any case, change was coming there, as in India, as a result of outside contacts.[91]

At the end of the *Grundrisse* and in the *Critique*, Marx indicated the value of studying India to gain insight into historical development. On the matter of common property in land, India provided "an array of the most varied forms of such economic communalism, more or less dissolved, but [good] . . . research would rediscover it as the starting point among all civilized peoples." From the study of Asiatic, and especially of Indian forms of common property, one could observe "how from the different forms of primitive common property, different forms of its dissolution have been developed."[92] India was the origin of communal ownership that could therefore be found among all European peoples at the beginning of their development.

In all the speculation, geographical and historical, about communal ownership and Oriental despotism, India was always at the core. Partly this was the consequence of the fact that Marx lived in London from 1849 until his death in 1883, and that Engels lived in Manchester and London for an even longer period until 1895. Marx acknowledged in his *Preface to a Critique of Political Economy* that London had been a favorable vantage point for the observation of bourgeois society and in *Capital* that England was used as the chief illustration in the development of his theoretical ideas.[93] It was also useful for Marx and Engels to reside in England, where they could draw on the work of British economists, official government reports, and parliamentary papers, to increase their knowledge and to formulate their opinions about India, Britain's major imperial possession at the time.

Throughout Marx's writings on Asia the influence of the British economists can be detected.[94] Adam Smith had written that water control systems were important, public works including roads and canals were noticeable, the economy of China was stationary, and the revenues of the rulers in many Asian countries came from a land tax or ground rents. James Mill, in his *History of India* had written of the "Asiatic form of government" as a distinctive type of system, different from feudalism, in which the sovereign was the supreme landlord.[95] John Stuart Mill in his *Principles of Political Economy* made some insightful comments on the bureaucracy of Oriental despotism.[96] From Richard Jones, lecturer on economics at the East India Company College at Haileybury, Marx took quotations regarding the unique access of the state and its officials to many important sources of income, the monuments built by that income, and the place of cities in Asia.[97]

Although Marx drew on these reputable sources and on a mass of official British government documents, his accuracy about Asia has been challenged by critics. Daniel Thorner argued that Marx was mistaken that communal property ever existed in either Mughal or post-Mughal India or that common cultivation in villages was the norm.[98] Much of the argument about the self-sufficiency, equality, and isolation of the Indian village; the importance of irrigation, especially by central government; and the role of the bureaucracy has been challenged.[99] Yet a necessary, if insufficient, retort to the critics is that the theory of the AMP, whatever the historical and factual errors, is not so much an abstraction of any real economic, social, or political system, as an ideal type with a particular set of characteristics. With this in mind, the model proposed by Marx of a distinctive mode of production can be analyzed.[100]

THE FEATURES OF THE ASIATIC MODE

The Village Community

In the AMP, and under Oriental despotism, people lived in "a social system of particular features," which was the result of two factors: the central government being responsible for the great public works and the domestic union of agriculture and manufacturing activities. It was a system of self-sufficient, isolated village communities, each with a unity of its own, forming "a little world in itself."[101] Though these communities might take different forms, they were "the solid foundation of Oriental despotism."[102]

Communities had little communication with each other. The inhabitants were bound to the village by custom, a bond that was strengthened by lack of an alternative. Each village produced what it needed, with the small surplus going "from time immemorial" as taxes to the central government in the form of compulsory labor and produce, the equivalent to rent. This surplus was used in turn by the government for public works. In each village community the individuals who were maintained at the expense of the whole community included the "chief inhabitant" who was judge, police, and tax-gatherer in one; the bookkeeper; legal prosecutor; the man who guarded the boundaries of the community; the water-overseer who distributed water for irrigation; the Brahmin conducting religious services; the schoolmaster; the astrologer; the smith, carpenter, potter, barber, washerman, and silversmith; and from time to time the poet.[103] If the population increased, a new community was founded, on the pattern of the old one, on unoccupied land.

Marx got many of his views on the village community from George Campbell's *Modern India*, published in 1852, and from a number of other writers and reports in the early nineteenth century. His list of village occupations is virtually identical, as Louis Dumont pointed out, to that in *The Philosophy of History* by Hegel who derived it from the British 1806 report on India by Thomas Munro, who had written that "every village is a kind of little republic."[104] Marx believed that the villages all produced the same kind of output with a fixed division of labor. Marx, following the report written by Mark Wilks, the fifth report from the Select Committee of the House of Commons on the Affairs of the East India Company (1812), outlined the list of officials and twelve occupations to be found.[105] That division of labor operated with "the irresistible authority of a law of nature," thus leading to a static condition.[106] Though Marx provided few other details about the functioning or the structure of the villages, he suggested that they sometimes differed, from the simplest procedure, land cultivated in common with the produce divided and spinning and weaving conducted in each family as subsidiary activities, to a more complex system in which the villagers tilled their own plots and used common pasture land.[107]

The Unity of Agriculture and Manufactures

Economic life in each village community was based on the unity of small-scale agriculture and home handicraft industry. This economic pattern was reproduced regularly in the same form. Village life rested on tradition, the villagers being bound by economic interests, kinship ties, and custom. In *Capital*, Marx explained that the social division of labor was a necessary condition for the production of commodities, but the reverse was not necessarily true: "In the primitive Indian community there is social division of labor without production of commodities." The economy of the village and of the AMP was organized to produce self-sufficiency, not commodities.[108] Most products were directly consumed by the community for use, not for exchange. Only surplus products became commodities, going as tribute to the despot and the state. Because they were spent by the ruler, these surpluses could not be accumulated as capital, the process that was at the heart of capitalism.[109]

Marx quoted Richard Jones to argue that no accumulation of capital took place. Because most people in India were self-sustaining peasants, no excess revenue was generated that could lead to accumulation. Also, there was no wage labor; labor was tied to the community. Wage labor arose from the disintegration of slavery and serfdom or from the decay of communal property, as among the Oriental and Slav peoples. It appeared as the dissolution, the destruction of relations in which labor was fixed in all respects, such as income, content, locality, and scope.[110]

In his analysis of the production and circulation of social capital, Marx explained that in capitalist production all products were transformed into commodities that were then transformed into money. In the ancient Asiatic and other ancient modes of production, the conversion of products into commodities, and therefore the conversion of men into producers of commodities, was of little importance, though it became more important as primitive communities approached dissolution.[111] The methods of production in the AMP were extremely simple and transparent as compared with bourgeois society.[112] Usury could, in the AMP, persist for a long time without leading to anything more than economic decay and political corruption. Moreover, every division of labor that was well developed and brought about by an exchange of commodities was founded on the separation of town and country.[113] The whole economic history of society was summed up in the movement of this antithesis. But the AMP was different: agriculture and handicrafts were not separated geographically but were carried out in the same village community. Though the portrayal of occupations in villages was mostly based on Indian conditions, Marx also applied it to China, where husbandry and manufacturing existed.[114] The difference between the two cases was that in India British control of landed property enabled the ruler to undermine the self-sustaining communities, whereas in China there was no force to wield this power.

Communal Ownership of Land

In their first newspaper articles and letters about India in 1853, Marx and Engels agreed that the key to the Orient was the absence of private property in land. An essential feature of Oriental society, and what was soon to be called the AMP or the "Oriental form," was communal property ownership, on which Oriental despotism was founded.[115] Wherever common ownership existed, Engels wrote to Karl Kautsky on March 2, 1883, be it of land, women, or anything else, it would necessarily be primitive. The subsequent process of development consisted entirely in the gradual dissolution of this primeval common ownership.[116] In the *Critique*, Marx criticized the "absurdly biased view" that primitive communal property was a specifically Slavonic phenomenon. It was an early form that could be found among Romans, Teutons, and Celts, and of which "a whole collection of diverse patterns [though sometimes only remnants survive] is still in existence in India."[117] Engels, in 1894, made a similar point that the common ownership of land was a form common to all peoples at a certain stage of development. He found it among all the Indo-European peoples in primeval times; it still existed in India.[118]

The two writers often made the point that common property, not private property, was the original historical form of ownership.[119] All Indo-Germanic peoples began with common property, according to Engels. This common property quietly persisted in India and Russia, under the most diverse forcible conquests and despotisms, and formed the basis of their societies and economies. This was an exemplification of the general proposition made by Engels in his *Preparatory Writings for Anti-Duhring* that, although all states were based on force, social and political variations could be explained by the different productive forces and distribution in states.[120]

But who owned the land in the AMP, the despot, the higher unity, officials, the village communities, the tribes? Marx and Engels gave varying answers. Marx, in his article of June 7, 1858, acknowledged that differences of opinion existed among British authorities about land tenure and private property in India, but thought they all agreed that in India, as in most Asiatic countries, "the ultimate property in the soil was vested in the government." His argument in *Capital* about labor rent in Asia rested on the view that direct producers there were under "direct subordination to a state which stands over them as their landlord and simultaneously as sovereign."[121] The state was then the supreme lord. Sovereignty in Asia consisted in the ownership of land concentrated on a national scale. No private ownership of land existed, but in reality there was both private and common possession and use of land. Engels provided a slightly different version: "In the whole of the Orient, where the village community or the state owns the land, the very term landlord is not to be found in the various languages. It was the Turks who first introduced a sort of feudal ownership of land in countries conquered by them in the Orient."[122]

Yet the argument is not altogether clear. In the *Land Tenure in India* article, Marx discussed the role of the *zamindars*, *talukdars*, or *sirdars* (different forms of holders of land) in the Indian economic system. Were they to be considered as landed proprietors or as mere tax gatherers?[123] Though Marx recognized that the claims of the *zamindars* and *talukdars* were to a certain extent legal, he appeared to favor the alternative view that "the property of the land was in the village corporations, in which resided the power of allotting it out to individuals for cultivation." In this view the two groups were only officers of the government, looking after the interests and collecting rent for the ruler.

In another place, Marx and Engels made a distinction between ownership and possession, between property rights held in an absolute sense and rights held in a more limited fashion. "In the Asiatic mode (at least, predominantly) the individual has no property but only possession; the real proprietor is the commune, hence property only as communal property in land."[124] In that mode the individual never became a proprietor but only a possessor; "he is at bottom himself the property, the slave of him in whom the unity of the commune exists." The original form of property in the "Oriental form, modified in the Slavonic" was direct common property. Again, in *Capital*, Marx held that in India, "no private ownership of land exists, although there is both private and common possession and use of land."[125]

A somewhat different emphasis on the issue of common ownership derived from their interest in anthropology. Marx spoke of tribal or common property rather than state property, in some passages in the *Grundrisse*.[126] The tribal community was not the result but the precondition of common application and use of the land. Engels asserted that in the early history of all civilized people, tribal and village communities existed with common ownership of the land, from India to Ireland. While giving in *The Mark* a short historical sketch of the primitive agrarian conditions of the German tribes, Engels generalized that "two fundamental facts govern the primitive history of all, or of almost all, nations: the grouping of the people according to kindred, and common property in the soil." He added that the Germans had brought the method of grouping people by tribes and gentes from Asia.[127]

Marx and Engels both recognized that if private property evolved in early societies, it was the result of altered relations of production and exchange brought about by external factors.[128] Barter with foreigners, more production of commodities for exchange, and increasing exchange within the communities all led to inequality in property ownership and to the undermining of the ancient common ownership of the land. Ironically, Engels argued that for thousands of years Oriental despotism and the changing rule of conquering nomad peoples had not injured the old communities, but foreign large-scale industry competing with the primitive home industry had brought those communities closer and closer to dissolution.[129] The condition of individuals in the AMP was one of "general slavery," though this was not the kind of slavery to be found in Greece and Rome. This general slavery was the consequence of the binding ties, the umbilical cord, between individuals and the community, resulting from communal property ownership and Oriental despotism, the embodiment of the unity of the community. Essentially a matter of labor tribute to the ruler, this form of slavery was different from that of individual slavery in which the worker was one of the factors of production for someone else.

Communal ownership of the land may have been the original form, but it was a fetter, a brake on agricultural production.[130] Engels explained that the Russian peasant lived in and had his being only in his village community, which was his whole world: the Russian word *mir* means both "world" and "peasant community." The parallel with the AMP is clear. For Engels, complete isolation of individual communities from one another was the natural basis for Oriental despotism from India to Russia.

Cities

Because the basis of the AMP lay in the village communities, cities were less important economically than in other societies, including earlier ones.[131] The Marxists pointed out the difference. Ancient classical history was the history of cities, but cities were based on landed property and agriculture; the city there "with its attached territory . . . forms the economic totality." By contrast, Asiatic history is "a kind of indifferent unity of town and countryside." Marx had spoken in *The German Ideology* of the antagonism between town and country that could only exist in the framework of private property. No such antagonism existed in the AMP because there was no clear distinction between town and country.[132]

Following the influential Bernier, Marx wrote that the large cities in the AMP must be regarded merely as royal camps, rather than as real cities, as an artificial excrescence on the actual economic structure. Towns like Delhi or Agra lived almost entirely on the army and were therefore obliged to follow the king if he went to war for any length of time. These towns were not like Paris, being little more than military camps and "only a little better and more conveniently situated than in the open country." Because in Asiatic societies the monarch appeared as the exclusive possessor of the surplus product of the countryside, entire cities arose that were really nothing but "wandering camps, through exchange of his revenue with the free hands, as Steuart [Sir James Steuart, the British economist] calls them." Cities in the proper sense were set up only at exceptionally favorable locations for foreign trade or where the head of state and his satraps exchanged their revenue (surplus product) for labor.[133]

Rent and Tax

In Marxist analysis a central, usually crucial, factor was the way in which the surplus product in a particular mode of production was extracted and allocated. For the most part in that analysis the AMP was differentiated from other systems because the surplus was concentrated in the hands of the Oriental despot, principally in the form of rent.[134] Marx spent some time reading and assessing the works on this issue by British economists, especially the book by Richard Jones, *The Distribution of Wealth and the Sources of Taxation*. He quoted from it extensively and presumably agreed with Jones that in precapitalist forms it was the landed proprietor, not the capitalist, who directly appropriated the surplus labor of other people. Rent appeared, especially among the Asiatic peoples, as the general form of surplus labor, of labor performed without payment in return.[135]

Rent and tax were one and the same. The reason, stemming from the common ownership of property, was that the state was landlord and sovereign. No tax existed that differed from the form of ground rent. The state taxes depended on the conditions of production. This mode of payment tended in turn to maintain the ancient forms of production. Individuals were treated politically and economically in the same way; what was common was that they were all subject to the state, the condition already categorized in the *Grundrisse* as general slavery.[136]

The Need for Irrigation

Early in their writings on India, Marx and Engels pointed to the crucial need for irrigation and water controls in Asiatic societies. Engels first wrote on the subject in his June 6, 1853, letter stating that "Artificial irrigation is [in the East] the first condition of agriculture and this is a matter either for the communes, the provinces, or the central government." Marx repeated the argument in his article of June 25, 1853, with one significant difference.[137] Comparing the Orient with Western Europe, where voluntary associations, in Flanders and

Italy, took care of maintaining adequate water, Marx wrote that in the East, where "civilization was too low and the territorial extent too vast to call into life voluntary association," the central power of government was necessary. The function of providing public works devolved on all Asiatic governments. The need to provide large-scale irrigation works and water control required bureaucratic and managerial control by a state capable of organizing a hydraulic system.[138]

Much of the controversy regarding the accuracy and value of the concept of the AMP stems from the assertion that the power of the Oriental despot came from this functional necessity, which required a strong state, rather than from his ownership of land or control of military force. Therefore Oriental despotism was a form of state that was not merely part of the superstructure but also performed vital economic functions.[139] Some Marxists cannot accept this activity by the state as a sufficient explanation for the origin or existence of a political and social structure. Orthodox Marxists tend to see the AMP concept as a denial of or too strong a qualification of the materialist conception of history because of the absence of any recognizable class struggle based on the relations of production, which in their orthodox theory gives rise to the political structure. Some of them, therefore, have exhaustively looked for evidence of the presence of classes in the AMP.[140]

Cooperation

The links among people in the labor process in early societies, including agrarian Indian communities, were based on common ownership of the means of production and on the ties of individuals to the "navel-strings of their tribes or communities, from which they had not been able to tear themselves free."[141] As a result, the links took the form of simple cooperation, different from the cooperation in capitalist systems that presupposed free wage laborers who sold labor power to capital, the essence of capitalism.[142] Marx at times appeared to differentiate cooperation and communal ownership in the AMP from that in other early societies where the sporadic application of cooperation on a large scale rested on direct relations of dominion and servitude. What Marx called the colossal effects of simple cooperation in the AMP could be seen in the gigantic architectural structures in the ancient Asiatic, Egyptian, and Etruscan countries. Marx accepted the statement of Richard Jones, in the latter's *Text-book of Lectures on the Political Economy of Nations*, that Oriental states, after supplying the expenses of their civil and military establishments, had a surplus that they applied to "works of magnificence or utility, and in the construction of these, their command over the hands and arms of almost the entire non-agricultural population has produced stupendous monuments which still indicate their power."[143] In Asian monarchies, the despot was able to direct the masses to build the "palaces and temples, the pyramids, and the armies of gigantic statues of which the remains astonish and perplex us." The fact that revenues in the AMP went to one or a few people made these undertakings possible.

Stagnation

A constantly recurring theme throughout this book has been the stagnation of Oriental societies. Aristotle and Montesquieu ascribed that stagnation to the passive and indolent nature of Oriental peoples. Burke and the Mills saw it as the result of following tradition and custom in Asian societies. Marx and Engels regarded it as the outcome of the AMP.[144] The Asiatic mode could not develop through internal mechanisms and therefore did not follow the dialectic of history as did other modes of production.[145] The "Oriental mutual complementation of agriculture and manufactures" and the self-sustaining cycle of the productive process meant the unchanging nature of the old forms of property in the AMP and of the community as a whole.[146] The small and extremely ancient Indian communities, some of which continued to exist, were based on the possession of the land in common, the blending of agriculture and handicrafts, and an unalterable division of labor.

The individual member of the village commune was "firmly rooted" to the community and could not be independent from it.[147] Labor in the AMP did not advance economic development or serve, as did the urban labor of the Middle Ages, as "a preparatory school for the capitalist mode of production."[148] The essence of the AMP was that the individual did not become independent of the commune. Asiatic countries, such as China and India, were marked by an absence of fixed capital and machinery necessary for economic development. Production did not have a cyclical nature as in capitalism.[149] It was for immediate consumption and not for exchange. Productivity was at a low level, as was circulation of money, and there was little connection between villages.[150] The interrelated factors – absence of accumulation because the surplus went to the Oriental despot, the lack of village initiative because there were no voluntary associations, the bondage of individuals to the soil, and the absence of wage labor and the persistence of primitive conditions of production – explained the inability to develop.[151] In the AMP, exchange or what Marx termed "the transformation of the product into a commodity" was of secondary importance. Exchange could only result from external influence: "Commodity exchange begins where the communities end, at the points of their contact with foreign communities or members of foreign communities."

Marx and Engels saw the old primitive communities remaining in existence for thousands of years – as in India and among the Slavs – before change came as a result of contact with the outside world.[152] The Oriental empires always showed an unchanging social infrastructure coupled with continual change in the political leaders and tribes. China was seen as a mummy preserved in a hermetically sealed coffin.[153] Engels spoke of Oriental ignorance, impatience, prejudice, vicissitudes of fortune, and favor inherent to Eastern courts. Yet these old countries, India and China, which had made no progress for thousands of years, were revolutionized as a result of the cheapening of Western products by industrialization. The only case where change was brought about by an internal despot rather than by external factors appeared to be Czarist Russia under Peter the Great.[154] In Marx's analysis, Peter transferred the capital to St. Petersburg because he recognized "the East was narrowly circumscribed by the stationary character and the limited relations of Asiatic peoples." He converted the state of Muscovy into Russia by changing it from a semi-Asiatic inland country into the paramount maritime power of the Baltic. The very simplicity in the AMP of the organization of production in the self-sufficient communities that constantly reproduced themselves in the same form and kept recurring was the key to the secret of the unchangeable character of Asiatic societies, despite the constant dissolution and refounding of Asiatic states and changes of dynasty.[155]

Backward

Perhaps influenced by Richard Jones and John Stuart Mill, Marx also saw the Orient as backward, as well as stagnant. In this, Marx, consciously or not, echoed Hegel's view of the East, as an area where "the principle of subjective freedom is lacking," and where despotism was appropriate to the "Dawn-Land of History." Engels in his 1859 review of Marx's *Critique* explained that his friend had struggled against Hegel's philosophical ideas and that Marx's "epoch making conception of history was the direct theoretical premise for the new materialist outlook."[156] Yet on Asia, Marx's implicit premises were close to the more explicit pronouncements of Hegel.[157] Asia was fixed, stationary, isolated from the great trends of history or even outside them. For Hegel, despotism was natural to Asia, though he qualified this in the case of China. India, however, was a "despotism without principles, without ethical or religious norms," the most arbitrary and dishonoring despotism. No consciousness of self, which might inspire the soul to revolt, stood in the way of Asian tyranny.[158] Everything was regulated, directed, and watched over from on high. Hegel also touched on a number of empirical features of Indian society, including one that was central for Marx, the permanence of its village structure, barely affected by the outside world. The fate of Asiatic empires was to become subject to Europeans.

In the *Principles of Communism* (1847), Engels had referred to all semibarbarian countries, including India and China, as having been more or less outside historical development until the present.[159] Again, in the *Communist Manifesto*, Engels and Marx, before they really knew much of Asia, had spoken in a general way of barbarian and semibarbarian countries and of the dependence of the East on the West. In one of his first writings on India, the article of August 8, 1853, Marx regarded India as a backward country with no known history. That history was merely one of successive intruders who founded their empires on the passive basis of an unresisting and unchanging society.

Earlier, in his June 25, 1853, article, Marx waxed ironic at the expense of "the idyllic village communities" that, among other things, restrained the human mind within the smallest compass, made it the unresisting tool of oppression, subjected it to tradition, and deprived it of grandeur and energies. He spoke in his strongest critical tone of "the barbarian egoism" that had witnessed the ruin of empires, unspeakable cruelties, and massacres. He saw in this Asiatic society "undignified, stagnatory and vegetative life," a passive sort of existence that evoked wild, aimless, unbounded forces of destruction and rendered murder a religious rite in Hindustan.[160] The religion of the Hindus had made them "virtuosi in the art of self-torturing; these tortures inflicted on the enemies of their race and creed appear quite natural (to them)."

The communities in India were contaminated by caste distinctions and slavery and subjected inhabitants to circumstances. This led to a brutalizing worship of nature and to degrading man who "fell down on his knees in adoration of Kanuman the monkey, the Sabbala, the cow."[161] Other Asian countries exhibited the same backwardness. In Persia the European system of military organization had been engrafted on Asiatic barbarity.[162] Marx talked of China as "the rotting semi-civilization" and of Chinese nationality "with all its overbearing prejudice, stupidity, learned ignorance, and pedantic barbarism."

Oriental Despotism

During the time when Marx was working on his major books on economics, he wrote both to Ferdinand Lassalle, the German socialist leader, on February 22,

1858, and to Engels, on April 2, 1858, that he was planning six related books, one of which would be on the state. That book was never written and, in spite of the efforts of later epigoni, there is little theoretical discussion of political systems and their organizational characteristics in the original Marxist writings. Marx had given a concise summary of the division of occupations in village communities, but he had little to say about the political structure of the AMP once he assumed it was despotic.[163] He accepted Bernier's view that the king is "the sole and unique proprietor of the realm in the Mughal Empire." The despotic ruler had sovereign power, especially over the court and his followers, though he had little contact with the villages.[164]

These village communes, Marx suggested in the *Grundrisse*, varied politically: despotic when the head was chief of the clan family, democratic when power was shared. Above the communes and their political arrangements stood the Oriental despot who incorporates "the higher unity" and wielded ultimate power in political, economic, religious, and military areas. Marx referred to him as the "patriarchal authority, the only moral link embracing the vast machinery of the state."[165] The stability of the AMP allowed that link to exist. Because the unity is the real owner and the real precondition of common ownership, it (may) appear as something separate and superior to the numerous real, particular communities. The despot here appears as "the father of all the numerous lesser communities, thus realizing the common unity of all."[166] Using different language, Engels made the same point in *The Frankish Period*.[167] The continued existence of the nation, arising from the early small village communities, depended on a state power that did not derive from these communities but confronted them as something alien and exploited them to an ever-increasing extent.

The precapitalist forms of production, Marx argued in *Capital III* provided "a firm basis for the articulation of political life [and their] constant reproduction in the same form is a necessity for that life."[168] In those forms most of the surplus product went to the rulers.[169] Again, political rule by the despot was linked to the economic form.[170] It also helped explain the continuing political rule as with "the conservation of the Ottoman Empire." Engels expressed this more simply in a letter to Bernstein of August 9, 1882: "The satrap, alias pasha, is the chief Oriental form of the exploiter, just as the merchant and the jurist represent the modern Western form."[171]

Engels tended for the most part to prefer the functional explanation of the Oriental despot. Marx in an early article had stated that not conquest by itself but the performance of public functions lent authority to the despots of the East and stabilized their rule.[172] Engels in his *Anti-Duhring*, after establishing that the exercise of a social function was everywhere the basis of political supremacy, explained that organs of authority, once established, made themselves more independent and more indispensable. The person chosen as the servant of society gradually changed into the lord, the lord emerged as an Oriental despot, or satrap, or as the dynast of a Greek tribe or chieftain of a Celtic clan. Yet, however large the number of despots who rose and fell in Persia and India, each was fully aware that above all he was responsible for the collective maintenance of irrigation throughout the river valleys.

WHY ORIENTAL DESPOTISM?

Marx and Engels from time to time alluded to factors that would explain the basis of Oriental despotism.[173] At the bottom was the mode of production in the self-sufficient village communities that constantly reproduced themselves in the same form or replaced themselves if they were accidentally destroyed. As described in the preceding text, this was the key to the static nature of Asiatic societies.[174] Marx quoted Sir Stamford Raffles, former governor of Java, "The inhabitants give themselves no trouble about the breaking up and division of kingdoms; while the village remains entire, they care not to what power it is transferred, or to what sovereign it devolves; its internal economy remains unchanged." With an unchanging social structure, the Oriental despot personified the state.

Only one fleeting reference to a psychological or biological factor is apparent in Marx's thoughts about different forms of government. Borrowing a thesis and a phrase from the economist Richard Jones, he remarked that peoples in different countries did not have the same predisposition toward capitalist production. "Some primitive peoples such as the Turks have neither the temperament nor the disposition" to it.[175] Marx made some brief, tantalizing references to other factors that might have had an impact on the origin and persistence of Oriental despotism. Echoing Montesquieu he refers to the size, and even the climate, of the area to be governed. Explaining the absence of landed property, even in its feudal form, in the Orient, Engels, in his June 6, 1853, letter to Marx, thought it was mainly due to the climate, taken in connection with the nature of the soil, especially with the great stretches of desert that extended from the Sahara straight across Arabia, Persia, India, and Tartary up to the highest Asiatic plateau.[176] By contrast, the mother country of *Capital* was not the tropical region with its luxuriant reputation but the temperate zone.[177] It was the necessity of bringing a natural force under the control of society, of economizing on its energy, of appropriating or subduing it on a large scale by the work of the human hand that played the most decisive role in the history of industry.

A second factor, never followed up or discussed analytically was religion. In his June 14, 1853, letter to Engels, Marx remarked, in the context of his argument about the sovereign as absolute landlord, that it seemed to have been the Muhammadans who first established the principle of "no property in land" throughout the whole of Asia.

A third factor, referred to from time to time, was tradition, which played a dominant role in political and economic relationships in early societies and sanctioned the existing order as law. At one point in *Capital*, Marx remarked that the "ancient Asiatic and other ancient modes of production are founded either on the immature development of man individually, who has not yet severed the umbilical cord that unites him with his fellow men in a primitive tribal community, or on direct relations of subjection."[178] The more general argument, especially as provided by Marx, in his article written on June 10, 1853, is that "the idyllic village communities, inoffensive though they may appear, have been the solid foundation of Oriental despotism." The sober picture Marx gave of the life and behavior of inhabitants – passive, subjugated, worshipping idols of the ruler – is already familiar. The ruler established the centers of distribution of the royal revenues and moved the capital city from time to time, causing the population to move also. This explained the vanished capitals in Asia.

A fundamental characteristic of those village communities was communal ownership.[179] For Engels, primitive communism furnished in India and Russia, and also in Java, was the "finest and broadest basis of exploitation and despotism." Discussing the state power in early small village communities, Engels made the point that the form taken by that power depended on the form of the communities at the time. When, as among the Aryan peoples of Asia and the Russians, agriculture was cultivated by the community for the common account and no private property existed, the state power was despotic.[180]

Elsewhere Engels gave a related explanation for the existence of Oriental despotism when discussing whether the *obshchina*, the village community system in Russia, might lead directly to a socialist regime.[181] It was the complete isolation of the individual communities that created the natural basis for Oriental despotism.[182] From India to Russia this village community society, wherever it had prevailed, had always produced despotic rule.

In the afterword to the 1873 second German edition of *Capital* Marx confessed that in his chapter on value he had "coquetted with the modes of expression" peculiar to Hegel.[183] He certainly did so in his most picturesque reference to the Oriental despot. The image was that of the "all embracing unity" the proprietor of land, who stood above the village communities.[184] These communities sent their surplus in tribute and in labor for the "glorification of the unity, in part the real despot and in part the imagined tribal being, the god."[185]

This theological attribute of the despot was rarely mentioned elsewhere, but one interesting relevant passage appeared in Marx's discussion of the rule of Napoleon III, where he put forward the generalization that the most trying governmental position was that of a civilian at the head of a despotic military state.[186] In the Orient, Marx continued, the difficulty was more or less met by transforming the despot into a god, above the level "common to himself and his swordsmen." Elsewhere, Marx had written that the state was personified in the Oriental despot, a personification that engendered a belief in his absolute power.

The most hotly disputed explanation for the existence of Oriental despotism is the functional one.[187] First Engels, in his June 6, 1853, letter, and then, quickly, Marx, in response and in his article of June 25, 1853, saw the crucial need for irrigation systems and thus for a ruler, "the despotic government poised above the lesser communities." Marx, however, emphasized more than Engels had done the role of central government to perform this function. Some structural Marxists have challenged the functional argument in two ways. They hold that crucial characteristics of the AMP, such as communal ownership and expropriation of the surplus by a higher unity, were not confined to those societies requiring irrigation. They also argue that large-scale irrigation controls were present not only in the AMP but also in non-Asiatic countries and areas such as Lombardy, Holland, Spain, and Egypt, as well as in India and Persia.

Both Marx and Engels argued that all Asiatic governments had the functions of providing public works.[188] Compared with their discussions of the various aspects of the AMP from a social and economic point of view, Marx and Engels had little to say about the political organization or structure of Oriental despotism.[189] Marx, in the *Grundrisse*, did refer to possible differences in governmental arrangements in tribal bodies, which could take either a more despotic or a more democratic form.[190] The starkest commentary on Oriental government, given in 1853, was the statement on its simple organization. In Asia, generally from time immemorial, only three departments of government, those mentioned in the preceding text, were established: finance, war, and public works. Parenthetically, Marx argued that British rule in India had continued the functions of finance and war but had neglected that of public works.[191] This helped explain the poor state of agriculture in that country. When the public works in India fell into disrepair, vast expanses once magnificently cultivated became arid, were ruined, and trade was destroyed.

In an article of September 9, 1854, on *Revolutionary Spain*, Marx made another point about the centralizing character of Oriental despotism by allusion and comparison.[192] He explained that the absolute monarchy in Spain, unlike other European absolute monarchies, prevented rather than fostered the growth of common interests on which "alone a uniform system of administration and the rule of general laws can be created." Spain therefore resembled Asiatic forms of government not the other European ones.

During the last two centuries Marx and Engels have been among the more prominent of those writers whose ambition has been to make history intelligible by finding what Isaiah Berlin called large patterns or regularities in the procession of historical events.[193] In these patterns they envisaged the Orient as a region with a historical background and a socioeconomic and political system qualitatively different from the West. Previous writers and analysts dealing with Asian countries tended to focus on the prominent role of the ruler, the Oriental despot, in the life of those countries. The two Marxists, in consonance with their general approach to analysis of historical development and contemporary societies, concentrated their discussion of the AMP on socioeconomic features rather than on political factors or the relationship between the ruler and his subjects in the intellectual structure Marx and Engels created.[194]

They wrote, mostly in their newspaper articles on the empirical issues of the day, with considerable insight on a variety of topics and on political and governmental policies concerning the Asian countries, especially India. Yet they never dwelt on theoretical analysis of political rule or compared Asian political institutions or the interrelationship between the individual and the state with Western systems in the same way or with the depth they exhibited in comparing socioeconomic formations or forms of property ownership. In particular, the role of the Oriental despot is made clear, but little is revealed of the activities or nature of his political and administrative functions.

The contribution of Marx and Engels to the discussion of Oriental societies has been important not only for its insight and suggestive comments but also for its effect on later Marxist theoreticians and activists. That contribution was the creation, with some qualification, of a coherent and consistent pattern of a distinctive form of society. To ideas and information they had garnered from previous writers, who influenced much of their work on Asia, and from contemporary documents on the region, Marx and Engels added their own reflections, sometimes changing emphases, and their general comparisons, making up a systematic overall theory of the AMP. Some of these comparisons were used negatively to suggest a system that contrasted with the essence and elements of the capitalist system. This comparison is reflected in discussion of topics such as free labor, private property, division of labor, separation of the worker from the land, commodity production, commodity exchange, use of money, capital accumulation, extraction of surplus value, and the effect of temperate climatic zones. But other features of the AMP, especially the communal village system, the unity of agriculture and handicrafts, the stagnant society, and the Oriental despot, are attributes that are not necessarily related to Marx's primary concern with capitalism.

For analysts of Marxism, the AMP has been important in at least two ways. First, it was an example of the complexities of historical analysis, illustrating or implying the possibility of different paths of development in the past or in the present. Equally important is that the AMP portrays a society in which political power appears to be autonomous and not the result, as in the usual Marxist explanation of that power, of class conflict and domination by the class owning the means of production. Partly because the AMP differs from the mainstream of Marx's writings it has occasioned considerable critical comment from Marxists and less ideologically oriented analysts. Some of the criticism is justifiable, but the extent of it is somewhat surprising. Ernest Gellner wittily pointed out that commentary on classical antiquity or primitive tribalism is hardly crucial testing grounds for appraisal of Marxism.

Yet, cogent criticisms of the concept of the AMP are valid. Analysis of the AMP does not always have the clarity or easy comprehensibility one would like, particularly on the differences between the AMP and other early societies, and between state property and communal or tribal property. At times, the location of "Oriental" appears to go beyond normally accepted geographical boundaries. A related problem is the changing emphasis on specific features of the AMP in different writing, because Marx and Engels were influenced by others' research on their subject during a thirty-year period.[195] Nevertheless, in spite of a particular emphasis at one point or another, the essential features, whether it is the self-sufficient village, the method of extraction of surplus labor, the communal property, or the Oriental despotism, remain always as part of the analysis.

To what extent does the Marxian analysis correspond to the realities of Oriental societies, economies, and politics? Experts in the field of Oriental societies have pointed out the factual mistakes or too strong generalizations that cannot bear the freight of the empirical statements in the writings on the AMP, though they often stemmed from the works of British administrators in India, government documents, and the general reading by Marx and Engels. Thorner, in particular, listed factual errors, and pointed out that Marx was mistaken in saying that communal property had ever existed in either Mughal or post-Mughal India. Others have remarked that there is no necessary relationship between elements of the AMP, such as absence of private land ownership and need for state control of irrigation and Oriental despotism.[196] Anderson went even further by arguing that the whole Marxist picture of the Indian villages was inaccurate except for the union of agriculture and crafts, which was common to all preindustrial rural communities.[197] Moreover, the villages were not egalitarian communities but rather were based on caste differences, a topic Marx mentioned but ignored for the most part.

Yet Anderson's argument is too strong in suggesting that the AMP was essentially a generic residual category for non-European development.[198] Marx and Engels were not Orientalists in the sense of specialized scholars in the field of Oriental societies, but neither were they ignorant or lacking in perspective of that area and of a distinctive type of society and political rule, the structure of Oriental despotism. More apt is Dumont's comment that Marx and the English historian Henry Maine were the two writers who drew the Indian village community into the circle of world history.[199] It may be excessive to hold that the views of Marx on the AMP are essential elements in his work and that without them the composition of *Capital* would have been unimaginable. A more modest claim is that the Marxist writings on the AMP have an important place in the perceptions of Oriental despotism by Western writers.

9

Max Weber: Patrimonialism as a Political Type

Max Weber (1864–1920) has few peers among European social theorists. His comparative historical studies of the structure, beliefs, and behavior patterns in the major civilizations in the world have influenced political and sociological analysts for more than a century No one in the social sciences can ignore his formulations, contributions, and original insights in the discussion of concepts such as rationalization, charisma, legitimacy, class, status, power, and bureaucracy. Less well known is his concept of patrimonialism, his version of Oriental despotism. There is no dispute about the genius of Max Weber and his honored place in early twentieth-century European thought, but legitimate differences exist about the essence and major thrust of his writings. Weber's multifarious publications on so many varied subjects illustrate an extraordinary intellectual mastery and an iridescent approach to complex social and political issues. They exemplify scrupulous integrity if not always total limpidity.

Beginning as a student of law in Heidelberg in 1882, whose first teaching appointment was in that field in 1892, Weber also studied economic and social history in Berlin (1884–5), in 1895 was nominated to a professorship of economics in Freiburg, and then in 1897 to a post in political science and to a chair at Heidelberg. Only at the end of his life, after a breakdown, travel abroad (including to the United States), and work as an independent scholar, did he receive in 1919 an appointment in sociology in Munich. In his last years he was active in politics, particularly in the German Democratic Party, acted as an adviser to the German delegation to the Versailles peace conference, and advised on the post–World War I Weimar constitution. He was also cofounder of the German Sociology Society and co-editor of a major sociological journal.[1]

Weber's erudition and scholarship, insights and theories, embraced a remarkable diversity of subjects, themes, and disciplinary approaches.[2] His grasp, in a relatively short life disturbed by serious personal problems from time to time, extended to all the social sciences, to philosophy, and to the humanities. Mere listing of the subjects on which Weber wrote and lectured is revealing: methodology of the sciences; the nature of scientific inquiry; interpretation of social action; comparative sociology and social structure; ancient and modern religions and their related institutions and beliefs, church, sect, charisma, and mysticism; political sociology and morphology, comparing regimes and societies at different times and places, including subjects such as legitimacy, class, status, party, and administrative organization; the processes of rationality and bureaucratization; leadership and ethical responsibility; democratic politics, contemporary German politics; the mutual interaction between economics and political and legal institutions; development of rationality and capitalism in the West and the lack of similar development in the Orient; sociological foundations of music; structure of political organizations and typology of forms of political domination; and the concept of "ideal types."

Weber formulated significant theories and typologies but combined these with empirical data based on his historical research.[3] His insights sprang from empirical evidence in many historical periods and geographical settings. Among them were medieval commercial associations on which he wrote his doctorate in 1889: agrarian workers in the East Elbe area, Roman agrarian history, Russian politics after the 1905 revolution, Russian peasants, Oklahoma Indians, coins and minting in early China, the condition of workers in large-scale enterprises, and the religions of the world.[4] Whether Weber aimed at a value-free social science is an issue still disputed, if much less mordantly articulated in recent years. More important was his concern to understand and compare different cultures, religions, and societies in space and time, and to analyze conflicts of value. Weber suffered no postmodernist angst about attempting to understand other cultures in terms of the categories of his own culture.[5]

Weber was unassuming about his scholarship; he wrote, for instance, of his "modest hopes of contributing anything essentially new" to the rich discussion of the religion of Israel and Jewry.[6] Commentators have criticized Weber, sometimes with unctuous effrontery in light of the vast range of his writings, for lack of experience and inadequate documentation or inaccuracies on specific issues, and for methodological defects.[7] Yet Weber always candidly acknowledged his reliance on the existing literature written by experts on the subjects of his work. He is said to have replied to an academic critic, who complained that Weber wrote outside of his field, "I'm not a donkey, and I don't have a field."

The richness of Weber's diversity of interests and subjects, the changes in his analytical focus, and the publication, a number posthumously, of uncompleted and fragmented manuscripts – only two of his important works were published in his lifetime – make it difficult to find any unified theme, or even a single major one, at the core of his voluminous writing. Even his major work, translated into English as *Economy and Society* and never completed in polished form because of his early death, has been criticized as a collection of concepts, which did not convey a substantive unity.[8]

Intrepid or fastidious commentators regretting that Weber left "nothing more than a series of unrelated fragments" have sought to create a mosaic within which these "fragments" can be placed.[9] The quest for that mosaic, the Holy Grail of Weber, has occasioned a miscellany of its own. What is that hidden essence? Is it a doctrine about values; the origins and development of modernity; rationalization as the key to social change; value-free social science; or the comparative study of world religions, sociology of domination, the meanings of social action, the inner logic of the rationalization process in the sphere of religion, the emergence of Western rationalism, the autonomous role of ideal, particularly religious factors, and the typology of legitimate political authority?

The search for the "real" Weber continues. Was he a prophet of despair because of the fears, expressed near the end of his life, about the ironic consequence of bureaucratization leading to "disenchantment" of the world and the "iron cage" and a possible "plebiscitarian leader-democracy" to maintain political order as traditional values were disappearing? Or was he the philosopher of modernity because of his emphasis on development through rationalization and the various forms of rationality? He does not fit comfortably in any familiar position nor can he be pigeonholed as a neo-Kantian, German idealist, positivist, historicist, Nietzchean, or nationalist. Whoever the "real" Weber was, the formidable problem of interpretation of his ideas remains. Explication is difficult because Weber did not always provide unqualified or wholly consistent definitions of his concepts or clarifications of his historical insights.[10] Nor were his writings a model of linear clarity even on major themes. Marianne Weber, his widow, acknowledged the lack of a "lucid sentence structure," explaining it by his wealth of ideas.[11] Even a brilliant, sympathetic analyst like Raymond Aron confessed he was not sure what Weber meant by "ideal types."[12]

It is also reasonable to comment that "direct references to the dimension of historical time" are infrequent in his discussion of "pure types." Weber warned that concepts should not be regarded as "empirically valid or real effective forces."[13] Weber did not offer simple or unilateral explanations of phenomena in the historical process or a unilinear view of the causes of social change. He made few direct references to Marx in his work but he did reject "most emphatically" economic determinism, the "so called materialistic conception of history," which he found an inadequate formula for the causal explanation of historical reality.[14] No one factor could be the "true" cause of another. Marx's view that "the economic is in some sense the ultimate point in the chain of causes is completely finished as a scientific proposition."[15]

In discussing causality Weber was not dogmatic, providing no simple answer. "Groups that are not somehow economically determined are extremely rare. The degree of this influence varies widely and, above all, the economic determination of social action is ambiguous – contrary to the assumption of so-called historical materialism. The structural forms (*Strukturformen*) of social action follow 'laws of their own,' and they may in a given case always be codetermined by other than economic causes. However, at some point economic conditions tend to become causally important, and often decisive, for almost all social groups, at least those which have major cultural significance; conversely, the economy is usually also influenced by the autonomous structure of social action within which it exists. No significant generalization can be made as to when and how this will occur. However, we can generalize about the degree of 'elective affinity' between concrete structures of social action and concrete forms of economic organization."[16]

For Weber no single determination of social action was historically valid, and no single group, which had been accorded privileges, social honor, and esteem and would embody a distinctive style of life, was the formative force in any society.[17] Different influential social "carriers" appeared in various societies: Confucian literati in China; monks in early Buddhism; Brahmans forwarding Hindu salvation doctrine; independent cultural strata in ancient Judaism; warrior nobles in Islam.[18] Weber saw the historical process as the outcome of multicausal factors. He argued neither an idealist nor a materialist interpretation of history. No automatic or consistent answer could be given to the question whether individual actions were oriented by "other-worldly" ideas or by socioeconomic conditions beyond their control. Weber's pluralistic position was expressed in a speech in 1910, saying that if "we look at the causal lines, we see them run, at one time, from technical to economic and political matters, at another from political to religious and economic ones. There is no resting place."[19] The most well-known formulation of his general position is found in his writing, *The Social Psychology of the World Religions*. He wrote, "Not ideas, but material and ideal interests, directly govern men's conduct. Yet very frequently the 'world images' that have been created by 'ideas' have, like switchmen, determined the tracks along which action has been pushed by the dynamic of interest. 'From what' and 'for what' one wished to be redeemed and, let us not forget, 'could be' redeemed, depended upon one's image of the world."

Throughout his work, Weber deals with this complex interaction of multiple factors. Among them are *Herrschaft* (the word variously translated but here used as "dominion"), religions, power, conflict, competition, status groups, geography, historical events, technological changes, customs, interests, beliefs, values, economic relations, culture, open markets, legitimacy, power of the state, and governmental structure.[20] Examples of complex interaction can be found at many points. In his early writing he argued that no "enclosed cyclical movement, nor any unequivocally mono-linear evolution" could explain the development of Mediterranean-European civilization.[21] In his early analysis of East Elbian agriculture Weber argued that social structure in that area was "a matter of reciprocal effects in which the purely economic factor does not by any means play the leading role. Population distribution, division of trades, division of land, the legal forms of the organization of labor . . . have a much more decisive significance" than particular economic conditions. At the same time he saw economic changes as the main explanation for the decline of the Roman Empire.[22] Climate helped the development of the economy in Northern Europe in the Middle Ages. Geography conditioned the lack of development of "economic rationalism" and "rational life methodology" in Asia.[23]

The most famous and controversial application of Weber's views on interaction of multiple factors is in *The Protestant Ethic and the Spirit of Capitalism* with its discussion of factors contributing to the rise of capitalism. Weber did not argue that Protestantism, particularly Calvinism, had produced or "caused" the rise of capitalism. Rather he was concerned with what he called "the elective affinity" between capitalism and Protestantism, and with those beliefs and outlook that led Calvinists to try to implement God's purposes in economic and social activity through dedication to one's calling (*beruf*). Economic development in the West was interrelated with the Protestant ethic and behavior patterns of worldly asceticism, thriftiness, and capital accumulation. Yet the Reformation cannot be deduced "as a historically necessary result from certain economic changes." Nor could Weber accept that the spirit of capitalism "could only have arisen as a result of certain effects of the Reformation, or even that capitalism as an economic system is a creation of the Reformation."[24]

Weber's multicausal approach was pertinent in explaining the emergence of a culture of individualism, which resulted from the coincidence of various factors, religious, economic, and social, that led to the development of behavior patterns of responsibility for one's own salvation, and taking action to change aspects of the world through pragmatic and rational activity. The last factor included the work discipline of Protestants, the product of particular social conditions and pressures, a discipline that was less present, if not absent, in other cultures where work was regarded as necessary only to provide an acceptable level of consumption or in cultures that were, as in Asia, imbued with attitudes of passive fatalism or mystical contemplation.[25]

Did Weber suggest or evaluate a hierarchy of cultures in the world, or adopt an evolutionary scheme in which history passes through particular stages of development? Indications of such a scheme appear in his works, which stressed the importance of rationality, defined in varying ways, as a fundamental feature of the Occidental way of life.[26] Yet Weber did not advocate a teleological theory of the historical process or a unilinear evolutionary model or even express a moral preference for Western-style development with its characteristics of increasing rationality, bureaucratization, and modernization.

Weber wrote that historical reality always appeared in mixed forms, and spoke of the continuous stream of actual phenomena. Referring to the historical compromises between secular and religious power and to the shifting distribution of power in societies, Weber was conscious that "fateful events play a tremendous role."[27] A powerful hereditary monarch, for example, might have turned the Western church into an institution similar to the Eastern, and "without the Great Schism [usually dated 1054] the decline of hierocratic power might have never occurred in the way it actually happened." No simple theory or conceptual tool could encompass the diversity of phenomena or concrete reality. Scientific explanation needed selection and abstraction. To help understand "the complex interaction of innumerable historical factors" and to compare social, political, and religious systems and forms of individual behavior and motives, Weber devised the concept of "ideal type." This concept was to be a methodological conceptual tool, not a model, an ethical or moral imperative, or a correspondence to concrete, empirical reality. It was a guide to research, a means by which the analyst could organize, explain, and interpret historical phenomena, could "analyze historically unique configurations or their individual components in terms of generic concepts."[28]

In an early work Weber had explained that "only clear, unambiguous concepts can smooth the way for any research that wishes to discover the specific importance of social and cultural phenomena." To this end Weber later proposed the concept of the "ideal type."[29] Rarely if ever, he warned, would real phenomena correspond exactly to a pure "ideal type," which, however, "must be in the realm of probability . . . must be somewhere a close empirical approximation . . . a working hypothesis."[30] Weber, unlike Marx, did not seek general "laws" of society or economics or stages of history.[31] The ideal type was an abstraction, neither testable nor predictive that aimed to bring "order into the chaos of those facts, which we have drawn into the field circumscribed by our interest."[32] The ideal type can be seen as a combination or alternation between sociological generalization of fundamental concepts and interpretation and explanation of history.[33]

In formulating his ideal type concepts of social and political systems Weber chose certain traits from a particular historical reality and form of behavior. In what is perhaps his fullest and clearest explanation of his concept of the ideal type Weber wrote that it "is formed by the one-sided accentuation of one or more points of view and by the synthesis of a great many diffuse, discrete, more or less present and occasionally absent concrete individual phenomena, which are arranged according to those one-sidedly emphasized viewpoints into a unified analytical construct. In its conceptual purity, this mental construct cannot be found empirically anywhere in reality. It is a utopia. It has the significance of a purely ideal limiting concept with which the real situation or action is compared and surveyed for the explication of certain of its significant components. Such concepts are constructs in terms of which we formulate relationships by the application of the category of objective possibility. By means of this category, the adequacy of our imagination, oriented and disciplined by reality, is judged."[34] Weber's analysis of patrimonialism, or Oriental despotism, must be seen in this light.

Weber may have been influenced by German idealism but he cannot accurately be regarded as an adherent of it. Yet linked to his formulation of ideal types is the concept, current in late-nineteenth- and twentieth-century German speculation, of *Verstehen*. For Weber this meant interpretive understanding of social behavior for explanation of its causes, its course, and its effect.[35] Such understanding involves classification of behavior, and Weber posits four categories in that classification: *zweckrational* (rational means to rational ends), *wertrational* (rational means to irrational ends), *affektual* (action guided by emotion), and *traditional* (action guided by custom and habits). He also cautioned that this kind of understanding needed to be controlled by the normal method of empirical tests.[36]

The construct of the ideal type was the basis for Weber's analysis of three "pure" types of political domination and the principles of legitimation on which they are grounded. At the start he made clear that the actual nature of domination occurring in historical reality constituted combinations, mixtures, adaptations, or modifications of those "pure" types.[37] Weber explained domination as the probability that certain specific commands or all commands will be obeyed by a given group of persons. Authority is defined as legitimate forms of domination, which subordinates accept and obey because they regard them as legitimate. Every genuine form of domination implies a minimum of voluntary compliance. In his major work on comparative political analysis Weber posited three types of legitimate domination: traditional, charismatic, and legal or rational.[38]

The traditional type rests on a belief "in the sanctity of everyday routines."[39] This means traditional rights of a dominant individual or group are accepted, and the system is based on custom, precedent, inviolable norms of conduct, and the sanctity of authority. The dominant ruler might be a priest, clan leader, family head, or an elite group.

The charismatic type is one in which people submit to a ruler because of their belief in the extraordinary and exceptional qualities, such as sanctity, heroism, character of leadership, of a specific individual regardless of whether these qualities are actual, alleged, or presumed. In different societies the qualities might be attributed to the sorcerer, the prophet, the leader of hunting expeditions, the warrior chieftain, the "Caesarist" ruler, or to the head of a political party. Charismatic rule becomes legitimate with the belief that the ruler possesses magical powers, can perform miracles, gains victories, seeks the welfare of the governed, can perform heroic deeds, or has a divine mission. Subjects accord the ruler devotion, perhaps stemming from distress as well as enthusiasm.[40]

A legal-rational type of domination is one in which normative rules and the right of those exercising authority to issue commands on the basis of those rules is accepted as legitimate. This legal domination is based on a system of rational rules, enacted by accepted procedure and by bureaucratic administrative techniques and the application of the same rules to all members of the community. Obedience by citizens is not to an individual person but to the law, to legal codes, rights, and rules.

The three ideal types of domination in Weber's formulation are not specifically linked to each other in some logical sequence of development, nor are they chronologically related in a continuing historical process. Exact geographical locations for the different types are never made completely clear, apart from the legal-rational type that is characteristic of modern, developed Western societies.

A crucial preoccupation of Weber's was the presence or absence of rationalization in different societies and the impact of this factor on development. Implicit in much of his work was a comparison or contrast between Occidental and Oriental societies concerning beliefs, and religious, political, economic, and social institutions based on this perspective. Weber did not formulate pure ideal types of Occidental and Oriental society. Existing political systems constituted combinations, mixtures, adaptations, or modifications of pure types. He rejected the idea that all "concrete historical reality could be exhausted in a conceptual manner."[41] However, he did emphasize the process of rationalization in all aspects of Western civilization, science, law, military organization, capitalist economics, business, bureaucratic administration, political system, music, and the absence of that process in Oriental societies.

Weber acknowledged that the concept of rationalization was subject to different interpretations. "There is, for example rationalization of mystical contemplation . . . just as much as there are rationalizations of economic life, of technique, of scientific research, of military training, of law and administration. Furthermore, each one of these fields may be rationalized from many different ultimate points of view and toward many different ultimate ends, and what is rational from one point of view may be irrational from another. Hence rationalizations of the most varied character have existed in various departments of life in all civilizations."[42] Recognizing "the peculiar rationalism of Western culture," he asks, "Why did not the scientific, the artistic, the political, or the economic development" in Oriental societies "enter on that path of rationalization which is peculiar to the Occident?"

Weber saw the process of rationalization as present in all areas of life in Western societies. It infused the sciences and mathematics. Art was based on rational perspective. The formal legal system, originating in Roman legal theory, was rational, universal in application, impersonal, nonarbitrary, and based on a distinction between secular and sacred rules, which resulted in order, predictability, and regularity of procedures. Law in Western systems did not depend on magic, morality, or religion. Weber saw the dominance of magic in non-Western societies as one of the most serious obstructions to the rationalization of economic life.[43] Like science, the state, and social institutions, music conditioned by a specifically shaped rationality took a unique form in the Occident. Western music is based on calculable rules, on a rational structure of notation, standardized instruments, harmonic chords, and counterpoint composition.[44]

Interrelated with the process of rationalization in Weber's analysis is Western capitalism, particularly industrial capitalism, a form of enterprise that requires organization of labor aiming at a mass market and dependent on correct calculation, efficiency, and technological innovations. It also requires among other things, a free market, rational bookkeeping, stock exchange, a middle class, and private property. Business is separated from the household. Moreover, industrial capitalism must be able to count on the continuity, trustworthiness, and objectivity of the legal order, and on the rational, predictable functions of legal and administrative agencies.[45]

In a striking passage Weber delineates the uniqueness of the Western world. "Only the Occident knows the state in the modern sense, with a constitution [*gesatzter Verfassung*], specialized officialdom, and the concept of citizenship.

Beginnings of this institution in antiquity and in the Orient were never able to develop fully. Only the Occident knows rational law, made by jurists and rationally interpreted and applied, and only in the Occident is found the concept of citizen (*civis Romanus*, *citoyen*, *bourgeois*) because only in the Occident does the city exist in the specific sense of the word. Furthermore, only the Occident possesses science in the present-day sense of the word. Theology, philosophy, and reflection on the ultimate problems of life were known to the Chinese and Hindu, perhaps even of a depth not reached by the European; but a rational science and in connection with it a rational technology remained unknown to those civilizations. Finally, Western civilization is further distinguished from every other by the presence of men with a rational ethos for the conduct of life. Magic and religion are found everywhere; but a religious basis for conduct that, when consistently followed, had to lead to a specific form of rationalism is again peculiar to Western civilization alone."[46]

The state in the modern, essentially Western, sense is characterized by certain features: a constitution and written documents, regular elections, separation of powers, limits on exercise of power, monopoly of the legitimate use of force and coercion, protection of rights, autonomous cities able to legislate for themselves, impartial judiciary, and "specialized officialdom."[47] Weber was always concerned about the last, a bureaucratic administration composed of specialized, trained officials.[48] The ideal was a "spirit of formalistic impersonality . . . without affection for enthusiasm. The dominant norms are concepts of straightforward duty without regard to personal considerations. Everyone is subject to formal equality of treatment; that is, everyone in the same empirical situation." Implementing equality before the law requires abstract regularity of the exercise of authority. Weber's analysis of bureaucratic structure is now classic and influential in the contemporary study of administration: official functions bound by rules, hierarchical organization, specified spheres of competence, specialized training, appointment on basis of competence, and decisions recorded in writing.

Weber in a pessimistic moment also saw the negative side of the process of bureaucratization and rationalization and of "the tremendous cosmos of the modern economic order."[49] The process "depersonalizes" itself by excluding love, hatred, and every purely personal feeling from the execution of official tasks. Modern culture required the emotionally detached, professional expert. The machinery of bureaucratic organization, like that of modern industrial production, was solidified human spirit, with functions assigned to a multitude of specialized experts, rigid regulation of competence, and hierarchical pattern of obedience to the appropriate superior authority. This might lead to "the iron cage of future serfdom in which men will have to live helplessly, like the fellahin in ancient Egypt, if they consider an efficient, that is to say rational, bureaucratic administration, which also provides for their needs, as the only and ultimate ideal that is to determine the nature of their own government." Borrowing the term from Schiller, Weber uses "disenchantment" to portray the irony of the rationalization process in which the belief in and the power of magic has broken down. "Not summer's bloom lies ahead of us, but rather a polar night of icy darkness and hardness."[50]

The contrast between the Western movement to modernity and economic capitalism, and the absence or delay of such movement in the Orient, was crucial for Weber. Scattered throughout his writings are discussions of various factors present in Western and absent in Oriental history that might explain the difference: Greek scientific rationalism; Roman juridical rationalism; Hebrew prophetic pronouncements; autonomous cities and political structures able to legislate and not simply be the tools of imperial rulers; independent universities; voluntary associations; stable rights of property in regard to land; competitive pressures fostering changes in economic organization and activity; and religious beliefs that helped lead to fundamental changes in the social and cultural structure. For Weber, Oriental societies lacked a "particular mentality" for development, modernity, and capitalism.[51]

Why did the Orient not enter on that path of rationalization, in science, art, politics, and economics, familiar in the Occident? The question is more pointed for Weber because he acknowledges the Orient's important contributions to world culture, in science, paper, printing, mathematics, grammar, in the past. The sobriety, thriftiness, and acquisitiveness present in Puritanism was present in China to some extent but did not amount to a "capitalist spirit." Only the Puritan rational ethic with its supramundane orientation brought economic rationalism to its consistent conclusion. Confucian rationalism meant adjustment to the world; Puritan rationalism meant mastery of the world.[52] To provide an answer Weber examined different features of the Oriental experience: religion, psychological attitudes, and belief systems; economic behavior and the prefeudal form of land ownership; the social framework including the strong kinship ties and caste system; ancestor worship and filial piety; the lack of a rational administration and judiciary; and the political systems, dictatorial, despotic, patrimonial, and "Caesaro-papist."[53] The last term implies a system where the king regards himself also as a cleric and becomes head of the church; by contrast a theocracy is a system where the priest becomes king.

THE DIFFERENT TRADITIONAL POLITICAL SYSTEMS

In Weber's sweeping generalizations, all forms of traditional authority – patriarchal, patrimonial, "sultanic" despotism, bureaucratic state order – rested on a similar social order: members of the lord's household, and the plebeians, those who lacked possessions or social honor of their own or who were entirely chained to the lord in material terms. The staff of the ruler did not have defined areas of competence or impersonal rules or arrangements of rational hierarchy, training, and promotion as in legal-rational systems.[54]

Within his "ideal type" of traditional authority Weber differentiated three specific subdivisions: gerontocracy, patriarchalism, and patrimonialism. In Weber's first two subdivisions, the most elementary forms of traditional domination – an individual or a group, a priest, clan leader, family head, or elite – exercised authority as a private prerogative without any real administrative staff.[55] He performed functions on behalf of the group as a whole.

The first two types differ in that gerontocracy, a group of elders cognizant of traditions was not, as was patriarchalism, primarily a kinship or an economic group or one where power was exercised by a particular individual designated by inheritance. In different works Weber spoke of patriarchalism as a system whose legitimacy rested on tradition, on "a belief in the sanctity of everyday routines," and in the norms that derive from tradition. The roots of patriarchal domination grew out of the master's authority over his household, the *patria potestas*, familiar from Rome. "Patriarchalism means the authority of the father, the senior of the house; the sib elder over the members of the household and sib; the rule of the master and patron over bondsmen, serfs, freed men; of the lord over the domestic servants and household officials; of the prince over house and court officials, nobles of office, clients, vassals; of the patrimonial lord and sovereign prince over the 'subjects.' "[56] In this kind of regime the head of the household, who had inherited his position and ruled for life, ruled despotically over wife, children, and slaves; property rights were exclusively vested in him.

The lord directly controlled administration through people personally dependent on him, including slaves, servants, domestic officials, personal "favorites," and those who received "prebends," in money or in kind. Weber uses the word *prebend*, originally an ecclesiastical term, to indicate allowances in kind or rights to land, which were nonhereditary forms of support, benefices granted by the ruler on a personal basis. Anyone could rise to the highest positions, such as the Grand Vizier, personal physician, or astrologer. In this kind of extended family, belief in and acceptance of authority was based on personal relations that were perceived as natural in the close and permanent living together of all dependents of the household in a "community of fate."[57] If there was piety toward tradition and obedience to the master, a regime of traditional authority also was bound by the precedents handed down from the past and to this extent was oriented to rules, but these were not akin to the impersonal rules of a legal-rational system. The ruler was dependent on the willingness of individuals, chosen by him, to comply with his orders in the same way as they respect the head of the family. In return, the ruler rendered services for them and did not exploit them. The ruler limited excessive interference with people or his demands for services and gifts.

Obedience in patriarchalism was owed not to enacted rules but to the individual who occupied the position of authority by tradition or who had been chosen for it by the traditional master. Internal conflict was minimized because of the strength of the *sib* (kinship) ties that enforced obedience and instilled respect for authority. Everyday needs in politics and religion were handled by the patriarchal structure, which was based on habituation, respect for tradition, piety toward parents and ancestors, and the servants' personal faithfulness.[58] Patriarchal domination stemmed from strictly personal loyalty and a belief "in the inviolability of that which has existed from time out of mind."

PATRIMONIALISM AND SULTANISM

Patrimonialism, the third form of traditional authority, was a system in which the entire realm was the private domain of the ruler, the political extension of the royal household. The crucial characteristic was that the ruler, usually designated by process of inheritance, controlled an administrative staff and military force, which were his purely personal instruments.[59] They did not come from kinship or clan groups nor did they constitute a corporate group. They stemmed from imperial household servants who served at the pleasure of the ruler to whom they were obedient.

In systems based on gerontocracy and patriarchalism, the master had no personal staff. In patrimonialism, which at the extreme became what Weber called *sultanism*, an administration and a military force were purely personal instruments of the master. His authority was a personal right, and he could exploit it as he liked. By controlling his supporters, slaves, "coloni," conscripted subjects, mercenary bodyguards, and patrimonial troops, he could broaden the range of his arbitrary power and grant grace and favor beyond those members of the household who were available in patriarchal and gerontocratic systems. Weber made a significant distinction. Where domination was primarily traditional, though exercised by the ruler's personal autonomy, it was patrimonial. Where it operated primarily on the basis of arbitrary discretion, it was sultanism. Both, however, had a personal staff, a retinue of slaves, clients, and retainers. Sultanism, a system of absolute authority, was characterized as the most extreme form of personal arbitrary will, almost free of traditional limitations. The ruler in this kind of regime was dependent on the military, his personal instrument, which he provided with material and financial resources from his own storehouses and revenue. The inherent problem for sultanism in the Ottoman Empire was in its dependence on the personal military force, such as the Janissaries. That force held down the sultan's subjects, but it could be a danger to the ruler if it became unreliable.

ADMINISTRATION IN PATRIMONIALISM

In Weber's view, the patrimonial personal staff would usually include the house priest, the ruler's personal physician, and those responsible, as in the Ottoman court until the nineteenth century, for managing the functions necessary for ensuring supplies of food and wine, clothing, armor, and revenues. This staff was responsible for household and official functions. Weber points out that the patrimonial origin of Indian officials is expressed in the name *Amatya* (house companion).[60] No clear lines of administrative functions were laid down. Their assignment was the personal affair of the ruler. In India, even administrative and court offices were not kept separate, and the jurisdictional spheres of a bewildering manifold of offices were fluid, indeterminate, irrational, and subject to chance influences.[61] In general, the patrimonial office lacked the legal-rational separation of the "private" and the "official" sphere.[62] The ruler's political power was part of his personal property. The exercise of power by officials was based on a mixture of obligatory behavior, sacred tradition, and personal discretion.

Law making in a patrimonial state stemmed from this juxtaposition of inviolable traditional prescription and completely arbitrary decision making by the ruler.[63] Unshakeable sacred tradition accompanied a realm of prerogative and favoritism.[64] Arbitrary rule inevitably resulted in favoritism and impeded rational administration and economic development. Arbitrary and discretionary authority depended on personal considerations: on the attitude toward the specific applicant and his concrete request, and on purely personal connections, favors, promises, and privileges on a case-to-case basis. Military and judicial authority was exercised without any restraint by the master as part of his patrimonial power.[65]

Weber made clear that patrimonial bureaucracies lacked those features common to legal-rational systems. There was no regular appointment or promotion process on an impartial basis; technical or specialized training; fixed salary; and procedural regularity in functions to be performed. Official titles did not indicate the function to be performed:[66] their meaning seemed to change quite arbitrarily as in Assyria. Decisions were made ad hoc throughout the range of the ruler's powers. The ruler demanded unconditional administrative compliance from his officials. Their loyalty to office was not an impersonal commitment to impersonal tasks but a servant's loyalty to a ruler to whom they had an obligation of fealty. Rights and privileges derived from the ruler's grant or favor.

Officials came from two different sources. In what Weber called "patrimonial recruitment," persons in the staff were related to the chief by traditional ties of loyalty.[67] They included kinsman, slaves, and dependents who were officers of the household such as the chamberlain in Europe, the head eunuch in the Orient, the executioner in Africa, and the ruler's personal physician and astrologer. Recruitment might also be "extra-patrimonial." This source included personal favorites; those who were vassals of the ruler; and freemen who voluntarily entered into a relation of personal loyalty as officials.

The patrimonial ruler recruited his officials at the beginning almost wholly from those who were personally dependent, slaves and serfs, and he could be absolutely sure of their obedience. However, the ruler was obliged, because of increased administrative needs, rivalries, and jealousies of those who had risen in status and power, or the growing task of governing large areas, to go beyond his group of personal dependents. The danger here for the ruler was that these officials might begin to challenge his authority, as the military force might also do.

Who were the officials? The list in China included the Grand Astrologer, Grand Augur, Grand Physician, superintendent of the palace, commander of the palace guards, and controllers of dikes and canals.[68] At one point in Chinese history, in the third century, the antitraditionalist autocrat opposed the socially influential educated group, the literati. Pure absolutism was ushered in, a rule based on personal favorites regardless of descent or education, a characteristic of Oriental sultanism.[69] Eventually, the old families, the literati, the army, and the peasant sibs revolted violently against this harsh sultanism. From this revolt emerged the principle of "enlightened" patrimonialism, that personal merit should qualify a man for office, but that principle made slow headway. Patrimonialism became the structural form fundamental to the Confucian spirit.[70]

A variant in this general analysis of patrimonialism was what Weber calls "estate-type domination" (*Standische Herrschaft*), a form of patrimonial authority under which the administrative staff appropriated certain powers and economic assets.[71] This appropriation might be administered by a group or by individuals who owned property or whose functions were based on heredity. These groups or individuals could thus limit the lord's discretion in selecting his administrative staff and in executing the administrative process. Examples of this estate-type control were the feudal knight, the count (or lord), and the Indian *jagirdar*.

PATRIMONIALISM GEOGRAPHICALLY

Where were the patrimonial systems located? No clear picture, either of geographic area or historical period, emerges, but references appear in a number of Weber's works. In no particular order patrimonialism is observed by him in areas ruled by sultans, the Safavid empire in Iran, the ancient Egyptian empire, especially during the New Kingdom period, Assyria, Babylon, the Hyksos and the Hittites empires, the Ming empire in China, the Tokugawa Shogunate in Japan, Mughal India and the empires of Akkad, the Mongols, Abbasides and the Mamluks, early Germanic and Slavic European tribes, late Roman and Byzantine empires, and the Ottoman Turks.

Weber held that the first consistent patrimonial-bureaucratic administration was in ancient Egypt.[72] Originally it was staffed solely with royal clients, servants attached to the pharaoh's court. Later, officials had to be recruited from the outside, from the ranks of the scribes, the only group technically suited for it. All Egyptians were dependent on a centralized Oriental despotic system that regulated river control and vast construction projects, required compulsory labor, and imposed penalties and punishments. To perform these tasks the pharaoh, who possessed an economic monopoly, mobilized his subjects by the thousands. The pharaoh's power depended on his control of both the army, equipped and provisioned out of royal supplies and storehouses, and of appointed officials. The needs of the pharaoh were met by provisions in kind supplied by the mobilized labor force.

India was not a pure example of patrimonialism.[73] Its history varied between the condition of petty kingdoms, territorial fiefs and hereditary economic rights, prebends and a stratum of landlords, and kingdoms that lacked central entrepreneurs and the condition of central, patrimonial empires whose rulers engaged in trade and controlled prices, and sometimes registered all inhabitants, required them to have passports, controlled their lives, and appointed relatives as regents of state territories. The ruler restricted activity and pleasures that might interfere with the will to work and used spies to report on the private lives of subjects. Yet he was also conscious of and restricted by the caste system and the chief religions: Hindu, especially the Brahmans, and Islam.

FEUDAL AND PREBEND SYSTEMS

Weber contended that East and West had taken different economic paths paralleled by different social and political structures. In medieval times the West had feudal economies, primarily oriented to land, and a manorial system of estates. Feudal systems could lead to the development of capitalism. Land rights were inherited; individuals obtained privileges and fiefs by law and contract, which allowed them certain governing powers; rights and duties were allocated on the basis of relevant standards of honor of a particular social group; and lords provided military service for the ruler in return for protection.

The essence of manorial feudalism, in this decentralized system, was status consciousness, resting on notions of honor as the basis of fealty, military fitness, and seigneurial, knightly conduct manifested by courage, loyalty, and heroism. The warriors supplied their own weapons and exercised power in areas given them on a hereditary basis. In this system of reciprocal obligations of the ruler and his subjects, officials were not personal dependents but individuals with a certain degree of authority who swore an oath of fealty to the ruler. Central government thus tended to be weaker than in Oriental systems, which lacked or retarded the growth of autonomous institutions.

In contrast to the West, Oriental systems were not based on estates or feudal aristocracy but on prebendal relationships, which meant certain rights to land ownership, allowances, and support. The important distinction for Weber was that these rights were conditional, not inherited, thus allowing the ruler to control his subjects or subordinates in an arbitrary way. The patrimonial ruler tried to prevent benefices from becoming hereditary rights, thus maintaining a strong central system. At various points Weber provided examples of nonhereditary benefices in Oriental systems. They included the income of the Turkish *spahis*, Japanese *samurai*, tax income of certain districts administered by officials in China, tax collection by Indian tax farmers, and army recruitment by *condottieri*. In India, the king farmed out tax collection in return for a fixed lump sum to people who became a class of landlords, *Zamindari* in Bengal and *Talukdari* in Oudh.[74]

In general, subjects obtained from their patrimonial rulers certain rights: allowances in goods or money, the right to use land in return for services, and appropriation of property income and fees.[75] The problem for the ruler was that some of these rights might result in a degree of personal and economic independence from the ruler. In addition, payment to mercenaries, or grants of land, especially if they became hereditary, might lead to the development of an incipient feudal system.

In Weber's analysis, the distinction between feudalism and patrimonialism from an economic point of view was never absolute. A significant qualification of his general argument arose if the patrimonial ruler could not pay his mercenaries and therefore had to give them access to revenues and tax payments of subjects, or had to transfer to the military official the position, originally independent of the military office, of the tax official who received a fixed remuneration.[76] The patrimonial ruler therefore tried to counter the social prestige and any independent power of local officials and tried to oppose an autonomous status for any possible feudal aristocracy or economically independent bourgeoisie.[77]

Preventing officials from gaining power in their own right became a problem from a practical point of view, especially that of geography. Territories near the center of the patrimonial empire formed the ruler's dynastic land holdings and were directly administered by patrimonial court officials.[78] However, for financial reasons, costs that could not be paid out of the ruler's own reserves, or because of administrative necessity, the outlying provinces were administered in patrimonial fashion by governors chosen by the ruler who might exercise strong powers of their own. These governors did not pass on all contributions made to the ruler but only the surplus remaining after local demands had been met. As the servants of the ruler became more numerous and organized, they gained some independent authority and limited the ruler's power by contractual arrangements.

Patrimonial political structures differed from patriarchy and feudal systems, based on stereotyped and fixed relationships between lord and vassal.[79] Weber's distinction between the two forms is crucial. Feudalism, with its contracts, personal fealty, and importance of manorial lords, tended to lead to a decentralized system. Patrimonialism prevented the emergence of decentralization and might lead to sultanic despotism. Both might include tradition as a fundamental element but patrimonialism also embodied discretionary power and arbitrariness.[80] The ruler was suspicious of every attempt of his officials to become autonomous and decided the extent to which he should delegate authority.

DESPOTISM AND STRUGGLE FOR POWER

Patrimonialism was Weber's "ideal type" of despotism, but, as in all other political systems, it was not devoid of struggles for power among the ruler, officials, and local notables and groups, and between the center and the periphery of the country. The struggle was never fully resolved, taking different forms with varying consequences in the countries that Weber examined. Patrimonial power was despotic, but it had limitations and took different forms. Weber used as an example the role of the Indian king whose administration was essentially confined to raising manpower for the army and raising taxes. He sought to maintain a balance in the country, avoiding dependence on any one interest group by using officials from different strata groups. To maintain support the ruler granted concessions. He commissioned, in a form of military prebend, an individual to recruit soldiers for him and then gave or leased that person the yields from land revenue. Similarly, in a form of a tax prebend, the ruler farmed out the right to collect taxes to an individual who in return gave him an agreed upon sum. In a general way, a "consensual community" existed by which people who were not personal servants accepted the ruler as legitimate provided he exercised power on traditional lines.

In China a measure of decentralization and local autonomy resulted from a number of factors. The Chinese ruler had a relatively small number of officials in the central government. The lack of knowledge of local conditions and languages by central officials, the size of the country, the distance of local officials and governors from the center of authority, and the inadequacy of transport all led to a degree of independent activity outside the center.[81] The main group exerting local power in the villages was the *sib*, the kinship group of tribal elders, a hereditary mobility linked with an ancestor cult and piety in the family. The institution of the *sib* operated in the administration of the smallest political units as well as in economic associations. The patrimonial rule from the central government sometimes clashed with the sibs' strong counterbalance from below.[82] These local interests, including guilds as well as the system of lineage of hereditary rights, tried to prevent economic and administrative changes if these posed a threat to their interests and resisted centralized control and hindered change. Fortunately for the central ruler those local groups did not unite against him or form a united status group. The patrimonial administration took serious notice of the attitude of the merchants' guilds only in a "static" way and when the maintenance of tradition and of the guilds' special privileges was at stake.[83] The literati, the cultured status group, did challenge sultanism and the eunuch system that supported it; the struggle between literati and sultanism lasted two millennia.[84] The literati were particularly threatened by the harem system because of the fact that emperors who were not of age when they succeeded to the throne were under the tutelage of women in the harem.

In India the patrimonial prince vied with the guild membership, which was at times powerful but which he, with the aid of the Brahmans, mastered. The great king, Ashoka (273 BC–232 BC), consolidated the ancient petty kingdoms under his rule and leveled the political power of the groups that had status and power. Religion also was used by contending groups, prince, priests, and monks, as an instrument to exert power over the masses.[85]

In general, the patrimonial ruler faced a variety of political and administrative problems and potential challenges.[86] To retain power and to deal with actual or potential challenges, the patrimonial ruler used a variety of political and organizational devices. Wherever possible the ruler tried to avoid monopolization of offices by groups that had status by appointing people dependent on him.[87] Administrative functions might be split among officials to prevent any from becoming too powerful. New or special tasks were given to favorites. Officials were appointed only for short terms. The office of military commander was separated from that of the tax collector or tax farmer. Officials were excluded from areas where they had relatives or where they owned land or were natives, and they were continually transferred. Spies and controllers, such as the Chinese censors, supervised them.

Competition was encouraged between provinces and among officials. Competing offices might be created in the same district. Examinations for officials and awards of certificates of conduct fostered competition and prevented the emergence of an elite group. If at all possible, benefices granted would not become hereditary rights. The ruler also might employ celibates for certain important positions. To enforce his authority, the ruler made regular visits through the country. All officials, in addition to their administrative tasks proper, had to attend the ruler when he traveled. They might be obliged to come to the court from time to time or send their sons there. To foster economic prosperity, the ruler might grant a monopoly for some economic pursuits and require the individual and his heirs to fulfill obligations and obey the ruler.[88] The prince also had a fiscal and military interest by granting small holdings to support peasant families thus preventing their exploitation by local lords. In the fluid power relationship in India, the king sometimes made use of distinguished secular nobles or priestly officials; at other times, the king appointed lower-class people to political positions. The patrimonial ruler employed as officials not only Brahmans, but also scribes of lower castes such as the *Shudra*.[89]

PATRIMONIALISM AND THE ECONOMY

Weber did not see the patrimonial economy as wholly in the hands of the ruler nor envisage a consistent pattern of intervention and control. The servile population performed obligatory services for the ruler, and their villages bore the burdens of providing resources.[90] The individual peasant, in countries such as Egypt, Mesopotamia, and Japan, was bound not only to the soil but also to his village, a situation Weber compared to that in the Russian *mir*. The needs of the ruler had to be met, wholly or mainly in kind. But rulers also tried to impose taxation. Weber illustrated the double burden by describing the Egyptian system of grain banks to which peasants contributed their whole production system and at the same time had to pay monetary taxes, particularly in Ptolemaic Egypt.

The prince controlled the money economy in a number of ways. He had his own means of production and trade for his own use and also for the market, as in Egypt and Babylonia. The household of the prince and the industrial establishment were thus intertwined: this was the "*oikos*-economy." A second method was for the prince to farm out collection of taxes to "adventurers," as in India; the ruler took a fixed amount of the receipts and the rest went to the administrative officials. A third device was the ruler's assignment of taxation to soldiers; this occurred when the prince was unable to pay the soldiers. As a result, Turkish soldiers from the tenth century on developed into a military nobility. Weber saw the political functions of securing money by private contractors, officials, or soldiers as the basis of what he called "Oriental feudalism." Allocation of the tax revenues of land and people to the troops of the slave army, whose arbitrary behavior meant legal insecurity of the taxpaying population, could paralyze commerce and the money economy; since the period of the Seljuks (1050–1150), the Oriental market economy had declined or stagnated.[91]

In some passages Weber wrote, as Marx had done, of the consequences for politics and religion that resulted from the need to regulate water in some Oriental economies, especially China, Asia Minor, and Egypt. In the Western world, settlements resulted from the clearing of land. Water control and irrigation were established for systematic and organized husbandry to use. In the Orient, the strong central regulation of water was undertaken for quite different reasons: the need for defense against nomads, a source of revenue, and the need to regulate the great river valleys, which flooded regularly and therefore required construction of dikes, dams, and canals. These large-scale enterprises required strong government and an organized administration to provide compulsory labor, supplies, and storage facilities. In China, the power of patrimonial officialdom was based on river regulation and tremendous military fortifications.[92]

In the Middle East, as in the empire of Thebes, because of the need for water regulation the king required an organized bureaucracy: those in Egypt and Mesopotamia were the oldest officialdom in the world established for this purpose. The result was the servile position of the population in relation to the prince: obligatory services of all the dependents and the liability of villages for the expense. The water question not only required the existence of the bureaucracy but also affected military activity. The military campaigns of the Assyrian and Babylonian kings were mainly hunts to obtain slaves to build canals and bring stretches of the desert under tillage. In China, as in Egypt and Mesopotamia, the need to control the rivers was a decisive factor for the economy, the inception of central authority, and the creation of a patrimonial officialdom.[93] The countries differed: in northern China, priority was given to dike construction against floods or canal construction to provide inland water transport, while in the Middle East canals for irrigation were most important.

In these countries, the need for water and its regulation had consequences for the nature of religion there. The God of the Middle East was modeled on the king who "created" the harvest. The supreme Deity was promoted there as the King of Heavens who had "created" man and the world from nothing and demanded obedience from everyone. In China the fact that the emperor was simultaneously and primarily high priest demarcated the system from that of the Western Holy Roman Empire where religious and secular rule were separated. As high priest, the Chinese emperor was essential for maintaining cultural cohesion among the individual states. His imperial authority partly originated from the magical charisma associated with his regulation of water.[94]

Weber held that the patrimonial state left economic life alone, at least as far as production and the profit economy were concerned. In China, the government confined itself to the care of the tide and maintenance of the water routes, necessary for the production of rice. It had no "commercial policy" in the modern sense.[95] The economy was left to itself to a large extent. The government did not have to cope with a self-conscious bourgeois class as in the West and took little notice of merchants' guilds. The ruler did not oppose any new property arrangement as long as it did not lead to a new power exercising independent authority.

Weber summarized the factors that prevented or obstructed the development of capitalism in patrimonial societies and indicated some of the various ways that patrimonialism financed its domination, pointing out three in particular.[96] One was by the *oikos-economy*, which was maintained by the local ruler to satisfy needs and was based wholly or primarily on contributions in kind and by compulsory services. The development of a market system was obstructed, money mostly used for consumption, and thus capitalism could not emerge. A second mode was the ruler's obtaining the services of socially privileged groups. This also limited the development of markets because property and productive capacity of these people were largely preempted for the ruler's needs. A third way was resort to monopolies; here again opportunity for the development of markets was limited. Weber concluded that opportunities for profit were only in the hands of the ruler and his administrative staff.

Patrimonial rulers often fostered organization of associations collectively responsible for public duties. Guilds and other groups became responsible for services or contributions of their members. They gained privileges in return for duties.[97] Nevertheless, residents were personal dependents of the despotic patrimonial ruler, bound to their occupation and subject to his arbitrary will and to central political control. This was particularly noticeable in Egypt. The need for forced labor, performance of public duties in residential localities, and tax payments meant that all the country was regarded as the household of the pharaoh. The ruler relied on his army and officials, maintaining them out of his storehouses and treasury, and sometimes giving them land grants and benefices, allowances in kind. The degree of despotism in the system depended on whether the army and officials could limit the exercise of arbitrary authority.

MILITARY SUPPORT

The patrimonial prince was supported by military forces recruited from various sources.[98] Soldiers could be patrimonial slaves, retainers living on allowances, or *coloni*. Pharaohs and Mesopotamian kings, as well as other powerful private lords in antiquity and in the Middle Ages, employed their *coloni* as personal troops; in the Orient serfs branded with the lord's property mark were also used. A second group was slaves who did not take part in agricultural production. The Islamic caliphate and Oriental rulers relied for centuries on armies of purchased slaves. The Abbasids, who ruled in Baghdad into the thirteenth century (750–1258), bought and militarily trained Turkish slaves who were tied to them. In later generations, from the thirteenth to the sixteenth centuries a military group, such as the Mamlukes, arose from Turkish and Egyptian slaves. The difficulty for the regime, especially in Egypt, was the growing strength and independence of the troops, partly because they became hereditary and partly because they were given land in place of pay. Beginning in the thirteenth century the Mamlukes became, more than the nominal ruler, the real effective power. In a sense, the patrimonial regime at this point took on aspects of feudalism because the troops were now in possession of land from which they obtained income from taxes and as landlords.

A third type of support came from the conscription, from the fourteenth century, by the Ottoman rulers of boys from conquered peoples who were tribal or religious aliens, mostly from southeastern Europe, for the professional army of Janissaries. Recruited at ages between ten and fifteen, the boys were drilled for about five years, got Islamic religious instruction, and were incorporated into the army. The Janissaries became a powerful and privileged group, monopolizing senior military positions. A fourth type was mercenaries, who often became bodyguards of the ruler and who were paid in kind, especially in precious metals. The ruler therefore had to have resources to pay them, either by trading or producing for the market or by levying monetary tributes on the subjects. In a fifth type, the patrimonial ruler might rely on persons who had been granted land, but who rendered military rather than economic services.

The monarch's troops in the ancient Orient were partly recruited in this fashion. Weber specifically alludes to the "warrior caste" of Egypt, the Mesopotamian fief-warriors, the Hellenistic cleruchs (the special type of colonies of Athenians who provided a military garrison in a conquered country), and the Cossacks.

A class factor was present in recruitment. In this system whenever individuals were recruited or conscripted from subjects, rather than from tribal aliens or pariah castes, they came from the property-less or nonprivileged parts of society, and especially from the rural masses. Soldiers were conscripted for permanent service, not just for occasional campaigns. Socially and economically powerful individuals were exempt because they were indispensable to the rationalization of the economy. The royal army was patrimonial, a purely personal army of the prince, because it was equipped and maintained out of supplies and revenues belonging to the ruler. However, many intermediate forms existed between such a pure patrimonial army and military organizations based on self-equipment and self-provisioning, especially when land had been granted. The ruler's authority rested on more than his military power, but his dilemma was that he, a personal despot, required a strong military force to maintain his rule. Because he was so dependent on the army, difficulties for the regime might arise in the event of his death or military defeats. Such was the case in the Roman Empire and under Oriental sultanism. The result was the sudden collapse of a patrimonial regime and great political instability. To a large extent, this was the fate of rulers in the Middle East, the classic location of "sultanism."

FATHER OF HIS PEOPLE

The patrimonial ruler sought the goodwill of his subjects. He appeared in the guise of the protector of the people against privileged status groups and the guardian of the welfare of his subject; he claimed to be not the warrior-king but the good king, "the father of his people." This feature of patrimonial regimes differed from the feudal system where the welfare of tenants was only important for the lord when it was a matter of economic survival, and where the landed aristocracy was the crucial privileged group.[99] Feudalism was always domination by the few who had military skills. Unlike feudal systems, which could afford to forego to a large extent the goodwill of subjects, patrimonialism was domination by one individual and strongly depended on that goodwill, if it could not rely on its alien troops for protection. Unlike feudalism, which was characterized by the free camaraderie of solemnly promised fealty, patrimonialism was based on an authoritarian relationship of father and children. The king in India declared that all subjects, regardless of religious belief, were his "children."[100] The Emperor Ashoka in that country, after expressing regrets for "unavoidable" butchery during which many pious people were killed, portrayed his regime as an ethical and charitable ideal of a welfare state, working for the public welfare in order that his subjects should be "happy" and "attain heaven."

Weber also referred to the legends of the welfare state in Egypt and the later Mesopotamian great kingdoms.[101] These legends described the various charitable policies instituted by various kings such as Nebuchadnezzar, Cyrus, and Darius. They claimed that no waif had been harmed nor any poor man; no hereditary land had been taken away; and that no inordinate taxation had been imposed. The ethic of charity was part of the patrimonial welfare policy and was, Weber wrote, projected into the heavenly rule of the world. This policy was developed first by the petty patrimonial princes and feudal lords of the Middle Kingdom of Egypt, and then systematized by the scribes, priests, and priestly influenced moralists in accordance with what Weber called a "hierocratic welfare policy." The concern for the welfare of his people was related to the ruler's economic policy. He did not object to people acquiring property through rational methods; he favored this if it did not establish new powers that gained independent authority. Typical of patrimonialism was the rise of men from poverty, from slavery and lowly service for the ruler, to the precarious all-powerful position of the favorite.

WHY NO CAPITALISM?

One historically important factor in the development of strong, centralized patrimonial bureaucracies was trade.[102] This happened in the Mongolian empire and the kingdoms of the Teutonic Migration. The general pattern was that tribes who lived adjacent to territories with a highly developed money economy invaded these, took their precious metals, and founded new polities on these territories. Weber made clear that the causal influence of trade on the formation of political associations was not unequivocal, but often there was a connection between trade and the rise of a simple chief to the rank of a prince. By contrast, in feudal systems trade was on the whole quite antagonistic to the tight-knit structure of the feudal hierarchy.

Various factors hindered economic development in the Orient, though some factors such as private wealth, internal commerce, and some external commerce might have favored the emergence of a capitalist economy. In patrimonial systems, no capitalist entrepreneurs emerged, and the accumulation of capital, especially landed wealth, did not primarily derive from rational profit making. The power of all Oriental rulers was based on their possession of precious metals in raw or finished form. But, Weber also argued, the origin of a patrimonial political ruler and strong centralized bureaucracies was to a considerable extent the result of trade, especially foreign trade over which the ruler might have a direct monopoly or from which he might benefit through tariffs, tolls, and other tributes.

The Oriental economy was basically stagnant or had declined. In Egypt, for example, the system appeared as a single, large *oikos* ruled patrimonially by the pharaoh, and the administration always retained characteristics of the *oikos* economy.[103] The needs of the patrimonial ruler were met wholly or mainly in kind, by labor, gifts, food, and taxes from subjects. Economic relationships tended to be strictly tradition based, obstructing development of markets, especially where the ruler controlled monopolies. Though priority was given to the ruler's needs, the economy did at times expand, and the ruler might obtain income from profit-making enterprises as did the pharaohs in Egypt on a large scale.

In China, where the economy was also stationary, capitalism failed to develop for a number of reasons, mostly related to the structure of the state but also related to the Confucian worldview, its ethic, and its effect on economic behavior.[104] Rational entrepreneurial capitalism was handicapped not only by the lack of a formal law, a rational administration and judiciary, and the ramifications of a system of prebends but also by the lack of a particular "mentality" and the attitude rooted in the Chinese "ethos" and peculiar to a stratum of officials and aspirants to office.

One factor hindering development was the character of the city, which in China and throughout the Orient lacked political autonomy. Its inhabitants did not try to obtain a charter that might guarantee its freedom. In sharp contrast with Western societies, cities in China and India could not legally make contracts, either economic or political, could not file law suits, and could not function as corporate bodies. The great Middle Eastern cities, such as Babylon, were completely at the mercy of the royal bureaucracy. The prosperity of Chinese cities did not primarily depend on the citizens' enterprising spirit in economic and political ventures but rather on the imperial administration, especially those involved in water regulation. Weber also commented, in his analysis of administrative ethos and style of life, that patrimonialism was interested in public peace, the preservation of traditional means of livelihood, and the satisfaction of subjects. It was alien to and distrustful of capitalist development, which would revolutionize existing social conditions.[105] Another general factor affecting development was fiscal arbitrariness, especially in sultanism, and lack of calculability because of the irrationalities in the general administration, including that of law and taxation. The development of markets was limited. In a patrimonial regime only certain types of capitalism were able to develop: some trading, tax farming, lease and sale of offices, provision of supplies for the state and the financing of wars, and, under certain circumstances, capitalist plantations and other colonial enterprises. But these could not lead to a full capitalist system.

THE SOCIAL FRAMEWORK

Development was also hindered by the social framework in the various countries of the Orient. Ritualistic considerations affecting caste and clan organizations prevented the emergence of a firm economic policy, autonomous urban institutions or cities, or a solid middle class, all conditions necessary for capitalist enterprises. Weber illustrates this by the presence of castes in India and sibs in China.

In discussing the Indian social framework and politics, Weber held that some industry existed there, but it was extremely unlikely that industrial capitalism could ever have originated because of the caste system. Weber called that system "closed status groups," which were based on social honor and heightened traditionalism and therefore hindered the development of economies based on competition and open markets as in Western societies.[106] The caste order was a product of Brahmanical thought and could not have lasted without Brahman influence. Each caste had its own dharma, a ritually required way of life and a work pattern based on the inherited trade of its members. This limited the role of merchant and craft-guild organizations, which in the West allowed apprentices free choice of masters and changes of trade. The caste system, with each caste having its own ethical and ritual obligations, also precluded fraternization of the guilds that led to fraternization of the citizenry. It was one of the constitutive principles of the castes that there be ritually inviolable barriers against complete commensalism (sharing a common table) among different castes.

Caste was also linked with kinship social relationships, with clans that had different levels of status and authority, a form of "clan charisma." Caste and clan mutually reinforced traditionalism in Indian social life and determined relationships on the basis of birth and hereditary occupation. In Weber's formula, the magical charisma of the clans contributed greatly to caste estrangement; the caste order served greatly to stabilize the *sib*. The caste system hindered the development of guilds on Western lines. That was why the beginnings of guild organizations in the cities in India had not led to city autonomy of the Western type, nor, after the development of the great patrimonial states, to social and economic organization of the territories corresponding to the "territorial economy" of the West.

In China, the powerful lineage body was the *sib*, the cohesive kinship group that protected individuals connected to it against economic hardships. The *sib* was a self-sufficient unit with military and judicial capabilities.[107] The ancestor cult, ascribing power to the ancestral spirits, was the only folk cult that was not managed by the Caesaro-papist government and its officials. Instead it was managed by the head of the household, as the house priest, with the assistance of the family. Family piety, resting on the belief in spirits, was by far the strongest influence on man's conduct. The *sib* ties prevented the formation of impersonal contract relationships, the type needed in capitalism. Weber argued that a great achievement of ethical (European) religions was to shatter the fetters of the *sib*. In the Orient the *sib* claimed the right to impose sanctions on its members and enforced this claim. It withstood the ruthless encroachments of the patrimonial administration and its activities. That administration was confronted with a resolute and traditional power that was stronger because it operated continuously and was supported by the most intimate personal associations.

RELIGION AND THE RULER

Patrimonialism and religion were interconnected; the ruler was the head of spiritual forces as well as of the social order. Imperial authority emerged from his magical charisma, but he had to prove this magical charisma through military success by securing good weather for harvest and by guaranteeing internal order. The Chinese monarch was the old rainmaker of magical religion, translated into ethics. He had to prove himself as the "Son of Heaven." Economic development was unlikely to occur in this setting; the patrimonial regime prevented social change because it rested on filial piety and on religious authority, both of which preserved tradition.

The Chinese situation was even more complex because of the role of the literati, Confucianism, and kinship groups. The literati as a group had been the ruling stratum in the country and had contributed to its stability.[108] The literati lived by a strict code, rigid and formal, sought self-perfection, and were skilled at writing, the basis of their prestige. They were the products of Chinese education, which had a ritualistic and ceremonial character and a traditionalist and ethical one. The literati were qualified for office on the basis of that education and by examination. They were, in China, the bearers of progress to a rational administration, based on the concept of "public office," the ethos of official responsibility. Possessing a monopoly of literacy and political office, the literati did not challenge traditional social relations or administrative methods. Regarding religion as a useful way of domesticating the masses, they helped maintain the stability of the state religion and that of the economy.

Confucian rationalism meant rational adjustment to the world not its transformation; Puritan rationalism meant rational mastery of the world. The Confucian way of life was rational but, unlike Puritanism, was determined from without rather than from within. This did not release the "capitalist spirit" as it was found in the modern economy. The Confucian "mentality" with its autonomous laws was strongly counteractive to capitalist development. The Confucian ideal of "gentility" was preferred to that of "vocation." Confucian ethics at its core rejected professional specialization, modern expert bureaucracy, and special training; above all, it rejected training in economics for the pursuit of profit. Unlike Puritanism, where the inward state of the believer led to a certain way of life, the Chinese religion, linked as it was to magic, emphasized an ethic where demands were made by external factors. The fact that Confucianism was anchored in magic meant the inviolability of tradition.

In a general comment, in his analysis of China and India, Weber discussed the traditional factors that accounted for the strength of kinship ties in those countries, the nationwide bureaucracy in China, and the lack of political autonomy in Asian cities, partly through the unbroken *sib* power and partly through caste alienation. The origin of a rational and inner-worldly ethic was associated in the West with the appearance of thinkers and prophets who appeared in a social context which was alien to Asiatic cultures.[109] Without that context in Western societies in which civic status groups of the cities were important, neither Judaism, nor Christianity, nor Hellenistic thinking was conceivable.

RELIGION AND POLITICS

A significant part of Weber's thought and writing was devoted to the sociology of religion. Examining the major world religions he sought to understand their inner orientations, their effect on conduct, their connection with social and political life, and the differences between Western and Eastern religions. It is useful to start discussion of Weber's thoughts on this issue by viewing his comparative statement in his own words.

"The Occidental church is a uniformly rational organization with a monarchical head and a centralized control of piety. That is, it is headed not only by a personal transcendental god, but also by a terrestrial ruler of enormous power, who actively controls the lives of his subjects. Such a figure is lacking in the religions of Eastern Asia, partly for historical reasons, partly because of the nature of the religions in question. . . . The Asiatic hierarchs in Taoism and the other hereditary patriarchs of Chinese and Hindu sects were always partly mystagogues, partly the objects of anthropolatric veneration, and partly – as in the cases of the Dalai Lama and Tashi Lama – the chiefs of a completely monastic religion of magical character. Only in the Occident, where the monks became the disciplined army of a rational bureaucracy of office, did other-worldly asceticism become increasingly systematized into a methodology of active, rational conduct of life. Moreover, only in the Occident was the additional step taken – by ascetic Protestantism – of transferring rational asceticism into the life of the world. The inner-worldly order of dervishes in Islam cultivated a planned procedure for achieving salvation, but this procedure, for all its variations, was oriented ultimately to the mystical quest for salvation of the Sufis."[110]

In addition, the Occidental kind of religious rulership, the clerical hierarchy or "hierocracy," as Weber termed it, "lived in a state of tension with the political power and constituted its major restraint; this contrasted with the purely Caesaro-papist or purely theocratic structures of antiquity and the Orient. In the Occident, authority was set against authority, legitimacy against legitimacy, one office charisma against the other, yet in the minds of rulers and ruled the ideal remained the unification of both political and hierocratic power."[111] In Weber's analysis, Occidental and Oriental religions took different paths. Confucianism and the Roman Church were "the two greatest powers of religious rationalism in history."[112] Hinduism and Brahmins had their own rational system of thought. However, Oriental religions did not give rise to an ethic that fostered economic development, individual rights, or limitation of political power. Nor did they emphasize the separation of the secular and the sacred as did Western religions, thus enabling political and intellectual development outside the church. Nor did a powerful priesthood or group of prophets emerge to challenge patrimonial bureaucracy.

Contrary to frequent misinterpretation, Weber did not hold that the spirit of capitalism arose as a result of the Reformation or that capitalism as an economic system was a creation of the Reformation. He did speak of "elective affinities" between religious beliefs and ethics and socioeconomic factors.[113] Whatever the interpretation of *The Protestant Ethic*, it is apparent that Calvinism, belief and practice, with its implicit call for rational mastery of the world, affected social, political, and economic behavior and the move to modernity, the emergence of modern society, and capitalist economics. The Calvinist, Weber wrote, "strode into the market-place of life, slammed the door of the monastery behind it, and took to penetrate just the daily routine of life, with its methodicalness, to fashion it into a life in the world, but neither of nor for this world."[114] Weber recognized that the popular religions of Asia "left room for the acquisitive drive of the tradesman," among other things.[115] Nevertheless, no motivation toward a rational system for the methodical control of life flowed from them in accordance with divine commandments. Nor was there development toward modern capitalism or the evolution of a "capitalist spirit."

Weber drew the contrast. "The Occidental sects of the religious virtuosos have fermented the methodical rationalization of conduct, including economic conduct. These sects have not constituted valves for the longing to escape from the senselessness of work in this world, as did the Asiatic communities of the ecstatics: contemplative, orgiastic, or apathetic." In a striking passage he compares the various popular religions of Asia, which, in contrast to ascetic Protestantism, see the world as a "great enchanted garden, in which the practical way to orient oneself, or to find security in this world or the next, was to revere or coerce the spirits and seek salvation through ritualistic, idolatrous, or sacramental procedures. No path led from the magical religiosity of the non-intellectual classes of Asia to a rational, methodical control of life. Nor did any path lead to that methodical control from the world accommodation of Confucianism, from the world-rejection of Buddhism, from the world-conquest of Islam, or from the messianic expectations and economic pariah law of Judaism."[116]

The consequence was that Oriental religions did not challenge existing institutions or orthodoxy. In the Christian West salvation was viewed as ethical justification before God, which ultimately could be accomplished and maintained only by some sort of active conduct within the world. For the Asiatic, the world was something simply presented to man, something that had been in the nature of things from all eternity; for the Occidental, the world is a work that had been created or performed, and not even the ordinances of the world are eternal. Occidental Rome developed and maintained a rational law; the relationship of man to God became a sort of legally defined subjection. The Oriental religions posited an impersonal divine power or a God standing within a world that was self-regulated by the causal claims of *Karma*.

The Western churches rejected or limited ecstatic procedures and individually planned procedures for attaining salvation, thus becoming one of the sources for a strictly empirical rationalism with a thoroughly practical political orientation. Labor emerged as the distinctive mark of Christian mysticism and as an instrument of hygiene and asceticism. Ascetic Protestantism translated rational asceticism into the life of the world. The Protestant ethic proposed that the world was the place in which to fulfill duties by rational behavior according to the will of an absolutely transcendental God. Worldly success was construed as a sign that God's blessing rested on sober, purposive behavior not oriented exclusively to worldly acquisition.[117]

Eastern religions fostered contemplation rather than practical activity. In India, religion hindered the rationalization of conduct in life, and thus did not allow the community to achieve the "spirit of capitalism." Hinduism, with its dogma of the unalterability of the world order, allocated positions on the basis of ritual and rigid social doctrine. Latent within Buddhism, in a sense a "democratic" religion, was its devaluation of the worldly order in general. That devaluation led to a passive attitude, which was intensified by patrimonialism and made it easier for the regime to control its subjects. Neither of the two religions in India led to social action as in the West.[118]

Weber viewed Hinduism not as a fixed dogma but as ritual practices tied to caste; salvation was related to an individual's fulfillment of obligations to his caste. Two basic principles reinforced rigidity in social behavior and were a barrier to social innovations that it dreaded. The first principle was the *samsara* essential belief: the soul was immortal and was reincarnated, and there was a transmigration of souls. The other was the *karma* doctrine, the most consistent theodicy ever produced by history. This doctrine stated that everything existed in an immutable, eternal order and cycle, and that the world was a strictly rational, ethically determined, well-ordered cosmos. As long as the *karma* doctrine was intact, revolutionary ideas or progressivism was inconceivable. It was impossible to shatter traditionalism, based on caste ritualism anchored in *karma* doctrine, by rationalizing the economy.[119]

The Hindu Brahmans, like the members of the Chinese bureaucracy, accepted the providential power of the harmonious and rational order of the world. The Hindu sacred scriptures made no distinction between ritual and ethical sins and enjoined ritual obedience as virtually the sole method of atonement. As a consequence, the pattern of everyday life was structured by traditionalism. The Brahmans, however, did not attempt to rule Indian society or to establish a theocratic regime. They did not make ethical judgments about the regime, as long as they were reasonably treated. With their belief in union with the divine, the Brahmans sought salvation through rejection of the world and by achieving a state of mystical knowledge. They withdrew from the world, rather than attempting to master it. They did not challenge secular rulers, try to form a political group, or encourage an economy of free labor. Admired for their mystical knowledge and their magical powers, the Brahmans bound Hindus to traditional ways of life and to avoidance of social or economic change. They also accorded legitimacy to the patrimonial ruler.

Patrimonialism in China was grounded not only in the ethic of the literati and the piety of the masses but also on Confucianism with its ideal of propriety, emphasis on emotional control, filial allegiance to ancestors, belief in the lack of tension between nature and Deity, and acceptance for adjustment to the world and its orders and conventions. Society was conceived as one large patrimonially ruled community.[120] The Confucian ideal was watchful self-control, self-observation and reserve, propriety not acquisitiveness, and the dignified bearing of the gentleman. But this ideal did not lead to expressions of individuality.

Confucianism was a rational ethic that reduced confrontation with the world to a minimum. It viewed the world as the best of all possible worlds; human nature was disposed to be ethically good. The literati, holding official positions, did not advance economic activity, lest it disturb harmony. Rigid sacred tradition was coupled with favoritism and prerogative. Family piety facilitated and controlled the strong cohesion of the *sib* associations. The state required the patrimonial subject to adhere to the ancestor cult, worldly piety, and docility.[121] Weber compared the two religions in China. Taoism differed from Confucianism in that it held that magical and animist factors were pervasive. Its nonliterate and irrational character was even more traditionalist than Confucianism; magic, not adjustment to the world, was decisive for man's fate. All Asian religions (or their "soteriology") found *gnosis* (spiritual knowledge) to be the single way to the highest holiness and the single way to correct practice. This knowledge was not a rational implement of empirical science such as that which made possible the rational domination of nature and man, as in the Occident. It was mystical knowledge that led to a realm of the rationally unformed, to the devaluation of the world and its drives.

Weber was interested in the relation of religions to economic rationalism, particularly that type of rationalism that, since the sixteenth and seventeenth centuries, had come to dominate the Occident as part of civic life. A rational economy was a functional organization oriented to money prices and a competitive market. The more the world of the modern capitalist economy followed its own immanent laws, the less it had any relationship with a religious ethic that furthered brotherhood. Religions of salvation regarded with profound suspicion the impersonal economic forces that were specifically opposed to brotherliness.

Belief in magical traditions or mysticism had been a constant part of psychological consciousness. But only ascetic Protestantism completely eliminated magic and the supernatural quest for salvation.[122] It alone created the religious motivations for seeking salvation, primarily through immersion in one's worldly vocation and through the fostering of a capitalist spirit. By contrast the East lacked "a particular mentality" that led to a capitalist spirit. Hinduism, for example, did not lead to a secular ethic or to a capitalist spirit but rather to mystic contemplation or passive asceticism. For the Asiatic religions, the world was something simply presented to man; for the Occidental, even the

Occidental mystic, the world was a work that had been created or performed.[123]

ISLAM AND THE ORIENT

Islam was one of the six major world religions about which Weber wrote as part of his study of sociology of religion, domination, and law. His discussion of Islam consists of scattered remarks throughout his writings, not the full work he had intended but never wrote. Most of his comments are concentrated on the early years of Islam up to the period of the Abbasids (750–1258).[124] Weber wrote relatively little about Islam during the Ottoman and Mughal periods. For both specialized information on Islam and general insights he relied to a considerable degree on the work of well-known European scholars, especially Carl Heinrich Becker, founding editor of *Der Islam*, the Hungarian Ignaz Goldziher, Julius Wellhausen, and the Dutch Calvinist scholar Christian Snouck Hurgronje.[125] Most of Weber's remarks on Islam appear to stem from research between 1911 and 1914.

What is important in Weber's writings on Islamic societies is not any detailed treatment of the character of the Islamic religion but his analysis of the political and social structure of Islamic societies in the context of his discussion of such issues as patrimonialism, domination, charisma, prebendal and feudal societies, bureaucracy, status groups, and the development of capitalism. Studying the origin of Islam in Mecca and Medina in the seventh century, Weber regarded Muhammad not as the kind of prophet like Buddha, an exemplary man demonstrating the way to religious salvation, but rather, like Zoraster, as an ethical prophet.[126] The latter was an instrument for the proclamation of a god and his will, preaching as one who has received a commission from god and who demanded obedience as an ethical duty.

Islam, for Weber, was never a religion of salvation.[127] The god it taught was a lord of unlimited power, though merciful, the fulfillment of whose commandments was not beyond human power. Weber lists the chief ordinances of Islam and makes the point they are essentially political in character: ending private feuds in order to increase the group's striking power against external foes; regulating sexual relations; prohibition of usury; obtaining taxes for war; and support for the poor. The ordinances also imposed requirements for everyday living, distinctive clothing, rules about food and drink, and restrictions on gambling, which affected attitudes toward speculative business enterprises. Equally political was the only required dogma: recognition of Allah as the one god and of Muhammad as his Prophet.

Weber argued that originally Muhammad addressed his message to the urban strata, but his doctrine soon was taken up by a warring tribe. Weber held that Islam emerged in "pietistic urban conventicles" whose members tended to withdraw from the world. However, from its origin in Medina and subsequently, the religion was transformed into a national Arabic warrior religion and into one that strongly emphasized status such as the members of powerful families whose conversion made possible the decisive success of the Prophet. In his comparative discussion of the primary carriers or propagators of world religions, Weber held that in Islam "the warrior seeking to conquer the world" played that role. The Prophet spent most of his time in psychological preparation of the faithful for battle in order to maintain a maximum number of warriors for the faith. Jihad for salvation was translated into a movement for world domination and social prestige.

In a crucial comparison, Weber laid out the differences in belief in predestination between Christianity and Islam. In Puritanism, predestination affected the fate of the individual in the world beyond, and salvation came by maintaining ethical integrity in the affairs of everyday life. By contrast, predestination in early Islam determined not the fate of the individual in the world beyond but rather the uncommon events of this world and the fate of warriors especially during wars of faith.[128] This belief explains the fearlessness of the warrior but did not promote rationalization of daily life. Unlike the Puritan or Calvinist requirement for disciplined daily conduct as a "calling" in the service of God, which led to economic and social development, Islam required performance of the five daily prayers and other pillars of the faith. This ritual reinforced a static society and did not lead to changing the social order.

Politics and religion in Islam were interrelated from its beginning. Muhammad's actions, in essence holy war, forced the subjugation of the unbelievers to his political authority and to the economic domination of the faithful.[129] Unbelievers, if they belonged to other religions, were not exterminated but were taxed: their survival was considered desirable because of the financial contribution they would make. Religious war for Muslims, to an even greater degree than for Christians during the Crusades, was essentially an enterprise directed toward the acquisition of large holdings of real estate because it was primarily oriented to securing feudal revenue. Prophetic Islam became a religion with the characteristics of a distinctively feudal spirit.

Weber selected key words or phrases to define the role of the world religions and their interrelationship with society. In Confucianism it was "mentality," in Indian religions "the spirit of the caste system," and in Protestantism an "ethic." For Islam the key was the "warrior ethic." This meant the attainment of wealth and its display, a lack of interest in reshaping the world, and the absence of a clerical hierarchy. Islam differed from the other world religions in its particular interrelation of religion and politics. Related to Islam as a religion incarnating a warrior ethic was the concept of holy war (*jihad*), and the division of the world into the House of Islam and the House of War (the infidels). The most pious adherents of early Islam became the wealthiest, enriched with military booty. The wealth was displayed in luxurious raiment, perfume, and meticulous beard-coiffure. Muhammad completely rejected every type of monasticism, though not all asceticism, and opposed chastity, a precept that Weber surmised might have sprung from personal motivations. Weber suggested that the promises in ancient Islam pertaining to this world were martial promises: wealth, power, and glory were the rewards of war, and Islam's image of heaven was a soldier's sensual paradise. Orthodox Islam's conception of sin was a composite of ritual impurity, ritual sacrilege, and disobedience to the injunctions of the Prophet. Weber added that Islam accepted slavery, serfdom, the subordination of women, and polygamy; expressed disesteem for women; and kept religious requirements simple.

For Weber Islam did not require a comprehensive knowledge of the law. The ideal personality type was not the scholarly scribe but the warrior. Weber, however, acknowledged ascetic sects existed among Muslims and contrasted the Umayyads and their enjoyment of the world to the Islamic warriors maintaining rigid discipline in the fortresses located in conquered areas. Then there was the essentially irrational "dervish religion" of Sufism with its orgiastic and mystical elements, which Weber saw as adulterating mainstream Islam.[130] The asceticism of the dervishes was not, like that of ascetic Protestants, a religious ethic of vocation; the religious actions of the dervishes had little relationship to their secular occupations.

Islam, Weber argued, never really overcame the divisiveness of Arab tribal and clan allegiances as was shown by the internal conflicts of the caliphate; in its early period it remained the religion of a conquering army composed of tribes and clans.[131] The structure of Islam was also divided by the split between the Sunni and Shi'ite movements. That split arose because Muhammad had died without male heirs. His followers therefore could not found the caliphate on the basis of hereditary charisma, and during the Umayyad period (661–750) developed it in what opponents considered to be an outright antitheocratic manner. Shi'ism, which recognized the hereditary charisma of the descendants of Ali, son-in-law of Muhammad, and hence accepted the infallible doctrinal authority of the Iman, was antagonistic to orthodox Sunna, which was based on tradition and *idshma* (consensus ecclesiae).

Islam's dependence on a warrior class as its social carrier limited the growth of autonomous cities and the emergence of an independent burgher class; this contrasted with development in the West where the autonomous city was associated with urban piety, legal autonomy, occupational associations, and political involvement. Weber argued that only the West knew how to create a state in the modern sense, with a professional administration, specialized officialdom, and law based on the concept of citizenship.[132] Citizenship signified membership in the state and certain political rights. The notion of citizenship was unknown in the world of Islam, as it was in India and China. The city produced art and science; in economics it was the seat of commerce and industry; in politics it was the seat of government; and in military affairs it was a fortified post. Outside the Western world, cities were sites for government administration and military headquarters. But only in the West were there cities in the sense of a unitary community, with their own laws and courts, and autonomous administrations. In the Western city urban citizenry claimed the right to end seigneurial domination; this was the great – the revolutionary – innovation that differentiated the medieval Occidental city from all others. This new social form had free citizens governed by a "special law exclusively applicable to them and who thus form a legally autonomous status group."

Why did not cities in the sense of a political community exist outside the West? Weber gave different answers. Unlike the Western organization for defense, in the East the army of the prince was older than the city. There was no army of the people, feudal army, polis army, and medieval guild to set up an army. The king expressed his power through a military monopoly. The establishment of the city, in the Western sense, was restricted in Asia, partly because of the castes. In contrast to Christianity, which had helped destroy clan association, Islam "remained the religion of a conquering army structured in terms of tribes and clans."[133]

In Middle Eastern and Egyptian antiquity, cities were fortresses or official administrative centers with royal market privileges. In early Mesopotamia some city kingdoms existed, but with the growing power of the military kingdom, politically autonomous cities, Western-style bourgeois stratum, and urban law did not develop. In the cities of the Arabian coast, urban patrician families retained a rather unstable autonomy for a time, but their power did not lead the city to consolidate into a separate and independent association.[134] Weber's general conclusion was that in Asian and Oriental settlements that had some of the economic characteristics of "cities," only clan associations and sometimes occupational associations took organized action but never as a collective body of urban citizens. In Asia, and in Africa, nothing was known of corporate "burgher rights."[135]

The warrior bellicosity continued. After the final dissolution in 833 of the Arabian tribally organized theocratic levy whose religious zeal had been responsible for the great conquests, the caliphate and most units resulting from its dissolution relied for centuries on armies of purchased slaves. Islam had "characteristics of a distinctly feudal spirit," but Islamic regimes were prebendal, not feudal. On this issue, Weber was influenced by the distinguished scholar C. H. Becker who explained that the Islamic warrior's fief originated from payment for his services as a mercenary soldier or from tax farming.[136] The patrimonial ruler sometimes had to give the unpaid mercenaries direct access to the tax payments of his subjects. He also appointed military officials (emirs) as tax officials who drew fixed incomes. The benefices from tax farming came from different sources: revenues of a village or district, grants of land to supporters, or confiscation of taxes of subjects by emirs or soldiers. These prebendal arrangements differed from Western feudalism and did not lead to Western-style capitalism, nor did the theocratic and patrimonial Kadi-justice with its arbitrary, subjective judgments and decision making and legal uncertainty lead to a Western type of legal system.

Theocratic judicial administration necessarily interfered with the operation of a rational economic system and organization of work and technology.[137] The modern capitalist enterprise rested primarily on calculation and presupposed a legal and administrative system whose functioning could be rationally predicted, because of its fixed general norms. Capitalist enterprise could not exist where there was Kadi-justice, adjudication according to the judge's opinion in a given case, or according to other irrationalities of law and administration in Islamic societies. Weber saw the warrior religiosity in early Islam as antithetical to bourgeois activity. Yet he also argued that industrialization was not impeded by Islam as the religion of individuals but by the religiously determined structure of the Islamic *states* (Weber's emphasis), their officialdom, and their jurisprudence.[138] He had already made the point that the patrimonial state lacked the political and procedural predictability indispensable for capitalist development, which needed rational rules of modern bureaucratic administration. Patrimonial arbitrariness had a negative anticapitalist effect.

Islamic law, Weber held, was a combination of rigidity, arbitrary decision making, and traditionalism. It emerged from various sources: the Koran, legal specialists (*faqih*) in Islamic jurisprudence who formed four law schools and brought together *hadith*, and Kadi-justice. The Koran contained a number of rules of positive law, such as those on marriage.[139] However, most legal prescriptions appeared as *hadith*, exemplary deeds and sayings of the Prophet, which were not committed to writing during the lifetime of the Prophet but were orally transmitted through time and constituted the *Sunna*, not an interpretation of the Koran but a tradition alongside it. Judges used the *fikh*, which came from the law schools and were collections of *hadith*, arranged by subject matter or by author. For a variety of reasons, systematic lawmaking, aiming at legal uniformity or consistency, was impossible. The sacred law could not be disregarded, nor could it, despite many adaptations, be really carried out in practice. The authoritative, but differing, opinions of *muftis*, who became officially licensed jurists, actually increased the irrationality of the sacred law rather than contributing to its rationalization.

Taking the concept from the German scholar Richard Schmidt, Weber referred to "Kadi-justice," informal subjective judgments rendered in terms of concrete ethical or other practical valuations. This was used when individual cases could not be decided by tradition or revelation. Kadi-justice had no rational rules of decision. Weber commented that the coexistence of strict traditionalism and of arbitrariness and lordly discretion were frequently found in countries, not only in Islamic societies. But with Kadi-justice, predictability of decisions was at a minimum. If religious courts had jurisdiction over land cases, capitalistic development of the land was impossible. In the West a unique relationship developed between sacred and secular law. Canon (Church) law had been a model for secular law to follow: the most significant contributions of Canon law were the recognition of informal contracts, freedom of testation, and the conception of the corporation. The Church was the first institution in the legal sense to be a public legal organization and to formulate the idea of a "juristic personality."

The contrast between Islamic and Western law was stark. In Islamic law judgments were deduced from the sacred book, arbitrary decisions of the ruler, and the varying views of the Kadi-judges, who had jurisdiction over all legal matters involving Muslims. In Western law secular and sacred elements were separated, and legal experts were trained in and upheld a rational formal law. Wherever sacred law or immutable tradition held sway, in China and India as well as in Islamic territories, it impeded legal unification and consistency.[140] No *lex terrae*, Western common law, was possible. Weber commented that in all the great Islamic empires of the present time a dualism of religious and secular administration of justice existed: the temporal official stands besides the *Kadi*, and the secular law beside the *sharia*. Weber generalized that the secular courts in Islamic societies were not concerned with the prohibitions of the sacred law but decided according to local custom, because systematization of secular law was prevented by the continuous intervention of spiritual norms.

The arbitrary nature of law in Islamic societies illustrated Weber's major point that the patrimonial state lacked the political and procedural predictability indispensable for capitalist development. He argued that monopolies existed in many states, but they were more frequent and pervasive in patrimonial states.[141] Weber mentioned the extensive scale of such monopolies in Egypt, the Middle East, Far East, and the late Roman Empire. Public financing was both negative and positive; the government imposed financing on certain status groups yet also granted concessions to private trade or craft monopolies for high fees, a share in profit, or a fixed annuity. Negative financing was carried through most comprehensively by the most rational patrimonial-bureaucratic empires of antiquity: Egypt, the late Roman Empire, and the Byzantine monarchy.[142] The Egyptian economy of the pharaohs had a peculiar "state-socialist" strain that reduced considerably private capital formation and the possibility of capitalist acquisition.

A peculiar kind of artificial immobilization of wealth resulting from arbitrariness of patrimonial justice and administration was evident in the Islamic *wakfs*, the family trusts or endowments devoted to pious works on behalf of persons or organizations and institutions. Instead of being used for speculative investment, the capital of urban merchants in Islamic countries was put into the *wakfs*, thus immobilizing capital and property for the sake of security, because it was thought the ruler was not likely to disregard the *sharia* and the *ulama* and take *wakf* property. Weber also suggested a more controversial explanation for Islamic economic underdevelopment. The initial message of Muhammad, the Prophet, may have been ascetic self-control but the social carriers of Islam were Arab warriors, not likely to foster economic and political development as Western bourgeois entrepreneurs had done.

Critics of Weber, such as the French Marxist Maxime Rodinson, have argued that Weber did more than anyone else to systematize, transform into a theory, and base on learned arguments the view that the "listlessness" of Muslims, the result of the fatalistic outlook of Islam, was responsible for the stagnation of Muslim societies.[143] Yet Rodinson and others misinterpreted Weber's intellectual position, which was more complex than they said. These critics, though not Rodinson himself, have constructed a discourse of something called "Orientalism" based on domination, and they ignore the more pluralist views of Weber who did not posit an "essentialist" position. Weber actually wrote that impediments to economic rationalism resulted from rigid traditions not from any lack of ability or "listlessness." True, he argued that such impediments had to be sought primarily in the domain of religion, insofar as they could not be located in purely political conditions. He also argued that Islam was different from other religions because of its interconnection of religion and politics. But he did not argue that Islam or the Islamic ethic was the only cause for legal irrationality, absence of a free market, or lack of autonomous cities. A more significant factor was the patrimonial domination that was responsible for Islamic political, economic, and legal instability or irrationality.[144]

The last word on Weber's work may be left to this extraordinary writer: "The primary task of a useful teacher is to teach his students to recognize 'inconvenient' fact. . . . I mean facts that are inconvenient for their party opinions. And for every party opinion there are facts that are extremely inconvenient, for my own opinion no less than for others. I believe the teacher accomplishes more than a mere intellectual task if he compels his audience to accustom itself to the existence of such facts. I would be so immodest as even to apply the expression 'moral achievement,' though perhaps this may sound too grandiose for something that should go without saying."

10

Conclusion

This book started with epigrams by Dr. Samuel Johnson. In the second of his piquant remarks he said that "there are two objects of curiosity, the Christian world and the Mahometan world. All the rest may be considered as barbarous." The writers discussed in this book exhibited a great deal of curiosity about one of his "objects," the Islamic world. In doing so they provided detailed information as well as valuable perceptions of that world and of the Orient. In his brilliant speech on the "perpetuation of our political institutions" to the Young Men's Lyceum of Springfield on January 27, 1838, Abraham Lincoln warned that memories of the past might be lost by the "silent artillery of time." Reacquaintance with the perceptions of our major writers regarding the two themes of this book, Oriental despotism and Islam, and regarding the symbiotic relationship between them may help prevent the erosion of knowledge of history of the Orient. They also help us understand the complex relationship between European and Oriental nations and societies, a relationship that has been distorted or simplified in some contemporary writing for polemical purposes, often anti-Western rhetoric, as can be seen from the previous chapters. The perceptions of our writers are not expressions of imperialist hubris nor are they manifestations of colonial humiliation of the Orient.

One can admit that the vocabulary of politics is sometimes vague and that attempts at definition may be inexact because the thing named often changes. Terms like *left* and *right* are hardly useful categories for meaningful political understanding today. The term *fascism*, as George Orwell pointed out sixty years ago, came to have little meaning other than something considered undesirable. Our six major writers, in their analysis of politics and religion in the Orient, coped with this problem of imperfection in definition and classification of political systems and in doing so provided coherent interpretations of the nature of despotism in the societies about which they wrote. In the process, they shed light on the characteristics of Islamic societies in the Middle East, and also in India and Algeria, and on Western countries' encounters with them. Their studies are not only important in their own right as part of Western intellectual history and for revealing the past, but they also help us understand the present state of Oriental societies. In particular, they remind us that knowledge of the history of the Middle East and of the cultural differences between the West and the East can help us comprehend the discourse and messages of some modern Muslim spokesmen. They also remind us that extreme theological doctrine has in the past and may again stir up apocalyptic passions and violence.

To appreciate fully the work of our writers it is essential to revisit the context out of which they wrote. Crucial in this context was the historical reality, so often ignored or minimized in some contemporary writing, especially in academic "post-colonial discourse" or "cultural studies" on the Orient, of the constant threat to Europe from Islam since its advent. Postcolonial contemporary writing appears less interested in this reality and in valid empirical evidence of the relationship between East and West during a millennium, than in emphasizing a colonial or imperialist attitude of the West during the last two centuries. Certainly Western intrusion and colonial control during these last two centuries has disrupted political and social behavior in Eastern societies, and perhaps led to an intellectual imperium. But in their narrative doctrinaire critics of Western policies and attitudes often depict a story that minimizes or omits the almost constant hostility and warfare, mostly the result of Islamic aggression, interrupted by intermittent periods of peace between Europe and Islamic countries during an era of a thousand years.

No doubt a guilt complex lingers to some extent in Western culture about Western attitudes and behavior toward the Orient in recent centuries, but it is salutary to recall two factors. First, the Orient was not a passive reactor to Western aggression toward the East. Only in the seventeenth and eighteenth centuries, for a number of reasons mentioned in the previous chapters, did the existence and activity of Islamic countries gradually cease to be a challenge to the West. Edward Gibbon could then believe that "the reign of independent barbarism is now contracted to a narrow span." Western attitudes in general were not those of imperialist aggression or desire to dominate, at least not until the nineteenth century, but were for the most part responses to the real continuing threats from the East. It is equally salutary to recall the arguments for and actions and initiatives by Westerners to foster what they considered desirable progressive change in Oriental societies. It seems perverse to argue, in this case as in others, that Western societies have rarely offered anything but imperialism, racism, or Eurocentric attitudes in dealing with "other" cultures.

Unlike early Christianity, Islam, though criticized, was not, for any prolonged period, the subject of oppression or persecution but was successful from its advent for a substantial amount of time. The threat it posed to Europe was territorial and religious. The first Muslim attacks were on "Christendom," the Western civilization and political area in which Christianity was the dominant religion, before the idea of "Europe" and "European identity" really developed. Islamic forces succeeded rapidly, in the Middle East and elsewhere, after the death of the Prophet Muhammad in 632; Jerusalem was quickly captured in 634, the Byzantine regime was challenged, and the Sasanian Empire of Persia destroyed. Egypt was conquered between 639 and 642. Islam spread to North Africa and to Spain, Portugal, and parts of Italy and France. In North Africa the process of the gradual conversion to Islam began in 701, and a decade later Islamic forces entered Spain. Much of the old Graeco-Roman world had been converted to Islam by the tenth century. Present-day manifestations of Islamic pride and fervor are rooted in that early era when a considerable part of the West was subjugated to Islam. The memory of that early period is manifest in the utterances of Muslim rhetoric during the last half century. Sayyid Qutb, the Egyptian intellectual regarded as the father of modern Islamic fundamentalism, and who spoke for the Muslim Brotherhood movement, wrote in his multi-volumned work *In the Shadow of the Koran*, which began appearing in 1952, that "Crusading . . . was an intellectual enemy. . . . [T]he Crusader spirit runs in the blood of all Westerners." More recently, Osama bin Laden declared that "the peoples of the East are Muslims. They sympathize with Muslims against the people of the West who are Crusaders."

An interesting early example of the subjugation and humiliation of Western countries by Muslims is shown in an incident that occurred in the ninth century. In a letter in 802 Nicephorus, Roman prince and Byzantine emperor (802–11) wrote to the Muslim caliph that he would no longer pay the tribute imposed by the caliph, which had been paid by the previous Byzantine ruler, for sparing Constantinople from Muslim attack. The caliph, Harun al-Rashid, replied to him: "Roman dog. I have read thy letter, O thou son of an unbelieving mother. Thou shalt not hear, thou shalt see my reply." The Muslim forces then proceeded to massacre many Christians in Heraclea, on the shore of the Black Sea. Nicephorus was obliged to make peace and continued to pay financial tributes.

Part of the response to the Islamic aggression of Arabs and Moors was the first Papal call in 846 for a Crusade to fight the enemies of Christ who had plundered the Holy Places in Palestine, had attacked Rome and sacked St. Peter's, and were, thirty-five years later, to sack the monastery of Monte Cassino. During the confrontations that followed the West recovered some of the lost territories, evicting the Muslim conquerors from Sicily, mainland

Italy, and from Spain after centuries of struggle. But Jerusalem was again lost to Christian rule in 1187. At the beginning of the thirteenth century Pope Innocent III countered this renewed Islamic domination by speaking of Islam as the beast of the Apocalypse, urging in 1215 another crusade, against Muslim towns, as well as legal restrictions on Muslims living in Christian lands, and calling for missions to convert Muslims.[1] The early threat to Europe by Arabs and Moors became less potent as Western countries regained most, but not all, of the territories they had lost. Occasionally, the West made attempts at coexistence. One was the curious episode in 1219 when St. Francis of Assisi went to the Holy Land to see the Crusaders but also is said, though this is disputed, to have visited and entered into a dialogue at Damietta, in Egypt, with Malik al-Kamil, the Sultan of Egypt. The object of that possible visit remains unclear, and its outcome was apparently failure, except perhaps for the fresco by Giotto commemorating the supposed event.

More relevant for the writers in this book was the new wave of Islamic attacks, this time from the advance of the powerful Osmanli Turks, who had become masters of Anatolia in the fourteenth century and were soon to create the Ottoman Empire, into Europe. They reached as far as the gates of Vienna, the Balkans, Cyprus, Egypt, Belgrade, as well as Algeria and the town of Tunis. Those attacks led to a general perception by Europeans of the identification of Islam with the Ottoman Empire. Pope Nicolas V in 1453, echoing Pope Innocent III of a century earlier, spoke of the Ottoman ruler as the Antichrist, as the red dragon of the Apocalypse and called Christendom to arms but no new crusade was undertaken. Instead, Constantinople fell to the Turks the same year. Pope Leo X, in his letter of 1513 to Emperor Maximillian, saw "the Turk" as the perpetual enemy.[2] Because of this threat to Western territory, late-fifteenth- and early-sixteenth-century popes took all of Europe into account in formulating major policies. In Papal discussions at the time, war was considered against the Turk that "like a ferocious dragon moves forward in haste to devour us."

Fear of the Turks crept into literature. An amusing expression of this fear appears in Machiavelli's play, *Mandragola*, probably written in 1518. A character, a widow, asks the priest, "Do you think the Turk will come into Italy this year?" to which the priest answers, "Yes, if you do not say your prayers." By the middle of the fifteenth century the outposts of Latin Christendom had been reached by the Turks, and in 1542 Hungary had been overrun. The defense and counterattack by Europeans were largely successful, as discussed in earlier chapters, but their presence as a consequence in Islamic countries ironically later led to the charge of imperialism, a term coined by Europeans. Critics of Western behavior appear to forget that if European powers controlled Egypt for sixty-seven years and Syria for twenty-one years, the Ottoman Empire controlled Egypt for 280 years after 1517, Southern Spain was under Muslim control for 781 years, and Greece for 381.[3] Even more ironically, because the European counterattack was not wholly successful in regaining lost territory, Europe and European values in a sense have been defined by the territories not lost to Islamic conquests.

Certain contemporary problems seem to flow from that heritage of past threats from the Orient and the history of Islamic control over Western lands. The authors studied in this book perceived the nature of Islamic militancy up to the time they were writing. But after centuries of Ottoman dominance the balance of power was shifting. The West was making rapid advances in many fields, in science, commerce, industry, navigation, military weaponry, and political development. Islam no longer posed a serious challenge as the Ottoman Empire was losing military power over the West and was experiencing internal and external problems. Externally, the Russians had taken the Caucasus; France had annexed Algeria; Britain controlled India, the Gulf and Aden, and in 1840 recaptured Acre; and Western sea power was important for military and economic purposes. Internally, the Ottoman central power was losing authority; the system was corrupt and incompetent; the military were discontented; the sultan's role in substantive decision making had been reduced; and the economy was suffering from a sharp increase in prices and from inflation.

Yet, in spite of this history of Ottoman dominance, some critics of Western behavior portray the Orient as if it were the constant victim of Western imperialism. Current Islamic militant groups have adopted this false view. This false view, accompanied with memories of past Islamic and Ottoman power, has given rise to a new problem in European societies, one that did not present itself to our six writers. This stems from the increasing number of Islamic immigrants to European countries, some of whom are not fully integrated in their host societies or do not show inclination to become assimilated, do not define their identity other than by their religion, may not accept the legitimacy of non-Islamic values, and have memories of past Islamic glories. It is not irrelevant that the name "Muhammad" has been the most popular name for boys in some Western countries in recent years. In host countries questions have arisen of whether *sharia* law should be given legal authority, or whether existing law should be changed to satisfy the cultural traditions of immigrants. In some British cities *sharia* courts have been functioning, making decisions on issues of divorce, and, to a lesser degree, on issues of property, inheritance, and physical injury. It is still an open question whether these decisions can be considered officially part of the British legal system. This problem is compounded by the approval in some European countries of the controversial concept of multiculturalism, which aims at preserving cultural and ethical diversity in a society, and perhaps treating differences in cultures as unimportant, but which, in practice, may hinder integration of minority groups and may make discussion of them more difficult.

Our writers and observers in the book illustrate differences in past attitudes between people in the West and the East toward each other. Western Europeans were, for a variety of reasons, curious about and interested in the Orient: travelers, merchants, scholars, and ambassadors cast light on Eastern societies. The reverse for the most part was rarely the case. Furthermore the West, unlike the East, was willing to absorb ideas and commodities from abroad. One memorable result of Western curiosity was the import into Europe of coffee from Turkey, an act that may have reduced European alcoholism in the seventeenth and eighteenth centuries, and even today.[4] Academically, the serious study of Arabic by European scholars began early. In the economic world, Western countries, especially Britain and France, from the sixteenth century on competed for the large Oriental market, and merchants traveled to the East. Scholars and official Western envoys searched the Ottoman Empire for manuscripts and books, laying the foundation of large French royal collections, and for library collections in France, Oxford, and Cambridge; they were also interested in coins and medallions. In contrast, with rare exceptions, the Ottoman Empire showed little interest in Western languages and cultures until around the late eighteenth century when it felt threatened by the West. Knowledge of foreign languages was not deemed important for officials in the Ottoman Empire, which for a long time relied on translators, Europeans, Christians, and Jews, to deal with foreign communication. Moreover, as Charles Issawi pointed out, in the fields of science, technology, and economics, the Ottoman Empire for three centuries was not prepared to learn from Europe.

Until the eighteenth century the Ottoman Empire had limited diplomatic contact with Europe and no permanent representatives there, at a time when Europeans maintained some form of permanent diplomatic representation in the empire. The Ottomans sent only "envoys" to Europe who had largely symbolic functions in their temporary missions, usually a few months, in various European countries. The mission to Paris during 1720 and 1721 in a sense provided the first real Eastern observations of the practices of the West. That mission was charged with observing Western activities that might be useful to apply in the empire. Resident embassies of the Ottoman Empire were not opened until the last years of the eighteenth century, when they were established in London, Vienna, Berlin, and Paris.

ORIENTAL DESPOTISM

Through their perceptions, our writers make clear and, with some exceptions, agree on the essential features of the despotic nature of Oriental political regimes and on the arbitrary and often cruel power of the sultan and other rulers who controlled the palace, the court, central government, and appointment of officials. It is true that they sometimes also criticize the excesses of their own governments. After all, declaiming about present times is, as David Hume remarked, a propensity inherent in human nature. Yet however justifiable some of those criticisms were, especially of autocratic rule in France, far more important for our writers were the differences between their Western systems and the East. All the writers criticized the lack of individual freedom in Oriental governments and societies. They observed in those societies the absence of Western features such as free association, considerable self-governance, representative bodies, corporate bodies, institutions of local self-government, independent professional associations, political pluralism, rotation of power, minority rights, individual judiciary, popular sovereignty, fair meaningful elections, relative freedom for women, secular law in the sense that political institutions and policies are not connected with belief in or attachment to God, and a culture of diversity.

Our writers, Montesquieu, Mill, Tocqueville, and Burke, were all concerned with and recommended limits on the exercise of power in all systems, but they specifically noted that these were absent in Oriental systems. For Montesquieu, who provided the first systematic characterization and definition of Oriental despotism as a particular type of political regime, the recognition of the arbitrary and excessive power of that regime in the Orient and of the need to restrain human impulses strengthened his argument for the necessity of a separation of powers in European political systems. He explained that despotism and stagnation existed in the Orient for various reasons; he emphasized the Islamic religion with its fatalistic doctrine of predestination and the resulting passive nature of the population in Oriental societies as well as geographical and climatic factors. Burke regarded Oriental despotism as abhorrent and called for British rule to introduce modern law and regulations. At the same time he was troubled by the possibility that a democratic state such as Britain might be negatively affected by governing a despotic state. Tocqueville depicted Algeria as backward and chaotic as a result of long years of despotic rule by the Turks and believed that Islamic culture because of its traditionalism could not easily be merged with French progressive values. The two Mills, though they differed on the remedy and on whether Britain should exercise direct or indirect rule in India, were conscious of the inefficiencies and corruption of Oriental despotism; the intrigues, suspicions, and passions typical of Oriental societies; and the problems created by the caste system in India.

Related to the alternatives in dealing with Oriental despotism were two problems facing both Mills. One was the effect on them of the ambivalence, which at least the younger Mill shared, in British opinion about policy for India, which varied between proposals for a kind of benevolent control that would prepare Indians for independence and those suggesting greater controls, ensuring impartial justice, security, and material benefits. Were Indians incapable of ruling themselves and thus in need of some form of arbitrary government? Secondly, the opinions of the two Mills were part of a broader discussion, which had really started with Adam Smith in 1776, regarding the costs and benefits of colonial possessions. The antiimperialist Smith had argued that colonies were a heavy burden on the British taxpayer, distorted the allocation of funds, and increased the possibility of war and of political corruption. He was critical of the "showy equipage" of colonies, which would contribute neither revenue nor military force to the support of an empire.[5]

Jeremy Bentham, the Utilitarian philosopher, held that colonies in general were not advantageous to the mother country. They cost much, they yielded nothing, they bred corruption, and they increased the chances of war. At one point he suggested their emancipation, though he also thought that Britain could benefit Indians by reforming their legal system. Bentham's disciple James Mill similarly thought that colonization was a liability from which Britain got little in return; in general it meant a large expenditure, leading to lower investment, lower employment, and lower wages at home. He too held that colonies were a great source of wars and multiplied the causes and pretext of war. John Stuart Mill, an advocate of international free trade, was ambivalent on this issue. However, his main argument was that Britain had to rely on foreign trade and investment and had to deal with excess population at home; on the whole financing colonization was beneficial from an economic point of view because it would reduce the excess population at home and thus increase wages. In addition, the colonies were also useful as markets for British capital and as suppliers of cheap agricultural products. A further argument he advanced, one that was similar to that of Tocqueville, was a political one, that colonies increased the prestige of Britain. Separation from the colonies would greatly diminish that prestige that, Mill thought, was a great advantage to mankind. Taking account of the different positions one can conclude that imperialism was not automatically inherent in liberal ideology nor in the beliefs of all significant Europeans as the writings of Bentham, Constant, Diderot, Kant, and Adam Smith show.

Opposition to or caution about possession of colonies was manifest in Britain in the nineteenth century. One concern was that the method of ruling colonies might have an adverse effect on British constitutional political practice. This is evident in the strong position held by Richard Cobden, the British politician, an advocate of free trade who opposed British intervention against Russia in the Crimea. He held that accession of territory would be a source of weakness, not of strength. In 1860 Cobden warned that "we may become corrupted at home by the reaction of arbitrary political maxims in the East on our domestic politics, just as Greece and Rome were demoralized by their contact with Asia."[6]

Marx and Weber understood the nature of both Western and Oriental regimes and sought to answer the question of why capitalism had developed in the West but not in the East. Marx saw the perpetuation of despotism as the cause and the consequence of the inability of the Orient to move beyond the early stages of economic and social development due to the arbitrary and capricious nature of state intervention, the isolation of villages from each other, and the undifferentiated nature of the city and the countryside in Oriental societies. Weber, as did Marx, held that state controls over public works were an important factor in the emergence of Oriental despotism. He believed that adherence to the patrimonial tradition, Islamic fatalism, and the reality of the warrior nature of Islam were so strong that capitalism, the autonomous and free cities so necessary for capitalism, and a system of legally abstract justice could not develop. The Islamic religion stressed salvation through adjustment to the world and acceptance of fate rather than the search for salvation through mastery of the world as in the Protestant ethic. Like the Mills, Weber blamed the caste system as one reason for economic and social stagnation. Like Marx, Weber argued that the Orient had not experienced a period of Enlightenment comparable to that in the West and emphasized the conflation of priest and king in Oriental society, which they considered detrimental to the development of modern society.

Some years ago Francis Fukuyama proclaimed that liberal Western values had triumphed over ideological competitors in the world.[7] He argued that we had reached the end of history in the sense that we could not expect any more desirable process than the Western progress to modernity, characterized by institutions like liberal democracy and capitalism. At that time the Soviet Union was the defeated foe. The flow of history has now put Islamic militancy in the place of the Soviet Union as an ideological competitor on the world scene. From the perceptions of our authors and the information provided by observers discussed in this book one may pose some questions relevant today. Do those institutions of modernity work only in the West? Are Muslim societies particularly resistant to modernity? Can Western liberal democratic values be acceptable in the Islamic world? Is a democratic form of government viable in the

Arab Islamic world or is it alien to the mind-set of Islam, if that is seen as the law of God, promulgated by revelation? More precisely can public and private law in Arab Islamic countries go beyond the *sharia*? Is it the religion of Islam that is not compatible with the mixture of liberal democracy and popular sovereignty typical of contemporary Western systems, or is it other factors, such as cultural, economic, social, historical, and political ones, that are responsible for the apparent incompatibility?

THE QUESTION OF WESTERN INTERVENTION

A difficult problem for policy makers today, as is was in the time of our writers, is whether Western countries should help try, while recognizing there is no one correct way or formula in this regard, to introduce changes in social and political behavior or promote reforms or democracy in Arab and Islamic countries or intervene for humanitarian motives, and whether those countries can accept that introduction while maintaining religious and cultural integrity and governmental reliance on the *sharia*. The question is dealt with by a number of our writers, especially Burke, Tocqueville, James and John Stuart Mill, and Marx, with their various views on liberating people through education, science, and modernization. Was Western dominion over countries in the Middle East and East benign or harmful for those ruled? While controlling India Britain began a process of modernization: building roads, railroads, irrigation systems, and introducing more efficient methods in education, defense, and government operation.

James Mill, believing that British rule was beneficial for the Indians, proposed a simple form of arbitrary government, tempered by European honor and European intelligence. John Stuart Mill, though he changed his point of view from time to time, thought that Britain brought gradual improvement to India. In an unusually broad statement in his *Representative Government*, Mill wrote it was becoming universal for the more backward populations of the world to be held in direct subjection by the more advanced or to be under their complete political ascendancy. Inherent in Tocqueville's thoughts on Algeria is the case for France to promote a *mission civilisatrice*, the duty and the ideal for French administrators to bring Western civilization to less developed peoples.

Tocqueville's writings on this subject, though they may be controversial and unfashionable today, in their emphasis on French responsibility for "lifting people toward well-being and enlightenment" are nevertheless useful for considering the relationship between Western-style liberal democracy and any civilizing mission. For the Western world the question is still open as to whether attempts to introduce elements of real democracy beyond simply formal elections, such as creating a civil society, imposing limits on government power, establishing norms for the conduct of those exercising power, framing procedures to manage conflict, have been beneficial or harmful for Middle East countries. One might also ask whether those attempts are in the real interests of the West or are misconceived.

This issue confronted Burke in his dispute with Hastings over British rule in India. If an imperial power wanted to act, in Burke's phrase, under a "mantle of universal morality" to introduce change, should it respect the local values, customs, and law of the society it was administering or helping, or should it impose or advocate strict regulation to avoid chaos. The conservative Burke was respectful of indigenous practices. The dilemma was stark as shown by the example of the Mughal Emperor Aurangzeb, who seized power in 1658 and ruled for fifty years. He was a bigoted, religiously purist individual who left the empire in a fragmented condition, in which it remained until the British, particularly Hastings in the early years of British rule, tried to transform the existing practices and establish order and efficient administration in India. Tocqueville, in his usual understated manner, also confronted the problem of how a European power, in his case France, was to deal with the Muslim society in North Africa. For him that society was not uncivilized, but he considered it as a backward and imperfect civilization. His conclusion was cautious. Because that society had incorporated advances in the past it was not absolutely impenetrable to enlightenment. Marx and Engels also struggled with the problem; should British rule in India, which encouraged development, be praised or condemned?

THE PROBLEM OF DEVELOPMENT

This question is linked with the lack of development in Islamic societies. One may ask why did not the West become "Orientalized" after the early advances of the East and Islamic successes had put it ahead of the West? Islamic countries produced a greater bulk and variety of learned and scientific work in the ninth, tenth, and eleventh centuries, notably by the House of Wisdom, the royal library and translation institute in Baghdad that lasted until it was destroyed by the Mongols in 1258, than medieval Christendom produced in any similar length of time. An interesting example of this is the influence on Copernicus of Islamic astronomers, starting with Al-Khwarizimi whose work in 830 was important for algebra and algorithms. This was no Oriental dark age. Great minds contributed to culture: Avicenna (Ibn-Sina) (981–1037), physician, philosopher, and scientist; Averroes (Ibn-Rushd) (1126–98), philosopher and social scientist, who wrote important commentaries on Aristotle; and

Ibn-Khaldun (1332–1406), historian and social scientist. Arab scholars by their translations played a role in transmitting Greek thought to Christian areas. In the early Ottoman Empire, mathematics, astronomy, and geography flourished; in 1579 Istanbul had a famous observatory. Cordoba in Spain not only had a Great Mosque, a spectacular architectural feat, but also a central library with purportedly four hundred thousand books. The Orient was skilled in irrigation methods, paper making, technical and scientific knowledge, and mathematics. Anatolia had hospitals and charitable institutions as well as mosques. Volney spoke of the "eclipsed splendor of Asia."

But then a change occurred, as one of the acute and influential observers in this book, Ghiselin de Busbecq understood. In a letter of 1560, he commented on the Ottoman Empire saying that although in the past no nation had been less reluctant to adopt useful inventions of others, it could not bring itself to print books or set up public clocks. His remark was partly true. The innovation of printing had been brought to the empire in 1493 by Jews who had been expelled from Spain a year earlier. The printing presses were allowed to operate but were not allowed to print in Turkish or Arabic for more than two centuries. One reason among others was that printing was opposed by Islamic dignitaries. Only in 1729 was the first printing press in Turkish, organized by a Hungarian convert to Islam, put into service in the empire, at a time when the dominance of Europe in the world was evident. Newspapers, magazines, and book publishing then followed. Our writers make clear that the West was innovative, and was advancing in many fields, in technology and in modernity, while the East was stagnating, a fact that led to resentment and frustration. It lagged behind the West on fundamental issues. As discussed earlier, there was no comparable Enlightenment, basic freedoms were absent, science and technology were not advanced, and there was little economic and geographical mobility. Edward Gibbon, in his forceful prose, not only regarded European nations as "the most distinguished portions of the human kind in arts and learning" but also contrasted Roman magnificence with Turkish barbarism. One can still ask whether Oriental despotisms are correlated with economically static societies, and whether political change may occur as those societies become more developed economically. In the Eastern world the tension between tradition and modernity remains, as it did in the time of our writers.

The last related question is what will be the outcome of that resentment and frustration which continues? Our writers commented on the aggressive behavior of Muslim regimes in their time, and some tried to interpret the meaning and significance of *jihad*. Differences on the interpretation of *jihad*, stemming partly from political orientation as well as from intellectual scholarship, are still current. Our writers tended to see *jihad* as the heart of a militant ideology, pitting the House of Islam (*Dar al-Islam*) against the enemy, the House of War (*Dar al-Harb*). That implies the centrality of war for Muslims in the fight against pagans. Other, more benign, interpreters argue that *jihad* is really the struggle against the lower self of baser human impulses.

In his book, *L'Ancien Regime*, Tocqueville compared "the ideal ... the strange religion" of the French Revolution to Islam, both of which had "over-run the whole world with its apostles, militants, and martyrs." The Western world now has to ponder the atmosphere of missionary fervor and the aspects of regimes and organizations legitimized by religion. It must now consider whether a divide of civilization and religion now exists between the West and modern counterparts of Oriental despotism similar to that which separated Christian and Islamic countries, a confrontation that the writers in this book understood and interpreted.

Notes

Introduction: What's Past Is Prologue

1. Henri Pirenne, *Mohammed and Charlemagne* (New York: Norton, 1939).
2. Gutas, *Greek Thought, Arabic Culture* (London: Routledge, 1998) 12–14, 23–4.
3. G. E. von Grunebaum, *Islam: Essays in the Nature and Growth of a Cultural Tradition*, 2nd ed. (London: Routledge, 1961); Arnaldo Momigliano, *Studies in Historiography* (London: Weidenfeld and Nicolson, 1966); Partha Mitter, "Can We Ever Understand Alien Cultures?," *Comparative Criticism* 9 (1987): 3–34.
4. Gunnar Myrdal, *An American Dilemma* (New York: Harper, 1944), 1041.
5. François Furet, *In the Workshop of History*, trans. Jonathan Mandelbaum (Chicago: University of Chicago Press), 9–10; Georg G. Iggers, *Historiography in the Twentieth Century: From Scientific Objectivity to the Postmodern Challenge* (Hanover, CT: Wesleyan University Press, 1997), 12; Max Weber, *On the Methodology of the Social Sciences*, trans. Edward A. Shils and Henry A. Finch (Glencoe, IL: Free Press, 1949), 84, 94.
6. Maxime Rodinson, *La Fascination de l'Islam* (Nijmegen: Université Catholique de Nijmegen, 1978), 118–19.
7. Ernest Gellner, *Postmodernism, Reason, and Religion* (New York: Routledge, 1992), 23–6; Gellner, *Conditions of Liberty: Civil Society and Its Rivals* (London: Hamilton, 1994); Gellner, *Encounters with Nationalism* (Oxford: Blackwell, 1994), 56–7; Lawrence Stone, "The Revival of Narrative: Reflections on a New Old History," *Past and Present* 85 (1979): 7–9; Touraj Atabaki, "Beyond Essentialism: Who Writes Whose Past in the Middle East and Central Asia?," a lecture delivered at the University of Amsterdam, December 13, 2002.
8. Jean Baudrillard, *Selected Writings*, ed. Mark Poster (Stanford: Stanford University Press, 1988), 166–84.
9. Michel Foucault, *Power/Knowledge: Selected Interviews and Other Writings 1972–1977*, trans. and ed. Colin Gordon (Brighton, UK: Harvester, 1980).
10. Edward Said, *Orientalism* (New York: Pantheon, 1978); A. L. Macfie, ed., *Orientalism: A Reader* (Edinburgh: Edinburgh University Press, 2000); Asaf

Hussain, Robert Olson, and Jamil Qureshi, *Orientalism, Islam, and Islamists* (Brattleboro, UK: Amana Books, 1984); Bryan S. Turner, *Marx and the End of Orientalism* (London: Allen and Unwin, 1978), 7–9, 53–9; Martin Kramer, *Ivory Towers on Sand* (Washington, DC: Washington Institute for Near East Policy, 2001), 27–43; Bernard Lewis, *Islam and the West* (New York: Oxford University Press, 1993), 99–118; Mark F. Proudman, "Disraeli as an 'Orientalist': The Polemical Errors of Edward Said," *The Journal of the Historical Society* 4 (December 2005): 547–68; Maxime Rodinson, *Europe and the Mystique of Islam*, trans. Roger Veinus (Seattle: University of Washington Press, 1987), 131; Bill Ashcroft and Pal Ahluwalia, *Edward Said: The Paradox of Identity* (London: Routledge, 1999), 74–86.

11. Leslie Peirce, "Changing Perceptions of the Ottoman Empire: The Early Centuries," *Mediterranean Historical Review* 19, no. 1 (June 2004): 6–28; Jane Hathaway, "Rewriting Eighteenth-Century Ottoman History," *Mediterranean Historical Review* 19, no. 1 (June 2004): 29–53.
12. Robert Irwin, *For Lust of Knowing: The Orientalists and Their Enemies* (New York: Allen Lane, 2006), 2–3.
13. Emmanuel Sivan, *Interpretations of Islam: Past and Present* (Princeton, NJ: Darwin Press, 1985), 136; Donald P. Little, "Three Arab Critiques of 'Orientalism'," *Muslim World* 69 (1979): 110–31; James Clifford, *The Predicament of Culture: Twentieth-Century Ethnography, Literature, and Art* (Cambridge, MA: Harvard University Press, 1988), 260–1.
14. Andrew Schulz, "Moors and the Bullfight: History and National Identity in Goya's *Tauromaquia*," *The Art Bulletin* XC, no. 2 (June 2008): 195–217.
15. N. M. Penzer, *The Harem*, trans. M. Sahiner (Istanbul: Yaynlan, 2000), 102, 194, 257; Howard Crane, "Architecture, Ceremonial, and Power: The Topkapi Palace in the Fifteenth and Sixteenth Centuries," *Journal of the American Oriental Society* 116, no. 2 (April–June 1996): 327; Lisa Jardine and Jerry Brotton, *Global Interests: Renaissance Art between East and West* (London: Reaktion Books, 2000), 8–9; Richard Ettinghausen, "Der Einfluss der Angewandten Kunste und der Malerei des Islam auf die Kunste Europas," *Europa und der Orient 800–1900*, eds. Gereon Sievernich and Hendrik Budde (Berlin: Bertelsmann, Lexikon, 1989), 170–3.
16. William H. McNeill, *The Rise of the West*, quoted in John M. Hobson, *The Eastern Origins of Western Civilisation* (Cambridge: Cambridge University Press, 2004), 174.
17. Fernand Braudel, *The Mediterranean and the Mediterranean World in the Age of Phillip II*, vol. 2, trans. Sian Reynolds (London: Collins, 1972–73), 1187; Mehmet Bulut, "The Ottoman Approach to the Western Europeans in the Levant during the Early Modern Period," *Middle East Studies* 44, no. 2 (March 2008): 259–60.
18. Julian Ruby, "Picturing the Levant," in *Circa 1492: Art in the Age of Exploration*, ed. Jay A. Levenson (Washington, DC: National Gallery of Art, 1991), 78; Julian Ruby, "Mehmed," *Oxford Art Journal* 5 (1982): 3; J. Michael Rogers, "Europe and the Mediterranean World," *Circa 1492*, 69.
19. Roger Benjamin, *Orientalist Aesthetics: Art, Colonialism, and French North Africa, 1880–1930* (Berkeley: University of California Press, 2003).

20. Julien Ruby, *Venice, Dürer and the Oriental Mode* (London and Totowa: Islamic Art Publications, 1982).
21. Jardine and Brotton, *Global Interests*, 61.
22. Gülru Necipoğlu, "Suleyman the Magnificent and the Representation of Power in the Context of Ottoman-Hapsburg–Papal Rivalry," *The Art Bulletin* LXX1, no. 3 (September 1989): 402, 424–5.
23. John M. MacKenzie, *Orientalism: History, Theory, and the Arts* (Manchester, UK: Manchester University Press, 1995), 142–3, 170–1.
24. Steven Marcus, *The Other Victorians: A Study of Sexuality and Pornography in Mid-Nineteenth-Century England* (New York: Basic Books, 1966); Bernard Lewis, *A Middle East Mosaic* (New York: Random House, 2000), 354.
25. Montaigne, *Essays and Select Writings*, ed. Donald Frame (New York: St. Martin's,1963), 106, 197, 492.
26. Momigliano, *Studies in Historiography*, 128–37; Sivan, *Interpretations of Islam*, 145.
27. Maxime Rodinson, *Europe and the Mystique of Islam*, 44; Urs. Bitterli, *Cultures in Conflict: Encounters between European and Non-European Cultures, 1492–1800*, trans. Ritchie Robertson (Oxford: Polity, 1989); H. A. R. Gibb and Harold Bowen, *Islamic Society and the West: A Study of the Impact of Western Civilization on Muslim Culture in the Near East* (London: Oxford University Press, 1950–7); Donald F. Lach, *Asia in the Making of Europe*, vol. II (Chicago: University of Chicago Press, 1965–93), 30–45.
28. Robert Schwoebel, *The Shadow of the Crescent: The Renaissance Image of the Turk, 1453–1517* (Nieuwkoop: B. de Graaf, 1967), 226.
29. P. M. Holt, "The Study of Islam in Seventeenth and Eighteenth Century England," *Journal of Early Modern History* 2, no. 2 (May 1998): 114–19.
30. Johan Fück, *Die Arabischen Studien in Europa bis in den anfang des 20 Jahrhunderts* (Leipzig: Harrassowitz, 1955); Gernot Heiss and Grete Klingenstein, eds., *Das Osmanische Reich und Europe 1683 bis 1789: Konflikt, Entspannung und Austausch* (Vienna: Verlag für Geschichte und Politik, 1983), 135–41.
31. Philip Almond, "Western Perceptions of Islam: 1700–1900," *Australian Journal of Politics and History* 49, no. 3 (2003): 412–24; S. N. Mukherjee, *Sir William Jones: A Study in Eighteenth-Century British Attitudes to India*, 2nd ed. (Hyderabad, India: Orient Longman, 1987), 2–3.
32. Francesco Gabrieli, "Apology for Orientalism," *Diogenes* 50 (Summer 1965): 131–2.
33. Lisa Small, *Napoleon on the Nile* (New York: Dahesh Museum, 2006); Charles C. Gillispie, "The Scientific Importance of Napoleon's Egyptian Campaign," *Scientific American* 271, no. 3 (September 1994): 78–85; Henry Laurens, *Les Origines Intellectuelles de l'Expédition d' Égypte: L'Orientalisme islamisant en France, 1698–1798* (Istanbul: Isis, 1987); Henry Laurens, *L'Expédition d'Égypte, 1798–1801* (Paris: Colin, 1989); Christopher J. Herold, *Bonaparte in Egypt* (New York: Harper and Row, 1962).
34. Carole Hillenbrand, *The Crusades: Islamic Perspectives* (New York: Routledge, 2000), 273–4, 311, 391, 397.
35. Palmira Brumett, *Ottoman Sea Power and Levantine Diplomacy in the Age of Discovery* (Albany: State University of New York Press, 1994), 175–9.

36. John Victor Tolan, *Saracens: Islam in the Medieval European Imagination* (New York: Columbia University Press, 2002), 74.
37. Rogers, "Europe and the Mediterranean World," 69.
38. H. R. Trevor-Roper, *Hitler's Table Talk 1941–44* (London: Enigma Books, 2000), 504.
39. Clarence D. Rouillard, *The Turk in French History, Thought, and Literature, 1520–1660* (Paris: Boivin, 1941), 7, 37, 641–5; Samuel C. Chew, *The Crescent and the Rose: Islam and England during the Renaissance* (New York: Oxford University Press, 1937), 520; William H. McNeill, *The Rise of the West* (Chicago: University of Chicago Press, 1963), 486–8.
40. Caroline Finkel, *Osman's Dream: The Story of the Ottoman Empire, 1300–1923* (London: Murray, 2005); Ann Thomson, *Barbary and Enlightenment: European Attitudes towards the Magreb in the 18th Century* (Leiden, the Netherlands: Brill, 1987), 18; Halil Inalcik, *The Ottoman Empire: Conquests, Organization and Economy* (London: Variorum Reprints, 1978); Colin Imber, *The Ottoman Empire, 1300–1650: The Structure of Power* (New York: Palgrave Macmillian, 2002).
41. Christopher Tyerman, *God's War: A New History of the Crusades* (Cambridge, MA: Harvard University Press, 2006), xiii, 77–8, 81, 89.
42. Halil Inalcik, "The Turkish Impact on the Development of Modern Europe," *The Ottoman State and Its Place in World History*, ed. Kemal H. Karpat (Leiden, the Netherlands: Brill, 1974); Orhan Burian, "Interest of the English in Turkey as Reflected in English Literature of the Renaissance," *Oriens* 2 (1952): 209.
43. Lucette Valensi, *Venise et la Sublime Porte: la naissance du despote* (Paris: Hachette, 1980).
44. Selin Deringil, "The Turks and 'Europe': The Argument from History," *Middle Eastern Studies* 43, no. 5 (September 2007): 709–23; Michael Heath, "Unholy Alliance: Valois and Ottomans," *Renaissance Studies* 3, no. 3 (September 1989): 303.
45. Alexandrine N. St. Clair, *The Image of the Turk in Europe* (New York: Metropolitan Museum, 1973); D. M. Vaughan, *Europe and the Turk: A Pattern of Alliances, 1350–1700* (New York: AMS Press, 1976).
46. De Lamar Jensen, "The Ottoman Turks in Sixteenth Century French Diplomacy," *The Sixteenth Century Journal* XVI, no. 4 (Winter 1985): 452–8; Garrett Mattingly, *Renaissance Diplomacy* (Boston: Houghton Mifflin, 1971), 180.
47. Brumett, *Ottoman Sea Power and Levantine Diplomacy*, 25, 175.
48. Braudel, *The Mediterranean*, vol. 1, 886–7.
49. Mattingly, *Renaissance Diplomacy*, 179.
50. Daniel J. Vitkus, ed., *Piracy, Slavery, and Redemption: Barbary Captivity Narratives from Early Modern England* (New York: Columbia University Press, 2001), 6–7; Paul Baepler, ed., *White Slaves, African Masters: An Anthology of American Barbary Captivity Narratives* (Chicago: University of Chicago Press, 1999), 44.
51. Pierre Dan, *Histoire de la Barbarie et des Corsaires* (Paris: Rocolet, 1637), 284–7; Emanuel d'Aranda, *Rélation de la Captivité à Algier*, 1671.
52. Robert C. Davis, *Christian Slaves, Muslim Masters: White Slavery in the Mediterranean, the Barbary Coast, and Italy, 1500–1800* (New York: Palgrave

Macmillan, 2003), 23; Giles Milton, *White Gold* (New York: Farrar, Straus and Giroux, 2004); Stephan Clissold, *The Barbary Slaves* (London: Elek, 1977), 52; Ellen Friedman, *Spanish Captives in North Africa in the Early Modern Age* (Madison: University of Wisconsin, 1983); Robert C. Davis, "Counting European Slaves in the Barbary Coast," *Past and Present* 172 (2001): 87, 90.

53. Olafur Egilsson *The Travels of Reverend Olafur Egilsson*, trans. Kari S. Hreinsson and Adam Nichols (Reykjavik, Iceland: Fjolvi, 2008).
54. Daniel Panzac, *Barbary Corsairs: The End of a Legend, 1800–1820* (Leiden, the Netherlands: Brill, 2005), 10; Stanley Lane-Poole, *The Barbary Corsairs* (New York: Kessinger, 2004) (repr. 4th ed., London, 1890); G. N. Clark, "The Barbary Corsairs in the 17th Century," *Cambridge Historical Journal* 8, no. 1 (1944/1946): 22–35; Jurien de la Gravière, *Les Corsaires Barbaresques et la Marine de Soliman le Grand* (Paris: Plon, 1887).
55. James Parton, "Jefferson, American Minister in France," *Atlantic Monthly* 30, no. 180 (October 1872): 405–24.
56. Bernard Lewis, *The Muslim Discovery of Europe* (New York: Norton, 1982), 66–7.
57. Elie Kedourie, *Arabic Political Memoirs and Other Studies* (London: Cass, 1974), 1; Paul Coles, *The Ottoman Impact on Europe* (New York: Harcourt Brace, 1968), 162–3; Bernard Lewis, *The Emergence of Modern Turkey* (London: Oxford University Press, 1968), 37–8; Norman Itzkowitz, "Eighteenth Century Ottoman Realities," *Studia Islamica* 16 (1962): 85–91.
58. Asli Cirakman, *From the "Terror of the World" to the "Sick Man of Europe": European Images of the Ottoman Empire and Society from the Sixteenth to the Nineteenth Century* (New York: Peter Lang, 2001), 118, 206–16; Asli Cirakman, "From Tyranny to Despotism: the Enlightenment's Unenlightened Image of the Turks," *International Journal of Middle East Studies* 33 (2001): 49–68.
59. Harold Temperley, *The Crimea* (London: Longmans, Green, 1936), 272.
60. Rouillard, *The Turk in French History, Thought, and Literature*, 291.

Chapter 1 European Views of Islam and Their Correlation with Oriental Despotism

1. Albert Hourani, *Islam in European Thought* (New York: Cambridge University Press, 1991), 15; Jacques Waardenburg, *Islam: Historical, Social, and Political Perspectives* (Berlin: De Gruyter, 2002), 102–11, 211.
2. Maxime Rodinson, *Europe and the Mystique of Islam*, trans. Roger Veinus (Seattle: University of Washington Press, 1987), 6; Ibrahim Kalin, *Western Perspectives of Islam: Yesterday and Today* (Falls Church,VA: Muslim American Society, 2003); Philip Almond, "Western Perspectives of Islam, 1700–1900," *Australian Journal of Politics and History* 49, no. 3 (2003): 412–24; Richard Southern, *Western Views of Islam in the Middle Ages* (Cambridge, MA: Harvard University Press, 1962).
3. St. Thomas Aquinas, *Summa contra Gentiles*, bk. 1, ch. 6, sec. 4.
4. David R. Blanks and Michael Frassetto, eds., *Western Views of Islam in Medieval and Early Modern Europe: Perception of Other* (New York: St. Martin's Press,

1999), 11–53, 218–20; Norman Daniel, *Islam and the West* (Edinburgh: Edinburgh University Press, 1980), 285.

5. John Milton, *Paradise Lost* (New York: Baker and Scribner, 1851), 35.
6. Francis Bacon, "Of Goodness and Goodness of Nature," *Essays or Counsels, Civil and Moral*, ed. Michael Kiernan (Cambridge, MA: Harvard University Press, 1985), 39; Bacon, "An Advertisment Touching an Holy War Written in the Year 1622," *The Works of Francis Bacon*, coll. and ed. James Spedding, Robert Ellis, and Douglas Heath (Boston: Brown and Taggard, 1860–64), 7, 22.
7. Michel de Montaigne, *Les Essais*, ed. Pierre Villey (Paris: Presses Universitaires de France, 1978), bk. 2, ch. 29, 11.
8. Dorothee Metlitzki, *The Matter of Araby in Medieval England* (New Haven, CT: Yale University Press, 1977); Robert Schwoebel, *The Shadow of the Crescent: The Renaissance Image of the Turk, 1453–1517* (Nieuwkoop, the Netherlands: de Graaf, 1967).
9. George Sandys, *A Relation of a Journey Begun 1610* (London: Barrett, 1615), 52–53; Jonathan Haynes, *The Humanist as Traveler* (Rutherford, NJ: Farleigh Dickinson University, 1986).
10. Blaise Pascal, *Pensées* no. 240 (Paris: Hatchette, 1925).
11. Pascal, *Pensées*, nos. 298, 301–3.
12. Humphrey Prideaux, *The True Nature of Imposture Fully Displayed in the Life of Mahomet* (London: Curl, 1723).
13. Henry Stubbe, *An Account of the Rise and Progress of Mahometanism, and a Vindication of Him and His Religion from the Calumnies of Christians* (London: Luzac, 1911).
14. Elizabeth Labrousse, *Pierre Bayle* (Dordrecht, the Netherlands: Nijhoff, 1985); Joan-Pau Rubiés, *Oriental Despotism and European Orientalism: Botero to Montesquieu* (Leiden, the Netherlands: Brill, 2005), 160–1.
15. Voltaire, *Essai sur les moeurs*, republished (Paris: Garnier, 1963), vol. 2, 153, 213, ch. 197.
16. Louis de Jaucourt, *Encyclopédie* (Paris: André le Breton, 1751–20), vol. 4, 885–9.
17. Edward Gibbon, *The Decline and Fall of the Roman Empire*, vol. V (London: Methuen, 1898), ch. 50.
18. Karl Schlegel, *Philosophy of History*, trans. James B. Robertson (repr., London: Bell, 1893).
19. Jacob Burckhardt, *Reflections on History* (repr., Indianapolis: Liberty Classics, 1979), 66; Burkhardt, *Judgments on History and Historians* (repr., Boston: Beacon Press, 1958), 61–6.
20. Johann G. Herder, *Outlines of a Philosophy of the History of Man*, trans. from German by T. Churchill (repr., New York: Bergman, 1966), 584.

Chapter 2 Observant Travelers

1. Amanda Wunder, "Western Travelers, Eastern Antiquities," *Journal of Early Modern History* 7, no. 2 (2003): 96–7; Osier G. de Busbecq, *Life and Letters*, vol. II (London: Paul, 1881), 243.
2. Albert Hourani, *Islam in European Thought* (New York: Cambridge University Press, 1991), 57–8; for recent different views of the relations of the West and Asia

see Deepak Lal, *In Praise of Empires: Globalization and Order* (London: Palgrave Macmillian, 2004); Sheridan Prasso, *The Asian Mystique: Dragon Ladies, Geisha Girls, and Our Fantasies of the Exotic Orient* (New York: Public Affairs, 2005).

3. Carol A. Breckenridge and Peter van der Veer, eds., *Orientalism and the Postcolonial Predicament: Perspectives on South Asia* (Philadelphia: University of Pennsylvania Press, 1993), 8.
4. There is a wealth of books and articles on the travelers to the Orient. Among the most useful are Rosalind Ballaster, *Fabulous Orients: Fictions of the East in England 1662–1785* (Oxford: Oxford University Press, 2005); Gerald M. Maclean, *The Rise of Oriental Travel: English Visitors to the Ottoman Empire, 1580–1720* (London: Palgrave Macmillan, 2004); Joan-Pau Rubiés, *Travels and Ethnology in the Renaissance: South India through European Eyes, 1250–1625* (Cambridge: Cambridge University Press, 2000); Pierre Martino, *L'Orient dans la littérature français au XVIIe et au XVIIIe siècle* (New York: Franklin, 1991); Orhan Burian, "Interest of the English in Turkey as Reflected in English Literature of the Renaissance," *Oriens* 5, no. 2 (1952): 208–29; Pramod K. Nayar, "Marvellous Excesses: English Travel Writings and India, 1608–1727," *Journal of British Studies* 44 (April 2005): 213–38; M. C. Aune, "Elephants, Englishman and India: Early Modern Travel Writing and the Pre-Colonial Movement," *Early Modern Literary Studies* 11, no. 1 (May 2005): 1–35; Clare Howard, *English Travelers of the Renaissance* (London: Lane, 1914).
5. Among those travelers were Ralph Fitch (1583–1611), a jeweler who explored India and whose journey is obliquely referred to by Shakespeare in Macbeth; William Hawkins, captain of a ship that traded with India; Thomas Coryat (1577–1617), who walked through Turkey, Persia, and Mughal India, and was probably the first English nonmercantile tourist; George Sandys (1582–1645); William Lithgow; Thomas Dallam (1575–1630); Pietro della Valle; Francisco Pelsaert; Henry Maundrell (1665–1701), Protestant clergyman; Sir Henry Blount (1602–82); Sir Thomas Herbert (1606–82); Adam Olearius (1603–71), German cartographer whose views of Persian behavior influenced Montesquieu's *Persian Letters*; James Bruce (1730–94), Scottish student of Arabic and expert on Ethiopia; the German, Carsten Niebuhr (1733 –1815); Thomas Stephens; John Mildenhall; Nicholas Withington; Henry Lord; and Peter Mundy.
6. Yvelise Bernard, *L'Orient du XVIe siècle à travers les récits des voyageurs français* (Paris: L'Harmaltan, 1988); Glenn J. Ames and Ronald S. Love, eds., *Distant Lands and Diverse Cultures: The French Experience in Asia, 1600–1700* (Westport, CT: Praeger, 2003); Geoffrey Atkinson, *The Extraordinary Voyage in French Literature from 1700–1720* (New York: Franklin, 1969).
7. Michael Cook, ed., *Studies in the Economic History of the Middle East: From the Rise of Islam to the Present Day* (London: Oxford University Press, 1970); Bernard Lewis, *The Middle East and the West* (New York: Harper and Row, 1966), 48.
8. Ogier G. de Busbecq, *The Turkish Letters, 1554–1562*, new translation (Oxford: Clarendon Press, 1927).
9. Giovanni Botero, *Relations of the Most Famous Kingdoms and Commonwealths through the World* (London: Haviland, 1630); Donald F. Lach, "The Political

Thought of Giovanni Botero," in *Asia in the Making of Europe*, vol. II, bk. 2 (Chicago: University of Chicago Press, 1977), 235–52; Federico Chabod, *Scritti sul Rinascimento* (Turin, Italy: Einaudi, 1967).

10. Giovanni Botero, *The Travelers Breviat*, pt. II, bk. IV (London: Iaggard, 1601).
11. de Busbecq, *The Turkish Letters.*
12. Botero, *The Travelers Breviat*, 40–4.
13. Jean-Baptiste Tavernier, *Six Voyages* (London: Godbid, 1677) 2 vols.; Tavernier, *Travels in India* (New Dehli: Oriental Book Reprint Corp., 1977), vol 1, 306–12.
14. Ibid., vol. 2, 108.
15. Ibid., vol. 1, 579.
16. Paul Rycaut, *The Present State of the Ottoman Empire, 1668* (repr., Farnborough, UK: Westmead, 1972), 2–5, 69, 170; Linda T. Darling, "Ottoman Politics through British Eyes: Paul Rycaut's 'The Present State of the Ottoman Empire'," *Journal of World History* 5, no. 1 (Spring 1994): 71–97; Sonia P. Anderson, *An English Counsul in Turkey: Paul Rycaut at Smyrma, 1667–1678* (Oxford: Oxford University Press, 1989); P. J. Marshall, *Problems of Empire: Britain and India, 1757–1813* (London: Allen and Unwin, 1968).
17. Leslie P. Peirce, *The Imperial Harem: Women and Sovereignty in the Ottoman Empire* (Oxford: Oxford University Press, 1993).
18. François Bernier, *Travels in the Mughal Empire, 1656–1668* (repr., Delhi: Chand, 1968).
19. John (Jean) Chardin, *Voyages du chevalier Chardin en Perse et autres lieux de l'Orient* (Amsterdam: de Lorme 1711), vol. 1, 275–7.
20. Ibid., 42.
21. Ibid., vol. 2, 211–12.
22. Ibid., 39.
23. Andrew Hadfield, *Amazons, Savages, and Machiavels: Travel and Colonial Writing in English, 1550–1630: An Anthology* (Oxford: Oxford University Press, 2001); Anita Damiani, *Enlightened Observers: British Travelers to the Near East, 1715–1850* (Beirut: American University of Beirut, 1979); Ram Prasad, *Early English Travelers in India* (Delhi: Dass, 1965); Kate Teltscher, *India Inscribed: European and British Writing on India, 1600–1800* (New Delhi: Oxford University Press, 1995); Amanda Wunder, "Western Travellers, Eastern Antiquities," *Journal of Early Modern History* 7, no. 2 (2003); Rhoads Murphey, "Pre-Colonial English and European Writing on the Middle East," *Journal of the American Oriental Society* 110, no. 2 (April 1990).
24. Richard Knolles, *The General History of the Turks*, 3rd ed., printed (London: Islip, 1621).
25. Richmond Barbour, *Before Orientalism: London's Theatre of the East, 1576–1626* (Cambridge: Cambridge University Press, 2003), 22.
26. Knolles, *The General History of the Turks.*
27. Fynes Moryson, *Shakespeare's Europe, 1617* (repr., New York: Blom, 1967), 12.
28. Brandon H. Beck, *From the Rising of the Sun: English Images of the Ottoman Empire to 1715* (New York: Lang, 1987), 36.
29. George Sandys, *A Relation of a Journey, 1610* (London, 1615), 52–3; Jonathan Haynes, *The Humanist as Traveler* (Rutherford, NJ: Farleigh Dickinson University, 1986).

30. Barbour, *Before Orientalism*, 14.
31. Sandys, *A Relation of a Journey*, 66.
32. Haynes, *The Humanist as Traveler*, 66–7.
33. Sir Thomas Roe, *The Embassy of Sir Thomas Roe to the Court of the Great Mughal, 1615–1619*, ed. William Foster, 2 vols. (London: The Hakluyt Society, 1899).
34. Edward Terry, *A Voyage to East India, 1655* (repr., London, 1777), 91, 115.
35. Ibid., 158–9.
36. Ibid., 260.
37. William Eton, *A Survey of the Turkish Empire*, 3rd ed. (London: Cadell and Davier, 1801), 16–20.
38. William Robertson, *The Progress of Society in Europe* (Chicago: University of Chicago Press, 1972), 23; E. Adamson Hoebel, "William Robertson: An 18th Century Anthropologist-Historian," *American Anthropologist* 62 (1960): 648–55; P. J. Marshall and Glyndwr Williams, *The Great Map of Mankind: Perceptions of New Worlds in the Age of Enlightenment* (Cambridge, MA: Harvard University Press, 1982), 142.
39. Robertson, *The Progress of Society in Europe*, 144–6.

Chapter 3 Political Thinkers and the Orient

1. Karl Popper, *The Poverty of Historicism* (Boston: Beacon Press, 1957), 27–30.
2. Richard Koebner, "Despot and Despotism: Vicissitudes of a Political Term," *Journal of the Warburg and Courtauld Institutes* 14 (1951): 293–6; Franco Venturi, "Oriental Despotism," *Journal of the History of Ideas* XXIV (1963): 135; Melvin Richter, "A Family of Political Concepts: Tyranny, Despotism, Bonapartism, Caesarism, Dictatorship, 1750–1917," *European Journal of Political Theory* 4:3 (2005): 221–48.
3. Alain Grosrichard, *The Sultan's Court: European Fantasies of the East*, trans. Liz Heron (London: Verso, 1998); original version by Grosrichard, *Structure du sérial: la fiction du despotisme asiatique dans l'Occident classique* (Paris: Seuill, 1979), 19.
4. Aristotle, *The Politics*, trans. Ernest Barker (New York: Oxford University Press, 1958); Antony Andrewes, *The Greek Tyrants* (New York: Harper and Row, 1963).
5. Marsilius of Padua, *Defensor Pacis*, trans. Alan Gewirth (Toronto: University of Toronto Press, 1980), discourse 1, 3–8.
6. Niccolo Machiavelli, *The Prince*, trans. Luigi Ricci (New York: Random House, 1950).
7. Jean Bodin, *Six Books of the Commonwealth*, trans. M. J. Tooley (Oxford: Blackwell, 1955).
8. J-B. Bossuet, *La Politique tirée des propres paroles de l'Écriture sainte* (repr., Geneva, Switzerland: Droz, 1967) Ii: V4, 1709.
9. Thomas Hobbes, *The Elements of Law, Natural and Politic*, ed. F. Tonnies, 2nd ed. (London: Cass, 1969); Hobbes, *Leviathan* (repr., Oxford: Clarendon Press, 1958), pt. II, ch. 20.
10. John Locke, *Second Treatise of Government* (New York: Hafner, 1947), ch. XV.

11. Paul Hazard, *La Pensée européenne au XVIIIème siècle: de Montesquieu à Lessing* (Paris: Bolvin, 1946).
12. Isaiah Berlin, *Against the Current: Essays in the History of Ideas*, ed. Henry Hardy (London: Hogarth Press, 1979), 3–4.
13. Asli Cirakman, *From the "Terror of the World" to the "Sick Man of Europe": European Images of the Ottoman Empire and Society from the Sixteenth to the Nineteenth Century* (New York: Peter Lang, 2001), 118.
14. Nicolas Boulanger, *Recherches sur l'origine du despotisme Oriental* (repr., Paris: Belles Lettres, 1988).
15. C-F. Volney, *Travels through Egypt and Syria in the Years 1783, 1784, and 1785*, vol. II, trans. from the French (New York: Tiebout, 1798), 67–8.
16. C-F. Volney, *The Ruins, or a Survey of the Revolutions of Empires*, trans. from the French (Philadelphia: Lyon, 1799), 32–3.
17. Volney, *Travels*, vol. 1, 197–8.
18. Ibid., 186.
19. Volney, *Ruins*, 174; *Travels*, vol. II, 394–5.
20. John Trenchard and Thomas Gordon, eds., *Cato's Letters: Essays on Liberty, Civil and Religious, and Other Important Subjects*, ed. (New York: Da Capo Press, 1971).
21. Ros Ballaster, *Fabulous Orients: Fictions of the East in England, 1662–1785* (New York: Oxford University Press, 2005) 41.
22. Robert Halsband, ed., *Selected Letters of Lady Mary Wortley Montagu* (New York: Longman, 1970), 329; Robert Halsband, ed., *Complete Letters of Lady Montagu*, vol. 1 (Oxford: Clarendon Press, 1965), 1708–20, 318–20.
23. Carter V. Findley, *Bureaucratic Reform in the Ottoman Empire: The Sublime Porte, 1789–1922* (Princeton, NJ: Princeton University Press, 1980), 87.
24. Sir James Porter, *Observations on the Religion, Law, Government, and Manners of the Turks* (London: Nourse, 1768), 417.
25. Henry Vyverberg, "Limits on Nonconformity in the Enlightenment: The Case of Simon-Nicolas-Henri Linguet," *French Historical Studies* 6:4 (Autumn 1970): 479, 490.
26. Daniel Brewer, *The Enlightenment Past: Reconstructing Eighteenth Century French Thought* (New York: Cambridge University Press, 2008), 75.
27. A. H. Anquetil-Duperron, *Législation Orientale* (Amsterdam: Rey, 1778), 47–8; Frederick G. Whelan, "Oriental Despotism: Anquetil-Duperron's response to Montesquieu," *History of Political Thought* 22:4 (Winter 2001): 619–47.
28. Anquetil-Duperron, *Législation Orientale*, 119.
29. Bernard Lewis, *The Emergence of Modern Turkey*, 2nd ed. (New York: Oxford University Press, 1969), 437–8.
30. David Hume, *Political Essays*, ed. Charles W. Hendel (New York: Liberal Arts Press, 1953), 17–18.
31. David Hume, *Writings on Economics*, ed. Eugene Rotwein (Madison: University of Wisconsin Press, 1955), 88–9.
32. Alexander Dow, *The History of Hindustan, 1770*, vol. III (repr., New Delhi, 1973), vii, xx–xxi, 401.
33. Ibid., vol. 1, xii.
34. Ibid., vol. 2, 401.

35. Adolphus Slade, *Record of Travels in Turkey, Greece, etc.* (London: Saunders and Otley, 1833), 2, 114–15, 285, 302.
36. G. W. F. Hegel, *The Philosophy of History*, trans. J. Sibree (New York: Dover Publications, 1956), 103–5.
37. Hegel, *Philosophy of Right*, trans. T. M. Knox (Oxford: Clarendon Press, 1958), 270.
38. Hegel, *Philosophy of History*, 158.
39. Hegel, *Philosophy of Right*, 286.
40. Ballaster, *Fabulous Orients*, 48–9.
41. Joan-Pau Rubiés, *Oriental Despotism and European Orientalism: Botero to Montesquieu* (Leiden, the Netherlands: Brill, 2005), 113.
42. Ibid., 158.
43. Sir Charles Eliot, *Turkey in Europe* (London: Arnold, 1900).
44. William Hunter, *Travels in the Year 1792 through France, Turkey, and Hungary to Vienna* (London: White, 1796), 387.
45. Sir Thomas Roe, *The Embassy of Sir Thomas Roe to the Court of the Great Mughal, 1615–1619*, ed. William Foster, 2 vols. (London: The Hakluyt Society, 1899), 270.
46. François Bernier, *Travels in the Mughal Empire, 1656–1668* (repr., Delhi: Chand, 1968), 16.
47. John Chardin, *A New Description of Persia*, vol. 2 (London: Beltesworth, 1724), 257.
48. Richard Jones, *An Essay on the Distribution of Wealth* (repr., New York: Kelley, 1964), 127, 138–9.
49. Richard Jones, *Literary Remains: Lectures and Tracts on Political Economy* (New York: Kelley, 1964), 234.
50. Jones, *An Essay*, 119.

Chapter 4 The Oriental Despotic Universe of Montesquieu

1. Richard Koebner, "Despot and Despotism: Vicissitudes of a Political Term," *Journal of the Warburg and Courtauld Institutes* 14 (1951): 275–302; Franco Venturi, "Oriental Despotism," *Journal of the History of Ideas* 24 (1963): 133–42.
2. All citations from *L'Espirit des Lois* and *Lettres Persanes* of Montesquieu are from *Oeuvres Complètes*, ed. Roger Caillois, 2 vols. (Paris: Pleiade, 1949–51). *L'Esprit des Lois* (hereinafter referred to as *EL*); *Lettres Persanes* (hereinafter referred to as *LP*); *Oeuvres Complètes* (hereinafter referred to as OC). English translations used are *Persian Letters*, trans. C. J. Betts (Harmondsworth, UK: Penguin, 1973) and *The Spirit of the Laws*, trans. Thomas Nugent (New York: Hafner, 1966).
3. Montesquieu, "Quelques Réflexions sur les Lettres Persanes," *OC*, vol. 1, 129.
4. Robert Withers, "The Grand Signior's Serraglio" (after Ottaviano Bon) published in *Purchas, His Pilgrimages* (London, 1625; repr., Glasgow: Maclehose,1905), vol. 9, 322 ff.
5. A number of writers have made this point about Giovanni Paolo Marana's work, published in French as *L'Espion du Grand Seigneur dans les Cours des Princes*

Chrétiens (Paris: Barbin, 1684). See Ernest Jovy, *Le Précurseur et l'Iinspirateur direct des Lettres Persanes* (Paris: Leclerc, 1917); John Baum, *Montesquieu and Social Theory* (Oxford: Pergamon, 1979); and Marie-Louise Dufrésny, *Orient Romanesque en France, 1704–1789* (Montreal: Beauchemin, 1946). Similar devices to that of Marana were used by Charles Dufrésny with a Siamese observer, the London *Spectator* with Indians from Java, and Bayle in his 1702 *Dictionnaire Historique* with Japanese and Chinese visitors commenting on Western civilization. G. L. Van Roosbroek, *Persian Letters before Montesquieu* (New York: Institute of French Studies, 1932).

6. Dufrésny, *Orient Romanesque en France*, 163, 168; Roger Laufer, "La Réussite Romanesque et la Signification des 'Lettres Persanes' de Montesquieu," *Revue d'Histoire Littéraire de la France* 61:2 (1961): 193–6.
7. Montesquieu, *LP*. In recent years, many scholars have engaged in the search. They include Pauline Kra, "The Invisible Chain of the *Lettres Persanes*," *Studies on Voltaire and the Eighteenth Century* 23 (1963): 9; R. L. Frautschi, "The Would-be Invisible Chain in *Les Lettres Persanes*," *French Review* 40:5 (April 1967): 604–11; Theodore Braun, "'La Chaîne Secrète': A Decade of Interpretations," *French Studies* 42:3 (July 1988): 278–91.
8. Louis Althusser, *Politics and History: Montesquieu, Rousseau, Hegel and Marx* (London: NLB, 1972), 82–3; Georges Benrekassa, *Montesquieu, la Liberté et l'Histoire* (Paris: Livre de Poche, 1987), 121; Montesquieu, *Pensées*, ed. Louis Desgraves (Paris: Laffont, 1991), 1302, 1306.
9. Jean Starobinski, *L'Invention de la Liberté, 1700–1789* (Geneva, Switzerland: Skira, 1987), 56.
10. Carl Becker, *The Heavenly City of the 18th-Century Philosophers* (New Haven, CT: Yale University Press, 1932), 113; Isaiah Berlin, *Against the Current* (London: Hogarth, 1979), 131–2.
11. Emile Durkheim, *Montesquieu et Rousseau, Précurseurs de la Sociologie* (Paris: Rivière, 1953); Melvin Richter, "Comparative Political Analysis in Montesquieu and Tocqueville," *Comparative Politics* 1 (January 1969): 144–59; Melvin Richter, *The Political Theory of Montesquieu* (New York: Cambridge University Press, 1977).
12. Raymond Aron, *Eighteen Lectures on Industrial Society* (London: Weidenfeld and Nicholson, 1968), 52; Althusser, *Politics and History*, 54–5. Also, the introduction by Franz Neumann to *The Spirit of the Laws* (New York: Hafner, 1949), xxxiii–xxxix.
13. Gustave Lanson, "Le Déterminisme historique et L'idealisme social dans L'Esprit des Lois," *Revue de Métaphysique et de Morale* 23 (1916): 177–202; Charles J. Beyer, "Le problème du déterminisme social dans l'*Esprit des Lois*," *Romanic Review* (April 1948): 102–6.
14. Peter Gay, *The Enlightenment: An Interpretation* (London: Wildwood, 1973), 326.
15. Shelia Mary Mason, *Montesquieu's Idea of Justice* (The Hague, the Netherlands: Nijhoff, 1975), 284–5.
16. Françoise Weil, "Montesquieu et le Despotisme," paper delivered at conference, *Actes du Congrès Montesquieu*, 1955 (published by Bordeaux: Delmas, 1956), 191–2; Henri Barckhausen, *Montesquieu, ses idées et ses oeuvres* (Paris:

Hatchette, 1907), 65; E. Levi-Malvano, *Montesquieu e Machiavelli* (Paris: Champion, 1912), 99–100.

17. Berlin, *Against the Current*, 158–9; David Carrithers, "Montesquieu's Philosophy of History," *Journal of the History of Ideas* 47 (January 1986): 61–80; Melvin Richter, *The Political Theory of Montesquieu*, 72.
18. Patrick Brady, "*The Lettres Persanes* – Rococo or Neo-Classical?," *Studies on Voltaire* 53 (1967): 47–77.
19. Harold Laski, *Studies in Law and Politics* (New Haven, CT: Yale University Press, 1932), 33.
20. George C. Vlachos, *La Politique de Montesquieu* (Paris: Mont Chrestien, 1974), 61–4; Catherine Larrère, "Les Typologies des Gouvernements, chez Montesquieu," in *Etudes sur le XVIII siècle*, ed. Jean Ehrard (Clermont, France: University of Clermont, 1979); Nannerl O. Keohane, "Virtuous Republics and Glorious Monarchies: Two Models in Montesquieu's Political Thought," *Political Studies* 20:4 (December 1972): 383–6.
21. Montesquieu, preface to *EL*, *OC*, vol. 2, 229.
22. Gay, *The Enlightenment*, 327.
23. Max Weber, *The Methodology of the Social Sciences* (Glencoe, IL: Free Press, 1949), 100–2; Melvin Richter, ed., *Essays in Theory and History* (Cambridge, MA: Harvard University Press, 1970), 80; Ernst Cassirer, *The Philosophy of the Enlightenment* (Princeton, NJ: Princeton University Press, 1951), 210.
24. Sergio Cotta, *Montesquieu e la scienza della società* (Turin, Italy: Ramella, 1953), ch. 3.
25. Voltaire criticized Montesquieu in many places: *Supplément au Siècle de Louis XIV* (1753), 113; *Essai sur les Moeurs* (1756), ch. 93; *Dialogues entre A, B, C* (1768); and *Pensées sur le Gouvernement*. Many of his statements are in *Commentaire sur L'Esprit des Lois* (1778). See J. H. Brumfitt, *Voltaire, Historian* (London: Oxford University Press, 1958), 111–21.
26. Robert Shackleton, *Essays on Montesquieu and on the Enlightenment* (Oxford: Voltaire Foundation, 1988), 39.
27. Berlin, *Against the Current*, 138; Aron, *Eighteen Lectures*, 50.
28. Henri Barckhausen, *Montesquieu: L'Esprit des Lois et les Archives de la Brède* (Geneva, Switzerland: Slatkine, 1970); Barckhausen, *Montesquieu, ses idées et ses oeuvres d'après les papiers de la Brède* (Geneva, Switzerland: Slatkine, 1970).
29. Muriel Dodds, *Les Récits de Voyages Sources de l'Esprit des Lois de Montesquieu* (Paris: Champion, 1929); Baum, *Montesquieu*, 35–6.
30. Berlin, *Against the Current*, 140.
31. Lawrence M. Levin, *The Political Doctrine of Montesquieu's Esprit Des Lois: Its Classical Background* (Westport, CT: Greenwood, 1973), 61–5.
32. Gay, *The Enlightenment*, 327; M. P. Masterson, "Montesquieu's Grand Design: The Political Sociology of 'Esprit des Lois'," *British Journal of Political Science* 2 (July 1972): 287–90; Berlin, *Against the Current*, 140.
33. Peter T. Mancias, "Montesquieu and the Eighteenth-Century Vision of the State," *History of Political Thought* 2:2 (Summer 1981): 317–20; Henry J. Merry, *Montesquieu's System of Natural Government* (West Lafayette, IN: Purdue University, 1970), 179–80; Melvin Richter, "Toward a Concept of Political Illegitimacy," *Political Theory* 10:2 (May 1982): 208–9.

34. Xenophon, *Memorabilia.* 4.6; see W. E. Higgins, *Xenephon, the Athenian* (Albany: State University of New York Press, 1977), 60–1 ; Xenophon, *Cypropaedia* (Cambridge, MA: Harvard University Press, 1914) 2 vols., i, iii, 18.
35. Joseph Dedieu, *Montesquieu* (Paris: Hatier, 1966), 104.
36. Bodin, *Six Livres de la République*, vol. 2, 2.
37. Dedieu, *Montesquieu*, 104–5; Shackleton, "Montesquieu et Doria," *Essays*, 93–101.
38. Joseph Dedieu, *Montesquieu et la tradition politique Anglaise en France* (Paris: Gabalda, 1909), 329–6.
39. Pierre Martino, *L'Orient dans la Littérature Française au XVII et au XVIII Siècles* (Paris: Hatchette, 1906), 138–9.
40. Richter, *Political Theory*, 73.
41. Anne M. Cohler, *Montesquieu's Comparative Politics and the Spirit of American Constitutionalism* (Lawrence: University Press of Kansas, 1988), 71–5.
42. Montesquieu, *The Spirit of the Laws*, trans. Thomas Nugent (New York: Hafner, 1949), 62.
43. Judith Shklar, *Montesquieu* (New York: Oxford University Press, 1987), 46.
44. One of the most controversial theories in this regard is Montesquieu's concept of the effect of climate on human behavior and politics.
45. Montesquieu, *Mes Pensées*, 1476, *OC*, vol. I, 1354. The consequence of hot climates is that Asia is weak and has slavery compared with a strong Europe, which has liberty (*EL*, vol. XVII, 3).
46. Orest Ranum, "Personality and Politics in the *Persian Letters*," *Political Science Quarterly* 84:4 (December 1969): 613.
47. Among the many writers on this parallel of the seraglio and despotic government are Alain Grosrichard, *Structure du sérial. La fiction du despotisme asiatique dans l'Occident classique* (Paris: Editions du Seuil, 1979); Aram Vartanian, "Eroticism and Politics in the Lettres Persanes," *Romantic Review* 60 (1969): 23–33; Laufer, "La Réussite Romanesque," 197–200; Jean Starobinski, *Montesquieu par lui-même* (Paris: Editions du Seuil, 1979), 66–9.
48. Grosrichard, *Structure du sérial.*
49. Vartanian, "Eroticism and Politics," 23–8; Mark Waddicor, *Montesquieu and the Philosophy of Natural Law* (The Hague, the Netherlands: Nijhoff, 1970); Roger B. Oake, "Polygamy in the Lettres Persanes," *Romantic Review* 32 (February 1941): 59.
50. Marshall Berman, *The Politics of Authenticity* (New York: Atheneum, 1970), 7–8.
51. Julien J. Lafontant, *Montesquieu et le problème de l'esclavage dans l'Esprit des Lois* (Sherbrooke, Quebec: Naaman, 1979), 85–6.
52. Montesquieu, "Réflexions sur la Monarchie Universelle," *OC*, vol. 2, 24, repeats the argument of the servile spirit in Asia.
53. Ibid., 23–4.
54. Mark Hulliung, *Montesquieu and the Old Regime* (Berkeley: University of California Press, 1976), 38–9.
55. *Mes Pensées*, 1475, OC, vol. 1, 1353; Paul Venrière, "Montesquieu et le monde Musulman, d'après L'Esprit des Lois," *Actes du Congrès Montesquieu*, 1955 (Bordeaux: Delmas,1956), 175–89.

56. Montesquieu, *Mes Pensées* 2186, OC, vol. 1, 1568.
57. Vernière, *Montesquieu et l'Esprit*, 179–80.
58. Bernard Lewis, *The Muslim Discovery of Europe* (New York: Norton, 1982), 128–30.
59. *The Complete Letters of Lady Mary Wortley Montagu*, vol. 1, 1708–20, ed. Robert Halsband (London: Oxford University Press, 1965), 338–9.
60. Althusser, *Politics and History*, 82–3.
61. Iris Cox, *Montesquieu and the History of French Laws* (Oxford: Voltaire Foundation, 1983), 168–71.
62. Merry, *Montesquieu's System of Natural Government*, 179–80.
63. C. E. Vaughan, *Studies in the History of Political Philosophy before and after Rousseau* (Manchester, UK: Manchester University Press, 1960), vol. 1, 265.
64. Merry, *Montesquieu's System of Natural Government*, 181–3.
65. Nannerl O. Keohane, *Philosophy and the State in France* (Princeton, NJ: Princeton University Press, 1980), 407.
66. "Le gouvernement despotique est uniforme partout: il saut aux yeux," Montesquieu, *Mes Pensées* 1793, OC, vol. I, 1429.
67. Montesquieu, *Considérations sur les causes de la grandeur des Romains et de leur decadence* (Paris: Oster, 1964), cited as *Considérations*.
68. Alred Cobban, *A History of Modern France* (Harmondsworth, UK: Penguin, 1961), 126.
69. Robert Shackleton, *Montesquieu: A Critical Biography* (London: Oxford University Press, 1961), 301.
70. John Plamenatz, *Man and Society*, vol. 1 (New York: McGraw-Hill, 1963), 284; Neumann, *The Spirit of the Laws*, liii–lv.
71. Peter V. Conroy Jr., *Montesquieu Revisited* (New York: Twayne, 1992), 83.
72. Vartanian, "Eroticism and Politics," 23.
73. *Mes Pensées* 1822, *OC*, vol. 1, 1436.
74. E. J. Hundert and Paul Nelles, "Liberty and Theatrical Space in Montesquieu's Political Theory," *Political Theory* 17:2 (May 1989): 240.
75. Thomas Macaulay, *Critical and Historical Essays*, vol. 1 (London: Longman, 1843), 106–8.
76. Many writers have made this point, starting with Voltaire, Anquetil-Duperron, Bentham, and James Mackintosh (*Miscellaneous Works*, vol. 1, 359–60). More recently, the point is made by A. Lortholary, *Les Philosophes du XVIII Siècle et la Russie* (Paris: Boivin, 1951); Tzvetan Todorov, "Droit Naturel et Formes de Gouvernement dans 'L'Esprit des Lois'," *Esprit* 75 (March 1983): 44; Jean Ehrard, *Politique de Montesquieu* (Paris: Colin, 1955), 107; Mark H. Waddicor, *Montesquieu: Lettres Persanes* (London: Arnold, 1977), 56; and Vernière, *Montesquieu et l'Esprit*, 187–8. A valuable statement on the nature of the Ottoman state and society is by Halil Inalcik, "Comments on 'Sultanism': Max Weber's Typification of the Ottoman Polity," *Princeton Papers* 1 (1992): 49–72.
77. Bernard Lewis, *The Emergence of Modern Turkey*, 2nd ed. (New York: Oxford University Press, 1969), 443–4.
78. Starobinski, *Montesquieu par lui-même*, 66.

Chapter 5 Edmund Burke and Despotism in India

1. Edmund Burke, *Abridgment of English History*, *Works* (Boston: Little, Brown, 1839) vol. 5, 583 and *Appeal from the New to the Old Whigs*, vol. 3, 454. The influence of Montesquieu on Burke is discussed in a number of works including C. P. Courtney, *Montesquieu and Burke* (Oxford: Blackwell, 1963) and F. T. H. Fletcher, *Montesquieu and English Politics (1750–1800)* (repr., Philadelphia: Porcupine Press, 1980).
2. John Morley, *Edmund Burke* (repr., New York: Arno Press, 1979), 25–6. Burke discussed the matter of his inconsistency in *Appeal*, vol. 3, 374–5.
3. Edmund Burke, *Works* (Boston: Little Brown, 1839), 3: 27.
4. Alan Ryan, "Who Was Edmund Burke?" *The New York Review of Books* (December 3, 1992): 37–43.
5. For some of the considerable diversity of interpretations of Burke in recent years see F. P. Canavan, *Edmund Burke: Prescription and Providence* (Durham: North Carolina Press, 1987); Daniel E. Ritchie, ed., *Edmund Burke: Appraisals and Applications* (New Brunswick, NJ: Transaction Publishers, 1990); Peter J. Stanlis, *Edmund Burke: The Enlightenment and Revolution* (New Brunswick, NJ: Transaction Publishers, 1991); Russell Kirk, *Edmund Burke: A Genius Reconsidered* (Peru, Indiana: Sudgen, 1988); Carl B. Cone, *Burke and the Nature of Politics*, 2 vols. (Lexington: University of Kentucky Press, 1964); C. B. Macpherson, *Burke* (New York: Hill and Wang, 1980).
6. Conor Cruise O'Brien, *The Great Melody: A Thematic Biography of Edmund Burke* (Chicago: University of Chicago Press, 1992), xxvi.
7. *The Writings and Speeches of Edmund Burke* (hereinafter referred to as *WS*), ed. by different scholars (Oxford: Clarendon Press, 1981), vol. V, 314–15.
8. Speech of February 16, 1788 in *WS*, vol. VI, 317.
9. *WS*, vol. V, 145, First Report Select Committee: "Observations," February 5, 1782.
10. Ibid., 383.
11. Ibid., 175.
12. Ibid., 190–1.
13. Ibid., 404.
14. P. E. Roberts, "The East India Company and the State, 1772–86," in *The Cambridge History of India*, vol. 5, ed. H. H. Dodwell (London: Cambridge University Press, 1929), 182.
15. G. W. Forrest, ed., *Selections from the State Papers of the Governors-General of India* (Oxford: Blackwell, 1910), vol. 1, 4.
16. Roberts, "The East India Company and the State," 188.
17. *WS*, vol. II, 396.
18. P. J. Marshall, *The Impeachment of Warren Hastings* (New York: Oxford University Press, 1965), 1.
19. *WS*, vol. II, 372–3.
20. Ibid., 392.
21. Edmund Burke, *Works*, 9 vols. (Boston: Little, Brown, 1839), 8, 569–70.
22. Frank O'Gorman, *Edmund Burke: His Political Philosophy* (London: Allen and Unwin, 1973), 99.

23. O'Brien, *The Great Melody*, 267.
24. *Works*, vol.8, 210 (speech on June 5, 1794).
25. Lucy S. Sutherland, "The East India Speculations of William Burke," in *Politics and Finance in the Eighteenth Century* (London: Hambledon, 1984), 368.
26. P. J. Marshall, *Impeachment*, 4–5. On the financial relationship, Sutherland, "The East India Speculations," 327–59.
27. Edmund Burke, *The Correspondence of Edmund Burke* (Chicago: University of Chicago Press, 1958–78), vol. IX, 237–8.
28. *WS*, vol. V, 389.
29. *Works*, vol. VIII, 64.
30. Sutherland, "The East India Company and Eighteenth Century Politics," 159.
31. *WS*, vol. V, 393.
32. *Correspondence*, vol. IV, 449.
33. *WS*, vol. V, 383.
34. Speech on May 7, 1789 in Edmund Burke, *The Works of Edmund Burke*, 8 vols (London: Bohn, 1854–89), vol. VII, 448–9.
35. *Works*, vol. VIII, 524, 571.
36. *Speeches of the Managers and Counsel in the Trial of Warren Hastings*, ed. E. A. Bond (London: Longman, 1861) vol. IV, 359.
37. *Correspondence*, vol. IX, 62.
38. Thomas Macaulay, *Essays on Warren Hastings* (Boston: Ginn, 1910), 188.
39. Fletcher, *Montesquieu*, 217.
40. Francis said that Burke had written both the reports, the Ninth on June 25, 1783 and the Eleventh on November 18, 1783, except "for a few pages . . . and some other articles" for which Burke had asked, and that he had corrected the whole "in minor particulars and lapses of expression." Quoted in *WS*, vol. V, 194.
41. Sophia Weitzman, *Warren Hastings and Philip Francis* (Manchester, UK: Manchester University Press, 1929), 171; *WS*, vol. VI, 7.
42. *Correspondence*, vol. V, 241–3.
43. Ibid., vol. V, 241.
44. Ibid., vol. VIII, 424.
45. First Report Select Committee: "Observations," February 5, 1782, *WS*, vol. V, 170–2.
46. *WS*, vol. VI, 351.
47. Ibid., 66.
48. *Works*, vol. VIII, 145.
49. O'Brien, *The Great Melody*, 272; Gerald W. Chapman, *Edmund Burke: The Practical Imagination* (Cambridge, MA: Harvard University Press, 1967), 271; Marshall, *Impeachment*, 186.
50. *Correspondence*, vol. VIII, 414.
51. Letter to Henry Dundas, October 8, 1792, *Correspondence*, vol. VII, 247.
52. *WS*, vol. V, 136.
53. Ibid., 141.
54. Ibid., 386.
55. Ibid., 384.
56. Ibid., 386.

57. Ibid., 401.
58. Ibid., 433.
59. Ibid., 463.
60. Ibid., 512–13, 537. On this issue, Morley, *Edmund Burke*, 205–7.
61. O'Brien, *The Great Melody*, 361.
62. Stanley Ayling, *Edmund Burke: His Life and Opinions* (London: Murray, 1988), 177.
63. *Works*, vol. VIII, 221 (speech on June 5, 1794).
64. Macaulay, *Essays on Warren Hastings*, 191.
65. *Correspondence*, vol. IV, 344–5.
66. *Correspondence*, vol. VIII, 426.
67. *Correspondence*, vol. V, 204.
68. *WS*, vol. VI, 275–6, 454.
69. Letter to Philip Francis, November 19, 1790, *Correspondence*, vol. VI, 171.
70. Ibid., 192.
71. *Correspondence*, vol. IX, 213–14.
72. Letters to Lord Loughborough, March 17, 1796, vol. VIII, 432; to Earl Fitzwilliam, June 21, 1794, vol. VIII, 553; and to Sir Hercules Langrishe, May 26, 1795, vol. VIII, 254.
73. O'Brien, *The Great Melody*, 30.
74. *WS*, vol. VI, 275.
75. *Works*, 8, 488.
76. *Speeches*, vol. IV, 384; *Works*, 8, 72, 94, 112.
77. *WS*, vol. VI, 46.
78. *WS*, vol. V, 477.
79. *Works*, 8, 507, 571–2.
80. P. E. Roberts, "The Impeachment of Warren Hastings," in *The Cambridge History of India, British India 1497–1858* vol. 5, ed. H. H. Dodwell (London: Cambridge University Press, 1929), 309.
81. Marshall, *Impeachment*, 189.
82. P. E. Roberts, *History of British India under the Company and the Crown*, 3rd ed. (London: Oxford University Press, 1952), 170.
83. Macaulay, *Essays on Warren Hastings*, 175.
84. Michael Edwardes, *Warren Hastings: King of the Nabobs* (London: Hart-Davis, 1976), 196–7.
85. Cone, *Burke and the Nature of Politics*, vol. II, 158–60; Vincent Smith, *The Oxford History of India*, 4th ed (Delhi: Oxford University Press, 1958), 514.
86. G. R. Gleig, *Memoirs of the Life of Warren Hastings*, 3 vols (London: Bentley, 1841), vol. III, 310.
87. Smith, *The Oxford History of India*, 507.
88. G. W. Forrest, *Selections from the State Papers of the Governors-General of India* (Oxford: Blackwell, 1910–26) vol. II, 61.
89. Ibid., 78–9.
90. *The Defence of Warren Hastings at the Bar of the House of Commons* (London: Stockdale, 1786), 105–6.
91. Forrest, *Selections*, 94–5.

92. C. C. Davies, "Warren Hastings and the Younger Pitt," *English Historical Review* 70 (October 1955): 616.
93. Quoted in M. E. Monckton Jones, *Warren Hastings in Bengal, 1772–1774* (Oxford: Clarendon Press, 1918), 151.
94. Ibid., 329.
95. The *Defence*, op.cit. 4.
96. J. L. Brockinton, "Warren Hastings and Orientalism," in *The Impeachment of Warren Hastings*, eds. Geoffrey Carnall and Colin Nicolson (Edinburgh: Edinburgh University Press, 1989), 91.
97. Eric Stokes, *The English Utilitarians and India* (Oxford: Clarendon Press, 1959), 3, 35.
98. Edward Thompson and G. T. Garratt, *The Rise and Fulfillment of British Rule in India* (New York: AMS Press, 1971), 124.
99. For different assessments of Akhbar's administrative ability and his despotism, W. W. Hunter, *A History of British India* (London: Longmans, 1899–1900), 350; and Smith, *The Oxford History of India*, 359.
100. Weitzman, *Warren Hastings and Philip Francis*, 2.
101. S. M. Edwardes and H. L. O. Garrett, *Mughal Rule in India* (Delhi: Chaud, 1962), 120.
102. Ibid., 242.
103. H. H. Dodwell, "The Development of Sovereignty in British India," in Dodwell, *Cambridge History of India*, vol. V, 589–608.
104. O'Brien, *The Great Melody*, 285.
105. Lucy S. Sutherland, "New Evidence on the Nandakuma Trial," in *Politics and Finance*, 244–45; Smith, *The Oxford History of India*, 505–6.
106. *WS*, vol. V, 2, 14.
107. William Fullarton, *A View of English Interests in India* (London: Cadell, 1787), 253.
108. *WS*, vol. V, 110–13.
109. Ibid., 141.
110. *WS*, vol. VI, 307–8.
111. *WS*, vol. V, 392.
112. Ibid., 171.
113. *WS*, vol. VI, 353.
114. *Works*, 8, 71.
115. *WS*, vol. VI, 309–10.
116. *Works*, 8, 47.
117. Ibid., 71.
118. Ibid., 73.
119. Carnall and Nicolson, *Impeachment of Warren Hastings*, 2–3.
120. *Speeches*, vol. IV, 367–9.
121. Ibid., 360.
122. Ibid., 656.
123. Ibid., 387.
124. *Speeches*, vol. II, 358.
125. *WS*, vol. VIII, 285, 288.
126. *WS*, vol. VI, 310–11.

127. Ibid., 311.
128. Burke referred to John Z. Holwell, *Interesting Historical Events Relative to the Provinces of Bengal and the Empire of Indostan*, 2nd ed. (London, 1766–67).
129. Macaulay, *Essays on Warren Hastings*, 159.
130. Among the many works pointing out the nature of the rulers are Keith Feiling, *Warren Hastings* (London: Macmillan, 1954), 13–14, 110 and Penderel Moon, *Warren Hastings and British India* (New York: Macmillan, 1949), 12.
131. Stokes, *English Utilitarians and India*, 1.
132. *Speeches*, vol. II, 532.
133. *WS*, vol. VI, 110 (Burke on June 1, 1786 speaking on the Rohilla war).
134. Romila Thapar, "Interpretations of Ancient Indian history," *History and Theory* 7 (1968): 318.
135. *Works*, 8, 50.
136. *Speeches*, vol.II, 533–5.
137. D'Herbelot, *Bibliothèque Orientale* (Paris, 1617), 888.
138. *Speeches*, ii, 535.
139. Tavernier, *Travels in India* (New Delhi: Oriental Books Reprint Corp., 1977) bk. 2, ch. 1.
140. Montesquieu, *L'Esprit des Lois*, vol. XVII, 5.
141. *Speeches*, ii, 543.
142. *WS*, vol. VI, 353.
143. Ibid., 469.
144. Ibid., 470.
145. Marshall, *Impeachment*, 91–2.
146. Ibid., 180.
147. Courtney, *Montesquieu and Burke*, 91–2.
148. *WS*, vol. VI, 267.
149. *Works*, 8, 64–5.
150. Ibid., 40.
151. Ibid., 43; *WS*, vol. VI, 350.
152. Stanlis, *Edmund Burke*, 34.
153. *WS*, vol. VI, 353.
154. *Speeches*, iv, 371 (May 28, 1794).
155. *WS*, vol. VI, 354.
156. Ibid., 364.
157. Ibid., 459.
158. Stanlis, *Edmund Burke*, 3.
159. Appeal from the New to the Old Whigs, *Works*, vol. 3, 349.
160. C. E. Vaughan, *Studies in the History of Political Thought* (Manchester, UK: Manchester University Press, 1939), 42–44.
161. *WS*, vol. V, 477.
162. Ibid., 537.
163. *WS*, vol. VI, 350.
164. Ibid., 350, 470.
165. O'Gorman, *Edmund Burke*, 104–5; Peter J. Stanlis, "Burke and the Natural Law," in Ritchie, *Edmund Burke*, 209–37.
166. *WS*, vol. VI, 346.

167. Ibid., 351.
168. Ibid., 302.
169. Ibid., 478.
170. Marshall, *Impeachment*, 181–2; G. R. Gleig, *Memoirs of the Life of Warren Hastings*, vol. I, 401.
171. *Speeches*, vol. IV, 387.
172. P. J. Marshall, "Empire and Authority in the later Eighteenth Century," *Journal of Imperial and Commonwealth History* 15 (January 1987): 105–22.
173. Gleig, *Memoirs of the Life of Warren Hastings*, vol. II, 15.
174. *Works*, 8, 41.
175. Ibid., 44.
176. Ibid., 60.
177. Ibid., 421.
178. Ibid., 48.
179. Gleig, *Memoirs of the Life of Warren Hastings*, vol. II, 30 (letter to Lawrence Sullivan, March 21, 1776).
180. Ibid., 148 (letter to Alexander Elliott, February 10, 1777).
181. Gleig, *Memoirs of the Life of Warren Hastings*, vol. I, 400.
182. Ibid., vol. II, 19.
183. Stokes, *English Utilitarians and India*, 5–7.
184. Lynn Zastoupil, "J. S. Mill and India," *Victorian Studies* 32:1 (Autumn 1988): 38.
185. Duncan Forbes, "James Mill and India," *Cambridge Journal* 5 (October 1951): 20–1.
186. Javed Majeed, *Ungoverned Imaginings* (Oxford: Clarendon Press, 1992), 11–46.
187. Ibid., 27.
188. Ibid., 29–30.
189. Thomas Macaulay, speech on India Bill, 1833, *Forbes*, 23.
190. James Mill, *The History of British India* (London: Madden, 1858) 10 vols., vol. 1, xxiii.
191. James Mill, "Voyage aux Indies Orientale," *Edinburgh Review* 15 (1810): 363–84.
192. Mill, *History*, vol. II, 84.
193. Ibid., 110.
194. Ibid., 166–7.

Chapter 6 Alexis de Tocqueville and Colonization

1. Sheldon S. Wolin, *Tocqueville between Two Worlds: The Making of a Political and Theoretical Life* (Princeton, NJ: Princeton University Press, 2001); André Jardin, *Tocqueville: A Biography*, trans. Lydia Davis (New York: Farrar Straus Giroux, 1988); Hugh Brogran, *Alexis de Tocqueville: A Life* (New Haven, CT: Yale University Press, 2006); Roger Boesche, *Tocqueville's Road Map: Methodology, Liberalism, Revolution, and Despotism* (Lanham, MD: Lexington Books, 2006); Raymond Aron, *Les Étapes de la pensée sociologique* (Paris: Gallimard, 1967); Isaiah Berlin, "The Thought of de Tocqueville," *History* 50:169 (1965): 199–206.

2. Letter to Pierre-Paul Royer-Collard, August 14, 1846; *Oeuvres Complètes* (Paris: Gallimard, 1952–95) vol. XI, 109 (hereinafter referred to as OC); *Memoirs* I, 373.
3. OC, vol. XI, 33–6, 89–92.
4. OC, vol. XV, 2, 309.
5. OC, vol. XIII, 1, 377.
6. Ibid., 2, 13.
7. Harold Laski, "Alexis de Tocqueville and Democracy," in *The Social and Political Ideas of Some Representative Thinkers of the Victorian Age*, ed., F. J. C. Hernshaw (New York: Barnes and Noble, 1967), 101.
8. Tocqueville, *Democracy in America*, vol. 2 (New York: Knoff, 1945), 14, 74.
9. OC, vol. II, 2, 346–7.
10. Ibid., 1, 42.
11. Tocqueville, *Recollections* (London: Henry, 1896), 62.
12. OC, vol. X, 106.
13. Letter to Beaumont, March 23, 1853, OC, vol. VIII, 3, 95.
14. OC, vol. VI, 1, 31–2.
15. Ibid., 1, 293–4.
16. M. C. M. Simpson, ed., *Correspondence and Conversations of Alexis de Tocqueville with Nassau William Senior*, vol. 2 (New York: Kelley, 1968), 262–5.
17. Seymour Drescher, *Dilemmas of Democracy: Tocqueville and Modernization* (Pittsburgh, PA: University of Pittsburgh Press, 1968), 2.
18. Tvetan Todorov, "Tocqueville's Nationalism," *History and Anthropology* 4 (1990): 361.
19. OC, vol. II, 90.
20. Tocqueville, "Ecrits et discourse politiques," OC, vol. III, 1, 214–15.
21. OC, vol. III, 2, 265.
22. Ibid., 2, 290–1.
23. OC, vol. VI, 2, 91.
24. OC, vol. III, 2, 256–65, 280.
25. OC, vol. XI, 90–1.
26. Letter to J. S. Mill, March 18, 1841, OC, vol. VI, 1, 335.
27. OC, vol. VI, I, 37–8. Letter to Henry Reeve, March 22, 1837.
28. Among the more interesting comments on this issue are Matthew Mancini, *Alexis de Tocqueville and American Intellectuals: From His Time to Ours* (Lanham, MD: Rowman and Littlefield, 2006), 19; André Jardin and J. J. Chevalier, introduction to OC, vol. III, 1, 9; Melvin Richter, "Tocqueville on Algeria," *Review of Politics*, 25, no. 3 (July 1963): 364; Michael Hereth, *Alexis de Tocqueville: Threats to Freedom in Democracy* (Durham, NC: Duke University Press, 1986), 158; Tzvetan Todorov, "Tocqueville's Nationalism," *History and Anthropology* 4 (1990): 366.
29. Letters, OC, vol. XIII, 1, 339, 343.
30. OC, vol. III, 1, 129–53; vol. VIII, 1, 429–30.
31. OC, vol. VI, 1, 98.
32. Ibid., 1, 314.

33. *OC*, vol. III, 1, 131.
34. Ibid., 1, 154–62.
35. Ibid., 1, 153.
36. *OC*, vol. XIII, 2, 28.
37. *OC*, vol. III, 1, 151.
38. Letter to Gobineau, October 22, 1843, *OC*, vol. IX, 69; vol. V, 2, 206–7.
39. *OC*, vol. III, 1, 173–4.
40. *OC*, vol. XIII, 2, 28–9.
41. *OC*, vol. III, 1, 187.
42. *OC*, vol. IX, 69.
43. Ibid., 243–4.
44. Tocqueville, *Democracy in America*, vol II, 283.
45. *OC*, vol. III, 1, 292–307; speech in Chamber of Deputies, June 9, 1846, and May 24, 1847 Report.
46. Ibid., 1, 298.
47. Letter to A. F. De Corcelle, September 26, 1840, *OC*, vol. XV, 1, 151.
48. *OC*, vol. III, 1, 224; letter to Louis de Kergorlay, May 23, 1841, *OC*, vol. XIII, 2, 85.
49. Ibid., 1, 225.
50. Ibid., 1, 329.
51. Ibid., 1, 153; vol. XV, 1, 224–5; vol. III, 2, 260.
52. *OC*, vol. V, 2, 191.
53. *OC*, vol. XV, 1, 224–5.
54. Ibid., 1, 219–21.
55. *OC*, vol. III, 1, 235–7.
56. Ibid., 1, 213.
57. *OC*, vol. V, 2, 211; vol. III, 1, 289.
58. *OC*, vol. 3, 1, 139–53.
59. *OC*, vol. IX, 245.
60. *OC*, vol. III, 1, 54; letter to J. S. Mill, November 14, 1839, *OC*, vol. VI, 1, 326; Tocqueville, *Democracy in America*, vol. 1, 372.
61. *OC*, vol. III, 1, 57, 77.
62. Ibid., 1, 112–26.
63. Ibid., 1, 330.
64. Ibid., 1, 59, 105–7; Todorov, "Tocqueville's Nationalism," 360.
65. Letter to Reeve, September 14, 1843, *OC*, vol. VI, 1, 72–3.
66. Letters to Nassau Senior, February 21, 1835, *OC*, vol. VI, 2, 69; to Lady Theresa Lewis, October 18, 1857, Memoir 2, 387; *OC*, vol. II, 389; *OC*, vol. VI, 1, 230.
67. *OC*, vol. VI, 2, 206; vol. III, 1, 457, 478–80, 494–5.
68. *OC*, vol. III, 1, 450, 495.
69. Letter to Reeve, January 30, 1858, *OC*, vol. VI, 1, 252–4.
70. Ibid., 1, 57–8.
71. *OC*, vol. IX, 243.
72. *OC*, vol. VIII, 1, 592.
73. Letter to Corcelle, October 11, 1846, *OC*, vol. XV, 1, 219.

Chapter 7 James Mill and John Stuart Mill: Despotism in India

1. Letter to Joseph Blanco White, April 15, 1853, *Collected Works of John Stuart Mill*, vol. XII, ed., J. M. Robson (Toronto: University of Toronto Press, 1977), 259 (hereinafter referred to as *CW*).
2. Letter to Robert Barclay Fox, August 3, 1840, *CW*, vol. XIII, 441.
3. Letter to Alexis de Tocqueville, May 11, 1840, *CW*, vol. XIII, 434.
4. J. S. Mill (hereinafter referred to as JSM), "De Tocqueville on Democracy in America II," *CW*, vol. XVIII, 159.
5. Letters to Tocqueville, December 30, 1840 and August 9, 1842, *CW*, vol. XIII, 458–9, 536–7.
6. James Mill, quoted in Ryuji Yasukawa, "James Mill on Peace and War," *Utilitas*, 3, no. 2 (November 1991): 179–97.
7. Trevor Lloyd, "John Stuart Mill and the East India Company," in *A Cultivated Mind: Essays on J. S. Mill Presented to John M. Robson*, ed. Michael Laine (Toronto: University of Toronto Press, 1991), 48.
8. JSM, "Autobiography," *CW*, vol. I, 27.
9. Ibid., 22–3, 26–9.
10. George D. Bearce, *British Attitudes towards India, 1784–1858* (Oxford: Oxford University Press, 1961), xx.
11. Lynn Zastoupil, *John Stuart Mill and India* (Stanford: Stanford University Press, 1994), 14.
12. Thomas Macaulay, *The Works of Lord Macaulay*, vol. XI (New York: Longman, 1898), 555.
13. James Mill (hereinafter referred to as JM), *The History of British India*, vol. XXV, abridged version, ed., William Thomas (Chicago: University of Chicago Press, 1975).
14. Ibid., 228.
15. Ibid., 197.
16. Gyan Prakash, "Post-Orientalist Third World Histories: Perspectives from Indian Historiography," *Comparative Studies in Society and History*, vol. 32 (1990): 384–5.
17. Ibid., 385.
18. Javed Majeed, *Ungoverned Imaginings: James Mill's "The History of British India" and Orientalism* (Oxford: Clarendon Press, 1992), 29.
19. Javed Majeed, "James Mill's 'The History of British India' and Utilitarianism as a Rhetoric of Reform," *Modern Asian Studies* 24 (1990): 210.
20. Majeed, *Ungoverned Imaginings*, 30–5.
21. S. N. Mukherjee, *Sir William Jones: A Study in Eighteenth-Century British Attitudes to India* (Bombay: Orient Longman, 1987), 115.
22. Majeed, *Ungoverned Imaginings*, 29.
23. Mukherjee, *Sir William Jones*, 127.
24. Ibid.
25. Majeed, *Ungoverned Imaginings*, 30.
26. David Kopf, *British Orientalism and the Bengal Renaissance: The Dynamics of Indian Modernization, 1773–1835* (Berkeley: University of California Press, 1969), 99.

27. JM, 233.
28. Ibid., 241.
29. Majeed, *Ungoverned Imaginings*, 5.
30. JM, 227–8.
31. Ibid., 223–4.
32. Ibid., 229.
33. Ibid., 190.
34. Ibid., 33.
35. Ibid., 45.
36. Ibid., 157–8.
37. Ibid., 274–5, 278–9, 287–8.
38. Ibid., 183.
39. Ibid., 248–9.
40. Ibid., 224.
41. Ibid., 209, 378–86, 478–81.
42. Ibid., 57–9, 236–7.
43. Ibid., 304.
44. Ibid., 264.
45. Ibid., 534.
46. Ibid., 394.
47. Walter Bagehot, "Review of Principles of Political Economy," *The Prospective Review* IV, no. 16 (1848): 460–502.
48. JSM, "Autobiography," *CW*, vol. I, 249.
49. JSM, letter to Thomas Carlyle, December 22, 1833, *CW*, vol. XII, 200; also, letter of April 28, 1834, *CW*, vol. XII, 224.
50. JSM, letter of February 9, 1869, *CW*, vol. XVII, 1560; letter of January 14, 1870, *CW*, vol. XVIII, 1687.
51. *CW*, vol. I, 249.
52. *CW*, vol. XXX, 52–5; Abram L. Harris, "John Stuart Mill: Servant of the East India Company," *Canadian Journal of Economics and Political Science* 30, no. 2 (May 1964): 185–202.
53. Martin I. Moir, Douglas M. Peers, and Lynn Zastoupil, *J. S. Mill's Encounter with India* (Toronto: University of Toronto Press, 1999), 208–9.
54. JSM, letter to Henry Taylor, undated 1837, *CW*, vol. XVII, 1970; Zastoupil, *John Stuart Mill and India*, 31, 42.
55. JM, *History*, 394; Eric Stokes, *The English Utilitarians and India* (Delhi: Oxford University Press, 1959), 56, 65–8.
56. JSM, *CW*, vol. XIX, 400–1.
57. JSM, *CW*, vol. XXIX, 395.
58. JSM, *CW*, vol. XI, 313; vol. XX, 24; vol. XXI, 34; vol. XXV, 1099.
59. JSM, *On Liberty*, ed., David Spitz (New York: Norton, 1975), 67–8.
60. JSM, "Principles of Political Economy," *CW*, vol. II, 169.
61. JSM, *CW*, vol. XIX, 401; vol. XXI, 335.
62. JSM, "Principles of Political Economy," *CW*, vol. II, 319.
63. JSM, letter to Charles Dupont-White, April 6, 1860, *CW*, vol. XV, 691.
64. JSM, *CW*, vol. XVIII, 197.
65. JSM, *CW*, vol. II, 18–20.

66. Ibid., 14, 168; vol. XVIII, 224–72; vol. XIX, 337–8, 410.
67. JSM, *CW*, vol. II, 403.
68. JM, *History*, 130–3.
69. JSM, *CW*, vol. II, 320.
70. Ibid., 416.
71. Ibid., 12–13.
72. Ibid., 327–8.
73. JSM, *CW*, vol. X, 233; Robert Kurfirst, "John Stuart Mill on Oriental Despotism Including its British Variant," *Utilitas* 1, no. 8 (March 1996): 73–87.
74. JSM, letter to Charles W. Dilke, February 9, 1869, *CW*, vol. XVII, 1560.
75. Ibid., 1536–7.
76. JM, *Edinburgh Review* XVI (April 1810): 155.
77. JM, Testimony to Select Committee, February 16, 1832; Zastoupil, *John Stuart Mill and India*, 22.
78. JM, "Essay on Colony," supplement to the *Encyclopaedia Brittanica*, first published 1823.
79. Ibid., 18.
80. JSM, letter to J. E. Cairnes, June 15, 1962, *CW*, vol. XV, 784.
81. JSM, *CW*, vol. XXX, 13–15.
82. JSM, letter to William W. Ireland, June 22, 1867, *CW*, vol. XVI, 1282.
83. JSM, letter to David Urquhart, October 4, 1866, *CW*, vol. XVI, 1205–6.
84. JSM, *CW*, vol. XXX, 15, 19–30, 114.
85. Thomas Macaulay, *Selected Writings*, eds., John Clive and Thomas Pinney (Chicago: University of Chicago Press, 1972), 242–4.
86. JSM, *CW*, vol. VIII, 911–12; Don A. Habibi, *John Stuart Mill and the Ethic of Human Growth* (Dordrecht, the Netherlands: Kluwer Academic Publishers, 2001), 182–3.
87. Majeed, *Ungoverned Imaginings*, 140–1.
88. JSM, letter to Henry Taylor, undated 1837, *CW*, vol. XVII, 1970.
89. Bearce, *British Attitudes towards India*, 285; Trevor Lloyd, "John Stuart Mill and the East India Company," 44–79; Zastoupil, "John Stuart Mill and Indian Education," *Utilitas* 3, no. 1 (1991): 77–9.
90. Robin J. Moore, "John Stuart Mill and Royal India," *Utilitas* 3, no. 1 (May 1991): 88.
91. JSM, *CW*, vol. XXX, 201.
92. Ibid., 117.
93. JSM, *CW*, vol. X, 233; vol. XXI, 335.
94. JSM, *CW*, vol. XIX, 388, 407, 410.
95. JM, *Works*, vol. XVIII, 23; vol. XIX, 387, 418–19, 567, 577; vol. XXX, 49.
96. *Works*, "The Spirit of the Age," (April 3, 1831); vol. XIX, 573; vol. XXII, 289.
97. *Works*, vol. XXX, 201; JSM, *On Liberty* (New York: Norton, 1975), 11
98. *Works*, vol. XVIII, 224; vol. XXI, 118–19.
99. *Works*, vol., XXVII, 34,
100. *Works*, vol. XXVII, 647.
101. *Works*, vol. XXX, 111, 152.
102. *Works*, vol. XIX, 567.
103. Zastoupil, *John Stuart Mill and India*, 93.

104. Ibid., 53.
105. JSM, *CW*, vol. XXVIII, 234; vol. XIX, 574; Douglas M. Peers, "Imperial Epitaph: John Stuart Mill's Defense of the East India Company," *Moir*, 210.
106. JSM, *CW*, vol. XXX, 79–80, 85.
107. Ibid., 155.
108. Ibid., 120–5.
109. Ibid., 49–50.
110. Ibid., 574; vol. XXIII, 678.
111. Among the critics are Uday Singh Mehta, *Liberalism and Empire* (Chicago: University of Chicago Press, 1999); Eddy M. Souffrant, *Formal Transgression: John Stuart Mill's Philosophy of International Affairs* (Lanham, MD: Rowman and Littlefield, 2000); Beate Jahn, "Barbarian Thoughts: Imperialism in the Philosophy of John Stuart Mill," *Review of International Studies* 31 (2005): 599–618; Bhikhu Parekh, "Decolonizing Liberalism," in *The End of 'isms? Reflections on the Fate of Ideological Politics after Communism's Collapse*, ed., Alexander Shtromas (Oxford: Blackwell, 1994), 85–103; Mark Tunick, "Tolerant Imperialism: John Stuart Mill's Defense of British Rule in India," *Review of Politics* 68 (2006): 586–611.

Chapter 8 Karl Marx: The Asiatic Mode of Production and Oriental Despotism

1. Karl Marx, *Capital*, 3 vols. (Chicago: Kerr, 1909).
2. Joshua A. Fogel, "The Debates over the Asiatic Mode of Production in Soviet Russia, China, and Japan," *American Historical Review* 93, no. 1 (February 1988), 79; Anne M. Bailey, "The Renewed Discussion on the Concept of the Asiatic Mode of Production," in *Anthropology of Pre-Capitalist Societies*, eds. Joel S. Kahn and Josef R. Llobera (London: Macmillan, 1981), 89–107; Jean Suret-Canale, *L'Afrique noire occidentale et centrale, géographie, civilisations histoire* (Paris: Editions sociales, 1958), 94; Barry Hindess and Paul Hirst, *Pre-Capitalist Modes of Production* (London: Macmillan, 1975), 178.
3. Among the more interesting of these discussions are Jean Chesneaux, "Ou en est la discussion sur le mode de production Asiatique," *La Pensée* 138 (March–April 1968): 47–57 and Chesneaux, "Le mode de production Asiatique: une nouvelle étape de la discussion," *Eirenne* 111 (1964): 131–69; Maurice Godelier, preface to *Sur les Sociétés Précapitalistes* (Paris: Editions Sociales, 1970) and Godelier, "Les écrits de Marx et d'Engels sur le mode de production asiatique," *La Pensées* 114 (January–February 1964): 56–66; Anthony Giddens, *A Contemporary Critique of Historical Materialism* (London: Macmillan, 1981); Heinz Lubasz, "Marx's Concept of the Asiatic Mode of Production: A Genetic Analysis," *Economy and Society* (1984): 456–83; Ferenc Tokei, *Essays on the Asiatic Mode of Production* (Budapest: Akademiai Kiado, 1979); Maurice Bloch, *Marxism and Anthropology* (Oxford: Oxford University Press, 1983); Gianni Sofri, *Il Modo di Produzione Asiatico* (Turin, Italy: Einaudi, 1969); Stephen P. Dunn, *The Fall and Rise of the Asiatic Mode of Production* (London: Routledge and Kegan Paul, 1982); Bryan S. Turner, *Marx and the End of Orientalism* (London: Allen and Unwin, 1978); Kimio Shiozawa, "Marx's View of Asian Society and His 'Asiatic

Mode of Production'," *The Developing Economies*, vol. IV (September 1966); Donald Lowe, *The Function of 'China' in Marx, Lenin, and Mao* (Berkeley: University of California Press, 1966).

4. Leo Yaresh, "The Problem of Periodization," in *Rewriting Russian History*, 2nd ed., ed. Cyril Black (New York: Vintage, 1962), 40; Teodor Shanin, ed., *Late Marx and the Russian Road* (New York: Monthly Review Press, 1983).
5. Eric Hobsbawm, ed., *Pre-Capitalist Economic Formations* (London: Lawrence and Wishart, 1964), 23.
6. Pierre Vidal-Naquet, "Karl Wittfogel et le concept de 'Mode de production asiatique'," *Annales* 14 (1964): 531–49.
7. Robert C. Tucker, *Philosophy and Myth in Karl Marx*, 2nd ed. (New York: Cambridge University Press, 1972), 204 and Robert C. Tucker, ed., *The Marx-Engels Reader* (New York: Norton, 1972), xxiv.
8. Karl Marx, *Grundrisse* (New York: Vintage, 1973), 105.
9. Engels to Marx, June 6, 1853, in Karl Marx and Friedrich Engels, *Collected Works* (hereinafter referred to as CW), vol. 39 (New York: International Publishers, 1975), 341.
10. F. Engels, *Herr Eugen Dühring's Revolution in Science* (usually referred to as *Anti-Dühring*), trans. Emile Burns (New York: International Publishers, 1939), 181.
11. Marx, "Contribution to the Critique of Hegel's Philosophy of Law," CW, vol. 3, 32.
12. Norman Levine, "The Myth of Asiatic Restoration," *The Journal of Asian Studies* 37 (1977): 75.
13. Godelier, *Sur les Sociétés précapitalistes*, 41–2.
14. Marx, letter to Arnold Ruge, May 1843, CW, vol. 3, 138.
15. Anne M. Bailey and Josep R. Llobera, eds., *The Asiatic Mode of Production: Science and Politics* (London: Routledge and Kegan Paul, 1981), 1–2.
16. Engels, June 6, 1853, CW, vol. 39, 335–42.
17. Marx, June 14, 1853, CW, vol. 39, 346–8.
18. Marx, December 28, 1846, CW, vol. 38, 96.
19. Ernest Gellner, *Spectacles and Predicaments* (Cambridge: Cambridge University Press, 1979), 322; Gellner, *Thought and Change* (Chicago: University of Chicago Press, 1964), 47–9.
20. Engels, "Karl Marx: A Contribution to the Critique of Political Economy," CW, vol. 16, 475.
21. Engels, "Principles of Communism," CW, vol. 6, 345.
22. Karl Marx, *Grundrisse*, 105–6.
23. Ibid., 107.
24. Ibid., 490.
25. Ibid., 472.
26. Hobsbawm, *Pre-Capitalist Economic Formations*, 10.
27. Shlomo Avineri, *The Social and Political Thought of Karl Marx* (Cambridge: Cambridge University Press, 1969), 112.
28. Marx, *Capital*, vol. III, 791.
29. Marx, "Critique of Political Economy," CW, vol. 28, 401; Marx, *Grundrisse*, 473.

30. Hobsbawm, *Pre-Capitalist Economic Formations*, 70, 83.
31. Ibid., 38.
32. Georges Sorel, *Illusions of Progress*, trans. John and Charlotte Stanley (Berkeley: University of California, 1969), xii.
33. Third draft to Vera Zasulich, *CW*, vol. 24, 364–7.
34. Hobsbawm, 58.
35. Engels, *Anti-Dühring*, 164.
36. Lawrence Krader, *The Ethnological Notebooks of Karl Marx*, 2nd ed. (Assen, the Netherlands: Van Gorcum, 1974), 179.
37. Brendan O'Leary, *The Asiatic Mode of Production* (Oxford: Blackwell, 1989), 94–5.
38. Engels, *The Origin of the Family, Private Property and the State*, 2nd ed., quoted in Tucker, *The Marx-Engels Reader*, 335.
39. Engels, "On Social Relations in Russia,"*CW*, vol. 24, 46; also, Engels, letter to Kautsky, February 16, 1884.
40. Bryan S. Turner, "Asiatic Thought" in *A Dictionary of Marxist Thought*, ed. Tom Bottomore (Cambridge, MA: Harvard University Press, 1983), 32.
41. Leszek Kolakowski, *Main Currents of Marxism* (Oxford: Clarendon Press, 1978) i, 350.
42. O'Leary, *The Asiatic Mode of Production*, 25; V. Kiernan, "Marx and India," in *The Socialist Register*, eds. R. Miliband and J. Saville (1967), 67; Hélène Carrère d'Encausse and S. Schram, eds., *Marxism and Asia, 1853–1964* (Harmondsworth, UK: Penguin, 1969), 8; Bloch, *Marxism and Anthropology*, 64.
43. First draft to Vera Zasulich, *CW*, vol. 24, 346.
44. Steven Lukes, *Marxism and Morality* (Oxford: Clarendon Press, 1985), 9–10; Engels, *CW*, vol. 16, 474–5; Donald Lowe, *The Function of 'China' in Marx, Lenin, and Mao*, 6–8.
45. Marian Sawer, "The Concept of Asiatic Mode of Production and Contemporary Marxism," in *Varieties of Marxism*, ed. Shlomo Avineri (The Hague, the Netherlands: Nijhoff, 1977), 337.
46. Marx, "Critique of Political Economy, *CW*, vol. 29, 275.
47. Shanin, *Late Marx*, 29.
48. Engels, "Preface to the 1888 English edition of the Communist Manifesto," *CW*, vol. 26, 517.
49. Letters of Engels to Joseph Bloch, September 21, 1890; to Conrad Schmidt, October 27, 1890; to Franz Mehring, July 14, 1893.
50. Haruki Wada, "Marx and Revolutionary Russia," in Shanin, *Late Marx*, 41, 59.
51. The four drafts of Marx's reply were not discovered until 1911 and were first published in 1924.
52. Second draft to Vera Zasulich, *CW*, vol. 24, 360.
53. This is made clear in a number of articles written for the *New York Daily Tribune* (hereinafter referred to as *NYDT*), especially those of January 23, 1857; April 10, 1857; and September 25, 1858.
54. Marx, "The British Rule in India," *NYDT*, June 25, 1853, *CW*, vol. 12, 128.
55. Marx, "The Turkish Question," *NYDT*, June 14, 1853, *CW*, vol. 12, 113; "The Future Results of British Rule in India," *NYDT*, August 8, 1853, *CW*, vol.12, 217–22.

56. Marx, *Capital*, vol. III, 451; Maurice Meisner, "The Despotism of Concepts," *China Quarterly* 16 (November–December 1963): 99–109.
57. Engels, "Abd-El-Kader," *NYDT*, January 22, 1848, CW, vol. 6, 472.
58. Marx, "The British Rule in India," June 25, 1853, CW, vol. 12, 126–8.
59. Marx, "The Anglo-Chinese Treaty," *NYDT*, October 5, 1858, CW, vol. 16, 31–2.
60. Marx, "Trade with China," *NYDT*, December 3, 1859, *CW*, vol. 16, 536–9.
61. M. C. Howard and J. E. King, *A History of Marxian Economics: Vol. I, 1883–1929* (Princeton, NJ: Princeton University Press, 1989), 134.
62. Fogel, "Debates over the Asiatic Mode," 79.
63. Marx, articles on the Turkish question, *NYDT*, April 19, 21, 1853, August 5, 1853; Engels, *On Social Relations in Russia*, 1875 and *Afterword 1894*, CW, vol. 24, 50; Marx, "In Retrospect," *Neue Oder-Zeitung*, January 2 and January 4, 1855, CW, vol. 13, 559.
64. Marx to Engels, November 7, 1868, *CW*, vol. 43, 154.
65. Marx and Engels, preface to 2nd Russian edition of the *Communist Manifesto*, CW, vol. 24, 426.
66. First draft to Zasulich, CW, vol. 24, 353.
67. Derek Sayer and Philip Corrigan, "Later Marx: Continuity, Contradiction and Learning," in Shanin, *Late Marx*, 89.
68. Preface to 2nd Russian Edition of *Communist Manifesto*, CW, vol. 24, 425–6.
69. Engels, afterword to "On Social Relations in Russia," CW, vol. 27, 433.
70. Tokei, *Essays on the Asiatic Mode of Production*, 20–1; Samuel Baron, "Plekhanov's Russia: The Impact of the West upon an Oriental Society," *Journal of the History of Ideas* 14, no. 3 (June 1958): 390–4; Joseph Schiebel, "Pre-Revolutionary Russian Marxist Concepts of Russian State and Society," in *Society and History: Essays in Honor of Karl August Wittfogel*, ed. G. L. Ulmen (The Hague, the Netherlands: Mouton, 1978), 318–23; Marx, letter to the editors of *Otechestvenniye Zapiski*, November 1877 (sent but not published until 1886).
71. Perry Anderson, *Lineages of the Absolutist State* (London: Verso Books, 1979), 484.
72. Marx, *Capital*, vol. III, 331; Marx, "On the Jewish Question," CW, vol. 3, 165.
73. First draft to Vera Zasulich, CW, vol. 24, 346.
74. Marx, "Theories of Surplus Value," CW, vol. 33, 340.
75. Ibid., 321.
76. Marx, "The Duchess of Sutherland and Slavery," CW, vol. 11, 488.
77. Krader, *Ethnological Notebooks*, 173.
78. Marx to Engels, March 14, 1868, CW, vol. 42, 547.
79. Engels to Kugelmann, February 17, 1870, CW, vol. 43, 434.
80. Engels, *Anti-Dühring*, 163.
81. Ibid., 149–50.
82. Ibid., 198, 203, 232.
83. Marx, introduction to first version of *Capita*l, CW, vol. 28, 25.
84. Third draft to Vera Zasulich, CW, vol. 24, 365–6.
85. Engels, letter to Edward Bernstein, August 9, 1882, CW, vol. 46, 301.
86. Engels, preparatory writings for *Anti-Dühring*, CW, vol. 25, 610–11.
87. Engels, "Afterword," CW, vol. 27, 421.

88. Engels, 1888 English edition of the *Communist Manifesto*, *CW*, vol. 26, 515–18.
89. Marx, "Trade with China," *NYDT*, December 3,1859, *CW*, vol. 26, 538; Lowe, *The Function of 'China'*, 25–6; Bernard Schwartz, "A Marxist Controversy on China," *Far Eastern Quarterly* XIII (February 1954): 143–54.
90. Engels, "Principles of Communism" (October 1847), *CW*, vol. 6, 345.
91. Marx, "Chinese Affairs, *NYDT*, July 7, 1862, *CW*, vol. 19, 216; Marx, "The Anglo-Chinese Treaty," *NYDT*, October 5, 1858, *CW*, vol. 16, 32; Marx to Engels, October 8, 1858, *CW*, vol. 40, 347.
92. Marx, *Grundrisse* (New York: Vintage Books, 1973), 882; *Capital*, vol. I, ch. 3; Marx, "Economic Manuscripts," *CW*, vol. 28, 29.
93. Tucker, *The Marx-Engels Reader*, 192.
94. Adam Smith, *The Wealth of Nations*, 348, 360, 362, 645, 687, 789; Umberto Melotti, *Marx and the Third World* (London: Macmillan, 1977), 52–3.
95. James Mill, *The History of India*, 2nd ed., ed. William Thomas (Chicago: University of Chicago Press, 1975), vol. I, 175.
96. John Stuart Mill, "Principles of Political Economy," CW,II
97. Richard Jones, *Lectures on the Political Economy of Nations* (Hertford, 1852) 77–8.
98. Daniel Thorner, "Marx on India and the Asiatic Mode of Production," *Contributions to Indian Sociology* 9 (December 1966): 57.
99. Anderson, *Lineages* (London: New Left Books, 1974), 492; Louis Dumont, *Religion, Politics, and History in India* (The Hague, The Netherlands: Mouton, 1966), 112–32; Timothy Brook, ed., *The Asiatic Mode of Production in China* (Armouk, NY: Sharpe, 1989).
100. Frederic Pryor, "The Asian Mode of Production as an Economic System," *Journal of Comparative Economics* 4 (1980): 420–42.
101. Marx to Engels, June 14, 1853, *CW*, vol. 39, 346–7; Marx, *CW*, vol.12, 219–20.
102. Marx, "The British Rule in India," *CW*, vol. 12, 132.
103. Marx, *Capital*, vol. 1, 337–8.
104. Nicholas B. Dirks, *Castes of Mind* (Princeton, NJ: Princeton University Press, 2001), 28.
105. Marx to Engels, June 14, 1853, *CW*, vol. 39, 347.
106. Marx, *Capital*, vol. I, 374–6.
107. Thorner, "Marx on India," 57; Marx, *NYDT*, February 9, 1853, *CW*, vol. II, 488.
108. Marx, *Capital*, vol. I, 49.
109. Marx, *Capital*, vol. II, 178; vol. I, 83.
110. Marx, *Capital*, vol. I, 625.
111. Robert Tucker, 223–4; Marx, *Capital*, vol. II, 34–5.
112. Marx, *Capital*, vol. III, 325.
113. Marx, *Capital*, vol. I, 387; Robert Tucker, 281.
114. Marx, "Trade with China," *NYDT*, December 3, 1859, vol. 16, 539.
115. Marx to Engels, June 2, 1853; Engels to Marx, June 6, 1853; Marx, "British Rule in India," *NYDT*, June 25, 1853.
116. Engels to Kautsky, March 2, 1883, *CW*, vol. 46, 451.
117. Marx, "Critique of Political Economy," CW, vol. 29, 275.
118. Engels, "Afterword," CW, vol. 27, 421.

119. Engels, "Preparatory Writings for Anti-Dühring," *CW*, vol. 27, 606.
120. Ibid., 613.
121. Marx, *Capital*, vol. III, 771–2, 790–1.
122. Engels, *Anti-Dühring*, 164, 198.
123. Marx, "Lord Canning's Proclamation and Land Tenure in India," *NYDT*, June 7, 1858, *CW*, vol. 15, 547.
124. Engels, *Anti-Dühring*, 150; Marx, *Grundrisse*, 484, 493, 497.
125. Marx, *Capital*, vol. III, 791.
126. Marx, *Grundrisse*, 400.
127. Engels, "The Mark," *CW*, vol. 24, 441.
128. Marx, *The German Ideology*, in *Writings of the Young Marx on Philosophy and Society*, eds. Loyd D. Easton and Kurt H. Guddat (Garden City, NY: Anchor Books, 1967), 446–7.
129. Engels, *Anti-Dühring*, 149–50.
130. Engels, "On Social Relations in Russia," *CW*, vol. 24, 46–7.
131. Marx, *Grundrisse*, 406–7, 479.
132. Marx, *The German Ideology*, 410.
133. Marx, "Outlines of the Critique of Political Economy," *CW*, vol. 28, 401.
134. Marx, "Theories of Surplus Value," *CW*, vol. 31, 174.
135. Marx, "Theories of Surplus Value," *CW*, vol. 33, 321.
136. Marx, *Capital*, vol. III, 790–1, 798; vol. I, 140.
137. *CW*, vol. 12, 126–8.
138. Marx, *Capital*, vol. I, 514.
139. Daniel Thorner, "Marx, India and the Asiatic Mode of Production," *Contributions to Indian Sociology* IX (December 1966): 33–66; Geoffrey de Ste Croix, *The Class Struggle in the Ancient Greek World* (London: Duckworth, 1981); Hindess and Hirst, *Pre-Capitalist Modes of Production*, 178–83; Benjamin Schwartz, "A Marxist Controversy on China," *Far Eastern Quarterly* XIII (February 1954): 143–54.
140. Maurice Godelier "*La notion de'Mode de Production Asiatique,*'" in CERM *Sur le "Mode de production asiatique"* (Paris: Editions Sociales, 1969); and Godelier, "The Asiatic Mode of Production," in Bailey and Llobera, eds., *The Asiatic Mode of Production*, 273.
141. Marx, *Capital*, vol. I, 316.
142. Ibid., 366–7.
143. Marx, *Capital*, vol. I, 315–16, 349–50; vol. II, 26.
144. Marx, "Outlines of the Critique of Political Economy," *CW*, vol. 28, 400.
145. Marx, *Grundrisse*, 486.
146. Marx, "Outlines of the Critique of Political Economy," *CW*, vol. 28, 418.
147. Ibid., 416.
148. Marx, "Theories of Surplus Value," *CW*, vol. 33, 356.
149. Ibid., 368.
150. Pryor, "The Asian Mode of Production," 420–42.
151. Marx, "Theories of Surplus Value," *CW*, vol. 33, 356.
152. Marx, "Chinese Affairs," *Die Presse*, July 7, 1862, *CW*, vol. 19, 216–18; Marx, *Capital*, vol. I, 358; Engels, *Anti-Duhring*, 167.

153. Marx, "Revolution in China and in Europe," June 25, 1853, CW, vol. 12, 95; Engels, "Principles of Communism," CW, vol. 6, 345; Engels, "Persia-China," NYDT, June 5, 1857, CW, vol. 15, 278–80.
154. Marx, "Revelations of the Diplomatic History of the 18th Century," published in *The Free Press* (1856–57), CW, vol. 15, 90–2.
155. Marx, *Capital*, vol. I, 338, 352.
156. Tucker, *The Marx-Engels Reader*, xviii.
157. Melotti, *Marx and the Third World*, 50–1.
158. Hegel, *Lectures on the Philosophy of History* (New York: Collier, 1902), ch. 2.
159. Engels, CW, vol. 6, 345.
160. Marx, "The British Rule in India," NYDT, June 25, 1853, CW, vol. 12, 132; Marx, "The Indian Revolt," NYDT, September 16, 1857, CW, vol. 15, 353–6.
161. Marx, "The British Rule in India," CW, vol.12, 132.
162. Engels, "Persia-China," NYDT, June 5, 1857, vol. 15, 279–82.
163. *Capital*, vol. I, 337–8.
164. Krader, *Ethnological Notebooks*, 289.
165. Marx, "Revolution in China and in Europe," NYDT, June 14, 1853, CW, vol. 12 94.
166. Marx, *Grundrisse*, 69.
167. Engels, "The Frankish Period," CW, vol. 26, 59.
168. Marx, *Capital*, vol. III, 732.
169. Ibid., 448.
170. Marx, *Capital*, vol. I, 140.
171. Engels, August 9, 1882 in CW, vol. 46, 301–2.
172. Marx, "The British Rule in India," NYDT, June 25,1853, CW, vol.12, 125–6.
173. Marx, *Capital*, vol. I, 338.
174. Ibid., 285.
175. "Theories of Surplus Value," CW, vol. 33, 356–7, 369.
176. Marx, *Capital*, vol. I, 647–9.
177. Ibid., 649.
178. Marx, *Capital*, vol. III, 793; vol. I, 91.
179. Engels to Kautsky, February 16, 1884, CW, vol. 47, 103; Engels, "The Frankish Period," CW, vol. 26, 59–60.
180. Engels, *Anti-Dühring*, 203; Engels, CW, vol. 25, 168.
181. Engels, CW, vol. 24, 46.
182. Marx makes a similar point about Spain in "Revolutionary Spain," NYDT, September 9, 1854, CW, vol. 13, 396.
183. Marx, *Capital*, vol. I, 29.
184. Marx, *Grundrisse*, 472–3.
185. Ibid., 473.
186. Marx, "Pelissier's Mission to England," NYDT, April 15, 1858, CW, vol. 15, 482.
187. Barry Hindess and Paul Hirst, *Pre-Capitalist Modes of Production* (London: Routledge, 1975), 207; Krader, *Ethnological Notebooks*, 274; Marian Sawer, "The Concept of the Asiatic Mode of Production and Contemporary Marxism," in *Varieties of Marxism*, ed. Shlomo Avineri (The Hague, the Netherlands: Nijhoff,

1977), 340; Ferenc Tokei, *Sur le mode de production asiatique* (Paris: Centre d'Etudes et de recherches Marxistes, 1969), 85–6.

188. Engels to Marx, June 6, 1853, *CW*, vol. 39, 340–1; Marx to Engels, June 14, 1853, *CW*, vol. 39, 346–8; Marx, "British Rule in India," *CW*, vol. 12, 126–8.
189. Robert C. Tucker, "Marx as a Political Theorist," in *Marx's Socialism*, ed. Shlomo Avineri (New York: Atherton, 1973), 136.
190. Marx, "Outlines of the Critique of Political Economy," *CW*, vol. 28, 401.
191. Marx, "The British Rule in India," *CW*, vol. 12, 127.
192. Marx, "Revolutionary Spain," *NYDT*, September 9, 1854, *CW*, vol. 13, 96.
193. Isaiah Berlin, *Historical Inevitability* (London: Oxford University Press, 1954), 5.
194. O'Leary, *The Asiatic Mode of Production*, 134.
195. Lucian Pye, *Asian Power and Politics: The Cultural Dimensions of Authority* (Cambridge: Belknap Press, 1985), 8.
196. Godelier in a number of his writings, especially the preface to *Sur les Sociétés Précapitalistes*.
197. Anderson, *Lineages*, 488–9.
198. Ibid., 494.
199. Dumont, *Religion, Politics, and History*, 80; Tokei, *Sur le 'mode de production asiatique*, 9.

Chapter 9 Max Weber: Patrimonialism as a Political Type

1. H. Stuart Hughes, *Consciousness and Society* (New York: Knopf, 1958), 292.
2. The bibliography on Weber's life and work is now voluminous in many languages. Among the more interesting in English are the following: Martin Albrow, *Max Weber's Construction of Social Theory* (Houndsville, UK: Macmillan, 1990); Stanislav Andreski, *Max Weber's Insights and Errors* (London: Routledge and Kegan Paul, 1984); David Beetham, *Max Weber and the Theory of Modern Politics*, 2nd ed. (Cambridge: Polity, 1985); Reinhard Bendix, *Max Weber: An Intellectual Portrait* (Garden City, NJ: Doubleday, 1962); Peter Breiner, *Max Weber and Democratic Politics* (Ithaca, NY: Cornell University Press, 1996); Andreas E. Buss, *Max Weber and Asia: Contributions to the Sociology of Development* (Munich: Weltforum, 1985); John P. Diggins, *Max Weber: Politics and the Spirit of Tragedy* (New York: Basic Books, 1996); Anthony Giddens, *Politics and Sociology in the Thought of Max Weber* (London: Macmillan, 1972); Anthony Giddens, *Capitalism and Modern Social Theory: An Analysis of the Writings of Marx, Durkheim and Max Weber* (Cambridge: Cambridge University Press, 1971); Ronald M. Glassman and Vatro Murvar, *Max Weber's Political Sociology: A Pessimistic Vision of a Rationalized World* (Westport, CT: Greenwood, 1984); Susan J. Hekman, *Max Weber and Contemporary Social Theory* (Oxford: Robertson, 1983); Wilhelm Hennis, *Max Weber: Essays in Reconstruction* (London: Allen and Unwin, 1988); Dirk Kasler, *Max Weber: An Introduction to His Life and Work* (Cambridge: Polity, 1988); Anthony T. Kronman, *Max Weber* (Stanford: Stanford University Press, 1983); Peter Lassman and Ronald Speirs, eds., *Max Weber, Political Writings* (Cambridge: Cambridge University Press, 1994); Karl Lowenstein, *Max Weber's Political Ideas in the Perspective of Our Time* (Amherst: University of Massachusetts Press, 1966); Kart Lowith, *Max*

Weber and Karl Marx (London: Allen and Unwin, 1982); Wolfgang J. Mommsen, *Max Weber and German Politics, 1890–1920* (Chicago: University of Chicago Press, 1984); Wolfgang J. Mommsen, *The Political and Social Theory of Max Weber* (Cambridge: Polity, 1989); Wolfgang J. Mommsen and Jurgen Osterhammel, eds., *Max Weber and His Contemporaries* (London: Allen and Unwin, 1987); Wolfgang J. Mommsen, *The Age of Bureaucracy: Perspectives on the Political Sociology of Max Weber* (Oxford: Blackwell, 1974); Talcott Parsons, ed., *Max Weber, The Theory of Social and Economic Organization* (New York: Free Press, 1964); Talcott Parsons, introduction to Max Weber, *The Sociology of Religion* (London: Methuen, 1965); Guenther Roth and Wolfgang Schluchter, *Max Weber's Vision of History, Ethics, and Methods* (Berkeley: University of California Press, 1979); W. G. Runciman, *A Critique of Max Weber's Philosophy of Social Science* (Cambridge: Cambridge University Press, 1972); Lawrence A. Scaff, *Fleeing the Iron Cage: Culture, Politics, and Modernity in the Thought of Max Weber* (Berkeley: University of California Press, 1989); Wolfgang Schluchter, *The Rise of Western Rationalism: Max Weber's Development History* (Berkeley: University of California Press, 1981); Wolfgang Schluchter, *Paradoxes of Modernity: Culture and Conduct in the Theory of Max Weber* (Stanford: Stanford University Press, 1996); Wolfgang Schluchter and Toby E. Huff, eds., *Max Weber and Islam* (New Brunswick, NJ: Transaction, 1999); Ralph Schroeder, *Max Weber and the Sociology of Culture* (London: Sage, 1992); Bryan Turner, *Weber and Islam: A Critical Study* (London: Routledge and Paul, 1974); Bryan Turner, *For Weber: Essays on the Sociology of Fate*, 2nd ed. (London: Sage, 1996); Marianne Weber, *Max Weber: A Biography* (New York: Wiley, 1975); Sam Whimster and Scott Lash, eds., *Max Weber, Rationality and Modernity* (London: Allen and Unwin, 1987); Sam Whimster, ed., *Max Weber and the Culture of Anarchy* (Houndsville: Macmillan, 1999); Dennis Wrong, ed., *Max Weber* (Englewood Cliffs, NJ: Prentice-Hall, 1970).

3. Mommsen, *The Political and Social Theory*, 200.
4. Diggins, *Max Weber: Politics and the Spirit*, 105; Mommsen and Osterhammel, *Max Weber and His Contemporaries*, 6–7.
5. Arnaldo Momigliano, "Two Types of Universal History: The Cases of E. A. Freeman and Max Weber," *Journal of Modern History* 58 (1986): 236.
6. Max Weber, *Ancient Judaism*, trans. Hans H. Gerth and Don Martindale (Glencoe, IL: Free Press, 1952), 425.
7. O. B. van der Sprenkel, "Chinese Religion," *British Journal of Sociology* 5 (1954): 272.
8. Friedrich H. Tenbruck, "The Problem of Thematic Unity in the Works of Max Weber," *British Journal of Sociology* 31, no. 3 (1980): 316–51.
9. Stephen Kalberg, *Max Weber's Comparative-Historical Sociology* (Cambridge: Polity, 1994), 127.
10. Max Weber, *The Methodology of the Social Sciences*, trans. Edward Shils and Henry Finch (New York: Free Press, 1949), 103.
11. Marianne Weber, *Max Weber: A Biography*, 350.
12. Raymond Aron, *Main Currents in Sociological Thought*, vol. 2 (Garden City, NJ: Anchor, 1968–70); Ernest Gellner, *Postmodernism, Reason and Religion* (London: Routledge, 1992), 145.

13. Weber, *Methodology*, 103.
14. Ibid., 68.
15. S. N. Eisenstadt, "Weber's Analysis of Islam and the Specific Pattern of Islamic Civilization," in Schluchter and Huff, *Max Weber and Islam*, 281–94; S. N. Eisenstadt, *Traditional Patrimonialism and Neo-patrimonialism* (Beverly Hills, CA: Sage, 1973).
16. Max Weber, *Economy and Society*, 3 vols., eds. Guenther Roth and Claus Wittich (New York: Bedminster, 1968) (hereinafter referred to as *ES*), 341.
17. Ibid., 936–7.
18. Max Weber, *The Religion of China: Confucianism and Taoism* (hereinafter referred to as *RoC*), trans. Hans H. Gerth (Glencoe, IL: Free Press, 1951), 107; Weber, *The Religion of India: The Sociology of Hinduism and Buddhism* (hereinafter referred to as *RoI*), trans. Hans H. Gerth and Don Martindale (Glencoe, IL: Free Press, 1958), 215–32; Weber, *Ancient Judaism*, 205–19.
19. Turner, *Weber and Islam*, 16.
20. Mommsen, *The Political and Social Theory*, 150.
21. Whimster and Lash, *Max Weber, Rationality*, 46.
22. Max Weber, quoted in Glassman and Murvar, *Max Weber's Political Sociology*, 95.
23. Kalberg, *Max Weber's Comparative*, 70; *ES*, 1091; *RoC*, 33.
24. Max Weber, *The Protestant Ethic and the Spirit of Capitalism* (hereinafter referred to as *PE*), trans., Talcott Parsons (New York: Scribners, 1958), 91.
25. David Beetham, "Max Weber and the Liberal Political Tradition," *Archives Européenes de Sociologie* 30 (1989): 316–17.
26. Mommsen, *The Political and Social Theory*, 146, 160–1.
27. *ES*, 1002, 1176.
28. Weber, *Methodology*, 68.
29. Hekman, *Max Weber and Contemporary*, 60; Sheldon Wolin, "Max Weber, Legitimation, Method, and the Politics of Theory," *Political Theory* 9 (1981): 401–24.
30. Max Weber, *Basic Concepts in Sociology*, trans., H. P. Secher (Secaucus, NJ: Citadel Press, 1962), 14.
31. Weber, *Methodology*, 75; Mommsen, *The Age of Bureaucracy*, 48.
32. Weber, *Methodology*, 105.
33. Max Weber, *From Max Weber: Essays in Sociology* (hereinafter referred to as *FMW*), trans. H. H. Gerth and C. Wright Mills (New York: Oxford University Press, 1958), 60; Roth and Schluchter, *Max Weber's Vision*, 124.
34. Weber, *Methodology*, 90, 93, 103.
35. Hughes, *Consciousness and Society*, 311; *ES*, 8–9, 57.
36. Hekman, *Max Weber and Contemporary*, 19.
37. *ES*, 216, 954; *FMW*, 299–300.
38. Max Weber, *The Agrarian Sociology of Ancient Civilizations* (London: New Left Books, 1976), 93, 393–9.
39. *FMW*, 297.
40. Ibid., 249.
41. *ES*, 216.
42. *PE*, 25–6.

43. Max Weber, *General Economic History* (hereinafter referred to as *GEH*), trans. F. H. Knight (Glencoe, IL: Free Press, 1950), 339, 341–2, 361; *PE*, 16; *RoC*, 329.
44. Wolfgang Schluchter, *Rationalism, Religion and Domination*, trans. Neil Solomon (Berkeley: University of California Press, 1989), 418.
45. *ES*, 1095.
46. *GEH*, 232–3.
47. *ES*, 904–5, 908.
48. Ibid., 225, 983.
49. Wolin, "Max Weber, Legitimation," 415.
50. *GEH*, 265.
51. *RoC*, 104.
52. Ibid., 247–8.
53. Ibid., 85, 99–100, 374.
54. Weber, *Political Writings*, 315.
55. *ES*, 234.
56. *GEH*, 47–51; *FMW*, 296; *ES*, 227.
57. *ES*, 1007–8.
58. Ibid., 1118.
59. Ibid., 231–2.
60. *RoI*, 74.
61. Ibid., 67.
62. *ES*, 1028–9.
63. Ibid., 1041.
64. *RoC*, 100.
65. *ES*, 1013.
66. Ibid., 1030.
67. Ibid., 228.
68. *RoC*, 264.
69. Ibid., 44.
70. Ibid., 47.
71. *ES*, 232–3.
72. Ibid., 1044.
73. *RoI*, 66–7.
74. Ibid., 69.
75. *ES*, 236.
76. Ibid., 1076.
77. Ibid., 1039–42, 1107.
78. Ibid., 1051.
79. Ibid., 1070, 1090.
80. Ibid., 1106–7.
81. Ibid., 1051.
82. *RoC*, 86.
83. Ibid., 137.
84. Ibid., 138–9.
85. *RoI*, 130, 235–6.
86. *ES*, 1038–40.
87. Ibid., 1027.

88. Ibid., 1022–3, 1058.
89. *RoI*, 72–5.
90. *GEH*, 57–9.
91. *ES*, 1016.
92. Ibid., 1047.
93. *RoC*, 20–1.
94. Ibid., 31.
95. Ibid., 136–7.
96. *ES*, 238.
97. Bendix, *Max Weber: An Intellectual Portrait*, 337.
98. *ES*, 1015–18.
99. Ibid., 1106.
100. *RoI*, 238.
101. Weber, *Ancient Judaism*, 257–8.
102. *ES*, 1092–3.
103. Ibid., 1013.
104. *RoC*, 13–16, 97, 100.
105. *ES*, 1109.
106. *RoI*, 39.
107. *RoC*, 86–7, 95.
108. Ibid., 108.
109. *RoI*, 337–8.
110. *ES*, 555.
111. Ibid., 1193.
112. Ibid., 537.
113. *PE*, 91.
114. Ibid., 154.
115. Max Weber, *The Sociology of Religion* (Boston: Beacon Press, 1969), 268–9 (hereinafter referred to as *SoR*).
116. *SoR*, 270; *FMW*, 291.
117. *SoR*, 77–8, 180, 183.
118. *RoI*, 240, 325, 330–1, 342.
119. Ibid., 121–3.
120. *RoC*, 152–3.
121. Ibid., 213–14, 227, 235–6, 331.
122. *SoR*, 269–70.
123. Ibid., 178, 182.
124. Schluchter, *Rationalism, Religion, and Domination*, 53.
125. Bryan Turner, *Social Compass* 25 (1978): 371–94.
126. *ES*, 447.
127. *ES*, 512, 624–6; *SoR*, 51, 148.
128. *SoR*, 204; *ES*, 574; *PE*, 227.
129. *ES*, 474.
130. Ibid., 555–6.
131. Ibid., 1138, 1244.
132. *GEH*, 313–14, 318.
133. *PE*, 100.

134. *ES*, 1230–3.
135. *RoC*, 16.
136. *ES*, 626, 1076.
137. Ibid., 823, 1394–5.
138. Ibid., 1095.
139. Ibid., 819–21, 823, 976.
140. Ibid., 822.
141. Ibid., 1097.
142. Ibid., 1095–6.
143. Maxime Rodinson, *Islam et Capitalisme* (Paris: Editions du Seuil, 1966), 91.
144. Turner, *Weber and Islam*, 13–14; Schroeder, *Max Weber and the Sociology of Culture*, 69.

Conclusion

1. John V. Tolan, *Saracens: Islam in the Medieval European Imagination* (New York: Columbia University Press, 2002) 195–6.
2. Kenneth Setton, "Pope Leo X and the Turkish Peril," *Proceedings of the American Philosophical Society*, 113, no. 6 (1969): 375–9.
3. Ibn Warraq, *Defending the West: A Critique of Edward Said's Orientalism* (New York: Prometheus Books, 2008).
4. Franco Cardini, *Europe and Islam*, trans. Caroline Beamish (Oxford: Blackwell, 2001) 130.
5. Adam Smith, *The Wealth of Nations* (New York: The Modern Library, 1937), 899.
6. Klaus Knorr, *British Colonial Theories, 1570–1850* (Toronto: University of Toronto Press, 1944), 359.
7. Francis Fukuyama, *The End of History and the Last Man* (New York: Free Press, 1992).

Select Bibliography

General Works

Abbattista, Guido S. "Empire, Liberty, and the Rule of Difference: European Debates on British Colonialism in Asia at the End of the Eighteenth Century," *European Review of History* 13:3 (2006): 473–98.

Anderson, Perry. *Lineages of the Absolutist State*. London: Verso, 1974.

Ballaster, Ros, ed. *Fables of the East: Selected Tales, 1662–1785*. Oxford: Oxford University Press, 2005.

Blanks, David R., and Michael Frassetto, eds. *Western Views of Islam in Medieval and Early Modern Europe: Perception of Other*. New York: St. Martin's Press, 1999.

Boesche, Roger. *Theories of Tyranny, from Plato to Arendt*. University Park: Pennsylvania State University, 1996.

Bonner, Michael David. *Jihad in Islamic History: Doctrines and Practice*. Princeton, NJ : Princeton University Press, 2006.

Bosworth, C. E. *The Islamic World from Classical to Modern Times: Essays in Honor of Bernard Lewis*. Princeton, NJ: Darwin Press, 1989.

Boulanger, Nicolas Antoine. *The Origin and Progress of Despotism in the Oriental and Other Empires of Africa, Europe, and America*. Amsterdam: Printed, 1764.

Boyd, Richard. *Uncivil Society: The Perils of Pluralism and the Making of Modern Liberalism*. Lanham, MD: Lexington Books, 2004.

Braudel, Fernand. *The Mediterranean and the Mediterranean World in the Age of Philip II*, trans. Sian Reynolds. London: Collins, 1972–73.

Burton, Jonathan. *Traffic and Turning: Islam and English Drama, 1579–1624*. Newark: University of Delaware, 2005.

Buruma, Ian and Avishai Margalit. *Occidentalism: The West in the Eyes of Its Enemies*. New York: Penguin Press, 2004.

Cannadine, David. *Ornamentalism: How the British Saw Their Empire*. New York: Oxford University Press, 2001.

Carlton, Eric. *Faces of Despotism*. Aldershot, UK: Scolar Press, 1995.

Chew, Samuel C. *The Crescent and the Rose: Islam and England during the Renaissance*. New York: Octagon Books, 1965.

Christensen, Stephen Turk, ed. *Violence and the Absolutist State: Studies in European and Ottoman History*. Copenhagen: Akademisk Forlag, 1990.

Franklin, Julian H. *Jean Bodin et la naissance de la théorie absolutiste*. Paris: Presses Universitaires de France, 1993.

Fuchs, Barbara. *Mimesis and Empire: The New World, Islam, and European Identities*. Cambridge: Cambridge University Press, 2001.

Furet, François. *In the Workshop of History*, trans. Jonathan Mandelbaum. Chicago: University of Chicago, 1984.

Gibb, H. A. R. *Mohammedanism: An Historical Survey*, 2nd ed. London: Oxford University Press, 1953.

Goitein, S. D. *Studies in Islamic History and Institutions*. Leiden, the Netherlands: Brill, 1968.

Goodwin, Jason. *Lords of the Horizons: A History of the Ottoman Empire*. New York: Holt, 1999.

Hanioglu, M. Sukru. *A Brief History of the Late Ottoman Empire*. Princeton, NJ: Princeton University Press, 2008.

Horowitz, Irving Louis. *Behemoth: Main Currents in the History and Theory of Political Sociology*. New Brunswick, NJ: Transaction Publishers, 1999.

Hourani, Albert. *Islam in European Thought*. New York: Cambridge University Press, 1991.

Howard, Deborah. *Venice and the East: The Impact of the Islamic World on Venetian Architecture 1100–1500*. New Haven, CT: Yale University Press, 2000.

Hutchins, Francis G. *The Illusion of Permanence: British Imperialism in India*. Princeton, NJ: Princeton University Press, 1967.

Inalcik, Halil. *The Ottoman Empire: Conquest, Organization and Economy*. London: Variorum Reprints, 1978.

Irwin, Robert. *Dangerous Knowledge: Orientalism and Its Discontents*. Woodstock, NY: Overlook Press, 2006a.

———. *For Lust of Knowing: The Orientalists and Their Enemies*. London: Allen Lane, 2006b.

Jones, Eric L. *The European Miracle*. Cambridge: Cambridge University Press, 1981.

Karpat, Kemal H., ed. *The Ottoman State and Its Place in World History*. Leiden, the Netherlands: Brill, 1974.

Labib, Subhi. "The Era of Suleyman the Magnificent: Crisis of Orientation," *International Journal of Middle East Studies* 10:4 (1979): 435–51.

Lal, Deepak. *In Praise of Empires: Globalization and Order*. New York: Palgrave Macmillan, 2004.

Lambton, Ann K. S. *State and Government in Medieval Islam: An Introduction to the Study of Islamic Political Theory: The Jurists*. Oxford: Oxford University Press, 1981.

Landes, David S. *The Wealth and Poverty of Nations: Why Some Are So Rich and Some So Poor*. New York: Norton, 1998.

Laurens, Henry. *Aux sources de l'Orientalisme: la Bibliothèque Orientale de Barthélemy d' Herbelot*. Paris: Maisonneuve et Larose, 1978.

Lewis, Bernard. *Islam and the West*. New York: Oxford University Press, 1993.

Lowe, Lisa. *Critical Terrains: French and British Orientalisms*. Ithaca, NY: Cornell University Press, 1991.
Makdisi, George. *Arabic and Islamic Studies, in Honor of Hamilton A. R. Gibb*. Cambridge, MA: Harvard University, 1965.
Millet, Claude. *Le despote Oriental*. Paris: Maisonneuve et Larose, 2001.
Persram, Nalini, ed. *Postcolonialism and Political Theory*. Lanham, MD: Lexington Books, 2007.
Richter, Melvin. "A Family of Political Concepts," *European Journal of Political Theory* 4:3 (2005): 221–48.
Robinson, Benedict Scott. *Islam and Early Modern Literature: The Politics of Romance from Spenser to Milton*. New York: Palgrave Macmillan, 2007.
Ruthven, Malise. *Islam in the World*, 3rd ed. Oxford: Oxford University Press, 2006.
Schwoebel, Robert. *The Shadow of the Crescent: The Renaissance Image of the Turks, 1453–1517*. Nieuwkoop, the Netherlands: de Graaf, 1967.
Southern, R. W. *Western Views of Islam in the Middle Ages*. Cambridge, MA: Harvard University Press, 1962.
Strauss, Leo. *On Tyranny, Including the Strauss-Kojève correspondence*, eds. Victor Gourevitch and Michael S. Roth. Chicago: University of Chicago Press, 2000.
Thomson, Ann. *Barbary and Enlightenment: European Attitudes towards the Maghreb in the 18th Century*. Leiden, the Netherlands: Brill, 1987.
Tibi, Bassam. *Islam between Culture and Politics*, 2nd ed. Basingstoke, UK: Palgrave Macmillan, 2005.
Valensi, Lucette. *Venise et la sublime porte: la naissance du despote*. Paris: Hachette, 1987.
Valiunas, Algis. "Encountering Islam," *Claremont Review of Books* 7:2 (Spring 2007): 32–9.
Von Grunebaum, Gustave E., ed. *Unity and Variety in Muslim Civilization*. Chicago: University of Chicago Press, 1955.
Waardenburg, Jean-Jacques. *l' Islam dans le miroir de l'Occident*. Paris: Mouton, 1963.
———. *Islam: Historical, Social and Political Perspectives*. Berlin: Gruyter, 2002.
Wittfogel, Karl A. *Oriental Despotism: A Comparative Study of Total Power*. New Haven, CT: Yale University Press, 1957.

Montesquieu

Actes du Congrès. *Montesquieu réuni à Bordeaux, 1955*. Bordeaux, France: Delmas, 1956.
Berlin, Isaiah. *Against the Current*. Princeton, NJ: Princeton University Press, 2001.
Boesche, Roger. "Fearing Monarchs and Merchants: Montesquieu's Two Theories of Despotism," *Western Political Science Quarterly* 43:4 (December 1990): 741–61.
Carrithers, David W. and Patrick Coleman, eds. *Montesquieu and the Spirit of Modernity*. Oxford: Voltaire Foundation, 2002.
Carrithers, David W., Michael Mosher, and Paul Rahe, eds. *Montesquieu's Science of Politics: Essays on the Spirit of Laws*. Lanham, MD: Rowman and Littlefield, 2001.

Cohler, Anne M. *Montesquieu's Comparative Politics and the Spirit of American Constitutionalism*. Lawrence: University Press of Kansas, 1988.

Conroy, Peter. *Montesquieu Revisited*. New York: Twayne, 1992.

Courtney, C. P. *Montesquieu and Burke*. Westport, CT: Greenwood Press, 1975.

Dobbs, Muriel. *Les récits de voyages, sources de 'L'Esprit des Lois' de Montesquieu*. Paris: Champion, 1929.

Fournal, Etienne Maurice. *Bodin, prédécesseur de Montesquieu; Étude sur quelques théories de la "République" et de "l'Esprit des Lois."* Geneva, Switzerland: Slatkine Reprints, 1970.

Gilson, David, and Martin Smith, eds. *Essays on Montesquieu and on the Enlightenment*. Oxford: Voltaire Foundation, 1988.

Grosrichard, Alain. *Structure du sérail*. Paris: Seuil, 1979.

Hirschman, Albert O. *The Passions and the Interests*. Princeton, NJ: Princeton University Press, 1977.

Juppé, Alain. *Montesquieu: le moderne*. Paris: Perrin Grasset, 1999.

Kaiser, Thomas. "The Evil Empire? The Debate on Turkish Despotism in Eighteenth-Century French Political Culture," *The Journal of Modern History* 72:1 (2000): 6–34.

Krause, Sharon. "Despotism in the Spirit of Laws," in *Montesquieu's Science of Politics: Essays on the Spirit of Laws*, eds. David W. Carrithers, Michael Mosher, and Paul Rahe. Lanham, MD: Rowman and Littlefield, 2001, 231–71.

Larrère, Catherine. "Les Typologies des Gouvernements chez Montesquieu," in *Études sur le XVIIIe siècle*, ed. Jean Ehrard. Clermont-Ferrand, France: Association des Publications de la Faculté des Lettres, 1979, 87–103.

Larrère, Catherine and Catherine Volpilhac-Auger. *1748, L'année de l'Esprit des Lois*. Paris: Champion, 1999.

Montesquieu, Charles de Secondat. *The Spirit of the Laws*, trans. Thomas Nugent. New York: Hafner Library of Classics, 1949.

———. *De l'Esprit des Lois*. Paris: Didot, 1872.

———. *Lettres Persanes*. Paris: Le Livre de poche, 1966.

———. *Considérations sur les causes de la grandeur des Romains et leur décadence*. Paris: Garnier-Flammarion, 1968.

———. *The Persian Letters*, trans. C. J. Betts. London: Penguin Books, 1973.

Mosher, Michael A. "The Particulars of a Universal Politics: Hegel's Adaptation of Montesquieu's Typology," *American Political Science Review* 78 (1984): 179–88.

Richter, Melvin. *The Political Theory of Montesquieu*. Cambridge: Cambridge University Press, 1977.

———. "Montesquieu's Theory and Practice of the Comparative Method," *History of the Human Sciences* 15:2 (2002): 21–3.

Schaub, Diana J. "Montesquieu on Slavery," *Perspectives on Political Science* 34:2 (2005): 70–8.

Shackleton, Robert. *Montesquieu, a Critical Biography*. London: Oxford University Press, 1961.

Starobinski, Jean. *Montesquieu*. Paris: Seuil, 1979.

Van Roosbroeck, Gustave L. *Persian Letters before Montesquieu*. New York: Franklin, 1973.

Vernière, Paul. *Montesquieu et l'Esprit des Lois ou la raison impure*. Paris: Société d' Édition d' Enseignment Supérieur, 1977.

Young, David. "Montesquieu's View of Despotism and His Use of Travel Literature," *Review of Politics* 40:3 (1978): 392–405.

Edmund Burke

Bass, Jeff D. "The Perversion of Empire: Edmund Burke and the Nature of Imperial Responsibility," *The Quarterly Journal of Speech* 81 (1995): 208–27.

Bernstein, Jeremy. *Dawning of the Raj: The Life and Trials of Warren Hastings*. Chicago: Dee, 2000.

Burke, Edmund. *The Writings and Speeches of Edmund Burke*. Boston: Little, Brown, 1901.

———. *The Speeches of Edmund Burke on the Impeachment of Warren Hastings*. London: Bell, 1902.

———. *On Government, Politics, and Society*, ed. B. W. Hill. New York: International Publications Service, 1976.

———. "India: The Hastings Trial, 1789–1794," in *The Writings and Speeches of Edmund Burke*, vol. 7, ed. Peter J. Marshall. Oxford: Clarendon Press, 2000.

Cambridge History of English and American Literature: Vol. XI, The Period of the French Revolution. New York: Bartleby, 2000.

Canavan, Francis. *Edmund Burke: Prescription and Providence*. Durham, NC: Carolina Academic Press, 1987.

Carnell, Geoffrey and Colin Nicholson, eds. *The Impeachment of Warren Hastings: Papers from a Bicentenary Commemoration*. Edinburgh: Edinburgh University Press, 1989.

Crowe, Ian, ed. *Edmund Burke: His Life and Legacy*. Dublin: Four Courts Press, 1997.

———. *An Imaginative Whig: Reassessing the Life and Thought of Edmund Burke*. Columbia:University of Missouri Press, 2005.

De Bruyn, Frans. "Edmund Burke's Gothic Romance: The Portrayal of Warren Hastings in Burke's Writings and Speeches on India," *Criticism* 29 (1987): 415–38.

Dirks, Nicolas B. *The Scandal of Empire: India and the Creation of Imperial Britain*. Cambridge, MA: Harvard University Press, 2006.

Fidler, David P. and Jennifer M. Welsh, eds. *Empire and Community: Edmund Burke's Writings and Speeches on International Relations*. Boulder, CO: Westview Press, 1999.

Lock, F. P. *Edmund Burke, Vol. 2, 1784–1797*. Oxford: Oxford University Press, 2007.

O'Brien, Conor Cruise. *The Great Melody: A Thematic Biography and Commented Anthology of Edmund Burke*. Chicago: University of Chicago Press, 1992.

Samet, Elizabeth D. "A Prosecutor and A Gentleman: Edmund Burke's Idiom of Impeachment," *English Literary History* 68:2 (2001): 397–418.

Stanlis, Peter. *Edmund Burke: The Enlightenment and Revolution*. New Brunswick, NJ: Transaction Publishers, 1991.

Whelan, Fredrick G. *Edmund Burke and India: Political Morality and Empire*. Pittsburgh, PA: University of Pittsburgh Press, 1996.

Tocqueville

Aron, Raymond. *Main Currents in Sociological Thought*, trans. Richard Howard and Helen Weaver. Garden City, NJ: Anchor Books, 1968.

———. *An Essay on Freedom*, trans. Helen Weaver. New York: New American Library, 1970.

———. *Defense of Political Reason*, ed. Daniel J. Mahoney. Lanham, MD: Rowman and Littlefield, 1994.

Benoît, Jean-Louis. *Comprendre Toqueville*. Paris: Colin, 2004.

Boesche, Roger. "The Dark Side of Tocqueville. On War and Empire," *The Review of Politics* 67:4 (Fall 2005): 737–52.

———. *Tocqueville's Road Map: Methodology, Liberalism, Revolution, and Despotism*. Lanham, MD: Lexington Books, 2006.

Boyd, Richard. "Tocqueville's Algeria," *Society* 38:6 (2001): 65–70.

Brogan, Hugh. *Alexis de Tocqueville: A Life*. New Haven, CT: Yale University Press, 2007.

Craiutu, Aurelian. "Tocqueville's Paradoxical Moderation," *The Review of Politics* 67:4 (Fall 2005): 599–629.

Dion, Stéphane. "La conciliation du libéralisme et du nationalisme chez Tocqueville." *La Revue Tocqueville/The Tocqueville Review* XVI:1 (1995): 219–27.

Drescher, Seymour. *Dilemmas of Democracy: Tocqueville and Modernization*. Pittsburgh, PA: University of Pittsburgh Press, 1968.

Furet, François. *Interpreting the French Revolution*, trans. Elborg Forster. New York: Cambridge University Press, 1981.

Gellner, Ernest. "The Civil and the Sacred," *Tanner Lectures*, Harvard University, March 1990.

Gershman, Sally. "Alexis de Tocqueville and Slavery," *French Historical Studies* 9:3 (1976): 467–83.

Goldstein, Doris S. *Trial of Faith: Religion and Politics in Tocqueville's Thought*. New York: Elsevier, 1975.

Jardin, André. *Tocqueville: A Biography*, trans. Lydia Davis. New York: Farrar Straus Giroux, 1988.

Kahan, Alan S. *Aristocratic Liberalism: The Social and Political Thought of Jacob Burckhardt, John Stuart Mill, and Alexis de Tocqueville*. New York: Oxford University Press, 1992.

Maguire, Matthew. *The Conversion of Imagination: From Pascal through Rousseau to Tocqueville*. Cambridge, MA: Harvard University Press, 2006.

Mancini, Matthew. *Alexis de Tocqueville*. New York: Twayne, 1994.

———. "Alexis de Tocqueville's Post-Civil War Reputation," *Society* 43:1 (November–December 2005): 75–81.

———. *Alexis de Tocqueville and American Intellectuals: From His Time to Ours*. Lanham, MD: Rowman and Littlefield, 2006.

Manent, Pierre. "Tocqueville philosophe politique," *Commentaire* 107 (2004): 581–7.

Mélonio, Française. *Tocqueville and the French*, trans. Beth G. Raps. Charlottesville: University Press of Virginia, 1998.

Nisbet, Robert. "Many Tocquevilles," *American Scholar* 46:1 (1976–7): 59–75.

Pappe, H. O. "Mill and Tocqueville," *Journal of the History of Ideas* 25:2 (1964): 217–34.

Pope, Whitney. *Alexis de Tocqueville: His Social and Political Theory*. Beverley Hills, CA: Sage, 1986.

Richter, Melvin. "Tocqueville on Algeria," *Review of Politics* 25:3 (1963): 362–98.

Salzmann, Ariel. *Tocqueville in the Ottoman Empire: Rival Paths to the Modern State*. Leiden, the Netherlands: Brill, 2004.

Spitzer, Alan B. "Tocqueville's Modern Nationalism," *French History* 19:1 (2005): 48–66.

Tessitore, Aristide. "Tocqueville and Gobineau on the Nature of Modern Politics," *The Review of Politics* 67:4 (Fall 2005): 631–57.

Tocqueville, Alexis de. *Oeuvres complètes*. Paris: Gallimard, 1952–95.

———. *L'Ancien régime et la Révolution*, ed. J. P. Mayer. Paris: Gallimard, 1967.

———. *Writings on Empire and Slavery*, ed. and trans.Jennifer Pitts. Baltimore: Johns Hopkins University Press, 2001.

Todorov, Tzvetan. *De la colonie en Algérie*. Brussels: Complex, 1988.

———. *Nous et les autres*. Paris: Seuil, 1989.

Welch, Cheryl B. "Colonial Violence and the Rhetoric of Evasion: Tocqueville on Algeria," *Political Theory* 31:2 (April 2003) 235–64.

———. *The Cambridge Companion to Tocqueville*. Cambridge: Cambridge University Press, 2006.

Wolin, Sheldon S. *Tocqueville between Two Worlds: The Making of a Political and Theoretical Life*. Princeton, NJ: Princeton University Press, 2001.

Zunz, Oliver, and Alan S. Kahn, eds. *The Tocqueville Reader: A Life in Letters and Politics*. Oxford: Blackwell, 2002.

James Mill and John Stuart Mill

Aron, Raymond. *Main Currents in Sociological Thought*, Vol. 1. New York: Basic Books, 1965.

Bearce, George D. *British Attitudes towards India, 1784–1858*. London: Oxford University Press, 1961.

Berlin, Isaiah. *Four Essays on Liberty*. New York: Oxford University Press, 1970.

Breckenridge, Carol A. and Peter van der Veer, eds. *Orientalism and the Postcolonial Predicament: Perspectives on South Asia*. Philadelphia: University of Pennsylvania Press, 1993.

Cannadine, David. *Orientalism: How the British Saw Their Empire*. Oxford: University Press, 2001.

Capaldi, Nicolas. *John Stuart Mill: A Biography*. Cambridge: Cambridge University Press, 2004.

Carlisle, Janice. *John Stuart Mill and the Writing of Character*. Athens: University of Georgia, 1991.

Collini, Stefan. *Public Moralists, Political Thought and Intellectual Life in Great Britain, 1850–1930*. Oxford: Clarendon Press, 1991.

Collini, Stefan, Donald Winch, and John Burrow. *That Noble Science of Politics: A Study in Nineteenth Century Intellectual History*. Cambridge: Cambridge University Press, 1983.

Dirks, Nicholas B. "Castes of Mind," *Representations* 37 (Winter 1992): 56–78.

Forbes, Duncan. "James Mill and India," *Cambridge Journal* (October 1951): 19–33.

Gray, John N. "John Stuart Mill: Traditional and Revisionist Interpretations," *Literature of Liberty* 2:2 (April–June 1979): 7–37.

Habibi, Don A. *John Stuart Mill and the Ethic of Human Growth*. Dordrecht, the Netherlands: Kluwer Academic Publishers, 2001.

———. "The Moral Dimensions of J.S. Mill's Colonialism," *Journal of Social Philosophy* 30:1 (1999): 125–46.

Halévy, Élie. *The Growth of Philosophic Radicalism*. Boston: Beacon Press, 1955.

Harris, Abram L. "John Stuart Mill: Servant of the East India Company," *The Canadian Journal of Economics and Political Science* 30:2 (May 1964): 185–202.

Hutchins, Francis G. *The Illusion of Permanence: British Imperialism in India*. Princeton, NJ: Princeton University Press, 1967.

Jones, H. S. "John Stuart Mill as Moralist," *Journal of the History of Ideas* 53 (1992): 287–308.

Krouse, Richard W. "Patriarchal Liberalism and Beyond: From John Stuart Mill to Harriet Taylor," in *The Family in Political Thought*, ed. J. B. Elshtain. Amherst: University of Massachusetts Press, 1982.

Kurfirst, Robert. "John Stuart Mill on Oriental Despotism including its British Variant," *Utilitas* 8:1 (March 1996): 73–87.

———. "John Stuart Mill's Asian Parable," *Canadian Journal of Political Science* 34:3 (2001): 601–19.

Laine, Michael, ed. *A Cultivated Mind: Essays on John Stuart Mill Presented to John M Robson*. Toronto: University of Toronto Press, 1991.

Laski, Harold J. "Introduction," in *Autobiography*, John Stuart Mill. Oxford: Oxford University Press, 1924.

Levin, Michael. *John Stuart Mill on Civilization and Barbarism*. London: Routledge, 2004.

Macaulay, Thomas. *Speeches*. London: Longmans Green, 1875.

Maine, Henry. *Village Communities in the East and West*, 7th ed. London: Murray, 1913.

Majeed, Javed. "James Mill's 'The History of British India' and Utilitarianism as a Rhetoric of Reform," *Modern Asian Studies* 24:2 (1990): 209–24.

———. *Ungoverned Imaginings: James Mill's the History of British India and Orientalism*. Oxford: Clarendon Press, 1992.

Makdisi, Saree. *Romantic Imperialism: Universal Empire and the Culture of Modernity*. Cambridge: Cambridge University Press, 1998.

Manent, Pierre. *An Intellectual History of Liberalism*, trans. Rebecca Balinski. Princeton, NJ: Princeton University Press, 1994.

Marshall, P. J. and Glynwr Williams. *The Great Map of Mankind: British Perceptions of the World in the Age of Enlightenment*. London: Dent, 1982.

Mehta, Uday. *Liberalism and Empire: A Study in the Nineteenth Century British Liberal Thought*. Chicago: University of Chicago Press: 1999.

Mill, James. "Affairs of India," *Edinburgh Review* 16 (April 1810): 127–57.

———. "War," *The Philanthropist* 3:11 (1813): 197–214.

———. *Collected Works*. Toronto: University of Toronto Press, 1963–91.

———. *The History of British India*, ed. William Thomas. Chicago: University of Chicago Press, 1975.

Moir, Martin I., Douglas M. Peers, and Lynn Zastoupil, eds. *John Stuart Mill's Encounter with India*. Toronto: University of Toronto Press, 1999.

Moore, R. J. "John Stuart Mill at East India House," *Historical Studies* 20 (1983): 497–519.

———. "John Stuart Mill and Royal India," *Utilitas* 3:1 (May 1991): 85–106.

Mukherjee, S. N. *Sir William Jones: A Study in 18th Century British Attitudes to India*. Cambridge: Cambridge University Press, 1968.

Pappe, H. O. "Mill and Tocqueville," *Journal of the History of Ideas* 25:2 (April–June 1964): 217–34.

Parekh, Bhikhu. "Liberalism and Colonialism: A Critique of Locke and Mill," in *The Decolonization of Imagination: Culture, Knowledge, and Power*, eds., Jan Nederveen Pieterse and B. Parekh. London: Zed Books, 1995.

———. *Rethinking Multiculturalism, Cultural Diversity, and Political Theory*. Cambridge, MA: Harvard University Press, 2000.

Pitts, Jennifer. *A Turn to Empires: The Rise of Imperial Liberalism in Britain and France*. Princeton, NJ: Princeton University Press, 2005.

Prager, Carol A. L. "Intervention and Empire: John Stuart Mill and International Relations," *Political Studies* 53:3 (2005): 621–40.

Prakash, Gyan. "Post-Orientalist Third World Histories: Perspectives from Indian Historiography," *Comparative Studies in Society and History* 32 (1990): 383–408.

Schultz, Bart. "Mill and Sidgwick: Imperialism and Racism," *Utilitas* 19:1 (March 2007): 104–30.

Schultz, Bart and Georgios Varouxakis, eds. *Utilitarianism and Empire*. Lanham, MD: Lexington Books, 2005.

Shtromas, Alexander, ed. *The End of 'isms? Reflections on the Fate of Ideological Politics after Communism's Collapse*. Oxford: Blackwell, 1994.

Smith, G. W., ed. *John Stuart Mill's Social and Political Thought*, vol. III. London: Routledge, 1998.

Souffrant, Eddy M. *Formal Transgression: John Stuart Mill's Philosophy of International Affairs*. Lanham, MD: Rowman and Littlefield, 2000.

Stokes, Eric. *The English Utilitarians and India*. London: Oxford University Press, 1963.

Sullivan, Eileen. "Liberalism and Imperialism: J.S. Mill's Defense of the British Empire," *Journal of the History of Ideas* 44 (1983): 608–13.

Tunick, Mark. "Tolerant Imperialism: John Stuart Mill's Defense of British Rule in India," *Review of Politics* 68 (2006): 586–611.

Urbinati, Nadia and Alex Zakaras, eds. *J. S. Mill's Political Thought: A Bicentennial Reassessment*. Cambridge: Cambridge University Press, 2007.

Yasukawa, Ryuji. "James Mill on Peace and War," *Utilitas* 3:2 (November 1991): 179–97.

Zastoupil, Lynn. *John Stuart Mill and India*. Stanford: Stanford University Press, 1994.

Marx

Aron, Raymond. *Introduction à la philosophie de l'histoire*. Paris: Gallimard, 1981.

———. *Le Marxisme de Marx*, eds., Jean-Claude Casanova and Christian Bachelier. Paris: Éditions de Fallios, 2002.

Avineri, Shlomo, ed. *Karl Marx on Colonialism and Modernization*. New York: Doubleday, 1969.

———. *Marx's Socialism*. New York: Lieber-Atherton, 1973.

———. *Varieties of Marxism*. The Hague, the Netherlands: Nijhoff, 1977.

Bailey, Anne M., and J. R. Llobera. "The Asiatic Mode Of Production: An Annotated Bibliography," *Critique of Anthropology* 1:2 (1974): 95–107.

Bailey, Anne M., and Joseph R. Llobera, eds. *The Asiatic Mode of Production: Science and Politics*. London: Routledge and Kegan Paul, 1981.

Bartolovich, Crystal, and Neil Lazarus, eds. *Marxism, Modernity, and Postcolonial Studies*. Cambridge: Cambridge University Press, 2002.

Berlin, Isaiah. *Historical Inevitability*. Loudon: Oxford University Press, 1954.

Bloch, Maurice. *Marxism and Anthropology*. New York: Oxford University Press, 1983.

Dunn, Stephen P. *The Fall and Rise of the Asiatic Mode of Production*. London: Routledge and Kegan Paul, 1982.

Fogel, Joshua A. "The Debates over the Asiatic Mode of Production in Soviet Russia, China, and Japan," *The American Historical Review* 93:1 (1988): 56–79.

Godelier, Maurice. *Sur les sociétés précapitalistes*. Paris: Editions Sociales, 1970.

———. *Perspectives in Marxist Anthropology*, trans. Robert Brain. Cambridge: Cambridge University Press, 1977.

Hindess, Barry, and Paul Q. Hirst. *Pre-capitalist Modes of Production*. London: Routledge, 1975.

Hobsbawn, Eric, ed. *Pre-Capitalist Economic Formations*. London: Lawrence and Wishart, 1964.

Jessop, Bob, ed. *Karl Marx's Social and Political Thought: Critical Assessments*. London: Routledge, 1990.

Krader, Lawrence. *The Asiatic Mode of Production: Sources, Development and Critique in the Writings of Karl Marx*. Assen, the Netherlands: Van Gorcum, 1975.

Lichtheim, George. *The Concept of Ideology, and Other Essays*. New York: Vintage Books, 1967.

Lowe, Donald. *The Function of "China" in Marx, Lenin, and Mao*. Berkeley: University of California Press, 1966.

Lubasz, Heinz. "Marx's Concept of the Asiatic Mode of Production: A Genetic Analysis," in *Karl Marx's Social and Political Thought: Critical Assessments*, ed. Bob Jessop. London: Routledge, 1990.

Mahoney, Daniel J. "Aron, Marx, and Marxism," *European Journal of Political Theory* 2 (2002): 315–27.

Mardin, Serif. "Power, Civil Society and Culture in the Ottoman Empire," *Comparative Studies in Society and History* 11:3 (1969) 258–81.

Marx, Karl. *Capital*, 3 vols. Chicago: Kerr, 1909.

———. *Grundrisse*. New York: Vintage Press, 1973.

Marx, Karl, and Frederick Engels. *Collected Works*. New York: International Publishers, 1975.

McLellan, David. *Karl Marx: A Biography*, 4th ed. Basingstoke, UK: Palgrave Macmillan, 2006.

O'Leary, Brendan. *The Asiatic Mode of Production: Oriental Despotism, Historical Materialism, and Indian History*. Oxford: Blackwell, 1989.

Piccone, Paul. "Reading the Grundrisse: Beyond 'Orthodox' Marxism," *Theory and Society* 2:2 (1975): 235–55.

Pryor, Frederic L. "The Asiatic Mode of Production as an Economic System," *Journal of Comparative Economics* 4:4 (1980): 420–42.

Rubel, Maximilien. *Marx critique du Marxisme*. Paris: Payot, 1974.

Sawer, Marian. *Marxism and the Question of the Asiatic Mode of Production*. The Hague, the Netherlands: Nijhoff, 1977.

Shanin, Teodor, ed. *Late Marx and the Russian Road*. New York: Monthly Review Press, 1983.

Sofri, Gianni. *Il modo di produzione asiatico*. Turin, Italy: Einandi, 1969.

Thorner, Daniel. "Marx on India and the Asiatic Mode of Production," *Contributions to Indian Sociology* 9 (1966): 33–66.

Tokei, Ferenc. *Essays on the Asiatic Mode of Production*. Budapest: Akademiai Kiado, 1979.

Turner, Bryan S. *Marx and the End of Orientalism*. London: Allen and Unwin, 1978.

Wolpe, Harold, ed. *The Articulation of Modes of Production: Essays from Economy and Society*. London: Routledge and Kegan Paul, 1980.

Vidal-Naquet, Pierre. "Karl Wittfogel et le concept de 'Mode de production Asiatique'," *Annales* 19 (1964): 531–49.

Vitkin, M. "The Asiatic Mode of Production," *Philosophy and Social Criticism* 8:1 (1991): 46–66.

Weber

Andreski, Stanislav. *Max Weber's Insights and Errors*. London: Routledge and Kegan Paul, 1994.

Bendix, Reinhard. *Max Weber: An Intellectual Biography*. Berkeley: University of California Press, 1977.

Breiner, Peter. "The Political Logic of Economics and the Economic Logic of Modernity in Max Weber," *Political Theory* 23:1 (1995): 25–47.

Burger, Thomas. *Max Weber's Theory of Concept Formation: History, Laws, and Ideal Types*. Durham, NC: Duke University Press, 1987.

Buss, Andreas E. *Max Weber and Asia: Contributions to the Sociology of Development*. Munich: Weltforum, 1985.

Diggins, John Patrick. *Max Weber: Politics and the Spirit of Tragedy*. New York: Basic Books, 1996.

Eisenstadt, S. N. *Traditional Patrimonialism and Modern Neo-patrimonialism*. Beverley Hills: Sage, 1973.

Gerth, H. H. and C. Wright Mills, eds. *From Max Weber: Essays in Sociology*. London: Routledge, 1991.

Hennis, Wilhelm. *Max Weber: Essays in Reconstruction*, trans. K. Tribe. London, Allen and Unwin, 1988.

Hoenisch, Steve. "*Max Weber's View of Objectivity in Social Science*," published in *Criticism.com*, 2003.

Huff, Toby E., and Wolfgang Schluchter, eds. *Max Weber and Islam*. New Brunswick, NJ: Transaction Publishers, 1999.

Kalberg, Stephen. "Max Weber's Analysis of the Rise of Monotheism: A Reconstruction," *The British Journal of Sociology* 45:5 (1994a): 563–84.

———. *Max Weber's Comparative-Historical Sociology*. Chicago: University of Chicago Press, 1994b.

Krader, Lawrence. *The Asiatic Mode of Production: Sources, Development and Critique in the Writings of Karl Marx*. Assen, the Netherlands: Van Gorcum, 1975.

Lassman, Peter, and Ronald Speirs, eds. *Weber: Political Writings*. Cambridge: Cambridge University Press, 1994.

Lough, Joseph W. H. *Weber and the Persistence of Religion: Social Theory, Capitalism and the Sublime*. London: Routledge, 2006.

Mommsen, Wolfgang. *The Political and Social Theory of Max Weber*. Chicago: University of Chicago Press, 1992.

Poggi, Gianfranco. *Weber: A Short Introduction*. Cambridge: Polity, 2006.

Ringer, Fritz. "Max Weber on the Origin and Character of the Western City," *Critical Quarterly* 36:4 (1994):12–19.

Sayer, Derek. *Capitalism and Modernity: An Excursus on Marx and Weber*. London: Routledge, 1991.

Schluchter, Wolfgang. *The Rise of Western Rationalism: Max Weber's Developmental History*, trans. Guenther Roth. Berkeley: University of California Press, 1981.

———. *Rationalism, Religion, and Domination: A Weberian Perspective*, trans. Neil Solomon. Berkeley: University of California Press, 1989.

Sica, Alan. *Max Weber and the New Century*. New Brunswick, NJ: Transaction Publishers, 2004.

Spinard, William. "Charisma: A Blighted Concept and an Alternative Formula," *Political Science Quarterly* 106:2 (1991): 295–312.

Turner, Bryan S. *Weber and Islam: A Critical Study*. London: Routledge, 1974.

———. *Max Weber: From History to Modernity*. London: Routledge, 1992.

Vidal-Naquet, Pierre. *La démocratie grecque vue d'ailleurs: essais d'historiographie ancienne et moderne*. Paris: Flammarion, 1990.

Weber, Max. *On the Methodology of the Social Sciences*, trans. and eds. Edward A. Shils and Henry A. Finch. Glencoe, IL: Free Press, 1949.

———. *General Economic History*, trans. Frank H. Wright. Glencoe, IL: Free Press, 1950.

———. *On Law in Economy and Society*, ed. Max Rheinstein. Cambridge, MA: Harvard University Press, 1954.

———. *The Religion of India: The Sociology of Hinduism and Buddhism*, trans. and eds. Hans H. Gerth and Don Martindale. Glencoe, IL: Free Press, 1958.

———. *The Theory of Social and Economic Organization*, trans. A. M. Henderson and Talcott Parsons. New York: Free Press, 1964.

———. *The Sociology of Religion*, trans. Ephraim Fischoff. Boston: Beacon Press, 1969.

———. *Economy and Society: An Outline of Interpretative Sociology*, eds. Guenther Roth and Claus Wittich, 2 vols. Berkeley: University of California Press, 1978.

———. *Max Weber on Capitalism, Bureaucracy, and Religion: A Selection of Texts*, ed. and trans. Stanislav Andreski. London: Allen and Unwin, 1983.

———. *From Max Weber: Essays in Sociology*, trans. H. H. Gerth and C. Wright Mills, new ed. London: Routledge, 1991.

Whimster, Sam. *Understanding Weber*. London: Routledge, 2007.

Index